Province of Quebec

FODOR'S TRAVEL GUIDES

are compiled, researched, and edited by an international team of travel writers, field correspondents, and editors. The series, which now almost covers the globe, was founded by Eugene Fodor in 1936.

OFFICES
New York & London

Fodor's Province of Quebec:

Editor: Langdon Faust
Area Editor: Pauline Guetta
Editorial Contributors: Bernadette Cahill, David Dunbar, Terri Foxman, Rosa Harris-Adler, Janet Kask, Kathe Lieber, Betty Palik, Heather Pengelley
Illustrations: Ted Burwell
Maps: Burmar Technical Corp., Pictograph

SPECIAL SALES

Fodor's Travel Guides are available at special quantity discounts for bulk purchases (50 copies or more) for sales promotions or premiums. Special travel guides or excerpts from existing guides can also be created to fit specific needs. For more information write Special Marketing, Fodor's Travel Guides, 2 Park Avenue, New York, N.Y. 10016

FODOR'S
PROVINCE OF QUEBEC

FODOR'S TRAVEL GUIDES
New York & London

Copyright © 1986 by Fodor's Travel Guides
ISBN 0-679-01396-2
ISBN 0-340-40076-5 (Hodder & Stoughton edition)
No part of this book may be reproduced in any form without permission in writing from the publishers.

The following Fodor's Guides are current; most are also available in a British edition published by Hodder & Stoughton.

Country and Area Guides

Australia, New Zealand & the South Pacific
Austria
Bahamas
Belgium & Luxembourg
Bermuda
Brazil
Canada
Canada's Maritime Provinces
Caribbean
Central America
Eastern Europe
Egypt
Europe
France
Germany
Great Britain
Greece
Holland
India, Nepal & Sri Lanka
Ireland
Israel
Italy
Japan
Jordan & the Holy Land
Kenya
Korea
Mexico
New Zealand
North Africa
People's Republic of China
Portugal
Province of Quebec
Scandinavia
Scotland
South America
South Pacific
Southeast Asia
Soviet Union
Spain
Sweden
Switzerland
Turkey
Yugoslavia

City Guides

Amsterdam
Beijing, Guangzhou, Shanghai
Boston
Chicago
Dallas & Fort Worth
Greater Miami & the Gold Coast
Hong Kong
Houston & Galveston
Lisbon
London
Los Angeles
Madrid
Mexico City & Acapulco
Munich
New Orleans
New York City
Paris
Philadelphia
Rome
San Diego
San Francisco
Singapore
Stockholm, Copenhagen, Oslo, Helsinki & Reykjavik
Sydney
Tokyo
Toronto
Vienna
Washington, D.C.

U.S.A. Guides

Alaska
Arizona
California
Cape Cod
Chesapeake
Colorado
Far West
Florida
Hawaii
I–95: Maine to Miami
New England
New Mexico
New York State
Pacific North Coast
South
Texas
U.S.A.
Virginia

Budget Travel

American Cities (30)
Britain
Canada
Caribbean
Europe
France
Germany
Hawaii
Italy
Japan
London
Mexico
Spain

Fun Guides

Acapulco
Bahamas
Las Vegas
London
Maui
Montreal
New Orleans
New York City
The Orlando Area
Paris
Puerto Rico
Rio
St. Martin/Sint Maarten
San Francisco
Waikiki

Special-Interest Guides

Selected Hotels of Europe
Ski Resorts of North America
Views to Dine by around the World

MANUFACTURED IN THE UNITED STATES OF AMERICA
10 9 8 7 6 5 4 3 2 1

CONTENTS

Foreword   vii

   Map of Quebec Province, viii–ix

Facts at Your Fingertips   1

   Facts and Figures, 1; Planning Your Trip, 1; Tourist Information, 1; Customs, 2; Tips for British Visitors, 3; What It Will Cost, 3; When to Go, 4; What to Pack, 5; Seasonal Events, 5; Language, 6; Hints to Motorists, 6; Hints to Handicapped Travelers, 7; National and Provincial Parks, 8; Camping, 9; Hunting, 9; Fishing, 10; Nature Watching, 11; Summer Sports, 11; Winter Sports, 11; Snowmobiles, 11; Spectator Sports, 12; Accommodations, 12; Bed-and-Breakfast, 13; Farm Vacations, 13; Hostels, 14; Restaurants, 14; Tipping, 15; Currency, 15; Credit Cards, 16; Time Zones, 16; Business Hours and Holidays, 16; Telephones and Emergency Numbers, 17; Postage, 17; Liquor Laws, 17; Traveling with Pets, 17; Metric Conversion Charts, 18

Introduction by Betty Palik   19
   Quebec History
   Quebec at Work
   The People of Quebec
   Quebec's Cultural Life
   Food, Food, Food

Winter in Quebec by Heather Pengelley   35

Montreal by Pauline Guetta   42
   Map of Montreal, 44–45
   Map of Downtown, 50–51
   Practical Information for Montreal, 53
   Map of the Métro, 56
   Map of Old Montreal, 62

Southern Quebec by David Dunbar   79
   Map of Southern Quebec, 83
   Practical Information for Southern Quebec, 84

Bas-St-Laurent, the Gaspé Peninsula, and the Magdalen Islands
by Pauline Guetta   93
   Practical Information for Bas-St-Laurent, the Gaspé Peninsula, and the Magdalen Islands, 96

CONTENTS

Quebec City by Janet Kask — 111
  Map of Quebec City, 114–115
  Practical Information for Quebec City, 118

Charlevoix by Pauline Guetta — 135
  Practical Information for Charlevoix, 138
  Map of Charlevoix, 139

The Laurentians and the Ottawa Valley by Bernadette Cahill — 150
  Practical Information for the Laurentians
  and the Ottawa Valley, 153
  Map of the Laurentians near Montreal, 154–155

Coeur-du-Quebec, de Lanaudière, and Portneuf by Kathe Lieber — 165
  Practical Information for Coeur-du-Quebec,
  de Lanaudière, and Portneuf, 167

Northern Quebec by Terri Foxman and Rosa Harris-Adler — 178
  Practical Information for Abitibi–Témiscamingue, 182
  Practical Information for Saguenay, Lac-Saint-Jean, and
    Chibougamau, 187
  Practical Information for the North Shore, 194
  Practical Information for Nouveau Quebec, 200

English-French Vocabulary — 203

Index — 207

FOREWORD

The Province of Quebec's location and history make it an ideal vacation spot for Americans—and anyone else. Just north of New England, it's easy to reach—even within a day's drive for many. But close though it is in miles, Quebec is a world apart culturally. The European character of its cities and villages is preeminent. As a walled city full of 17th- and 18th-century architecture, Quebec City seems more like an ancient European town than a relatively near neighbor of New York. Montreal is cosmopolitan and exciting. The country, whether populated with small villages and farms or real wilderness, is beautiful. You can stay at a grand resort or in a lovely inn (*auberge*)—or follow an outfitter into the Far North. Quebec is Canada's largest province, with myriad pleasures to offer travelers, at very reasonable prices, especially due to the Canadian-American dollar exchange rate.

Carry a good French-English dictionary (preferably one published in Quebec) and don't be shy. French is the established language here, but the tensions surrounding the language question in the 1970s have subsided. You'll meet lots of people who speak English well and many more who will make the effort to communicate with you using what English they know and what French you know.

In putting together this guide, we've received much kind and useful assistance from Quebecers. Normand Hall and Susanne Haase of Quebec Government House in New York have been helpful from the start. Paule Berube in Quebec City and Luce-Anne Tremblay in Charlevoix helped us appreciate the beauty and historical interest of the province. Also of assistance were Tourisme Quebec, the Greater Montreal Tourist and Convention Bureau, the Maison du Touisme run by the Quebec government in Montreal, the Quebec City Region Tourism and Convention Bureau, the Charlevoix Region Tourism Association, other regional tourism officers, Air Canada, VIA Rail, Québecair, Tilden Rent-A-Car; Voyageur bus lines, and researcher Mary Alice Daly.

Our writers, all members of PWAC—Canada's national association of professional free-lance writers—have displayed their professionalism and dedication in tracking down facts and checking details. Still, perfection is hard to come by in a complex and changing world. We'll value your comments. Write to us at Fodor's Travel Guides, 2 Park Avenue, New York, NY 10016, or 9–10 Market Place, London W1N 7AG, England.

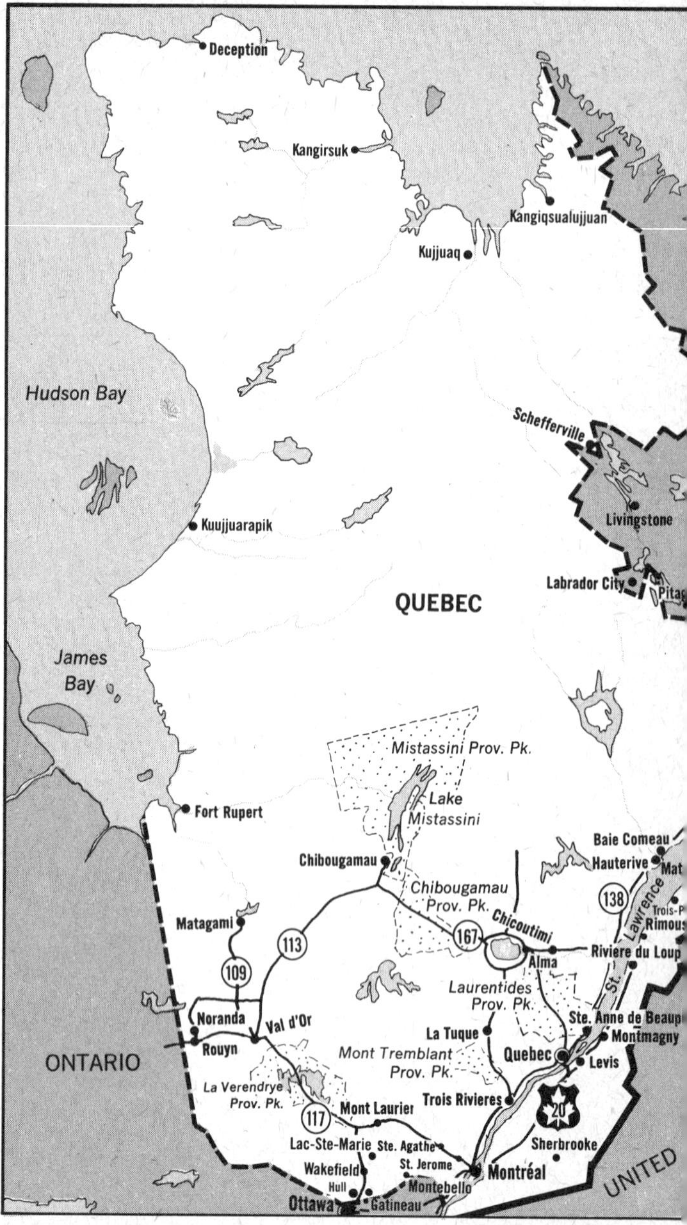

Deception
Kangirsuk
Kangiqsualujjuan
Kujjuaq
Hudson Bay
Schefferville
Kuujjuarapik
Livingstone
Labrador City
Pitag
QUEBEC
James
Bay
Mistassini Prov. Pk.
Lake
Mistassini
Fort Rupert
Baie Comeau
Chibougamau
Hauterive
Mat
Chibougamau
Prov. Pk.
138
Matagami
Chicoutimi
Lawrence
Trois-P
Rimous
113
167
Riviere du Loup
Alma
109
Laurentides
Prov. Pk.
St.
Noranda
Val d'Or
Ste. Anne de Beaup
La Tuque
Montmagny
Rouyn
Mont Tremblant
Quebec
ONTARIO
Prov. Pk.
Levis
La Verendrye
Prov. Pk.
Trois Rivieres
20
117
Mont Laurier
Lac-Ste-Marie
Ste. Agathe
Sherbrooke
St. Jerome
Wakefield
Montréal
UNITED
Hull
Montebello
Ottawa
Gatineau

PROVINCE OF QUEBEC

LANGUAGE/30

For the Business or Vacationing International Traveler

In 30 languages! A basic language course on 2 cassettes and a phrase book ... Only $14.95 ea. + shipping

Nothing flatters people more than to hear visitors try to speak their language and LANGUAGE/30, used by thousands of satisfied travelers, gets you speaking the basics quickly and easily. Each LANGUAGE/30 course offers:
- approximately 1½ hours of guided practice in greetings, asking questions and general conversation
- special section on social customs and etiquette

Order yours today. Languages available: YIDDISH (available fall '86)

ARABIC	INDONESIAN	PORTUGUESE
CHINESE	IRISH	VIETNAMESE
DANISH	ITALIAN	RUSSIAN
DUTCH	TURKISH	SERBO-CROATIAN
FINNISH	JAPANESE	SPANISH
FRENCH	KOREAN	SWAHILI
GERMAN	LATIN	SWEDISH
GREEK	NORWEGIAN	TAGALOG
HEBREW	PERSIAN	THAI
HINDI	POLISH	

To order send $14.95 per course + shipping $2.00 1st course, $1 ea. add. course. In Canada $3 1st course, $2.00 ea. add. course. NY and CA residents add state sales tax. Outside USA and Canada $14.95 (U.S.) + air mail shipping: $8 for 1st course, $5 ea. add. course. MasterCard, VISA and Am. Express card users give brand, account number (all digits), expiration date and signature.
SEND TO: FODOR'S, Dept. LC 760, 2 Park Ave., NY 10016-5677, USA.

FACTS AT YOUR FINGERTIPS

FACTS & FIGURES. Quebec, Canada's largest province, covers 1,540,687 sq km (594,860 sq mi); it is more than twice the size of Texas and almost three times larger than France. About 6.5 million people live in *la belle province*. Over 80 percent are French-speaking. Montreal, boasting a population of over 2.5 million, is the world's second largest French-speaking city. The provincial flower, which you will see on road signs, tourist information centers, and Quebec's sky-blue flag, is the white garden lily, or fleur-de-lis.

PLANNING YOUR TRIP. Whenever possible, plan ahead by writing to *Tourisme Quebec* (see "Tourist Information") for travel information. Ask for an accommodations guide, road and city maps, listings of attractions and seasonal events, and special interest publications. If you plan to attend a large convention while in Quebec, reserve accommodations early to avoid disappointment. Ask your travel agent about package tours to Quebec. These travel plans may save you money.

If you are a member of the Canadian or American Automobile Association (CAA or AAA), your local affiliate can help you plan your trip, advise you about road and weather conditions, and give you the addresses of Quebec branch offices where you can receive emergency help. (See "Hints to Motorists.")

Take along your passport (even though it is not necessary for American travelers), some valid identification that includes your current address, and major credit cards. If you are a student, bring your i.d.; if you are a senior citizen (over 65), bring your birth certificate so you can take advantage of discounts at many attractions.

TOURIST INFORMATION. Tourisme Quebec publishes a variety of brochures, maps, and directories to help visitors plan vacations. To obtain this helpful information, write *Tourisme Quebec*, Box 20,000, Quebec City, PQ G1K 7X2.

For your convenience the Quebec government maintains the following information offices in American cities: Délégation du Quebec, Peachtree Center Tower, 230 Peachtree St. N.W., Suite 1501, Atlanta, GA 30303 (404–581–0488); Délégation du Quebec, 100 Franklin St., 4th Floor, Boston, MA 02110 (617–426–2660); Délégation du Quebec, 35 East Wacker Dr., Suite 2052, Chicago, IL 60601 (312–726–0681); Délégation du Quebec, 700 South Flower St., Suite 1520, Los Angeles, CA 90017 (213–689–4861); Délégation du Quebec, 17 West 50th St., Rockefeller Center, New York, NY 10020 (212–397–0200); Bureau de tourisme du Quebec/Quebec Government Office of Tourism, 1300 19th St. N.W., Suite 220, Washington, DC 20036 (202–659–8990 or 8991).

In Canada a Gouvernement du Quebec tourism office is located at Toronto's Eaton Center, 20 Queen St. W., Suite 1004, Toronto, ON M5H 3S3 (416–977–6060).

If you live on the eastern seaboard from New England to South Carolina, from Long Island to Illinois and Ohio, telephone (toll free) 1–800–443–7000 for Quebec tourism information.

PROVINCE OF QUEBEC

In Canada you may dial the following toll-free telephone numbers for travel advice: from Ontario, New Brunswick, and P.E.I., 1–800–361–6490; inside Quebec, 1–800–361–5405; in Montreal, 873–2015.

Tourisme Quebec operates permanent information offices at 2 Place Ville-Marie, Bureau 70 (i.e. Office 70, corner of Cathcart and University), Montreal, PQ H2B 2C9 (514–873–2015) and at 12 rue Sainte-Anne (near Place d'Armes), Quebec City, PQ G1R 3X2 (418–643–2280).

The ministère du Loisir, de la Chasse, et de la Pêche (minister of recreation, hunting, and fishing) can provide much useful information on outdoor recreation in Quebec. Contact his office at 150 blvd. St. Cyrille Est, Quebec City, PQ G1R 4Y1 (418–643–2464).

CUSTOMS. The following information is subject to change, so do double check with tourist information offices before your trip. **Entering Canada.** Because of Canada's close ties with the United States, American visitors may take advantage of the world's most liberal customs regulations. Legal U.S. residents and citizens do not need a passport or visa to cross the Canadian border, only an acceptable form of identification (driver's license, birth certificate, social security card, certificate of naturalization, "green" card, or draft card).

If you are visiting from any other country except Greenland, St. Pierre, and Miquelon, you must possess a valid passport. It is your responsibility to find out whether an entry or reentry visa is required before you reach the Canada Customs gate. Officials will ask where you were born, where you live, where you are going, and why and how long you intend to stay.

Canada Customs allows British and American visitors to bring boats, trailers, hunting rifles, shotguns and 200 rounds of ammunition, cameras, radios, and typewriters into the country without paying duty. Your personal effects are, of course, exempt from taxes and duty. It is a good idea to carry proof of purchase for expensive camera and sports equipment, as well as medical and vehicle, and luggage or boat insurance.

Some items are restricted. Handguns and automatic weapons are strictly prohibited. Smuggling narcotics and other contraband items will land you in jail.

If you are driving a rented car, you must carry a copy of the rental contract with you.

Visitors over 16 may bring up to 50 cigars and 200 cigarettes into Canada duty-free. If you are over 18, you may import 1.1 liters (40 oz) of alcohol.

All plants must be examined for destructive insects by customs officials before entry. (See also "Traveling with Pets".)

Leaving Canada: U.S. visitors who stay in Canada longer than 48 hours and have claimed no exemptions in the past 30 days, may return with Canadian goods worth up to $400 (retail value in U.S. funds) duty-free.

Try to keep all your receipts together for easy reference. To avoid embarrassing delays at the U.S. customs counter, keep your Canadian purchases near the top of your luggage or in a separate suitcase.

To avoid surprises, check allowable fish and game limits at your U.S. customs office before leaving; register all cameras, lenses, scopes, binoculars, and electronic equipment.

FACTS AT YOUR FINGERTIPS

TIPS FOR BRITISH VISITORS. Although you will not need a visa to enter Canada, you must bring a valid passport or British Visitor's Passport. These documents are available in Britain for £15 and £7.50 respectively; the former is good for ten years while the British Visitor's Passport expires after one year. No health certificates are required.

Customs. If 18 or over, you may import your luggage and personal possessions, 50 cigars, a carton of cigarettes (200), almost a kilogram of pipe tobacco (2 lbs.); one bottle (40 fl. oz.) of wine or liquor, or a case of beer (24 pints), small amounts of perfume, and other goods worth $40 (Canadian). You cannot bring seeds, meats, plants, fruit, handguns, automatic weapons, or narcotics into the country.

When returning to the U.K. from Canada, you can take home the following goods duty-free: 200 cigarettes, 100 cigarillos, 50 cigars, or 250 grams of tobacco; one liter of alcohol over 38.8% proof, two liters under 38.8% proof, or two liters of sparkling or fortified wine and two liters of table wine; 50 grams of perfume and ¼ liter toilet water; other goods worth a total of £28.

Consulates. Although the British High Commission is located in Ottawa, the nation's capital, there are two British consulates in Quebec. In Montreal the Consulate Général de Grande Bretagne is located at 635 Dorchester Blvd. West (514-866-5863). In Quebec City, you will find an information office at 500 Grande Allée Est (418-525-5187).

Insurance. Because of the high cost of health care in Canada, you may want to get health and automobile-accident insurance from *Europ Assistance,* 252 High St., Croydon, Surrey CRO 1NF (01-680 1234).

Air Fares. Budget flights to Quebec operate from London to Mirabel International Airport north of Montreal. Also investigate cheap trans-Atlantic rates from London to New York combined with low-cost People Express flights from the nearby Newark, New Jersey, airport to Montreal's Dorval Airport. Check APEX and other money-saving fares before making your reservations and consult your travel agent about package tours.

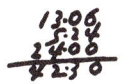

WHAT IT WILL COST. Quebec is one of the more expensive places for travelers, but that does not mean that you need a champagne budget to enjoy its many splendors. The proliferation of bed-and-breakfast and country inn accommodations makes it possible to travel through the province economically. While there are some campgrounds and trailer parks near Quebec cities, this form of accommodation is usually found in the province's recreational regions. Whether you are planning to "trip the light fantastic" or stay within a strict budget, booking accommodations ahead will help you to estimate your total vacation costs.

Quebec standards are high; so no matter what your accommodations are, you can usually expect to get what you pay for.

Allow a realistic amount for entertainment expenses and entrance fees to special attractions such as museums, galleries, parks or zoos, sports events, concerts, or plays. You will probably purchase souvenirs and gifts, clothing, and extra film while you are away. Remember to set sums aside for tips and emergencies.

Offset the relatively high cost of restaurant meals with casual picnics in picturesque city or roadside parks. To keep costs down, avoid hotel room-service charges.

Although there is no room tax or provincial tax on accommodations, Quebec charges a 9 percent sales tax on consumer goods and a 10% meal tax on orders

PROVINCE OF QUEBEC

over $3.26. (It is sometimes a good idea to ask for separate bills to avoid it.) There is no tax on books, clothing expenditures under $500, shoes under $125, and home furnishings under $500. (Note: throughout this guide, all prices are given in Canadian dollars.)

Typical Daily Budget for Two People

Hotel (moderate)	$75
Breakfast	$7
Sightseeing tour	$20
Lunch (inexpensive)	$10
Dinner (moderate)	$40
One cocktail each	$10
Museum or gallery	$10
	$172

WHEN TO GO. Quebec is a world within a world, where cities and towns have a uniquely European flavor, but a true North American style. You will feel at home here anytime, but your trip will be especially rewarding if you link it to some of the province's major seasonal events.

In Quebec winter is a time for activity, not hibernation. Hearty Quebecers practice the 4 s's: they ski, skate, snowmobile, and snowshoe. If that is not enough to keep you warm, then plan to celebrate at Quebec City's renowned Winter Carnival, the oldest in North America. City cultural activities blossom in winter, the perfect time to enjoy such indoor spectacles as the ballet, symphony, theater, opera, ice skating performances, and Quebec's two NHL hockey teams, the Montreal Canadiens and the Quebec Nordiques.

Spring thaw means only one thing in Quebec: maple syrup season. Everyone migrates to local *cabanes à sucre* to down a traditional feast of maple-soaked beans, bacon, potatoes, bread, omelets, *les oreilles de Christ* ("Christ's ears," crispy, deep-fried pieces of bacon rind), pancakes and deep-fried dumplings, or maple taffy rolled in snow.

Quebec comes alive in summer; in the cities you can lounge in sidewalk cafes, listening to street musicians play jazz or classical music. This is the time for fireworks and festivals, parades, and a host of summer outdoor activities. In Quebec's provincial parks you can fish, swim, sail, windsurf, hike, and camp.

There is no place more beautiful in the autumn than Quebec's forests; the brightly colored hillsides are a sight to behold. At country inns nearby you can enjoy gourmet meals before a brisk walk along naturally paved woodland paths.

Deciding when to visit Quebec depends on your interests and inclinations. Quebec offers excitement year-round. Whenever you come, prepare for wild temperature variations (see "What to Pack"). In summer air-conditioning will help to relieve you on hot, humid days. Northern evenings can be chilly. Severe winter blizzards and ice storms can transform the province's city core into trafficless wastelands and force stores to close. Salted streets will play havoc with leather boots and shoes; rubber "duck" boots are a wise choice for spring and fall travel wardrobes.

FACTS AT YOUR FINGERTIPS

Average Temperatures in Montreal

Month	Maximum C/F	Minimum C/F
January	−4°C/24°F	−13°C/8°F
February	−3°C/26°F	−12°C/10°F
March	2°C/46°F	−5°C/23°F
April	11°C/52°F	3°C/38°F
May	18°C/64°F	9°C/48°F
June	24°C/75°F	15°C/59°F
July	26°C/79°F	17°C/62°F
August	25°C/77°F	16°C/61°F
September	20°C/68°F	12°C/54°F
October	13°C/55°F	6°C/42°F
November	6°C/42°F	−1°C/30°F
December	−3°C/26°F	−10°C/14°F

WHAT TO PACK. From June to August temperatures are hot and sometimes stifling. Pack light, loose clothing that will keep you cool, as well as a hat, a light jacket or sweater, shorts, summer-weight pants, skirts and blouses, a bathing suit, and sunglasses. A collapsible umbrella and a light raincoat will protect you during occasional summer showers.

Deciding what to bring in spring (April to June) and fall (September to November) is more difficult. Temperature fluctuations are common during these seasons. Indian summer spells hot days and warm nights. Spring cold snaps are enough to convince the hardiest travelers that winter will never end. Pack a range of clothing for warm and cool weather: a warm coat, a light jacket, gloves, a hat, a few light summer outfits, warm sweaters, and waterproof boots that will not be damaged by salt. Nights are on the cold side, especially in the northern regions.

Quebec's winter temperatures are frigid; humidity seems to cut through your bones like a knife. Bring your warmest sweaters, heavy-weight clothing, a hat or toque, a scarf, gloves, lined, waterproof boots and, if you are planning outdoor activities, a heavy ski jacket, thick wool socks, a face protector, and long underwear. Interiors are very well heated, so be prepared to shed layers when you come inside.

Many of Quebec's restaurants and nightclubs have dress codes. For an evening on the town, gentlemen need a suit and tie while ladies need appropriately dressy clothing. Montreal, after all, is one of the fashion capitals of North America.

If you plan to visit the country from May to July, pack some black-fly repellent. Regular insect spray will protect you from nasty mosquitoes during the summer.

SEASONAL EVENTS. No one enjoys life more than the Quebecers. Each month a host of events, such as Quebec City's Winter Carnival and sugaring-off parties in the spring, or Montreal's jazz festival, beckons travelers to join the celebrations. The following chapters provide information on seasonal events. For more help in planning a timely visit, write Tourisme Quebec (see "Tourist Information") for a detailed schedule of regional activities.

PROVINCE OF QUEBEC

After arriving in Quebec, check local newspapers for theater, dance, music, and other happenings.

LANGUAGE. Although Canada is a bilingual country, the official language of Quebec is French. More than 80 percent of the province's inhabitants claim French as their native tongue. Travelers from outside Canada's borders are often surprised by the extensive use of *la langue Quebecoise*. All road signs, store signs, and billboards are French. Restaurant menus and tourist information, however, are available in English.

While most urban dwellers are bilingual, you may find that you are unable to communicate effectively in some rural areas. If you can speak a few words of French, do not hesitate to use them. It will add to your enjoyment of Quebec's international joie de vivre. Quebecers who are proficient in both languages will automatically switch to English if they sense your difficulty. Many Francophones feel as shy as you do about speaking another language but rest assured that a Quebecer will trot out every English word known to help the conversation along. In this province it is not unusual to hear two-way French-English exchanges.

If a passerby ignores your request for directions, it is probably because he or she does not understand or speak English at all; ask someone else. The majority of Quebecers love to greet visitors and make them feel welcome. If you know a few key words, however, it will help break the ice and you will enjoy your stay all the more.

You will find a list of common words and phrases at the end of this guide. Also it might be wise to invest in a good pocket dictionary once you reach the province; la langue Quebecoise is not the same as the language spoken in France. Centuries of isolation on the North American continent have preserved some ancient French expressions and integrated some English ones.

HINTS TO MOTORISTS. Before you leave home, investigate auto club memberships that provide helpful travel information, insurance coverage, and emergency and repair service. The *Canadian Automobile Association (CAA)* is affiliated with the *American Automobile Association (AAA)*, 8111 Gatehouse Rd., Falls Church, VA 22047, and will supply you with AAA services while you travel in Quebec.

A U.S. or international driver's license is valid in Quebec for six months; after that time you must apply for a Quebec driver's permit. For information contact the local *Régie de l'assurance automobile du Quebec* (Quebec Automobile Insurance Board). The Montreal address is Tour de l'est, CP 151, Bureau 1616, Montreal, PQ H5B 1B3 (514-873-8526).

If you drive your own car into Canada from the United States, you should get a Canadian Non-Resident Inter-Province Motor Vehicle Insurance Liability Card, which is available from insurance companies in the States. The best source of information and advice about automobile insurance is *The Insurance Bureau of Canada*, 181 University Ave., Toronto, ON M5H 3M7 (416-362-2031). Anyone who drives in Quebec must have a minimum of $50,000 liability insurance coverage for property damage caused by car accidents. Nonresidents who are injured in automobile accidents may be entitled to compensation under the Quebec Automobile Insurance Plan. Drivers must carry vehicle registration information in the car at all times. If you are driving a rented car, you must carry a copy of the rental contract that authorizes your use of that vehicle in Quebec.

FACTS AT YOUR FINGERTIPS 7

The use of seat belts is mandatory in Quebec. Drivers and passengers must buckle up for safety or face a $25 per person fine.

In 1980 Quebec joined the rest of Canada by trading miles for kilometers and gallons for liters. All road signs are metric. (See the metric conversion charts below.) Most rental cars have a metric speedometer and odometer.

Gas, sold by the liter, is more expensive here than in the United States or other Canadian provinces due to higher provincial taxes (at press time it averaged over 60 cents per liter or about $2.30 per gallon). There are 4.5 liters in a Canadian gallon and 3.8 liters in one American gallon. (See "Metric Conversion Charts" below.)

Quebec has a vast network of super highways called "autoroutes" that provide motorists with safe, rapid transportation. Quebec's autoroutes link with US interstates 87, 89, and 91, as well as trans-Canada routes 401 (Toronto) and 417 (Ottawa). Smaller scenic routes, marked by a brown sign with an eye surrounded by sun rays, were once trails blazed by explorers and pioneers who first settled the province. A list of roadside provincial tourist information offices are marked with a brown sign with a huge question mark.

On intercity highways, the speed limit is usually 100 km/hr (60 mph) unless otherwise posted. When driving in Quebec cities, be on your toes. The speed limit is 50 km/hr (30 mph) unless otherwise posted. In major centers, pedestrians have a nasty habit of routinely walking against traffic lights; you may have to honk your horn to get them to clear the road even when you have the right of way.

Study your road maps (available from Quebec tourist information offices) before starting out in your car. All road signs are in French. Here are some useful terms: *pont*, bridge; *cul-de-sac*, dead end; *rue* or *route barrée*, road closed; *entrée interdite*, access prohibited; *arrêt*, stop; *ligne d'arrêt*, stop line.

If you have a CB radio and intend to use it while motoring through Quebec, you will need a permit from the Director of Operations, Department of Communications, Ottawa, ON K1A 0C8; allow a few months to receive it prior to your departure.

Winter driving in Quebec is a challenge; always pack an emergency kit in case of breakdown. You will probably need winter tires outside major centers. Driving conditions vary from crisp, clean roads to extraslippery surfaces iced by freezing rain. To prevent skidding, remember to pump rather than lock your brakes. Leave an extra car length or two between you and the automobile in front of you. To check road conditions, especially in outlying areas, call "Etat des routes" (road conditions) listed under "Gouvernement du Quebec" in the blue information section of local telephone directories. On provincial highways the Quebec provincial police (Sûreté du Quebec) will help motorists who need aid.

HINTS TO HANDICAPPED TRAVELERS. Since the International Year of the Handicapped, Quebec is more aware of the special needs of physically handicapped travelers. Most public buildings, churches, restaurants, and hotels now have wheelchair access ramps, washrooms, and telephones. Bus, train, and airport terminals have automatic doors for easier entry. Sidewalks dip at corners to facilitate street crossing by wheelchair. Many of the province's tourism brochures include information for handicapped travelers.

In major centers, public transportation is available for wheelchair-bound travelers. Voyageur, the provincial bus company, offers interprovincial wheelchair transportation. Contact the nearest office listed in the local telephone directory's white pages, or write: Voyageur Inc., 505 blvd. de Maisonneuve Est, Montreal, PQ H2L 1Y4. Reserve access 24 hours ahead.

PROVINCE OF QUEBEC

If you plan a vacation, these handy reference guides may help: *Access to the World: A Travel Guide for the Handicapped* by Louise Weiss, from Facts on File, 460 Park Ave. S., New York, NY 10016, which covers travel by air, bus, train, car, and recreational vehicle as well as accommodations, tours, travel organizations, and more; *The Incapacitated Passengers Air Travel Guide* from The International Air Transport Association, 2000 Peel St., Montreal, PQ H3A 2R4, deals with international airline travel; *A Guide for the Disadvantaged* published by Transport Canada, Tower C, 21st Floor, Place de Ville, Ottawa, ON K1A 0N5.

NATIONAL AND PROVINCIAL PARKS. Parks Canada operates three national parks, 17 national historic parks and sites, and five heritage canals within Quebec. For information contact the regional office of Parks Canada, 3 Buade St., Box 6060, Haute Ville, Quebec City, PQ G1R 4V7 (418-648-4177).

For nature lovers the Mingan Archipelago, an 80-km-long group of islands off the Moyenne-Côte-Nord near Havre St. Pierre, is accessible by ferry. Here adventurers may wander among colonnades, eroded "flower pots," caves, and other prime examples of nature's handiwork. Seals and whales, shellfish, and colorful flora and fauna inhabit these rustic isles. Camping is controlled in this fragile environment; to obtain a free permit, contact the Parks Canada office, 1047 Dulcinée St., Box 1180, Havre St. Pierre, PQ G0G 1P0 (418-538-3331).

Forillon National Park. 146 de Gaspé Blvd., Box 1220, Gaspé, PQ G0C 1R0 (418-368-5505). Bird watchers will delight in the dazzling spectacle of sea and high-pitched cliffs at Forillon National Park in the Gaspé, one of Quebec's most popular tourist attractions. The peninsula provides a habitat for over 200 winged species. From seaside hiking trails, where the relentless gulf waters sculpt the picturesque cliffs, you may spot blue or humpback whales.

La Mauricie National Park. 465 5e rue, Box 758, Shawinigan, PQ G9N 6V9 (819-536-2638). This largely undeveloped and heavily forested reserve in the heart of Quebec is a paradise for canoe campers. There are three campgrounds with showers, toilets, fireplaces, and sewage disposal, as well as a group campground and primitive sites along canoe routes. You must obtain winter camping permits from the park superintendent.

At Parks Canada's **national historic sites** and parks you can explore everything from Lachine's fur trade to Quebec City's fortifications. Heritage canals not only satisfy your curiosity about the province's historic water routes but entice outboard and sailboat enthusiasts to explore the mighty St. Lawrence River and the network of Canadian nautical highways leading south to Lake Champlain. Contact Parks Canada's regional office for detailed information.

Quebec's **provincial parks,** wildlife and forestry reserves, and other territories contain more than 500 km of hiking, bicycling, walking, cross-country skiing, snowmobiling, and snowshoeing trails. Quebec is an outdoors enthusiast's dream; here you can canoe into the wilderness and camp by a remote lake where the loon's haunting call awakens you in the misty hours of dawn.

Swimming, hunting, fishing, golf, climbing, and underwater exploration are only some of the sports available in Quebec's provincial recreation areas. On-site services include snack bars, reception areas, trail maps, ski patrols, warming huts for cross-country skiers, equipment rental and repair shops, and more.

Quebec's ministère du Loisir, de la Chasse, et de la Pêche publishes a comprehensive guide entitled, *Quebec Parks and Wildlife Reserves, Activities and Services,* that describes all facilities, outlines park regulations and permit requirements, informs you how to reserve in-park accommodations, lists the

FACTS AT YOUR FINGERTIPS

current year's rates for swimming, camping, canoe or small boat rentals, golf, parking, accommodations, hunting and fishing, and provides detailed maps of park areas. For your copy, write to the ministère or contact the Quebec Tourist Information Bureau (see "Tourist Information"). A calendar of events is also available.

CAMPING. In Quebec most campgrounds and trailer parks are run by private owners but the ministère du Loisir, de la Chasse, et de la Pêche operates at least 60 campgrounds on provincial lands. All sites, general information, and regional camping and caravaning associations are listed in a free publication, "Quebec Camping," available from Tourisme Quebec, Box 20,000, Quebec City, PQ G1K 7X2 (see "Tourist Information").

The *Quebec Federation of Camping and Caravaning,* at 4545 Pierre de Coubertin, Box 1000, Postal Station M, Montreal, PQ H1V 3R2 (514-252-3001), represents the province's most ardent camping enthusiasts. It offers a wide range of services including publications, membership cards that entitle holders to small discounts, courses in camping basics, regional discovery programs, and rallies.

Space in many private campgrounds and trailer parks is prerented on a seasonal basis. It is wise to reserve camping or trailer sites in advance to avoid disappointment and last-minute scrambles.

Provincial park campgrounds have a variety of sites available from full-service, developed spaces to rustic, wilderness locales. Maximum stays are usually limited to 14 days. Group sites for nonprofit organizations are also available. At some provincial campgrounds you can purchase monthly or seasonal passes to campsites where you intend to set down roots for an extended stay. The maximum number of campers per site is six.

Senior citizens (over 65) camp for half-price in provincial parks and reserves. Special discounts are offered for stays longer than seven days, as well as monthly or seasonal campsite rentals. Canoe camping spots cost about $6 per night per site.

In Quebec parks and wildlife reserves, gas-powered motorboats are prohibited unless otherwise specified; only electric motors are allowed on pristine lakes and rivers. *Quebec Parks and Wildlife Reserves,* available from the ministère du Loisir, de la Chasse, et de la Pêche (see "Tourist Information"), lists powerboat restrictions. All boaters must wear life jackets.

No household pets are allowed to roam in provincial parks and reserves. Motorcycles, motorbikes, and recreational vehicles are allowed only on main access roads.

For information about camping in Quebec's three national parks, contact Parks Canada, Information Services, 3 Buade St., Box 6060, Haute Ville, Quebec City, PQ G1R 4V7 (418-648-4177).

HUNTING. An extensive network of paved roads provides easy access to the province's prime hunting destinations. Northern Quebec, where there is more than a half million square kilometers of wildlife habitat, is accessible by float plane.

Whether you have set your sight on moose, bear, deer, small game, caribou, waterfowl, goose, grouse, ptarmigan or pheasant, Quebec is the place to be. There are, however, a few hunter's guidelines to respect. You must purchase the appropriate hunting licenses before venturing afield. You will need a permit for each type of game hunted. The only exception is for Canadian residents who have a federal permit for hunting migratory game. Outfitters usually have all necessary permits available but we suggest that you inquire about this before your trip. You must show proof of previous hunting experience; a hunting license from your home province, state, or country, or a certificate from a recognized firearms safety training course will do. The prices of hunting permits are set each March; they are available anytime after that date from most sporting goods stores. Migratory bird hunting licenses can be obtained only at Canada Post offices.

For safety's sake, everyone except bowhunters and waterfowlers must wear 400 square inches or more of unbroken orange hunting clothing when on the trail. Adolescents over 12-years-old are authorized to hunt with firearms but, if under 16, they must be accompanied by an adult over the age of 18. Handguns are prohibited.

In the southern half of Quebec you may improve your odds for success by hiring an outfitter but the decision is up to you. North of 52 degrees latitude, however, nonresidents must book an outfitter and use the services of a guide. For a copy of Quebec's outfitters association directory, contact the tourist information office, the ministère du Loisir, de la Chasse, et de la Pêche (see "Tourist Information"), or the Quebec Outfitter's Association Inc., 482 blvd. St. Cyrille Ouest, Quebec City, PQ G1S 1S4 (418–527–1524).

To keep an accurate count of big game, hunters are requested to register caribou, moose, deer, and black bear kills within 48 hours of leaving the forest. Registration centers are located along major arteries leading to and from hunting regions and at float plane bases or local airports.

To help plan your Quebec hunting trip, request the following free brochures from Tourisme Quebec, Box 20,000, Quebec City, PQ G1K 7X2 (800–443–7000 in eastern U.S., 800–361–6490 in Ontario and Atlantic Canada, and ask for operator 400): "Quebec Hunting Guide," which contains estimated game populations, success ratios, hunting season information, firearms recommendations, bag limits, and prime hunting territories; "Quebec Fishing, Hunting, and Trapping," a summary of regulations, hunting zones, limits, and license costs.

FISHING. The sparkling waters of over one million virgin, wilderness lakes and rivers tempt anglers to cast for myriad sport fish. In the St. Lawrence River you can troll for fierce, fighting muskie. Spin for quick-jumping ouananiche, landlocked salmon, in the pristeen Lac-Saint-Jean or Lac Tremblant, or fly fish the magnificent, wild Gaspé rivers for Atlantic salmon. In Quebec's arctic regions, you can cast for the exotic char, whose whitish-pink flesh is a gourmet delight.

Rainbow, brook, brown, speckled, sea, lake, and the unique Quebec red trout are some of the sport fish that attract avid fly fishermen. A stubborn fighter, the smallmouth bass reaches weights of up to eight pounds. Walleye, more commonly called *doré* in Quebec because of its golden sheen, is plentiful. And the northern pike, weighing up to 30 pounds, will strike at almost any bait you care to offer!

Nonresidents must hire an outfitter and use a guide north of the 52nd parallel; south of this point, the decision is up to you. You must have a fishing license (available at most sporting goods stores) before unpacking your rod and reel. You can fish most species, including perch, whitefish, and sturgeon, in most places from June 15 to Labor Day. During the winter, ice fishing is popular. Perch, pike, and walleye swim the cool water under the lake ice around Montreal and Quebec City.

FACTS AT YOUR FINGERTIPS 11

Before planning your trip, write Tourisme Quebec, Box 20,000, Quebec City, PQ G1K 7X2 for copies of the following valuable guidebooks: "Quebec Fishing Guide," which highlights Quebec sport fish species as well as tackle, popular fishing methods, and general information; *Quebec Outfitters Association Directory* (see "Hunting"); and "Quebec Fishing, Hunting, and Trapping," a listing of regulations, limits, zones, and license costs.

NATURE-WATCHING. In spring and fall, skies at Cap Tourmente National Wildlife Reserve (see *Quebec City*, "National Parks") are white with 100,000 migrating Greater Snow Geese. In Montreal visitors can see kestrel and the rare peregrine falcon at the Macdonald College Raptor Center. Quebec's whale-watching capital is at the mouth of the Saguenay River, 175 km (108 mi.) from Quebec City. Every summer thousands of nature lovers crowd aboard cruises, hoping to catch sight of white beluga whales and the gigantic blues.

Nature interpretation programs are hosted by experienced naturalists in Quebec provincial parks during the summer.

SUMMER SPORTS. The Quebecers participate in every sport. In addition to fishing, hunting, and camping, water sports are very popular in Quebec; yachting, windsurfing, water skiing, and canoeing are only a few summer pastimes. You can swim in one of a thousand inland lakes at provincial parks. Along the St. Lawrence River there are beaches in quiet coves and bays. Avid sailors can write to the ministère du Loisir, de la Chasse, et de la Pêche (see "Tourist Information") for the free brochure *Randonnée nautique Quebec*.

Tennis, squash, and other racket sports are played throughout the province. Many resorts offer tennis weeks with instruction. In urban areas, public courts abound in small parks; these may be free of charge for local residents or playable for a small hourly fee. Quebec has many championship golf courses, so remember to bring your golf shoes.

Hiking, climbing, birdwatching, and other natural activities are available in Quebec's many provincial and national parks and reserves. Cycling and bicycle touring is becoming more popular, although there is still a chronic shortage of city paths.

WINTER SPORTS. The proliferation of winter sports in Quebec may surprise you. In the Laurentians alone, there are more than 2000 km of well-groomed cross-country ski trails. Each February more than 100 Nordic ski enthusiasts participate in the 140-km Lachute to Hull cross-country ski marathon. There are more than 95 alpine ski centers where you can enjoy a day's outing; most are located within two hours of Quebec's major urban centers.

Ice skating, tobogganing, snowmobiling, snowshoeing, and even dog sledding are popular ways to keep fit and warm during Quebec's long winter months. And, of course, there are those great Canadian pastimes: curling, broomball, and ball, or street hockey.

SNOWMOBILES. To snowmobile in Quebec, you must hold a membership card or daily pass issued by an authorized representative of a snowmobile club. Such passes are readily available from one of more than 260 local organizations. You must carry your snowmobile permit and registration certificate with you. Every snowmobile owner must maintain a minimum insurance coverage of

PROVINCE OF QUEBEC

$35,000, wear a protective helmet and only ride on marked snowmobile trails. Drivers under 18 may not cross public roads unless they have an automobile driver's licence. When your snowmobile is in operation, headlights and other running lights must be on.

For information about snowmobile tours offered by private companies, contact Tourisme Quebec (see "Tourist Information.") Request a copy of Quebec's Snowmobiling Guide and Transport Quebec's map of the Trans-Quebec Trail Network, including its nine circuit routes. The Canadian Council of Snowmobile Organizations may also help you to locate valuable regional resources. Write: 2596 de Vigny, Mascouche, Quebec, J7K 1W4 (or call 514–474–1177).

SPECTATOR SPORTS. When the Quebecers are not playing sports, they are watching them. Major league baseball, Canadian football and, naturally, national league hockey top the avid sports fan's list of must-see team events. At Montreal's Forum les Canadiens sail down the ice; in Quebec City les Nordiques stick-handle the puck past the Colisee's blue line. At Montreal's Olympic Stadium les Expos and their orange mascot Youppi face other national baseball league teams and les Concordes play a wild game of football against rival Canadian teams.

International cycling, equestrian, diving, boxing, wrestling, swimming, gymnastics, ice skating, and other competitions are held at Quebec's sporting arenas annually. In June you can thrill to the excitement of Grand Prix auto racing on Montreal's Île Notre Dame. Harness and thoroughbred racing tracks operate near major urban centers.

ACCOMMODATIONS. Quebec offers weary travelers a variety of accommodations, from modern, luxury hotels in Montreal and Quebec City to shared dormitory space in rustic youth hostels near the heart of Gaspé. Wherever you plan to travel, try to reserve ahead to avoid high-priced, unsuitable, last-minute accommodations. Do not settle for potluck, especially in the peak summer tourist season from June to September. To shake away the winter blues at Quebec City's "Carnaval," arrange for a place to stay at least four to six months in advance.

Daycare services, cribs or cots, and parking and laundry facilities may or may not be available. Usually there is a minimal extra charge for these services. When confirming your reservation, ask the hotelier for a comprehensive list of what is included in the room cost. If you are traveling with a pet, always verify that the inn will accept it. Most Laurentian hotels, for instance, do not allow four-footed guests (guide dogs are the exception).

Many popular inns, hotels, and motels accept long-distance telephone reservations that are confirmed with an immediate deposit on a credit card (American Express, Visa, or MasterCard are usually accepted). If you plan to stay at a hotel or motel affiliated with a major international chain, you may be able to book accommodations through the member hotel in your hometown.

In some cases, innkeeper's prices reflect the meal-accommodation package offered. The American Plan (AP) includes three meals daily. You can expect breakfast and an evening meal on the Modified American Plan (MAP) and a light breakfast of croissant and coffee on the European Plan (EP).

Price Categories. All accommodations in this guide are divided into five categories—*Super Deluxe, Deluxe, Expensive, Moderate,* and *Inexpensive*—based on the price of a double room. The price range for each classification varies from one region to another. A moderate hotel in an urban area, for

FACTS AT YOUR FINGERTIPS 13

example, may seem costly when compared to its countryside counterpart. In every chapter the appropriate price ranges (in Canadian dollars) for each category are clearly stated before each list of establishments.

Lilies and Forks. The provincial government rates all inns and hotels, awarding up to six lilies for comfort, and four forks for cuisine, ambiance and service. The lilies mean: one for basic comfort; two for average comfort; three for good comfort; four for above-average comfort; and five for very good comfort. Hotel restaurants are classified with awards of forks, as follows: one fork for satisfactory cuisine, service and ambiance; two forks for good; three for very good; 4R for excellent (on a regional basis); and four for excellent. The government inspectors do not throw their forks around lightly, so even one or two forks can mean that the cuisine is quite good. Perhaps the waiters or waitresses did not wear fancy uniforms, or the décor may lack excitement. In general, restaurants with more forks charge more for meals.

Country Inns. Quebec has some delightful country accommodations, from fine old manors to charming, new inns. An excellent reference guide to 100 pensions, auberges, hotels, and chalets, Pauline Guetta's *Inns and Manoirs of Quebec* is available from Deneau Publishers, 760 Bathurst St., Toronto, ON M5S 2R6 (416–530–1035) or most travel bookstores for about $10.

BED-AND-BREAKFAST. Scattered in a variety of settings and sites, these guest houses are usually family homes with a pleasant atmosphere and clean, comfortable rooms. Whether situated by a meandering country stream or in a bustling city core, the style, standards, and price of these accommodations vary widely. Private bathrooms are a luxury; in most places the facilities are down the hall. Breakfast arrangements vary; the hostess may serve a homemade French Canadian meal with pancakes, preserves, Canadian back bacon, and other delights, or ask you to prepare a do-it-yourself meal with supplied ingredients.

Two terrific guidebooks will help you to find bed-and-breakfast accommodation in Quebec. John Thompson and Pat Wilson's handy *Traveller's Guide to Bed-and-Breakfast Places in Canada* has over 40 provincial listings, from Auguste and Anne Simard's 800-acre dairy farm in Lac-St.-Jean to a 110-year-old Victorian antique-furnished town house overlooking the heart of Montreal (available from Grosvenor House, 1456 Sherbrooke St. W., 3rd Floor, Montreal, PQ H3G 1K4, for about $12). A guide to farm vacations, country inns, and B&Bs, *Les Sejours et Les Promenades à la ferme, les gîtes du passant et les tables champêtres* is published and distributed free by the ministère du Loisir, de la Chasse, et de la Pêche (see "Tourist Information"). An English edition of this free guidebook may be available in 1986.

FARM VACATIONS. Quebec is one of eight Canadian provinces that offers farm tours and holidays. The Quebec Ministry of Agriculture and the Agricotour Association sponsor these interesting, low-cost options for travelers. In spring you can harvest the sugar bush, steaming sap until it condenses to sweet maple syrup. In autumn, when foliage is ablaze, rural settings are the perfect vantage point. About 150 farm families participate in the program. A night's accommodations with hearty country meals may cost as little as $20 per adult, $15 per child. Farm vacation spots are listed in *Les Sejours et les Promenades à la ferme, les gîtes du passant et les tables champêtres,* available free from the ministère du Loisir, de la Chasse, et de la Pêche. For complete information about the farm vacation program, contact the *Fédération des*

PROVINCE OF QUEBEC

Agricotours du Québec, 4545 av. Pierre de Coubertin Box 1000, Postal Station M, Montreal, PQ H1V 3R2 (414–252–3000).

HOSTELS. This inexpensive alternative is not limited to youths; hosteling is an international way of life. In Quebec, there are at least 24 hostels ranging in price from $7 to $12 for a night's accommodation. The Fédération Quebecois de l'Ajisme is part of the International Youth Hostel Federation's worldwide network. If you purchase a membership card (adults, $15; youths under 18, $9), you are entitled to a slight reduction in rates from 50 cents to $2. Write to the *American Youth Hostels Association, Inc.,* 1332 Eye St. N.W., Washington, DC 20005.

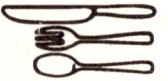

RESTAURANTS. Whether you enjoy a croissant and espresso at a sidewalk cafe, sample North America's finest nouvelle cuisine, or order *poutine,* a streetwise mix of homemade french fries *(frites)* from a fast-food emporium, dining in Quebec is an unforgettable experience. You do not simply "eat out"; restaurants are an integral slice of Quebec life.

Montreal is undoubtedly the culinary capital of North America. Over 3,000 restaurants invite hungry travelers to sample international cuisine. Name a country–its national dishes are served here. Local chefs specialize in the finest haute cuisine outside France (for considerably better prices than you will find overseas). Do not assume that Quebec's culinary classics are limited to its major centers; chefs at some Laurentian inns have won international acclaim for their gourmet expertise.

This is the land of maple syrup and blueberries, French onion soup and deep-dish apple pie. Quebec is the birthplace of habitant cooking: hearty bean cassoulets, rich *tourtières,* and other stick-to-the-ribs fare.

Wherever you dine, make your reservations early. At the province's finest restaurants you must book early in the week for Friday and Saturday night. Waiters and waitresses in the province's best restaurants have a sixth sense about excellent service; local standards are generally high. Dress codes vary from one restaurant to another; it is always wise to check in advance. Expensive restaurants often require gentlemen to wear a jacket and tie. In summer dress does not automatically become more casual. Few, if any, restaurants will accept bare feet or bare-chested males.

Most American hamburger chains—McDonalds, Burger King, and Wendy's—operate in Quebec. You will find Chi-Chi's Mexican restaurants and Baskin-Robbins ice cream parlors in major cities. The popular St. Hubert Bar-B-Que and Swiss Chalet chicken-and-rib chains also are well represented.

Restaurant Categories: In this guide, restaurants are divided into five categories—*Super Deluxe, Deluxe, Expensive, Moderate,* and *Inexpensive*—determined by the price of a full dinner for one, without beverage, tax, or tip. The price ranges represented by categories vary from one region to another; a moderately priced meal at a Montreal restaurant may seem expensive in Val-David. In every section, Canadian dollar values for each classification are clearly stated before the listings.

Space and availability of information has limited our listings; restaurants not included may be very worthwhile. In large urban areas, restaurants are also categorized by type of cuisine: French, Greek, Italian, Chinese, Canadian, etc.

Provincial rating system—forks: See above, under "Accommodations."

FACTS AT YOUR FINGERTIPS 15

TIPPING. Attentive, courteous, and efficient service in restaurants, hotels, and drinking establishments is usually rewarded with a monetary expression of your appreciation—a tip. In Quebec patrons who are pleased with restaurant service generally add 10 to 15 percent to the bill as a sign of approval.

Taxi drivers usually expect a similar amount. Unfortunately, often you must pay for the ride before the driver fetches your bags or opens your door, so small tippers may have to fend for themselves. Even a hefty tip will not guarantee good service.

In hotels bellhops usually receive 50 cents per bag while room service and other hotel service personnel will usually accept $1. It is not necessary to tip hatcheck or behind-the-counter staff. If you stay more than a night, expect to leave $1–$2 per person for the cleaning staff.

Never feel obliged to leave a tip when service is rude, sloppy, or extraordinarily slow. If someone is thoughtful and particularly prompt, a good tip is clearly in order.

If the low service standard spoiled your meal or ruined your trip, write the reason for your dissatisfaction on the bill and do not leave a tip. You will feel better and the person responsible for the sloppy job will get the message.

CURRENCY. The Canadian dollar comes in denominations of $1, $2, $5, $10, $20, $50, $100, etc., and is divided into 100 cents. Each dollar denomination sports a different color; the $1 bill is grey-green, $2 bills are pink, $5 bills are blue, $10 bills are purple, $20 are orange-green, $50 are orange, etc.

Common coinage varies in shape and size: copper pennies (1 cent) brandish maple leaves; the small, silver dime (10 cents) harbors the famous Bluenose schooner; the slightly bigger nickel (05 cents) frames the Canadian beaver, and the large quarter (25 cents) carries the proud profile of a caribou.

The value of the Canadian dollar is established by international money markets; at press time, about $1.40 Canadian buys a U.S. dollar, so American travelers have greater buying power. Although U.S. currency is accepted in Canada, you will find it simpler to exchange funds for Canadian dollars at your local bank. The exchange rates at Canadian banks or foreign exchange firms are often 5 to 10 percent higher than those offered in local shops and restaurants. Hotels will usually exchange money for guests.

Unless otherwise indicated, all prices in this guide are listed in Canadian dollars.

There are no restrictions on the amount of foreign capital that you can carry in and out of Quebec.

To safeguard your funds, buy traveler's checks before your trip. Most merchants will cash American Express checks outright; Visa traveler's checks, issued and honored by the Royal Bank of Canada, National Banque du Canada, Toronto Dominion Bank, and Canadian Imperial Bank of Commerce are also very popular. The Bank of Montreal is MasterCard's Canadian affiliate. Thomas Cooke traveler's checks are represented by the Permanent Trust Company and the Toronto Dominion Bank. (For banking hours, see "Business Hours.")

PROVINCE OF QUEBEC

CREDIT CARDS. Plastic money is as popular in Quebec as it is elsewhere in the world. Credit cards are easier to carry than cash and are handy in financial emergencies. When you receive your monthly statement, you will find that funds spent in Quebec have been converted to your national currency, providing you with a kind of discount.

All major credit cards are accepted. American Express Visa, and MasterCard are the most widely used cards throughout the province; Carte Blanche and Diner's Club are often accepted by hoteliers and restaurateurs. We have used the following abbreviations in this guide: AE, V, MC, CB, and DC.

TIME ZONES. Two time zones divide Quebec. East of Havre St. Pierre on the St. Lawrence River's north shore and on the eastern half of Anticosti Island, visitors set their watches to Atlantic Time. If you are traveling to Montreal, Quebec City, or points west of Havre St. Pierre, through Gaspé or the western half of Anticosti Island, adjust your watch to Eastern Time, which is one hour behind Atlantic Time.

When you arriving from London, England, visitors must set *back* their clocks by five hours (EST). If you are coming from New York, Florida, or Bogota, Columbia, you will not lose or gain any sleep. West Coast inhabitants from Los Angeles or Vancouver must adjust their watches *ahead* by three hours.

From the last Sunday in April to the last Sunday in October, most Quebec towns and cities switch to daylight saving time, which is one hour ahead of both Eastern and Atlantic Time. During these months, British travelers will suffer a six-hour jet lag.

BUSINESS HOURS AND HOLIDAYS. Business hours vary from city to city but retail stores are usually open from 10:00 A.M. to 6:00 P.M., Monday to Wednesday, 10:00 A.M. to 9:00 P.M. on Thursday and Friday, and 10:00 A.M. to 5:00 P.M. on Saturday.

You may eat, drink, and be merry in Quebec's major centers on Sundays but outside tourist areas or attractions, like Old Montreal *(Vieux Montréal),* you cannot shop or buy more than a few groceries. Drinking establishments, movie theaters, and restaurants open around noon.

In most small centers, retail stores close on one weekday; the local chambre de commerce will provide you with more detailed information about business hours.

Standard banking hours, from 10:00 A.M. to 3:00 P.M. during the week, are observed. Some branches offer extended service on evenings and Saturdays. You will find bank branch information in the yellow pages. Travelers from the United States who use automatic teller machines should contact their financial institution to discover which Canadian banks with branches in Quebec accept bank cards.

Quebec financial institutions, government offices, and large corporations observe the following provincial and national holidays: *New Year's Day* and the following day, January 1 and 2; *Good Friday,* the Friday preceding Easter; *Easter Sunday; Easter Monday,* the day following Easter; *Victoria Day* (Dollard Des Ormeaux Day), the third Monday in May; *Saint Jean Baptiste Day,* June 24; *Canada Day,* July 1; *Labor Day,* the first Monday in September; *Thanksgiving Day,* the second Monday in October; *Christmas,* December 25; and *Boxing Day,* December 26. Local retail stores may or may not open on these holidays.

FACTS AT YOUR FINGERTIPS 17

TELEPHONES AND EMERGENCY NUMBERS. Three area codes crisscross the province: Montreal and its environs, 514; Quebec City, Gaspé, and eastern Quebec, 418; Eastern Townships and northern Quebec, including Hull, 819. For directory information, call 411 locally or (area code)–555–1212.

Bell Canada, Quebec's telephone company, charges 25 cents for local pay telephone calls. Have lots of change handy if you plan to make long distance calls; to do so, dial 0–(area code)–telephone number direct within Canada and the United States, or dial 0 for operator-assisted calls.

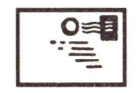

POSTAGE. Within Canada postal rates are 34 cents for letters and postcards under 30 grams. Mail destined for the United States must bear stamps worth at least 39 cents. Postcards and letters to Europe cost 68 cents for the first 20 grams, $1.05 for up to 50 grams, and $1.65 for up to 100 grams.

You will find bright red mailboxes marked "Postes Canada" on almost every street corner. Local post office branches appear under the federal government's Canada Post Coporation listings in the blue section of city telephone directories. Look for the red and white Postes Canada sign in drugstore or convenience store windows; these locales sell stamps and provide other postal services. Post offices are generally open from 8:00 A.M. to 5:45 P.M., Monday to Friday, and from 9:00 A.M. to noon on Saturdays.

LIQUOR LAWS. The minimum drinking age in Quebec is 18. The province's public drinking hours are the most liberal in Canada. Taverns and brasseries serve liquor from 8:00 A.M. to midnight, Monday to Saturday. All other licensed establishments are open from 11:00 A.M. to 3:00 A.M. daily.

Beer and Quebec wines are sold at corner grocery stores *(dépanneurs)* throughout the province. The sale of liquor and imported wines is regulated by the provincial government and distributed through "Société des Alcools" stores, which are open from 10:00 A.M. to 6:00 P.M., Monday to Wednesday, 10:00 A.M. to 9:00 P.M. on Thursday and Friday, and 10:00 A.M. to 5:00 P.M. on Saturday. Provincial liquor stores close on Sundays and holidays.

If you plan a night on the town, walk, ride public transit, or take a taxi to your hotel. Quebec has tough antidrunk-driving laws. If motorists exceed the legal blood alcohol limit of 0.08 percent, they face stiff fines, a few hours behind bars of a different kind, and risk losing their driver's licenses.

TRAVELING WITH PETS. Although your cat may enter Canada as easily as you can, dogs over four months old must have a rabies certificate issued within the last 12 months by a licensed vet. Vaccinations must be administered no less than 30 days before crossing the border.

Before leaving home, check accommodations guides to find out whether hotels and motels en route will accept pets. When you reserve, be sure to mention your pet.

Many Canadian cities, towns, and parks have leash and poop-and-scoop laws; please respect them. Make sure that your dog or cat wears an identification tag in case it wanders off.

PROVINCE OF QUEBEC

Pets are strictly prohibited in Quebec provincial parks and campsites. Dogs are not allowed to roam in wildlife reserves and must be restricted to a vehicle while traveling through the park.

Never leave your cat or dog in a parked car on a hot day; the torrid internal temperatures can prove fatal. Keep windows open a crack to allow fresh air to circulate. Offer your pet a bowl of water often and exercise it periodically. Pack its favorite food, dish, and toys.

METRIC CONVERSION CHARTS. First, a simplified list; then, some useful charts: 1 inch = 2.54 centimeters; 1 foot = 12 inches = 30.48 centimeters; 1 yard = 3 feet = 0.9144 meters; 1 ounce = 28.35 grams; 1 pound = 453.59 grams; 2.2 pounds = 1 kilo; 1 U.S. gallon = 3.75 liters; 1 hectare = 2.47 acres; 1 square kilometer = .3861 square miles.

Kilometers and Miles

This simple chart will help you to convert to both miles and kilometers. If you want to convert from miles into kilometers read from the center column to the right; if from kilometers into miles, from the center column to the left. Example: 5 miles = 8.0 kilometers, 5 kilometers = 3.1 miles.

Miles		Kilometers	Miles		Kilometers
0.6	1	1.6	12.4	20	32.2
1.2	2	3.2	18.6	30	48.3
1.9	3	4.8	24.8	40	64.4
2.5	4	6.3	31.0	50	80.5
3.1	5	8.0	37.3	60	96.6
3.7	6	9.6	43.5	70	112.3
4.3	7	11.3	49.7	80	128.7
5.0	8	12.9	55.9	90	144.8
5.6	9	14.5	62.1	100	160.9
6.2	10	16.1	124.3	200	321.9

Tire Pressure Converter

Pounds per Square Inch	16	18	20	22	24	26	28	30	32
Kilogrammes per Square Centimeter	1.12	1.26	1.40	1.54	1.68	1.82	1.96	2.10	2.24

U.S. Gallons and Liters

Gallon	Liters	Gallon	Liters
1	3.78	6	22.71
2	7.57	7	26.50
3	11.36	8	30.28
4	15.14	9	34.07
5	18.93	10	37.85

INTRODUCTION

Bienvenue à la Belle Province

by
Betty Palik

Betty Palik is a journalist living in Montreal. She writes on a freelance basis for a variety of magazines and newspapers in Canada.

Of all the provinces of Canada, Quebec is the most changing, the most talked about, the most different, and the most proud of its difference.

What makes Quebec so different is its strong French heritage. Not only is French spoken everywhere (although English is spoken too), but many of the local customs and traditions have their roots in Roman Catholic France rather than in Anglo-Protestant Great Britain.

Quebec is an intriguing and remarkable province. Visitors love Quebec; for its French character, for its peacefulness and for its great beauty. And Quebec offers them many unique experiences. Quebec is so rich in places of historical interest that it is often called the "storied province." For those who love history and tradition, Quebec City is unlike any other in North America, with its old-world feeling, its ramparts and its winding, cobblestone streets. For those who seek religious inspiration, nowhere else in Canada are there so many important religious shrines for pilgrims, a vast number of silver-spired churches and splendorous cathedrals. For those who want fun and excitement, there is Montreal. It is as cosmopolitan as New York, as chic and as French as Paris, as booming and bustling as Tokyo. For those who yearn for the serenity and majesty of nature, that too is in Quebec, in its uncountable lakes, streams, and rivers, in its great mountains and deep forests, in its rugged coastline, and in its farmlands and villages, seemingly asleep under Quebec's blue and white fleur-de-lis flag.

Life in Quebec is lived according to the dictates of the seasons. Even though Quebecers are forever talking about the weather, of how yesterday was lovely and today is terrible, they are as thrilled to see the first sprinkling of snow as they are at the arrival of the first robin and the appearance of crocuses in the garden. Quebecers might complain about the length of the winter, but nonetheless, they love winter for the activities it offers. Skating and ice hockey are loved by all, and practically every city and town park has a skating rink.

Even a great snowfall cannot impede the life of the province. Within a few hours after a storm, highways and roads are plowed and, when necessary, sanded and salted, and traffic moves with no difficulty.

When spring comes to Quebec in March, it slips in gently, with the days getting longer and the land warming gradually. Flowers come to life at the start of April and the trees green slowly. By mid-May in Southern Quebec the trees are lustrous and full, it is time for sunbathing.

Summers are warm and sometimes very hot. In the cities, the parks are filled with children and with office workers sprawled on the grass at lunchtime. Flowers bloom in front yards, window boxes, sidewalk planters, parks, and even on the highway medians. On the weekends, Quebecers flock to the rivers, lakes, and beaches for swimming, sailing, boating, and canoeing. They play baseball, football, and soccer; they jog, walk, or bicycle. They rush to play tennis or golf. Provincial and national parks are filled with campers, hikers, and picnickers. The air is heavy with the scent of evergreen trees and wildflowers.

By mid-September, autumn has arrived, the sun is not as hot, and the nights are cooler. Slowly the cold moves in and the leaves turn red and yellow, and finally by the end of October, they fall. The outdoor markets are brimming with freshly harvested fruits and vegetables. It is a season for canning and freezing and squirreling away for the winter. Camping, hiking, and fishing are still popular weekend activities, and the bicycles, footballs, and soccer balls are not put away till November. That is when the winter cycle begins again, when the rain and the grayness give way to snow and winter brightness.

Whatever the season, however, what strikes one the most are the numerous days of sunshine. Montreal, for example, records 100 more sunny hours a year than Paris!

QUEBEC HISTORY

In 1534 a young French sea captain named Jacques Cartier set out to find the Northwest Passage around the American continent to China, but he discovered eastern Canada instead. On his second trip the following year, he came back looking for gold. But this time he found a wide river, sailed down it, and arrived at Stadacona, an Indian village, on the site of Quebec City. He admired the location of the village perched on the cliffs overlooking a *kebec,* the Indian word for "narrowing of the waters." Then he sailed upstream, for he was intent on exploring, not empire building. He disembarked at Hochelaga (which became Montreal), where he was greeted by over a thousand surprised Indian natives.

First Inhabitants

About 22,000 years before Cartier was met by these natives, people from Asia began to spread across North America through what is now Alaska, from the Pacific to the Atlantic. They dispersed into tribes with varying languages, and by the time Cartier took his wrong turn, it was the fierce and mighty Iroquois who inhabited this region. Hochelaga consisted of about fifty long houses, frameworks of sticks covered with birch bark, in which many families dwelled.

The Iroquois lived south of the St. Lawrence River and east of it to the Richelieu River. Another large tribe, the Naskapi, hunted in the eastern part of the Quebec region. The members of this tribe who lived toward the south, between the St. Maurice River and present day Sept-Îles, were called Montagnais (mountain men) by the French. Other Indian tribes of southern Quebec were the Algonquin, Huron, Malecite and the Micmac. The Cree Indians roamed south of James Bay between the Naskapi and the Inuit (Eskimos), who lived west of Ungava Bay and along the shores of Hudson Bay. Once the fur trade began, the Algonquins and the Hurons carried beaver pelts in from the interior and sold them to the French. But the Iroquois, who coveted the fur routes, fought bitter wars against those tribes and also terrorized the French settlers. Eventually, after many battles, the French made peace with the Iroquois, but only towards the end of the 17th century.

French Cities

Seventy-three years passed after Cartier's visit before the French returned. Samuel de Champlain arrived in 1608 determined to build a French settlement close to where Stadacona was, with a commanding view of the river. His people built a two-story, wooden *"Habitation"*, on the riverbank beneath the cliffs of Cape Diamond. But because of Indian attacks, he then constructed a fortress atop the Cape and the inhabitants moved behind its protection. Champlain did more than any other explorer to explore and map the Atlantic coast, the northern United States and the Canadian interior. He also did much to encourage settlement in the vast region.

In 1642 Paul de Chomedey, Sieur de Maisonneuve, came to the island where Hochelaga once had existed, and to the mountain that Cartier had named Mont Réal, in order to establish a Jesuit mission for the Indians. He and his followers, including several missionaries, built a small palisaded settlement and named it Ville-Marie de Montreal. In gratitude for their success, they later erected a huge cross on the mountaintop. Today a brightly lit cross, visible for miles, stands on the site. Ville-Marie prospered due to a demand for furs in Europe. Her location was ideal, at the meeting of the mighty St. Lawrence and Ottawa rivers, and soon Ville-Marie was at the center of the fur lines running into the interior. Sixty years later, by the early 1700s, about 9,000 French colonists and native people lived in the town.

Throughout the 17th century, the French opened up Canada and most of the United States. They discovered and mapped a vast area stretching from Hudson Bay to the Gulf of Mexico. The adventurers who staked out this immense new territory of New France were the *coureurs de bois* (fur traders). Alongside the explorers traveled the missionaries, converting the Indians to Christianity. Among them were Pierre Radisson, Louis Jolliet, and the Jesuit, Jacques Marquette. There was also René Robert Cavalier de La Salle, who explored and named Louisiana, and Pierre Le Moyne d'Iberville, who colonized the state.

The Seigneuries

In 1663 King Louis XIV of France abolished the trading Company of One Hundred Associates and instead proclaimed Canada a crown colony. To bolster defenses he sent out the famous Carignan-Salières regiment. He also appointed a succession of military governors and civil intendants. The governors waged war or made peace, but the intendants founded settlements and established local industries.

Jean Talon, the first intendant, offered large grants of land, or *seigneuries,* to officers of the Carignan-Salières regiment if they settled discharged veterans on the land. In the same way he offered land to aristocrats in the colony if they promised to settle tenants or *habitants.*

INTRODUCTION

In return, the seigneur swore loyalty to the king, served in the military, maintained a manor house on the seigneury, ceded land to the habitants, built a flour mill and established a court to settle local grievances.

The land was allotted in a unique fashion. Rectangular strips, each about 1.6 km deep and about 60 mi wide, fronted a lake, road, or river bank. The houses and farm buildings were built along a road through the seigneury, giving the impression of a continuous village street. As the front *"rang"* filled up, further allotments were made in a second rang behind it. Thus married sons could open farms in the same seigneury as their fathers, and close family bonds developed between habitants of each locality. This pattern of long and narrow farms is still evident in the Quebec countryside. The habitants were not only close-knit, they were also deeply religious. The Roman Catholic Church took on an importance that went beyond religious functions. The priests and the nuns also acted as doctors, educators, and overseers of business arrangements between the habitants and between French-speaking traders and English-speaking merchants. An important doctrine of the church in Quebec was *survivance,* the survival of the French people and their culture. Couples were told to have large families, and they did. Ten and 12 children in a family were the norm, not the exception.

Talon also turned to France and sought settlers on promise of free passage and free land. There was a strong response from Normandy and the Île de France. Many hundreds of "King's Daughters"—orphans and the daughters of poor families destined to marry the settlers—also made the crossing. As an inducement to marriage, the administration provided wedding presents and relief from taxes.

Through these measures, the population of New France more than doubled between 1665 and 1672.

War with England

The first half of the 18th century saw a series of wars in Europe and in the New World between England and France. The Seven Years' War began in 1756. France sent the commander, Louis Joseph, Marquis de Montcalm, to secure the southern frontier of New France and consolidate the new territory of Louisiana. Leading a French/Indian expedition, he captured two British forts, securing the Ohio valley, and turning Lake Ontario into a French waterway. He fortified Fort Carillon (now Ticonderoga) on Lake Champlain and commanded the route north. But two years later the English captured Fort Louisbourg on Cape Breton Island, Fort Duquesne (Pittsburgh) and Fort Niagara. In 1759 the British dispatched to Quebec City a large invasion fleet carrying an army commanded by James Wolfe.

The British bombarded the city for weeks, reducing it nearly to rubble and attempted several times to land on shore. With the summer drawing to a close, Wolfe decided on one more attack. With about 4,000 men, he rowed upriver to a cove behind the city and climbed the cliff face in the darkness, bringing his army right against the walls of

Quebec and Montcalm's supply lines. The French had to emerge from their stronghold to battle on the Plains of Abraham.

The fate of Canada was decided in a vicious battle that lasted 30 minutes. The British won, but both leaders were mortally wounded. Today, overlooking the boardwalk, there is a unique memorial to these two army men—the only statue in the world commemorating both victor and vanquished of the same battle. A year later French troops, under François Gaston, Duc de Lévis of Montreal, marched on Quebec and defeated the British at Ste. Foy. Then they besieged the city of Quebec but were forced to withdraw when English ships arrived with supplies and reinforcements. The French were driven back to Montreal, where a large British army defeated them in 1760. Three years later the Treaty of Paris ceded Canada to Britain. France preferred to give up the new country in preference for her sugar islands, which were believed to be of more value. At that time all of the French civil administrators, as well as the principal landowners and business men, returned to France. Of the leaders of New France, only the Roman Catholic clergy remained behind, becoming even more important to the peasant farmers than ever before.

The Quebec Act

In 1774 the British Parliament passed the Quebec Act. It proclaimed an extension of Quebec's borders, hemming in the northernmost of the independence-minded British colonies to the south. It also gave full authority to the Roman Catholic Church, maintained the seigneurial landlord system, and provided for civil justice under the laws of Canada—in fact, French law. In general, it ensured the survival of the traditional Quebecois way of life.

War with the Americans

The American colonists were furious with the passing of the Quebec Act and hoped to incite a revolt in Quebec against British rule. When the American War of Independence broke out, an army set out to seize Canada. Led by General Richard Montgomery and Benedict Arnold in 1775, they did take over Montreal and set up their headquarters in the Château de Ramezay, home of the British governor (now a museum and tourist attraction).

But the French Canadians were underestimated by the invading Americans. They were true Royalists and devout Catholics, and had no sympathies for the "godless" republicans. So they stood with the English in Quebec City to fight off the invasions. Montgomery died in the attack and Arnold fled. The following year British forces arrived and recaptured Montreal.

The Creation of Upper and Lower Canada

A number of British and American settlers left Albany in New York and settled in Montreal. They began to press the authorities, as did other British colonists west of the Ottawa River, to introduce representative government.

The British responded with the Constitutional Act of 1791, which divided Quebec into two provinces, Upper and Lower Canada, west and east of the Ottawa. It provided for nominated legislative councils and elected assemblies, like those that had existed in the English colonies. The first election was held the following year.

Elected government was a novelty to the French Canadians who had never known democracy and who had been shielded from the French Revolution of 1789. But democracy suited them well and before long, there was rising demand for more rights. Heading the movement for greater rights was Louis Joseph Papineau, who was also leader of the French-speaking majority in the legislative assembly. He demanded that the English *château clique,* which made up the governor's council, should be subject to elections like the assembly. In 1834 he and his associates issued a long list of grievances, "The 92 Resolutions." Papineau lost the support of many of his own associates, and also that of the leaders of the church. The British responded with their own "ten resolutions" and refused elections to the council. The same year crops failed and unemployment spread. General unrest led to clashes between the English and young French *Patriotes* in Montreal. Soon a general insurrection broke out. Patriote irregulars fought British troops at St. Charles and St. Eustache near Montreal.

In spite of bad feelings, the upheavals led to major legislative changes in 1841. England passed the Act of Union, which produced a united Canada. Quebec was now known as Canada East, while Upper Canada became Canada West. Each sent an equal number of representatives to the elected assembly, but the governor was not responsible to the assembly, but rather to the Colonial Office in London. This continued to bridle both English and French members of the assembly.

The Growth of Montreal

Toward the end of the 1700s, the fur trade declined so much that Montreal almost faced economic disaster. But demand in Europe for lumber increased and Quebec had lots of it. As a result Montreal became the major trading center in British North America, helped by the fact that New York and New England had seceded from Britain.

Then the flood of immigration from Britain started, so much so that by the mid-1800s, Montreal had transformed into a predominantly English city. About 100,000 Irish immigrants came to work in Montreal's flour mills, breweries, and shipyards that had sprang up on the shores of the river and the Lachine Canal, begun in 1821. By 1861 working class Irish made up a third of Montreal's population. In the next 80 years Polish, Hungarian, Italian, Chinese, Ukrainian, Greek, Armenian, Spanish, Czech, Japanese, German, and Portuguese immigrants, escaping from poverty and political hardships, arrived by the thousands, seeking freedom in the New World.

Canada got its first bank in 1817, the Bank of Montreal, and world-renowned McGill University was founded in 1821. The French-language Université de Montreal was built in 1874. The stock exchange opened in 1874 in a pillared building in Old Montreal, which now houses the Centaur Theatre.

Confederation

By 1867 more than a half million immigrants had arrived from Europe, pushing Canada's population to over two million. Demand for union came from all the provinces of British North America to increase trade and economic prosperity, to increase their strength militarily in case of attack from the United States, to create a government capable of securing and developing the Northwest (the vast lands west of Canada West), and to make possible the building of a railway that would contribute to the realization of all these ambitions.

The Dominion of Canada was created on 1 July 1867 by an act of the British Parliament, known as the British North America (BNA) Act. It divided the Province of Canada into Quebec and Ontario, and brought in Nova Scotia and New Brunswick. Manitoba joined in 1870, British Columbia in 1871, Prince Edward Island in 1873, Alberta and Saskatchewan in 1905, and Newfoundland in 1949. The BNA Act also enshrined French as an official language. The Province of Quebec, like the other provinces, was given far-reaching responsibilities in social and civil affairs.

The Conscription Crisis

The entente between the French and English in Canada was viable until World War I strained it. At the outbreak of the war, the two groups felt equally supportive of the two European motherlands. Many volunteered. Even a totally French regiment was created, the Royal 22nd (Van Doos). But two things ended the camaraderie.

On the battlefields in Europe, Canadians, along with the Australians, formed the shock troops of the British Empire and died horribly, by the thousands. More than 60,000 Canadians died in the war, a huge loss for a country of 7½ million. In 1915 Ontario passed Regulation 17, severely restricting the use of French in its schools. It translated into an anti-French stand and created open hostility. The flow of French Canadians into the army became a trickle. Then Prime Minister Robert Borden ordered conscription of childless males to reinforce the ailing Canadian corps. A wider conscription law loomed in Ottawa. This led to an outcry in Quebec, led by nationalist journalist and politician

INTRODUCTION

Henri Bourassa (grandson of the patriot, Louis Joseph Papineau). The nationalists claimed that conscription was a device to diminish the French-speaking population. When, in 1917, conscription did become law, Quebec was ideologically isolated from the rest of Canada.

The crisis led to the formation of the Union Nationale provincial party in 1936, initially a reformist party. Under its leader Maurice Duplessis, it held control till 1960 and was characterized by lavish patronage, strong-arm methods, fights with Ottawa, and nationalistic sloganeering. Duplessis believed that to survive, the Quebecer should remain true to their traditions—a culture founded in religion and an economy founded in agriculture. Duplessis deterred industrial expansion in Quebec, which went to Ontario, and slowed the growth of reformist ideas until his death and the flowering of the Quiet Revolution.

The Quiet Revolution

The population of Quebec had grown to six million but the province had fallen economically and politically behind Canada's English majority. Under Duplessis and the Union Nationale party, French-language schools and universities were supervised by the church and offered courses in humanities rather than in science and economics. Francophones (French-speaking Quebecers) were denied any chance of real business education unless they attended English institutions. As a result, few of them held top positions in industry or finance. On a general cultural basis, the country overwhelmingly reflected Anglo-Saxon attitudes rather than the Anglo-French mixture.

In 1960 the Liberal Party under Jean Lesage swept to power. Though initially occupied with social reform, it soon turned to economic matters. In 1962 Lesage's minister of natural resources, René Lévesque, called for nationalization of most of the electricity industry, which up to then, was in private hands. This was the first step towards economic independence for Quebec. The financiers of Montreal's St. James Street, the heart of the business district, opposed it, but ordinary Quebecers were enthusiastic. In 1965 Lévesque's ministry established a provincial mining company to explore and develop the province's mineral resources.

Meanwhile American capital poured into Quebec, as it did everywhere else in Canada. With it came American cultural influence, which increased Quebecer's expectations of a high standard of living. English-speaking citizens remained in firm control of the large national corporations headquartered in Montreal. Indeed it became clear that they had no intention of handing power over to the French. Few Francophones were promoted to executive status. Successive provincial governments became increasingly irritated by the lack of progress.

The discontent led to a dramatic radicalization of Quebec politics. A new separatist movement arose that hoped to make Quebec a distinct state by breaking away from the rest of the country. The most extreme faction of the movement was the Front de Libération du Québec (FLQ). It backed its demands with bombs and arson, culminating in the kidnap-murder of Quebec Cabinet Minister Pierre Laporte in October 1970.

The federal government in Ottawa, under Prime Minister Pierre Elliot Trudeau, himself a French-speaking Quebecer, imposed the War Measures Act. This permitted the police to break up civil disorders, arrest hundreds of suspects, and led to the arrest of the murderers of Laporte.

The political crisis calmed down but it left behind vibrations that affected all of the country. The federal government redoubled its efforts to correct the worst grievances of the French Canadians. Federal funds flowed into French schools outside of Quebec to support French Canadian culture in the other provinces. French Canadians were appointed to senior positions in government and crown corporations. The federal government increased its bilingual services to the population dramatically.

In Quebec from the mid-1970s, the Liberal government and then the Parti Quebecois, elected in 1976, headed by René Lévesque, replaced the English language with the French language in Quebec's economic life. In 1974 French was adopted as the official language of Quebec. This promoted French language instruction in the schools and made French the language of business and government. The Parti Quebecois followed up in 1977 with the Charter of the French Language, which established deadlines and fines to help enforce the program to make French the chief language in all areas of Quebec life. The charter did bring French into the workplace; it also accelerated a trend for English companies to relocate their headquarters outside Quebec, particularly in and near Toronto. The provincial government is working to attract new investment to Quebec to replace those lost jobs and revenues.

The Parti Quebecois proposed to go further by taking Quebec out of confederation, provided that economic ties with the rest of Canada could be maintained. Leaders in the other provinces announced that such a scheme would not be acceptable. A referendum was held in 1980 for the authority to negotiate a sovereignty association with the rest of Canada. But Quebec voters rejected the proposal by a wide margin. In the last provincial elections, held in the fall of 1985, the Parti Quebecois government was itself defeated at the polls.

QUEBEC AT WORK

Twenty-five percent of Quebec's population lived on farms in 1941. By 1971 less than six per cent did; today, four to five percent do. Only ten percent of Quebec is suitable for agriculture. Most of the farming areas

INTRODUCTION

lie near the St. Lawrence River and in the Eastern Townships. Dairy farming is the most valuable agricultural sector, with swine production second. After that poultry, then beef production; fruit and vegetable farming (particularly apple); strawberry, corn, cabbage, and potato growing; followed by special ventures like sugar beet and tobacco growing.

The forests are Quebec's most abundant renewable resource. Ninety percent of forests are crown land (i.e., public land), the rest are private. A variety of trees grow in the province. The timber industry is lucrative and supports more than 500 sawmills, but the pulp and paper industry is much larger. Quebec produces more than one third of Canada's total pulp and paper. It is the world's second producer of pulp and paper after the United States. It produces 20 percent of the world's total newsprint, as well as great quantities of paper and cardboard. Newsprint alone heads Quebec's export list, and brings in $2 billion a year.

Quebec's mineral production has been rising steadily since 1970. In 1982 it totaled $2 billion. To Canada and the rest of the world, Quebec exports primarily asbestos (30 percent of the world's total), gold, iron, and copper, and it also mines zinc, gold, titanium, and building materials such as cement, stone, sand, and limestone.

Among Quebec's great assets is hydroelectricity, of which only a portion of the potential has been utilized. Nonetheless, hydroelectricity meets one third of the province's energy requirements. It has many dams and they are some of the largest in the world. The Manic-Outardes hydroelectric project in eastern Quebec and the La Grande project in the James Bay region are the most spectacular in terms of size and output.

The availability of hydroelectricity has enabled many smelters and refineries to be built in the province. Among them are Noranda's giant electrolytic copper refinery in Montreal east, and its electrolytic zinc refinery in Valleyfield. Aluminum smelters operate in Shawinigan, Arvida, Beauharnois and at Cap de la Madeleine. An integrated steel industry also operates in Port Cartier and Contrecoeur.

Manufacturing also adds greatly to Quebec's economy. The production of ironworks and iron implements have been strong in the province since the 1740s. The technology made it possible for other manufacturing to be set up, among them shipbuilding, railway, and locomotive building, an aviation industry, and snowmobile building. Quebec is also a world leader in manufacturing electronic (notably telecommunications) equipment. Montreal's Northern Telecom is a world-famous electronic company. In addition, building products, furniture, fixtures, textiles, clothing, leather goods, footwear, chemicals, petroleum, and coal products, as well as many foods and beverages, are manufactured in Quebec.

THE PEOPLE OF QUEBEC

Of Quebec's 6.4 million inhabitants, 5.3 million are French-speaking. They have retained their linguistic and cultural identity in a sea of over 200 million English-speaking North Americans. Quebec is very much part of the same New World as its neighbors on three sides, but at the same time it is different. For while Quebec is of North America, the majority of its people live and think in French.

But Quebec also has a large English-speaking population (706,000), particularly in Montreal, the Ottawa Valley, and the Eastern Townships. They are descendants of those English, Irish, and Scots who landed here after the conquest of New France, and of immigrants from other nations whose main language is English. English-speaking Montrealers founded and financed a variety of great institutions such as universities, museums, hospitals, orchestras, and social agencies, as well as a number of national and multinational corporations in the worlds of banking and finance, transportation, natural resources, and distilled spirits.

Half a million immigrants from Europe, Asia, Latin America, and the Caribbean also live in Quebec. People from 80 different countries have made their new homes in the province. In proportion to its population, this land, along with Canada, has welcomed the greatest number of fugitives from political and economic unrest over the past 20 years. Between 1968 and 1982, for example, there arrived 60,000 immigrants from Czechoslovakia, Haiti, Uganda, Lebanon, Chile, and Southeast Asia. A much larger wave of immigrants, from Italy, Greece, and Eastern Europe, had arrived following the Second World War.

Immigrant schoolchildren are assigned to the French school system but first they are taught French in special introductory classes. Newly arrived adults attend immigrant orientation and training centers (COFI's), where they learn French and receive vocational and social assistance. The ethnic communities also have created their own service associations and cultural and religious groups.

The native people of Quebec number more than 40,000. Nearly 30,000 of Quebec's Amerindians live in villages within reserved territories in various parts of Quebec where they have exclusive fishing and hunting rights. The Inuit people (Eskimo) number over 5,000 and live in villages scattered along the shores of James Bay, Hudson Bay, Hudson Strait, and Ungava Bay. They have abandoned their igloos for prefabricated houses, but even today they make their living by trapping and hunting. Many of them also make beautiful crafts and sculpture, highly prized by the whites in the south and abroad. These works of art are widely available in galleries and through specialized dealers.

Tourists should be careful not to confuse authentic Inuit art works with lower priced imitations sold in most gift shops and at airports.

The Inuit and Amerindians of the Far North (Cree and Naskapi), have a system of local and regional self-government. Natives in communities affected by the use of their James Bay territory for hydroelectric purposes also receive special restitution grants from Quebec and Ottawa.

Religious freedom is fundamental to Quebec society, and immigrants to Quebec have brought with them almost all the world's religious faiths.

Each segment of the population, French and English, has its own system of free public schools and colleges—Catholic, Protestant, Jewish, and nondenominational. There is also a private-school system, catering to some ten percent of the population. These private schools have tuition fees but they are also heavily subsidized by the government. In all schools, parents may choose to have their children receive religious instruction or a neutral type of moral instruction.

QUEBEC'S CULTURAL LIFE

The French Canadians of Quebec, often called "Latins of the North," have a wonderful ever-sparkling joie de vivre, especially at the more than 400 festivals and carnivals they celebrate each year. Even the long winter does not dampen their good spirits. The largest festival splash is on June 24, which was originally the Feast of Saint John the Baptist. Now it is called "La Fête Nationale," or National Day. Everyone celebrates the long weekend by building roaring bonfires and dancing in the streets.

February brings Quebec City's winter carnival, a two-week-long, noisy, and exciting party. Chicoutimi also has a winter carnival when residents of the city celebrate and dress up in period costumes. In September international canoe races are held in Mauricie and in August, an international swim gets underway across Lac-Saint-Jean. Trois-Rivières celebrates the summer with automobile races through its streets, and Valleyfield is the scene of international regattas.

Words and Music

In the early 1900s, Quebecers sang songs from France and the United States. Then came Félix Leclerc, who, in the 1950s, traveled the province with simple songs celebrating the uniqueness of Quebec. He sang of everyday life: of farmers, log drivers, and lumberjacks. The effect was to make Quebecers very proud of their heritage and culture. Then Gilles Vigneault rose to popularity with his traditional melodies and provocative lyrics. One by one, other *chansonniers* took their places on stage, and took on star stature. Then a sophisticated recording industry came into being around them. Some of the stars are Robert Charlebois, Pauline Julien, Diane Dufresne, Claude Léveille, Ginette Reno, Monique Leyrac and Céline Dion.

Then Raymond Lévesque established Quebec monologue as an art form. Other monologuists appeared, most notably Yvon Deschamps. Monologues and *chansons* took hold of French Quebecers' imaginations and were credited with helping to elect the separatist Parti Quebecois in 1976 by proclaiming to a wide audience that Quebec was for the Quebecers.

Their efforts were paralleled in literature. In 1960 a new kind of writing appeared, fierce and satirical. *The Impertinences of Brother Anonymous,* written by a teaching brother, Jean-Paul Desbiens, satirized the French educational system and thus sparked a fiery debate on the social, religious, and academic realities of the day. To be sure, French Quebec had its great writers before then; such as Roger Lemelin *(Plouffe Family)* and Claude-Henri Grignon *(Un Homme et son Péché),* but it was the work of Desbiens that began the creative flood of prose and poetry.

Novelists like Gabrielle Roy *(The Tin Flute),* Anne Hébert *(Kamouraska),* Marie-Claire Blais *(Une Saison dans la vie d'Emmanuel),* and Yves Thériault *(Agaguk)* came to attention. Their books were about the frustrations of Quebec society. Other novelists, like Hubert Aquin, Jacques Godbout and Réjean Ducharme, as well as dramatist Michel Tremblay, produced important reflections of Quebec society. These novels and plays are available in English translation.

Certainly not all Quebec writing is French. Many of Mordecai Richler's short stories and novels *(The Apprenticeship of Duddy Kravitz)* and Leonard Cohen's novels *(Beautiful Losers)* and poems *(The Spice-Box of Earth)* sprang from their experiences in Montreal. Hugh MacLennan of Montreal's McGill University, is one of the best-known novelists and essayists in Canada. His novels *Two Solitudes* (1945) and *Return of the Sphinx* (1967) are about interactions between French and English in contemporary Quebec. More recently, playwright David Fennario has written about English working-class Montreal *(On the Job),* and has won great acclaim.

Turning again to music, Quebec has two professional symphony orchestras—the Montreal Symphony conducted by Charles Dutoit (who succeeded Zubin Mehta) and the Quebec Symphony in Quebec City under Simon Streatfield. The McGill Chamber Orchestra also plays to large audiences as does the Opera du Quebec.

An international jazz festival has been held in Montreal every summer since 1977 and is on the way to becoming one of the major events of its kind. On the rock scene, groups like Offenbach, Harmonium, and April Wine take music created inside Quebec beyond her borders. On the disco scene, international favorites from Quebec include young René Simard, France Joly, Gino Socio, Geraldine Hunt, and Corey Hart.

INTRODUCTION

Stage and Film

There are a number of professional theater companies in the province, most of them in Montreal. They stage both classical and modern theater and also premiere Quebec productions. The best known are Théâtre du Nouveau Monde, Le Rideau Vert, La Nouvelle Compagnie Théâtrale, Le Théâtre de Quat'Sous, and the Centaur Theatre Company.

Classical and jazz ballet are extremely popular. Montreal's Les Grands Ballets Canadiens is frequently touring other nations and has a classical and modern repertoire. There are some 80 other dance companies in the province in addition to folk dance groups like the Feux-Follets and the Sortilèges.

Quebec's film industry is also aspiring for world attention. The National Film Board (NFB) of Canada, founded in 1939, trained many well-known directors and producers who are now working privately. Some of them are Gilles Carle, Michel Brault, and Claude Jutra. The NFB (its studios are located in Montreal), has won a number of Oscars and other international prizes for its excellent short animated features. Since 1970 many Quebec independent filmmakers, such as Denis Héroux *(Atlantic City)*, have won international acclaim.

Montreal is also the site of the annual Montreal Film Festival, international in scope, held in late August.

Visual Arts

Tourists in Old Montreal and Old Quebec are quickly attracted by artists they find working in the open, in the Paris tradition. These open-air artists are the most obvious evidence of Quebec's modern painters, of whom a number are well-known.

In the early 1900s, Quebec's impressionists, such as James Wilson Morrice, Maurice Cullen, and Marc-Aurèle Suzor-Côté, produced canvases that are highly prized. Then came Alfred Pellan, "Quebec's Picasso," who started the "Automatistes" school, largely impressionistic but with strong social and political overtones. In the center of this school was Paul-Émile Borduas, a painter who wrote "Le Refus Global" in 1948, a political manifesto demanding liberation and independence. In the 1950s Jean-Paul Riopelle, an abstract painter, gained international stature. Separate from this school was Jean-Paul Lemieux, whose nostalgic and impressionistic style has special appeal to Quebecers.

A second school emerged in the late 1950s, "Les Plasticiens," whose hard-edged style gained strength through the work of Guido Molinari. Recent years have seen a realist school emerging, characterized by painstaking devotion to detail. Graphic art is also flourishing.

In the field of sculpture, Quebec has produced wood carvings for its churches since the 17th century. Today this skill is kept alive by a sculptors' school run by Médard Bourgault in Saint-Jean-Port-Joli.

In addition, sculpture is produced by the Inuit in northern Quebec. Very moving and beautiful, they are made from stone, bone, or ivory. These works represent arctic animals, legendary and mythical beings, and hunting scenes. They are distributed through cooperatives run by the Inuit themselves and are sold in specialized galleries. Inuit carvings all bear an igloo tag and a number, issued by the federal government. The many lower priced imitations carved by whites in the south, and sold in gift shops and at airports, do not carry this tag of authenticity.

FOOD, FOOD, FOOD

No Canadian will disagree with the statement that Quebec has the best fast food in the nation. Hot dogs on steamed buns *(steamé)* and french fries with sauce *(frites avec sauce)* are sold everywhere in towns, cities, villages, and in little restaurants and *casse-croûtes* (snack bars) along the highways. *Poutine* is another Quebec fast food, probably unique to the world. It is french fries with sauce topped with curd cheddar cheese. It is salty, filling, and yummy. Barbecue chicken is also a fast-food specialty prepared deliciously in Quebec.

Traditional Quebec specialties are energy-rich foods, body-warming in the winter. *Tourtière,* the specialty of every French-Canadian home, is chopped pork or veal pie. And for special occasions in the country, *six-pâtes* is served: a deep dish pie filled with partridge, hare, quail, bacon, and potatoes flavored with cloves. *Ragoût de boulettes et de pattes de cochon,* is a homey meat ball and pig's feet stew. You should not leave the province without sampling Quebec pea soup *(soupe aux pois),* made with white beans, and every child's delight, *tart au sucre,* sugar pie flavored with maple syrup.

Montreal has an assortment of restaurants equaled nowhere else in North America except in New York City. Quebec City also has many fine restaurants, especially the French ones.

WINTER IN QUEBEC

by
Heather Pengelley

The snowy days of winter signal the start of special celebrations in Quebec. February cold snaps mark the season of Carnival. To ward of winter blues, Quebecers have adopted an old French-Canadian custom that has its roots in the tradition of Mardi Gras and other pre-Lent celebrations. Throughout the province, a number of winter festivals dull the chill edge of winter's onslaught.

The most notable vanquisher of winter's woes is the Quebec City Carnival, the largest celebration of its type in North America. Now in its 33rd year (1987), the grand fête encourages visitors to discover that no matter how harsh the weather may seem, the Quebec spirit, cultural heritage, and joie de vivre radiate an exceptional, unforgettable warmth.

Led by the Bonhomme, a jolly snowman sporting the traditional French-Canadian toque and multicolored woven sash, the carnival hosts a number of unique events including national and international snow sculpture competitions, sleigh rides, an all-night barbeque, automobile racing on ice, dogsled competitions, the hilarious bed races (competing teams push brass or metal bed frames through city streets to vie for the championship), lumberjack contests, the wild international canoe race, snowshoe competitions, and more. Join Bonhomme at the grand parades and balls, evening soirees, and international sporting events. Every outdoor sport that you can imagine, including torch-lit ski runs illuminated by grand fireworks displays, is exalted during the ten-day celebration. (For more information, see *Quebec City*.)

At Chicoutimi's Carnaval-Souvenir, it is the custom to wear a costume. For a complete list of the province's many winter celebrations, contact Tourisme Quebec (See *Facts at Your Fingertips,* "Tourist Information") before planning your mid-winter journey.

Winter in the City

Like strange flowers, Quebec's urban centers bloom under wintery snows. In Montreal, underground walkways that connect with the public transit Métro system protect travelers from the icy chill of northern winds. You can literally journey from the city's heart to its suburban limits without walking outdoors. Linked to major downtown shopping concourses and department stores, these tunnels are often lined with underground musicians who entertain passersby with traditional French-Canadian folk ditties, classical music, or swinging jazz.

Ballet, classical concerts, plays, and other cultural events crowd the wintertime calendar of events in Quebec's cities. The cold nights inspire a healthy, hearty nightlife of fine dining, dancing, nightclubbing, and romancing.

A Winter Paradise

If you prefer outdoor sports to the indoor variety, this is the place to be. Quebec's bustling cities and rolling countryside are treated to 200–275 centimeters (78–110 inches) of crisp, white snows annually. Every type of winter sport is practiced here: ice hockey, free-style and speed skating, tobagganing, alpine and nordic skiing, ice fishing, snowmobiling, automobile and motorcycle racing on ice, snowshoeing, sailing and windsurfing across frozen lakes, curling, dogsledding, and more. (For details about your favored outdoor activity, see the "Participant Sports" and "Spectator Sports" sections in each chapter.)

Snowmobile Country

Over 25 years ago, the sport of snowmobiling burst onto the winter scene when Joseph-Armand Bombardier first marketed his new invention, the Skidoo, on a grand scale. Today, Quebec boasts the world's most sophisticated network of immaculately groomed, well-marked snowmobile trails. The 28,000-kilometer (17,500-mile) system of double-lane rideways crisscrosses the Laurentian Shield, ice-bound lakes and rivers, maple forests, and the rugged, magnificent Quebec wilderness.

The 8,000-kilometer (5,000-mile) Trans-Quebec trail system's 20 interconnected highways provide an uninterrupted link to all picturesque regions of the province. En route service stations, snowmobile dealers and rental outlets, restaurants, and accommodations attend to your snowmobile touring needs. Five sections of this vast trail network extend into the United States in Vermont, New York, Maine, and New Hampshire. In Canada the Trans-Quebec system crosses the Ontario and New Brunswick borders.

In each of nine major snowmobiling regions, Quebec authorities have developed a donut-shaped circuit, color-coded with a triangular sign that bears the trail's special name, to offer winter vacationers enjoyable round-trip outings. All of these trails feed into the Trans-Quebec network.

The heart of snowmobile country is the Eastern Townships. At Valcourt, a visit to Bombardier's giant manufacturing facility and snowmobile museum should figure prominently in your travel plans. And, if you are in the area at the beginning of February, do not miss Valcourt's International Snowmobile Festival. Thousands of enthusiasts from around the world participate in North America's largest annual snowmobile meet. Located nearby, the first professional racing school for snowmobilers develops the driving skills of aspiring racers.

A few private snowmobile tour companies offer extensive snow-cruise packages. Whether you decide to face the challenging Devil's Mountain climb in the Ottawa Valley region or cruise from one comfy Laurentian inn or gourmet restaurant to another, these organizers will guide you along your chosen path. For sources of detailed information see *Facts at Your Fingertips,* "Snowmobiles."

Cross-country Skiing

Quebec's snow-carpeted hills and dales are tailor-made for winter action. Along narrow trails of quiet white, you will find a cross-country skier's paradise. Whether you ski on Mont-Royal in the heart of Montreal or ply the snows of the Gatineau or Morin Heights, the Laurentian mecca of nordic enthusiasts, you will appreciate the province's 2,000-kilometer (1250-mile) network of well-groomed, marked trails.

Some country inns, farm vacation sites, youth hostels, and hillside resorts specialize in cross-country ski packages. In many places you can ski right up to the doorstep of your chalet! In the Laurentians, Far Hills Inn at Val Morin nestles beside more than 80 kilometers (50 miles) of pretty trails that wind around small lakes, over gentle Laurentian slopes and through maple-sugar bush country. L'Esterel, the Alpine Inn and many other local resorts also border on a vast network of trails linked to the long Maple Leaf Trail that runs through this region. There are tracks for every type of nordic enthusiast, from novice to expert.

Most Laurentian alpine ski centers also offer well-groomed trails for nordic skiing and slopes where telemarkers can practice their wide, graceful turns.

In the Ottawa Valley, Chateau Montebello, the world's largest log cabin, is a cross-country ski mecca. Camp Fortune, near Ottawa, has over 200 kilometers (125 miles) of groomed, patroled trails. This region hosts the Canadian Ski Marathon, the ultimate test of cross-country endurance stretching 140 kilometers (87 miles) from Lachute to Hull, Quebec, each February. The Gatineau 55, an international cross-country ski marathon, is also held in this attractive valley setting.

More than 20 Quebec parks and reserves offer cross-country skiing facilities. You can glide along trails that last a few hours or plan a long trek with overnight accommodations en route.

For hearty, skillful adventurers, a number of challenging ski excursions in the Ottawa Valley's Petit Nation corridor, the Laurentians, the Eastern Townships, the Gaspé, and Charlevoix lead you along well-groomed tracks with trail-side shelters where you can camp overnight and prepare your meals. Each of these regions has hundreds of trails; whether you wander far afield or stay close to Quebec's major cities, you will find challenging tracks that travel through every type of terrain.

Alpine Skiing

From Gaspé's lofty, unexplored peaks to the small, cozy villages nestled at the base of Laurentian slopes, the spirit of alpine skiing in Quebec runs as deep as its snows. This sporty celebration of winter, enhanced by Quebec's joie de vivre, gives skiing à la française a special flavor that attracts downhill racers year after year. In the Laurentians, Eastern Townships, and Quebec City region, you can sample world-class ski resorts. The outlying areas of Charlevoix, the Ottawa Valley, and de Lanaudière offer more family-style, intimate skiing atmospheres.

Owl's Head as well as monts Sutton, Bromont, and Orford attract skiers south of Montreal to the Eastern Townships. With a 460 meter (1500-feet) vertical drop, 31 trails, more than 200 inches of snow and eight ski lifts including a quadruple chair, Sutton tops the list of popular ski hills in this region. Skiers weave through pretty, tree-lined glades between birch and other hardwoods.

If you are looking for a mountain with wide open spaces and dependable snow, try Mont Orford, only 20 minutes from Sherbrooke. This skier's paradise rises 540 meters (1,772 feet). Named after an Indian chief over 200 years ago, Owl's Head looms over narrow Lake Memphremagog, only a few miles from the Vermont border. Down its formidable 548-meter (1,800-foot) drop, 19 white rivulet trails tumble and curve around forest stands and rocky outcrops. Only 50 minutes

WINTER IN QUEBEC

from Montreal, Bromont offers skiing from 9 A.M. until 10:30 P.M. weekdays or 1:00 A.M. weekends under artificial light.

Say "Quebec City" to a local downhiller and you will elicit one sure response: "Mont Ste-Anne." Located but 30 minutes from the provincial capital past the icy cascade of Montmorency Falls and the Basilica of Ste-Anne-de-Beaupré, this pilgrimage site's 625-meter (2,650-foot) summit towers over the widening St. Lawrence River and peaceful Île d'Orleans. Sixteen lifts, including eastern Canada's only gondola, climb the 2,050-foot vertical to 32 perfectly groomed trails that cover three sides of the mountain. The most spectacular are a pair of expert runs, La S and La Super S, that cascade down the south side like elongated versions of Montmorency Falls. While one of these trails is groomed regularly, the other is left to grow moguls the size of small Japanese cars. Nearby La Crête, a long, wide run, was a 1984 Women's World Cup downhill course. On the backside, La Quanik, L'Anore, and La Paradeuse make you feel like part of the winter landscape. The 5-kilometer (3-mile) La Familiale on the southern face will ease novices into downhill mode. Snowmaking equipment now covers more than 80 percent of the mountain, but it is expected to expand to complete coverage within a few years.

Several smaller resorts nestle on the hillsides even closer to Quebec City. Stoneham, Le Relais (open since 1936), and Mont St. Castin offer skiers a choice of over 30 trails.

In Charlevoix you can enjoy Quebec's most unique alpine experience: bus skiing. Northeast of Ste-Anne-de-Beaupré, along the St. Lawrence River's north shore, you will find Le Massif de Petit-Rivière St-François. From the top of Quebec's largest vertical drop (800 meters or 2,624 feet), you ski with guides and 50 or 60 other people who are lucky enough to claim the virgin, three-peak massif for themselves. The exceptional view of the widening St. Lawrence River only adds to your appreciation of the mount's intermediate trails. At the base, a narrow road separates you and the mighty river. Once at the bottom, you are bused to the summit. About $23 buys you a ticket for 3,050 meters (10,000 feet) of skiing but make your reservations early!

In the backyard of the nation's capital, Ottawa, five ski areas lie in the Gatineau Hills. Camp Fortune, with fifteen trails and nine lifts, is the closest. A few kilometers down the road near Cantley is the Ottawa Valley's newest pearl, Mont Cascade, which bears 11 intermediate slopes. Half are lit for night skiing. At Edelweiss, a circular fireplace and spirited lodge await downhillers at the end of runs as long as 1,220 meters (4,000 feet). Near Wakefield, Vorlage is a tidy resort with a dozen more slopes. An hour north of Hull, Mont-Ste-Marie's 15 trails wind down a 381-meter (1,250-foot) drop on two mountainsides. At the base, L'Abri, designed by the same architect who planned Toronto's Ontario Place, blends into the attractive wilderness setting, sheltering vacationing families and convention executives alike.

In de Lanaudière, just 90 minutes north of Montreal, two small resorts with vertical drops just under 305 meters (1,000 feet) sit within the town limits of St-Donat. Mont Garceau's wide runs, loads of snow, and *sous-bois* or tree-lined glades attract every caliber of skier. Mont La Reserve's expert La Principale trail features challenging moguls that cascade through sous-bois. The scenic La Pente-Douce, for novice to intermediate skiers, meanders 2,400 meters (7,800 feet) from summit to base.

Mont Logan, a sprawling 1,128-meter (3,700-foot) giant in the Gaspé, usually harbors a snow base more than 6 meters (20 feet) deep. Carefully marked runs snake through the forests that flank the mountainside, skirting wide snowfields and frozen waterfalls. This snow-capped peak holds its snows until June.

Like other Chic Choc mountains, Mont Logan is only accessible by helicopter. Whether you test your skiing skills on the deep powder of monts Collins, Mattawee, Fortin, or Coleman, with vertical drops up to 825 meters (2,700 feet), you will experience the only heli-skiing operations east of the Rockies. Every run through the virgin snows differs; ski steep, snow-packed bowls or slalom through dense forests. Guides will choose trails to match your group's abilities and lead you down wilderness runs that stretch almost 8 kilometers (5 miles). Contact Tourisme Quebec or your travel agent for heli-skiing information.

The world's first rope tow was installed in Shawbridge, a Laurentian village only 45 minutes north of Montreal, in 1932. Since then, the Laurentians have dominated the Eastern North American ski scene, attracting thousands of eager downhillers annually. The concentration of more than 30 alpine ski centers in a 50-kilometer (30-mile) radius combines with such outstanding local amenities as luxury hotels, cozy inns, bargain hostelries, and more fine restaurants than are found in many North American cities.

The Laurentians are an alpine fantasyland. More than half of its ski hills have artificial snowmaking equipment to preserve top-flight skiing conditions from mid-December until Easter. Near the villages of Morin Heights, St Sauveur, Piedmont, Mont Rolland, Ste Adele and Val-Morin, avid skiers extend their hours of enjoyment well into the moon-lit hours, swooshing down shimmering slopes under bright artificial lights.

The pinnacle of the Laurentian ski experience is Mont-Tremblant. Its 914-meter (3,000-foot) vertical drop sits majestically at top of the Laurentian Autoroute, the skiers' highway, only 90 minutes from Montreal. Its summit, the highest locally, commands a spectacular panorama of lakes, valleys, and forests. Almost half of its picturesque runs are reserved for experts, the most renowned being the icy, well-moguled Expo and breathtaking Flying Mile. Novices can cruise almost 5 kilometers (3 miles) down Nansen. Intermediate skiers wind their way along the pretty Beauvallon, Beauchemin, or Lowell Thomas trails. Eleven lifts, including a quadruple, carry skiers up slopes and over snow-covered fir trees to Mont-Tremblant's 30 trails.

Founded as a wilderness retreat in 1906, Gray Rocks is the dean of the Laurentians. The resort's own 183-meter (600-foot) slope, Sugar

Peak, is always immaculately groomed. The home of the ski week, Gray Rocks is best known for its excellent ski school.

Mont Blanc, near St-Faustin, has 22 trails and the second highest vertical in the Laurentians. Only a 45-minute drive from Montreal, Ski Morin Heights and monts Gabriel, Olympia, Avila, Habitant, and St-Sauveur are family favorites; all of these hills offer night skiing. Rising between 168 meters (550 feet) and 214 meters (700 feet), their shimmering slopes are enhanced by artificial snowmaking equipment. Spread across four mountains, Le Chantecler's 195-meter (640-foot) drop offers skiers a choice of 22 trails, ten of which are fully illuminated at night.

Aside from the marvelous variety of skiing experiences, Laurentian hills specialize in top-flight ski instruction. Whether you enroll in a daily or weekly ski school program, you will learn the fine points of the sport under the guidance of qualified instructors certified by the Canadian Ski Instructor Alliance.

MONTREAL

by
Pauline Guetta

Pauline Guetta has contributed dozens of articles to national and international periodicals, including Reader's Digest *and the* Globe and Mail. *She is also former Canadian editor of the International Hotel Review and author of two other travel books on Quebec.*

Nearly half of Quebec's 6,000,000 people live in or near Montreal, with 2.5 million in the Greater Montreal area. It is an island city, 51 km (32 mi) long and over 16 km (10 mi) across at its widest. The city takes up 31 percent of the island, the largest in the St. Lawrence River, apart from Anticosti. To the northwest lie the Laurentians and the Ottawa Valley. Ontario lies to the west, Richelieu-South Shore to the south, and de Lanaudière to the northeast.

A City with a Past

LaSalle ... Jolliet ... Duluth ... Lamothe-Cadillac ... La Vérendrye ... Benjamin Franklin ... Benedict Arnold ... Montgomery ... Champlain ... Cartier ... Jeanne Mance ... Frederick Law Olmstead ... John F. Kennedy ... Queen Victoria ... Queen Elizabeth ... you will find all these names, familiar or distantly remembered, echoing through the *quartiers,* streets, and buildings of Montreal.

Remember Jacques Cartier? He was the French explorer who sailed 1600 km (1,000 mi) up the St. Lawrence River in 1535 to become the first white to see Montreal, the largest island in a small archipelago. The site already formed a metropolis, with 3,500 Indians living in what Cartier described as a "round village" surrounded by a stockade. A throng of over 1,000 natives greeted Cartier on his arrival.

The Indian village had vanished when Samuel de Champlain arrived 75 years later. Champlain set up a temporary trading post about a block west of the present Place Royale in Old Montreal.

Indians and Europeans alike settled here because three converging rivers made it a natural communications and transportation center. From here voyageurs could portage past the roiling, unnavigable Lachine rapids to rejoin the St. Lawrence further west, and press on to the continent's heart.

To the north and northwest, intrepid travelers found the Ottawa River (French, *Outaouais,* pronounced "Oot-away"). The Richelieu River led south to Lake Champlain and the headwaters of the Hudson River. All around lay a fertile plain, its soil deposited by the last ice age.

In 1639 a group of zealous lay Catholics—convinced that American Indians formed the lost tribe of Israel whose conversion would hasten Christ's second coming—formed the the Société de Notre-Dame de Montreal, to convert the natives to Christianity. In May 1642 Paul de Chomedey, sieur de Maisonneuve, landed with 40 settlers. Picked as carefully as today's astronauts, the group included Jeanne Mance, who set up the colony's first hospital. De Maisonneuve named the settlement "Ville-Marie de Montreal," later shortened to Montreal.

The little colony suffered from constant danger, as the Iroquois fought bitterly until the treaty of 1701. In spite of hardship from weather, war, and pestilence, settlers survived, and penetrated into the continent. Some sought furs and other valuable commodities, some explored for a direct route to China, and still others wanted converts, but all uncovered more and more of the new land.

Throughout the French regime Montrealers extensively explored and mapped the continent. Men like LaSalle, d'Iberville, Jolliet, Marquette, Duluth, Lamothe-Cadillac and La Vérendrye extended New France from Hudson Bay to the Gulf of Mexico and the Rocky Mountains. They discovered, explored, or settled at least 35 of the American

PROVINCE OF QUEBEC

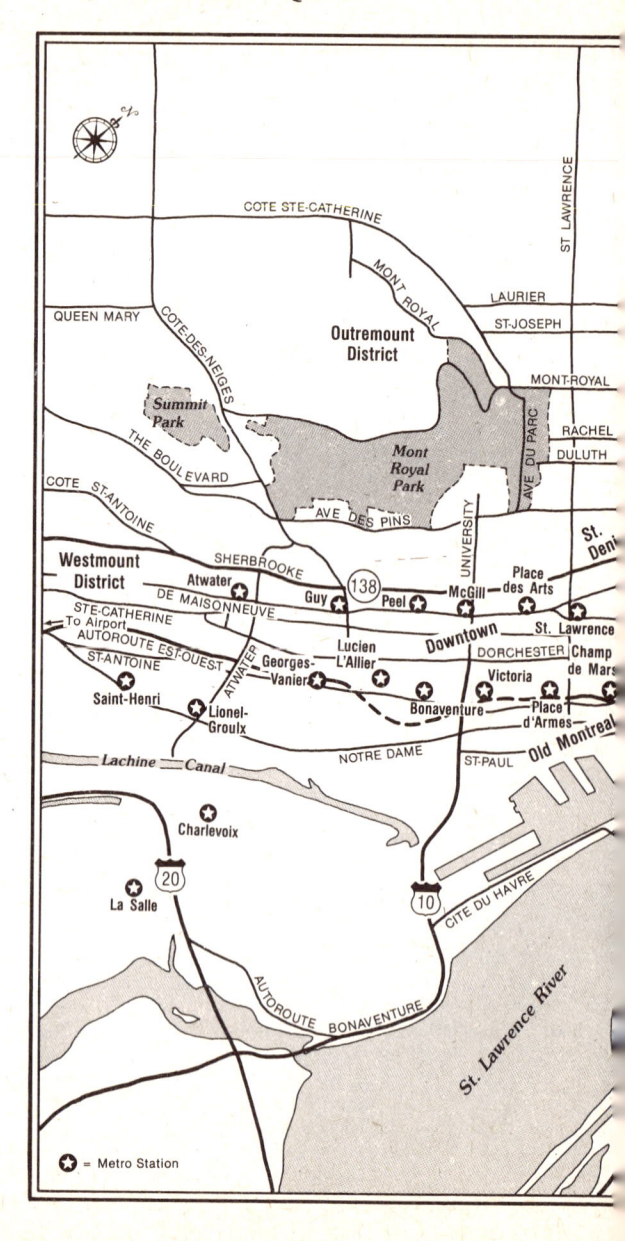

MONTREAL 45

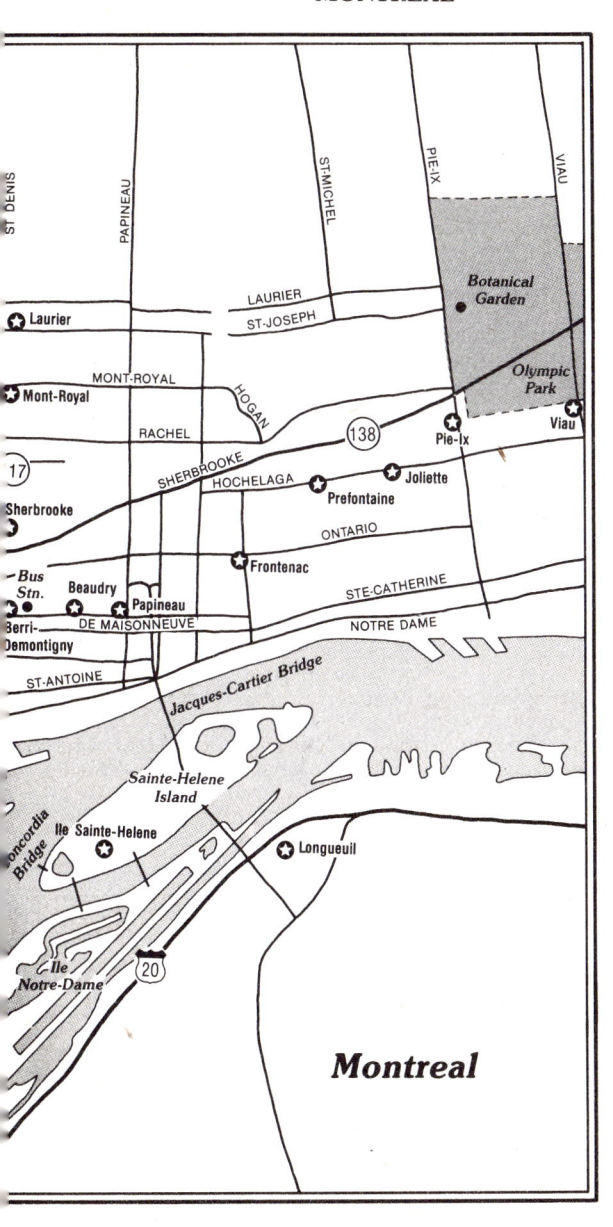

states, leaving 4,000 French geographical names throughout the United States to echo memories of their exploits.

During the 18th century, European powers strained to control the Americas. French and English colonies waged constant war, culminating in the English victory and the death of generals Wolfe and Montcalm at Quebec City in 1759, when Montreal became the capital of New France for the few months until, in 1760, François-Gaston de Lévis, successor to Montcalm, surrendered without a fight.

The French regime officially ended in 1763. With the Treaty of Paris, France gave rights to all North American land east of the Mississippi river to England, and ceded her territory west of the Mississippi to Spain. At that time Montreal's population had reached 5,000, almost entirely French.

Fifteen years later, because almost all Quebecers had French roots, members of the American Continental Congress in New England believed the inhabitants would welcome an American army to liberate them from the British. Accordingly, in November 1775 General Richard Montgomery led his Continental Army troops into a Montreal that had surrendered the day before. They headquartered at Château Ramezay (now a museum). Colonel Benedict Arnold and General Richard Montgomery, as well as Benjamin Franklin, stayed there. The French population, however, declined the invitation to become the fourteenth state. After suffering conclusive defeat at Quebec City, the Americans retreated from Canada in June 1776.

American forces also tried to take Montreal, and Canada, during the war of 1812–14, but in 1813 Colonel de Salaberry's forces beat them back at Châteauguay, just south of Montreal. Again, during the American Civil War, the North threatened to invade Canada after a party of twenty-odd Montreal-based Confederate soldiers raided St. Alban's in Vermont. Fortunately, good sense prevailed and no war ensued.

After the British conquest, a small group of Scots and English reorganized the fur trade, which dominated the city's economic life throughout the 18th century. Traders sent *coureurs de bois* and *voyageurs* out to trap and trade in the wilderness. In time, the smaller companies formed the North-West Company, competing with the older Hudson Bay Company of James Bay. Eventually, the rivals merged, but by then other forms of commerce and transportation evolved.

Development of Communications

Montreal progressed rapidly after it incorporated as a city in 1832. It became the capital of the United Canadas (Upper and Lower) with the 1841 Act of Union, but lost the title to Kingston, Ontario, in 1849. (Ottawa is now Canada's capital city.) Montreal, however, retained economic supremacy. As commerce in furs dwindled, lumber and then wheat became major exports. The city emerged as a shipping and railway giant. In 1867 Canadian provinces formed a confederation, and

MONTREAL

by 1900 Montreal, with a population of 370,000, formed the country's major metropolis.

Over the years tensions rose and fell between the city's two main groups. The Francophones saw that they needed to learn English to get ahead in the economic and, during the 1914–18 war, military world, while Anglophones could use their own language. The French felt discriminated against.

Since then—and particularly since the 1960s and early 1970s, when Quebec separatists agitated to make the province a separate state— French has become Quebec's official language. Separatist parties have dwindled through the years, until the Parti Quebecois, which had watered down its separatism to "sovereignty-association," suffered a major defeat, being almost wiped out in December 1985.

Now, in Montreal, all street signs, traffic directions, and all outdoor publicity, are in French only. Montreal is the world's second largest French-speaking city, after Paris. With the acceptance of the "French Fact," and a concerted effort to train and promote Francophones in business and government, racial tension in Montreal diminished. Now, about 70 percent of the population speaks French, with the majority of the remaining speaking English, and nearly all speaking at least a few words of one another's language.

Métro, Expo, Olympics

Recent decades brought Montreal vibrant international development, placing it in a global spotlight. In 1967 the city hosted North America's first officially recognized world's fair, Expo 67. Over 50 million people from 70 nations participated during the six-month run, recalled each summer with the ongoing Man and His World fair and the amusement park, La Ronde.

Also in 1967, the city constructed a colorful and efficient subway, the Métro. A building boom dramatically changed the city's skyline and added a new underground dimension.

The city hosted the 21st Olympic games in 1976, building a unique "flying saucer" stadium seating 72,358, and a complex that includes a six-pool swimming arena, and Vélodrome for cycling.

Economy

Montreal still ranks as a major inland port and the gateway to the St. Lawrence, the world's greatest inland waterway. The city also houses the headquarters of two giant railways, Canadian National and Canadian Pacific. Two large aircraft manufacturers, Pratt & Whitney and Canadair, provide jobs for thousands of the city's highly skilled aeronautic engineers and technicians.

An air transport center, Montreal serves as headquarters for the country's biggest airline, Air Canada, as well as the International Civil

48 PROVINCE OF QUEBEC

Aviation Organization, and the International Air Transport Association.

Manufactures include beer, cigarettes, clothing, foods, furs, furniture, pharmaceuticals, pulp and paper, railroad cars, trucks, shoes, skis, snowmobiles and snowplows, and much, much more.

Tourism

Each year, Montreal welcomes over 5,000,000 visitors. American travelers particularly appreciate that each U.S. dollar buys more than one Canadian dollar and that they can claim tax deductions for business expenses in Canada. Hosting national and international meetings forms an important part of the city's economy. In recent years Montreal has drawn millions of visitors to cultural attractions, such as the 1985 Picasso exhibit at the Montreal Museum of Fine Arts, the Egyptian treasures and artifacts of Ramses II, and festivals of art, movies, and music, as well as popular events like the annual fireworks show, La Ronde amusement park, and free dancing and band concerts in the cities' many parks.

One of the most trite, yet true, phrases used to describe Montreal is "joie de vivre." What else can people say? You do find "joy of life" here . . . in spades!

Exploring Montreal

People often compare Montreal with Paris. You will instantly recognize the Gallic heritage, particularly in people's love of fun, dedication to good food and wine, and, of course, the fact that everyone speaks French. But, in reality, comparing Montrealers to French people because they speak the same language is like saying that New Yorkers or Kansans resemble Londoners because they speak the same language and hold similar ancestry.

Montreal is . . . different. But it is clean and organized, so that most visitors feel safe and comfortable as they discover the city's charms. Most downtown hotel and restaurant employees speak excellent English. In other areas they try if they can, for Montrealers jealously guard their reputation as good hosts, happy to welcome you as their guest.

You will soon discover that Montreal holds many centers, or *quartiers,* each with its own charm. Of the island's two dozen or more quartiers here is a small selection:

Downtown, you will find boutiques, department stores, and museums. The Fifth Avenue/Regent Street area is Sherbrooke, roughly between University and St. Mathieu, and all streets between leading down to Dorchester. (Montrealers often leave off the rues, streets, and avenues, making street names serve equally well in French and English.) On Sherbrooke between University and McTavish, you will find the handsome collonade called the Roddick Gates, marking the

MONTREAL

entrance to McGill University's campus, which opened in 1821, and is one of the city's two English-language universities (with Concordia University on nearby de Maisonneuve).

Further west on Sherbrooke, at the corner of Drummond, you find the Ritz-Carlton Hôtel and, at Mountain Street, Holt Renfrew, an exclusive department store. The Montreal Museum of Fine Arts stands on the north side of Sherbrooke. Boutiques, galleries, and restaurants line the south side of Sherbrooke, and all the side streets. Indeed, Crescent, Mackay, and Bishop streets house some of the trendiest bars, restaurants, and clubs, while the Hôtel de la Montagne, a baroque luxury hotel enjoyed by many beautiful people, stands on Mountain.

Continuing west, past Guy and Atwater streets, you arrive in the City of Westmount, one of the 28 municipalities belonging to the Montreal Urban Community.

Westmount holds the Victorian municipal library (built to celebrate Queen Victoria's 1899 jubilee), pretty municipal greenhouses (free entry), and a bowling green. You will find many fine boutiques and restaurants, such as Les Près and Encore une Fois (health food—bring-your-wine) in the Victoria Avenue–Sherbrooke area. Similar delights abound on Greene Avenue, and in Westmount Square, where many European couturiers have boutiques.

Many handsome homes line the steep and winding roads leading up the slopes of Westmount, which is topped by a bird sanctuary and Westmount Lookout, from which you can see the St. Lawrence River and the Adirondack Mountains of New York. On the other side, you can see the main tower of the huge Université de Montreal (begun in 1928), designed by art déco architect Ernest Cormier.

Just over the border from Westmount, on the east side of Atwater, corner of Ste.-Catherine, stands the Montreal Forum, home of the Montreal Canadiens ice hockey team. From here take a cab a few streets down Atwater to browse among the antique stores on *Notre-Dame Ouest* between Atwater and McGill College avenues. They specialize in items like old duck decoys, Napoleonic mementos, and *junque.*

Back in the downtown area east of Crescent, Mackay, and Bishop streets, Ste.-Catherine boasts several major department stores including Ogilvy's (where a Scottish highlander pipes you out at closing time), Simpson's, Eaton's, The Bay, and Birk's. Within this area you will also find some of the world's finest (and most reasonable) furriers, many of whom produce furs for the world's great couture houses.

Further east on Ste.-Catherine stands the city's main performing arts center, Place des Arts (PdA) with three theaters seating a total of 5,000. Opposite PdA you will find Complexe Desjardins, with offices and the luxury Hôtel Meridien on the upper levels, and boutiques and restaurants circling a handsome atrium of plants and fountains at the center.

PdA and Complexe Desjardins link up to the "underground city," connected to the Métro, which reaches to the four corners of the city and under the St. Lawrence River to the south shore. Downtown

PROVINCE OF QUEBEC

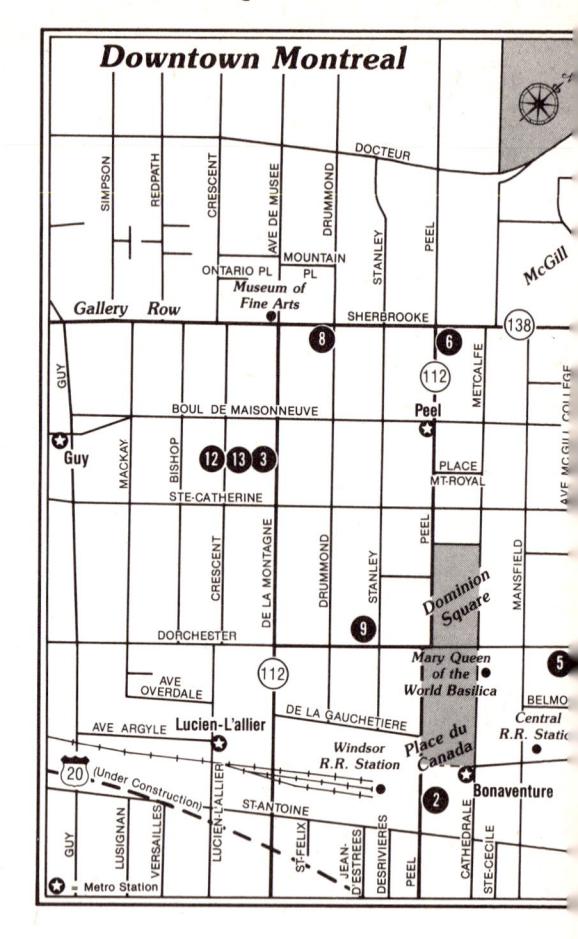

MONTREAL

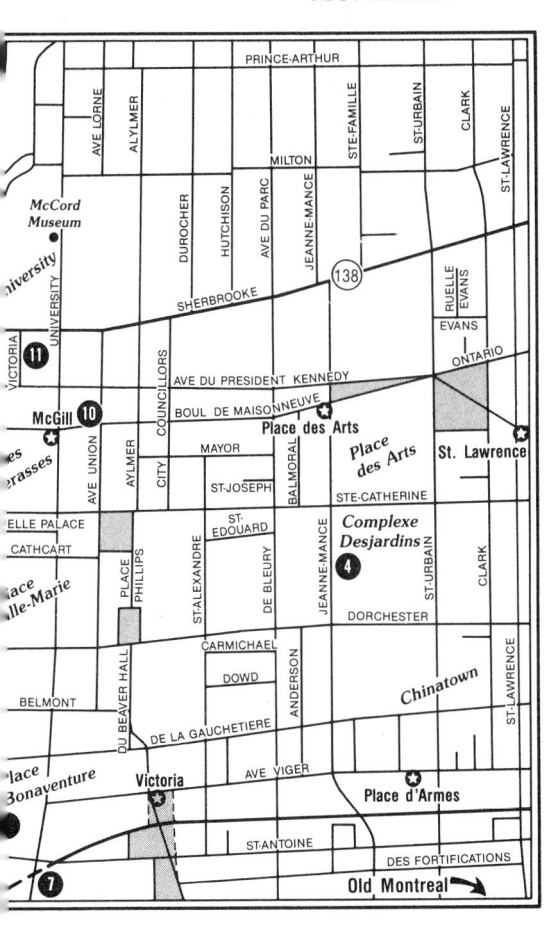

Points of Interest

Hotels
1) Bonaventure Hilton
2) Chateau Champlain
3) Hotel de la Montagne
4) Meridien
5) Queen Elizabeth
6) Quatre Saisons
7) Regence Hyatt
8) Ritz Carlton
9) Sheraton Centre

Restaurants
10) Biddles
11) Caveau
12) Les Halles
13) Thursday's

PROVINCE OF QUEBEC

pedestrian passageways lead to hotels and parking garages. Packed with shops, boutiques, cafes, street musicians (who must pass tests for permits to play), and bustling, well-dressed people, the underground city proves popular as well as practical—in bad weather no one need set foot outside.

Buildings linked this way include, Place Ville-Marie, hotels Château Champlain and Queen Elizabeth, and convention centers like the Palais des Congrès and Place Bonaventure. The latter also serves as a year-round merchandise mart and showcase for manufactures and industries. Atop you will find the Bonaventure Hilton International Hôtel, with its unusual year-round outdoor pool and country garden.

From here you can reach the city's Latin Quarter by Métro, surfacing at Berri-de Montigny station on St.-Denis Street. Main center for students is the modern University of Quebec at Montreal, which retains as its façade the historical old cathedral (St.-Jacques) that originally stood there. St.-Denis holds a typical student-quarter atmosphere, with book stores, art galleries, and bistros frequented by poets and artists. In summer musicians in town for the Jazz Festival gather for jam sessions, part of an outdoor frolic enjoyed by hundreds. Off St.-Denis, the 19th-century homes on St.-Louis Square surround a fountain and flower market. The square's west side leads to Prince Arthur, a pedestrian mall lined with restaurants, many of them inexpensive, and outdoor cafes, where you watch *le monde* go by to the strains of street musicians. Nearly every evening people flock to the area, heeding the invitation "bring your own wine" *(apportez votre vin)*, to enjoy one of Montreal's favorite activities—dining out.

From there you can take a cab to Place Jacques-Cartier in Old Montreal, many of whose historic sites are described elsewhere (See "Historic Sites").

Or, you might return via Métro to Place d'Armes station, and visit the Palais des Congrès and exhibition hall. Just outside, a stroll along LaGauchetière through Chinatown leads to Blvd. St.-Laurent (St. Lawrence Boulevard) and to Complexe Guy Favreau.

Within the city, you should also visit the Parc Lafontaine area, including the small zoo in the park, and Château Dufresne on the corner of Sherbrooke and Pie IX ("Pie Neuf," for Pope Pius Ninth), which holds fine collections of decorative arts. In this same area you will find the Botanical Gardens and Olympic Park site of the 1976 Olympic Games, and still a much-used sports center.

Other interesting areas include Plâteau Mont-Royal, on the east side of Mont-Royal, once mainly a Greek and Jewish area, but now, with the melting-pot effect, increasingly popular with all groups. Avenue Parc, in particular, is the newest "in" spot for nightlife, restaurants, and bistros. Neighboring Outremont, an area with many fine old houses, caters to the carriage trade, offering lively little restaurants, boutiques, the Cinéma Outremont (French repertory), and the ubiquitous bistros. To the east of the Plâteau, you will find the gradually changing blvd. St-Laurent (St. Lawrence), through which every immi-

MONTREAL

grant group passes. It, too, is gradually becoming more upscale—even the old fish market (Waldman's) has been bought by a grocery chain. But on the streets east of St-Laurent, you can still see rows of houses whose outside staircases twist up to second-story apartments, and marvel how generations of people can manage them in icy weather.

Outside the city you will find much to do, from the amusement park thrills of La Ronde on Île Ste-Hélène (accessible by the Métro of the same name), to the West Island towns usually referred to as "the Lakeshore." From Lachine (whose rapids roil in the St. Lawrence, ideal for rafting), the old road hugs the shoreline west to the tip of the island at Ste.-Anne de Bellevue and Senneville. Charming developments and old properties line the road, which winds through the picturesque old villages of Dorval, Pointe Claire, Beaurepaire, Baie d'Urfé, and Ste.-Anne de Bellevue. City and provincial tourist offices supply lists of sights outside the downtown area, including the Kahnawake Indian village in Caughnawaga (632–6030) on the south shore and the Legaré water Mill in St-Eustache to the north.

As you will see, Montreal's geography, food, wine, atmosphere, and, above all, the people, make it a city like no other. When you visit you are sure to agree with the local sentiment: "Vive la différence!"

PRACTICAL INFORMATION FOR MONTREAL

WHEN TO GO. You will find Montreal a year-round city of culture and activity with four distinct seasons. Winters can be brutal, particularly from January to mid-February. But although temperatures stay well below freezing from December through mid-March, the sub-zero (°F) weather alternates with January thaws and February warmups. The city efficiently controls snowfalls that would zap others for days. The heated "underground city," linked by fast, clean, and quiet Métro trains, helps you shop, dine, attend concerts and recitals, and return to your hotel or office without facing the cold. You do need winter boots, though, plus a warm coat, scarf, or hat, and gloves to step outside in winter.

Spring starts early in March, when maple sap rises and people head to the country for sugaring-off parties. You will find the first outdoor spring flowers in the Botanical Gardens some time in April. Temperatures inch up to the 40s and 50s, but you will need a warm coat or windproof jacket in case.

By May spring is in full bloom and, for Quebec's June 24 holiday, the streets are decked with flowers. The ducks return to the Ritz-Carlton Hotel's outdoor garden cafe. Children's-zoo animals move from winter quarters in Angrignon Park to Parc Lafontaine, and Montrealers take on a jaunty air.

In July temperatures zoom up to the 80s and 90s, but evenings usually stay pleasant. Everyone remains outdoors for free concerts, dancing, and children's shows in the public parks, or to take up an outdoor cafe vantage point to watch *le monde* go by.

Maple leaves turning fiery hues make fall spectacular. These cool, dry days prove ideal for horse-and-buggy calèche rides in Old Montreal or to explore "the Mountain"—Parc Mont-Royal. October and November still bring Indian sum-

54 PROVINCE OF QUEBEC

mer's last strains of warmish weather before everyone starts looking forward to winter sports again.

HOW TO GET THERE. By Plane. Some 60 airlines use Montreal's two commercial airports. *Dorval* receives mainly domestic flights. *Mirabel International Airport* handles overseas planes plus Nordair's Fort Lauderdale flights and two bargain lines, Washington, DC's *Presidential Airlines,* and *People's Express,* which flies daily from principal U.S. cities. Canada's main airlines include *Air Canada, CP Air, Wardair,* and *Quebecair,* which goes to Quebec City, New York, Boston, and many points within the province served by no other commercial line. Major American airlines flying into Dorval include: *American Airlines, Delta, Eastern, Republic, United,* and *U.S. Air.*

By Boat. The Montreal Yacht Club, Port Ste.-Hélène, CP 20, Station M, Montreal, PQ H1V 3L6. Open from mid-May to mid-October; facilities for boats up to 19.5 m (65 ft) long (871–1595).

By Bus. Bus companies including Greyhound, Voyageur, and Voyageur-Colonial, from throughout the U.S. and Canada use Montreal's downtown Voyageur Bus terminal, 505 Blvd. de Maisonneuve Est, Montreal, PQ H2L 4R6 (514–842–2281).

By Train. From Gare Centrale (Central Station) downtown on Dorchester Ouest at Mansfield (514–871–1331), VIA Rail trains leave for all Canadian destinations, and AMTRAK (800–426–8725 - or 4AMTRAK) serves U.S. cities. Commuter trains use both Central and Windsor Station, located on Peel at Lagauchetière streets.

By car. Montreal is accessible to all of Canada by the Trans-Canada Highway, ("the 401") also called *"la Transcanadienne"* and Autoroute 40 (*quarante,* pronounced "karant"). Three major expressways lead to the U.S.: Route 91 to Boston, Route 87 to New York, and Route 89 to Vermont.

To reach Montreal from the U.S. you will cross one of four bridges from the south shore—but not during rush hours, *s'il vous plaît!*

TOURIST INFORMATION. Before setting out, you can collect ample information by contacting the tourist information offices. The *Greater Montreal Convention and Tourism Bureau,*174 Notre-Dame Est, Montreal, PQ H2Y 1C2 (514–871–1595) or *Tourisme-Quebec,* Maison de Tourisme, 2 Place Ville-Marie, Room 70, Montreal, PQ H3B 2C9 (514–873–2015). From many parts of North America you can reach the province's tourist information hot line seven days a week, from 9 A.M.–5 P.M. In the U.S., 800–443–7000 serves 14 American states, including those in New England, New York, and the area as far south as South Carolina and Georgia, and to the west as far as Illinois and Ohio. In the Province of Quebec, dial the hot line at 800–361–5405; from Ontario and the Maritimes, dial 800–361–6490. Within the 514 area code, dial 873–2015.

In summer stop by the downtown information kiosk on the north side of Dominion Square, open mid-May to Labor Day, 9 A.M.–9 P.M. Year-round you can walk into the Greater Montreal Convention and Tourism Bureau, close to Montreal's City Hall, and the Maison de Tourisme (addresses above). At big hotels, the Montreal Convention Centre, and tourist kiosks, a video screen displays data on shows, sports, exhibitions, upcoming events, and history. Simply push a button on an Info-Montreal terminal for free access. Good sources for latest data on coming events include the Friday and Saturday editions of Montreal's daily papers, *La Presse* and *Le Devoir* in French, and *The Gazette*

MONTREAL 55

in English. You can also buy *Montreal* magazine (English). Many hotels and some restaurants give away *En Ville* (bilingual) and *Montreal Scope*. Wanderlust Publishing, Ltd., puts out *Montreal Cuisine*, with menus, prices, and recipes from great local restaurants; $12.95 at newsstands. Write Box 1471, Montreal, PQ H5A 1H5 (871-9122).

TELEPHONES. Montreal and surrounding areas' code is 514. You pay 25 cents for a local call on a public telephone, with no time limit. Reach directory assistance by dialing 411. Dial 1 plus the area code and local number you want for long-distance calls, or dial zero for operator assistance.

EMERGENCY TELEPHONE NUMBERS. For police, fire department, and ambulance (called "Urgence Santé"), dial 911; 24-hour drugstore service, 527-8827; dental clinic (523-2151), open seven days 8 A.M.-11 P.M.;*Montreal General Hospital* (937-6011); local *poison-control* centers are at the Montreal Children's Hospital (934-4456) and at l'Hôpital Ste.-Justine pour enfants (731-4931). Other emergency numbers: *Tél-Aide*—mental health assistance—(935-1101); *Suicide Action* (522-5777); *Psychiatric Clinic* (933-4223); *Alcoholics Anonymous* (376-9230); *Touring Club de Montreal*—AAA, CAA, RAC (288-7111).

SMOKING. The city prohibits smoking in department stores, movie houses, and theaters. Many restaurants and hotels set aside no-smoking areas. Montrealers consider it impolite to smoke in elevators and restaurants.

HOW TO GET AROUND. From the Airports. Dorval is 22.5 km (14 mi.) from downtown, and Mirabel 54.5 km (34 mi.). You'll easily find taxis at both airports.
From Dorval, fares run about $20 to the city. *Tour Autocar* (397-9999) buses leave Mon.-Fri. every 20 minutes, Sat., Sun., every half hour, for downtown Queen Elizabeth Hotel, stopping at Peel Métro station, Sheraton Centre, and Château Champlain, with more stops planned. Return trip makes same stops. Fare $6. If you travel light and do not mind stairs, take the bus and the Métro: Board autobus 204 for nearby Dorval Gardens Shopping Centre, then take express bus 211 to Lionel-Groulx (pronounced "groo") Métro station for the ride downtown, total fare $1 or one bus/Métro ticket. Limousine service is provided by *Samson Limousine Service* (631-5466) and *Murray Hill Limousine Service* buses. Call (937-5311). **From Mirabel,** taxis to downtown cost about $50. *Miracar* (397-9999) provides buses, at $9 per person, between the airport and Place Bonaventure Métro station (behind Central Station) with no stops; and between airports, also at $9. Many people arriving at Mirabel take the bus to Dorval, then bus or taxi downtown.

By Subway and Bus. You'll easily spot entrances to Le Métro, Montreal's safe, clean, and quiet underground transportation system, by the the foot-square signs with a large white arrow on a blue ground. There are five lines and 55 stations. Call 288-6287 for bilingual help to reach points served by the MUCTC (Montreal Urban Community Transit Commission). Le Métro runs 5:30 A.M. -1:30 A.M. daily. Fare $1, or six tickets for $5 at Métro stations. Bus drivers take only exact fare or tickets. Seniors, students with official Montreal ID cards, and local children travel at reduced rates.

By Taxi. You will find taxi stands clearly marked at points including hotels and shopping centers. Or you can easily hail a cab. Fares start at at $1.50, with

56 **PROVINCE OF QUEBEC**

$1.10 for each additional mile and 25 cents a minute for waiting. Montreal's major taxi companies include: *Diamond* (273–6331); *La Salle* (861–2552); *Champlain* (273–2435); *Co-op* (725–9885); *Regal* (484–1171); *Veterans* (273–6351); and *Taxico* (842–2133).

By Rental Car. Drivers renting cars must be over 21 years old, hold a valid driver's license, identification papers, and a credit card. Visitors from outside North America usually need passports. You can rent by day or week, and you usually pay mileage charges. You will find rental firms at the two main airports, railway stations, and major hotels. Main local car rental services include: *Avis Rent-a-Car* (514–866–7906); *Hertz* (514–842–8537); and *Budget-Rent-a-Car* (514–937–9121). For a local bargain, check out *Tilden Rent-a-Car* (514–878–2771). The phone directory's Yellow Pages list smaller companies renting cars or trucks. Read the contract carefully and check the insurance policy before signing.

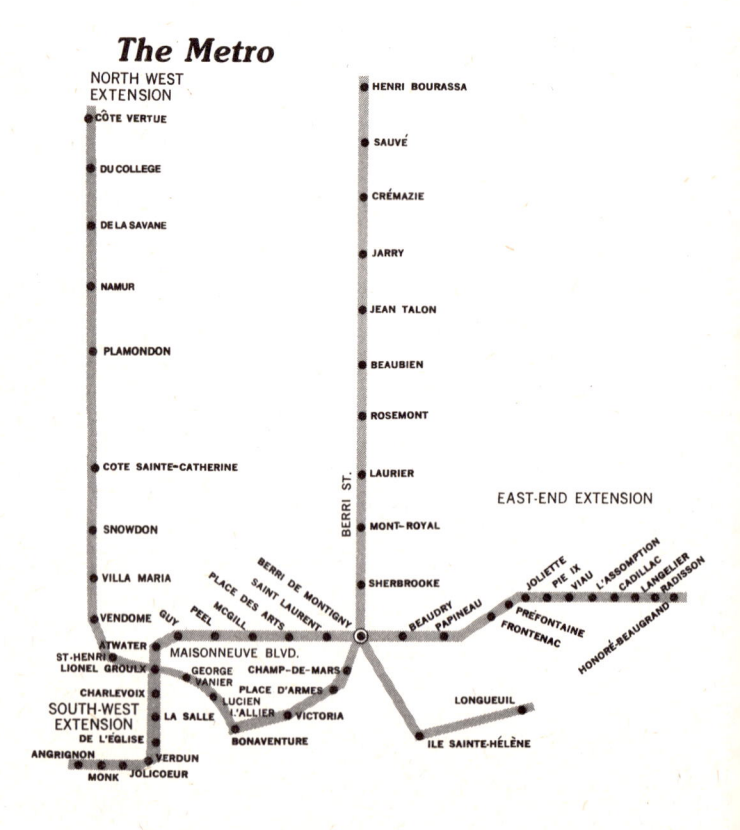

The Metro

NORTH WEST EXTENSION
- CÔTE VERTUE
- DU COLLEGE
- DE LA SAVANE
- NAMUR
- PLAMONDON
- COTE SAINTE-CATHERINE
- SNOWDON
- VILLA MARIA
- VENDOME
- ATWATER
- ST-HENRI
- LIONEL GROULX
- CHARLEVOIX
- SOUTH-WEST EXTENSION
- DE L'ÉGLISE
- ANGRIGNON
- MONK
- JOLICOEUR
- VERDUN
- LA SALLE
- LUCIEN L'ALLIER
- BONAVENTURE
- GEORGE VANIER
- PLACE D'ARMES
- VICTORIA
- CHAMP-DE-MARS
- MAISONNEUVE BLVD.
- GUY
- PEEL
- McGILL
- PLACE DES ARTS
- SAINT LAURENT
- BERRI DE MONTIGNY
- BERRI ST.
- HENRI BOURASSA
- SAUVÉ
- CRÉMAZIE
- JARRY
- JEAN TALON
- BEAUBIEN
- ROSEMONT
- LAURIER
- MONT-ROYAL
- SHERBROOKE
- BEAUDRY
- PAPINEAU
- FRONTENAC
- PRÉFONTAINE
- JOLIETTE
- PIE IX
- VIAU
- L'ASSOMPTION
- CADILLAC
- LANGELIER
- RADISSON
- HONORÉ-BEAUGRAND
- LONGUEUIL
- ILE SAINTE-HÉLÈNE

EAST-END EXTENSION

MONTREAL

HINTS TO MOTORISTS. Most Montreal streets follow a north-south, east-west grid pattern. Boulevard St-Laurent cuts the city from north to south. All numbers on streets such as Sherbrooke, Dorchester, and Ste-Catherine, which disect St-Laurent from east to west, start at One at St-Laurent. Numbers 10 east *(est)* and 10 west *(ouest,* pronounced "west") are respectively 10 lots east and 10 lots west of St-Laurent. Montrealers see the Laurentians (Les Laurentides) as north, although they are more northwest of the city. "Up" means north *(nord)* and "down" is south *(sud)*. In fact, the city is easy to navigate from downtown, since Mont-Royal ("the mountain") is always to the north.

All incoming highways lead to main streets, roads, and boulevards. Route markers show upcoming highways, bridges, and special tourist attractions. The Boulevard Metropolitain expressway crosses northern Montreal. Ville-Marie and Bonaventure expressways (autoroutes) cover the south and southwest sections. Décarie Expressway runs north to south linking with Metropolitain and Ville-Marie. Avoid driving during business rush hours, 7:30–9:00 A.M.; 3:30–6:00 P.M. Speed limit is 50 km/hour (30 mph) where traffic permits.

Montreal allows no right turn on red lights. All traffic moves on right side of road. Note that Montreal motorists and pedestrians often ignore one another's right of way. Pedestrians frequently jaywalk, risking fines.

Parking. Heed the no-parking signs—a red "P" in a black circle on posts and sandwich boards on the sidewalks during snow removal and street repairs. Meters, which take 25-cent pieces, stand well back on the sidewalk away from snow removal machinery. Signs specify rates and free-parking times. Snow removal signs: In winter, watch for no-parking lights on lamp standards during snow removal. The city tows away cars violating these signs. You will find parking lots available at varying rates. Auto club members (CAA and AAA) get full services from CAA Montreal, 1425 rue de la Montagne, Montreal, PQ H3G 2R7 (288-7111).

HINTS TO HANDICAPPED TRAVELERS. Write to The Greater Montreal Tourist Convention and Bureau, 174 Notre-Dame Est, Montreal, PQ H2Y 1B5 (871-1595), for the folder, "Useful Information for the Handicapped." Most restaurant guides and tourist pamphlets list facilities for the handicapped. Many streets have wheelchair ramps. Shopping centers and main tourist and entertainment centers allot primary parking areas to handicapped people's vehicles bearing special stickers. You can get wheelchair help from *Kéroul,* 4545 ave. Pierre de Coubertin, Montreal, PQ H1V 3N7 (252-3104), Mon.–Thurs., 9 A.M.–5 P.M.; Fri., 9 A.M.–noon. Reach the *Canadian National Institute for the Blind* (CNIB) at Suite 420, 1010 Ste-Catherine Est, Montreal, PQ H2L 2G3 (284-2040), Mon.–Fri., 8:30 A.M.–noon; 1–4:30 P.M. Reserve at least 24 hours ahead for transportation for people in wheelchairs from Voyageur Bus Service, 505 blvd. de Maisonneuve Est, Montreal, PQ H2L 1Y4 (514–842–2281).

SEASONAL EVENTS. March. Sample maple sugar products at *sugaring-off parties* on farms near Montreal (873-2015). **May.** The *Benson & Hedges International Fireworks Competition* lights up the skies for over a week late this month with classic and pyromusical fireworks. At La Ronde amusement park on Île Ste. Hélène. Tickets ($8–$15) through Ticketron or AMARC, Administration Pavilion, Île Notre Dame, Montreal, PQ H3C 1A9 (872-6212).

PROVINCE OF QUEBEC

In late May attend the *Montreal International Mime Festival,* when masters from a dozen countries lead 23 stage productions, 30 street shows, and five 40-hour workshops. Box 267, de Lorimier Station, Montreal, PQ H2H 2N6 (525-3390).

June. *Montreal International Music Competition* (872-5582 or 6211). Younger visitors enjoy the *Quebec International Puppet Festival* early in June, at the provincial children's theater, La Maison-Théâtre, 255 Ontario Est, Montreal, PQ H2X 1X6 (288-7211). Top Formula 1 drivers compete for the world championship at *Grand Prix Labatt of Canada.* Write to Grand Prix Labatt, Bassin Olympique, Île Notre-Dame, Montreal, PQ H3C 1A9 (871-1421). Late June comes *Montreal's International Jazz Festival,* with 800 musicians from 15 countries participating in a ten-day series of free indoor and outdoor shows. Besides big names, you will find many brilliant lesser-knowns, as well as acrobats, jugglers, and street performers. Tickets from Ticketron and from Montreal International Jazz Festival, 355 Ste-Catherine Ouest, Suite 301, Montreal, PQ H3B 1A5 (289-9472). Antique buffs note the annual three-day *antique show,* held each June in Place Bonaventure, Box 1,000, Montreal, PQ H5A 1G1 (933-6375). June 24 is *la Fête nationale des Quebecois,* Quebec's national Festival, formerly Saint Jean Baptiste Day, an official provincial holiday when neighbors get together for parades, street dancing, and bonfires.

July. The jazz beat (see June) continues, followed by giggles with the *"Just-for-Laughs Festival."* Over 60 comics from a dozen countries give four nights of English performances and five French. Tickets from Ticketron and Festival du Rire, 63 Prince Arthur Est, Montreal, PQ H2X 1B4 (845-3155). **August.** *Player's Challenge Tennis Championships.* The world's best players. Odd years (1987 and 1989) the men play; even years (1986 and 1988) the women take over. At Jarry Tennis Stadium. Tickets from $4 to $2,000 for a box for four. Player's Challenge Tennis Canada, 5253 ave. Parc, Suite 610, Montreal, PQ H2V 4P2 (273-1515). In late August Montreal's *International Film Festival* shows movies representing cinematography's every trend, in North America's only competitive film festival recognized by the International Federation of Film Producers' Assoc. Write to Festival des Films, 1455 blvd. de Maisonneuve Ouest, Suite 109, Montreal, PQ H3G 1M8 (848-3883).

September. *Montreal International Marathon,* a 42.195-km (26.2-mi) course. Some 11,000 take part. Registration, $10. Write to Montreal Marathon, Box 1570, Station "B", Montreal, PQ H3B 2L2 (879-1027). **October.** In Chinatown, *Festival of the Harvest Moon.*

TOURS. City tours by bus leave all year from Dominion Square on Peel below Dorchester. For sightseeing tours call *Murray Hill* (937-5311) or *Gray Line of Montreal* (280-5327). A company called *Les Montrealistes* Box 457, Station A, Montreal, PQ H3C 2T1 (744-3009) organizes bus and walking tours of cultural and tourist attractions in Montreal districts daily during summer. Throughout the year Les Montrealistes organize social programs for conventions and special groups, and trips to Quebec and Ottawa. *Guidatour,* Box 575, Station N, Montreal, PQ (844-4021) provides licensed guides, and escort services for arrivals and departures, and also organizes traditional and specialized tours for individuals and groups, in several languages.

Boat Cruises. *Montreal Harbor Cruises,* Box 1085, Place D'Armes, Montreal, PQ H2Z 2C7 (842-3871), run three vessels offering a variety of tours of the mighty St. Lawrence River from early May to late September. Prices range from about $5 for one-hour sunset cruises to over $20 for ten-hour cruises to Sorel

MONTREAL 59

(children half price). Choices include three-hour "Love Boat" cruises with live orchestra and Sunday breakfasts, and 90-minute moonlight cruises.

Calèche Rides. All year you can rent a horse-drawn carriage from starting points at Dominion Square, Place d'Armes or on Mont-Royal. You can hail a *calèche* in Old Montreal around Bonsecours and Gosford, and de la Commune streets. Hourly cost $20–$25 (844-1313 or 845-7995).

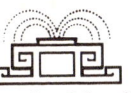

PARKS AND GARDENS. Angrignon Park. Métro station Angrignon, 3400 des Trinitaires, LaSalle, (872-2815). Winter home of the children's zoo, tobogganing, extensive cross-country ski trails, summer jogging, cycling paths. *Like all Montreal parks, closed from midnight to 6 A.M.*

Dominion Square. The city center, at Peel and Dorchester Ouest. Board your tour bus or *calèche* here, or relax between shopping and sightseeing. Summer outdoor art exhibits, square dancing, snacks in area south of Dorchester.

Île-Ste-Hélène. An island park reached by Métro (Île-Ste-Hélène station) or by car from Jacques-Cartier Bridge. In winter you can cross-country ski and snowshoe. In summer jog, walk, picnic, and swim in outdoor pools. Or spend the day at La Ronde Amusement Park and other nearby attractions such as the Alcan Aquarium.

Jardins botaniques (Botanical Gardens). (872-1400). On blvd. Pie IX, above Sherbrooke, are the world's third largest gardens after London's and Berlin's. A minitrain ride gives an overall view of some 20,000 different species of plant life displayed in 30 outdoor gardens and nine greenhouses. Unique collections include 1,000 varieties of bonsai (miniature trees) and 1,200 orchid varieties. Open daily 9 A.M.–6 P.M. Snackbars. Free admission to grounds. Admission to greenhouses; adults, $5, seniors, students, and handicapped, $1.

Lafontaine Park. rue Sherbrooke Est at Papineau (Métro Papineau) holds a lagoon where you can rent boats by the hour. Or visit the children's zoo and playground area.

La Ronde Amusement Park. Île-Ste-Hélène (Métro stop Île-Ste-Hélène) provides fun for all. You will find many attractions—games of chance, an old Quebec village with craft workshops, restaurants, and boutiques. Visitors of all ages will find something to please them, from nightclubs, cabarets, and discos to a fairyland for the very young. View the city and river from on high in the overhead minirail. Recent spruce-ups include Western Fort, giant water slides, an antique, hand-carved merry-go-round, live entertainment, and the world's highest double-tack roller coaster, aptly named "The Monster"—*"c'est terrifiant!"* Early May–late June, weekends, holidays only. Late June-Labor Day, Mon.–Sat, noon–2:30 A.M., Sun., holidays, 10 A.M.–midnight. Various admission packages range in price from about $5–$35 (for a family pass). For data on day passes, call 872-6222.

Les Floralies. On Île-Notre-Dame, via Métro to Île-Ste-Hélène (872-6222). Huge outdoor international flower show makes sweet-scented background for strolling musicians, free open-air concerts.

Mont-Royal. Known fondly as "the mountain" to Montrealers, topped by a 30.5-meter (100 ft) illuminated cross, Mont-Royal rises 233 meters (764 ft) above sea level in the heart of the city. The 19th-century landscape architect Frederick Law Olmstead, who also designed New York's Central Park and Boston's Franklin Park, insisted that Mont-Royal remain natural. Montrealers use their mountain park widely for recreation. They jog and hike all year round. In summer they cycle and folk-dance around Beaver Lake or stroll up to feed the ducks and sail miniature boats. In winter they use the little ski run, toboggan, and skate on the small lake. Other attractions include mounted police,

PROVINCE OF QUEBEC

horse-drawn carriage and sleigh rides, the Universal Museum of Hunting and Fishing, and a chalet lookout giving a panoramic view extending south to Vermont. Picnic and snackbar facilities. Get there by car, or number 11 bus from Mont-Royal Métro station. No public transport service to adjoining Westmount lookout or bird sanctuary topping Westmount. But by cab or car, turn up Belvedere Road from Côte-des-Neiges. From here, on a clear day you can see the Adirondack Mountains in New York State.

PARTICIPANT SPORTS. Montrealers' many sports vary with the season. In summer you will find **cycling**, on paths in some 20 areas, many in parks. Guided cycle tours of historic Lachine Canal, 2 P.M., Sat.–Sun., mid-May–mid-June; and daily, mid-June–Sept. (872-6211). Rent good bikes from Cycle Peel, 6665 St-Jacques, Montreal, PQ H2S 2M3 (486-1148). You can **jog** on Mont-Royal and in most other city parks.

Most **golf** clubs are private. Call 873-2015 for a list of courses. Public courses include: *Fresh Meadows,* 505 Golf Beaconsfield, Pointe-Claire, PQ H9W 2E5 (697-4036) and *Golf Le Village,* 4601 rue Sherbrooke Est, Montreal, PQ H1X 2B1 (872-2781). A nine-hole municipal course.

There are two **rafting** outfitters: *Lachine Rapids Tours Ltd.,* 105 rue de la Commune, Montreal, PQ H2Y 2C7 (284-9607 or 843-4745). Daily from Victoria Pier at rue Berri. Jet boat every two hours, May–mid-Sept., 10 A.M.–6 P.M. Daily rubber rafting, mid-June–mid-Sept. Adults, $25. Youths 10–18, $20. Minimum age 10. *Voyageur-Lachine,* from Quay 34, St.-Joseph Blvd. at 32nd Ave., Lachine (873-2015). Mid-May–Sept., 9 A.M.–7 P.M. Mon.–Fri., $15. Sat., Sun., $18.

You can play **tennis** all year in Montreal—in winter in indoor health clubs. Summer outdoor courts include: Parc Jeanne-Mance, north of avenue des Pins at avenue Parc; Parc Lafontaine, rue Sherbrooke Est at Calixa-Lavallée (872-6211).

You can **swim** only in pools—indoors or out. You will find great pools at the *Olympic Park* (252-4622); and *Île Ste-Hélène* (872-6211).

You will find many **curling clubs** in Montreal, including the continent's oldest (1807), Royal Montreal Curling Club, 1850 blvd. de Maisonneuve Ouest, Montreal, PQ H3H 1J8 (935-3411).

You can **skate** all winter at 27 illuminated outdoor rinks, 20 indoor arenas, and every neighborhood park maintains a skating and/or hockey rink. Try pretty *Angrignon Park,* 7050 de la Vérendrye Blvd., and *Beaver Lake* on Mont-Royal (872-6211).

Parc *Mont-Royal* provides a small **downhill ski** run. You will find **cross-country** trails and good snowshoeing throughout the city's parks and golf courses, notably: *Île Notre-Dame* and *Île Ste-Hélène,* (both at Man and His World) and *Parc Mont-Royal.* These, plus Angrignon, Ahuntsic, and Parc Lafontaine, also hold great **toboggan slides.**

SPECTATOR SPORTS. Hockey. The Canadian Ice Hockey Club, Les Canadiens, has won 22 Stanley Cups. Regular season, Oct.–Apr.; playoffs, Apr., May at The Montreal Forum, 2313 Ste. Catherine Ouest, Montreal, PQ H3H 1N1 (932-6181).

Football. Les Alouettes, Canadian football, Olympic Stadium, June–late Nov. Montreal football club, Box 100, Station M, Montreal, H1V 3L6 (253-8088). Tickets from $5 (bleachers)–$18.50.

MONTREAL

Baseball. Expos' Baseball Club plays at Olympic Stadium. Mid-Apr.–Oct. Montreal Baseball Club, Ltd., Box 500, Station M, Montreal, PQ H1V 3L6 (253-3434 or 800-351-0658).

Running. More than 11,000 people participate. Enthusiastic spectators line the route. (See "Seasonal Events.")

Tennis. Player's International and Player's Challenge. Parc Jarry hosts the world's greats in the Canadian men's and women's championships last two weeks of August. Men play odd years (1987 and 1989). Women play even years (1986 and 1988) (273-1515). (See "Seasonal Events.")

Auto Racing. Every year car racing greats compete in this Formula-One Canadian Grand Prix, mid-June, Île Notre-Dame (871-1421).

Harness Racing. Blue Bonnets race track, Jean Talon and Decarie Blvd. (Métro Namur). 7440 Decarie Blvd., Montreal, PQ H4P 2H1 (739-2741). Winter months and June.

HISTORIC SITES AND HOUSES. You will find much of Montreal's rich cultural legacy permanently preserved within the heritage area of Old Montreal, near the port, and around Place d'Armes. To explore the area thoroughly takes several days, but the city provides a free 22-page walking-tour guide detailing all the interesting points. Many older buildings now house collections of art and artifacts. (See "Museums" below.) Some of the city's special landmarks are listed here.

Bank of Montreal. 129 St-Jacques Ouest (877-6892). Montreal's oldest bank faces Place d'Armes. Worth a visit for its ornate, black marble-columned main hall. Numismatists find the tiny museum particularly interesting. Displays include a detailed reconstruction of the bank's first branch (featuring period office equipment), an extensive currency collection, and 19th-century mechanical savings banks. Mon.–Fri., 10 A.M.–4 P.M. Admission free.

Bonsecours Market (Marché Bonsecours). rue St-Paul, one of the city's oldest streets. The market, with its handsome dome and collonades, is the street's most impressive building, but all the neighboring buildings have been well restored and now house boutiques, offices, and restaurants. The restored market (1845) is now used as municipal offices.

Centaur Theatre. 453 St-François-Xavier (288-3161). English theater housed in Montreal's first Stock Exchange Building, colonnaded front.

Château Dufresne. 2929 Jeanne-d'Arc, corner of blvd. Pie IX (pronounced "Pinuff") and Sherbrooke Est (259-2575). A classic mansion, built in 1918 for the Dufresne family. Permanent and visiting exhibits of decorative arts, plus Victorian and Edwardian furnishings. Thurs.–Sun., noon–5 P.M. Adults, $2; students, 75 cents; seniors, $1; children under 12, handicapped, free.

Château Ramezay. 280 Notre-Dame Est (861-7182). Built in 1705 for Claude de Ramezay, France's eleventh governor of Montreal, it was the base of the American occupying forces in 1775-76. Benjamin Franklin slept here. Interior shows 18th-century nobleman's residence, complete with original furniture, household articles, prints, paintings, weapons, tools, and miscellany. Exhibits of fur trade, English influence, 19th-century Canadiana and Quebec's Indians. Tues.–Sun., 10 A.M.–4:30 P.M. Adults,$1; under 16 and seniors, 50 cents.

City Hall (Hôtel de Ville). 275 rue Notre-Dame Est, and opposite Château Ramezay, is a massive example of Renaissance architecture, adapted to 19th-century needs. Finished in 1877, it overlooks Place Vauquelin's pretty fountain and Champ-de-Mars, the old military training ground, now a city parking lot. The fine, domed old courthouse (1849) on the other side of Place Vauquelin, houses CIDEM, Montreal's economic development department, and home of

PROVINCE OF QUEBEC

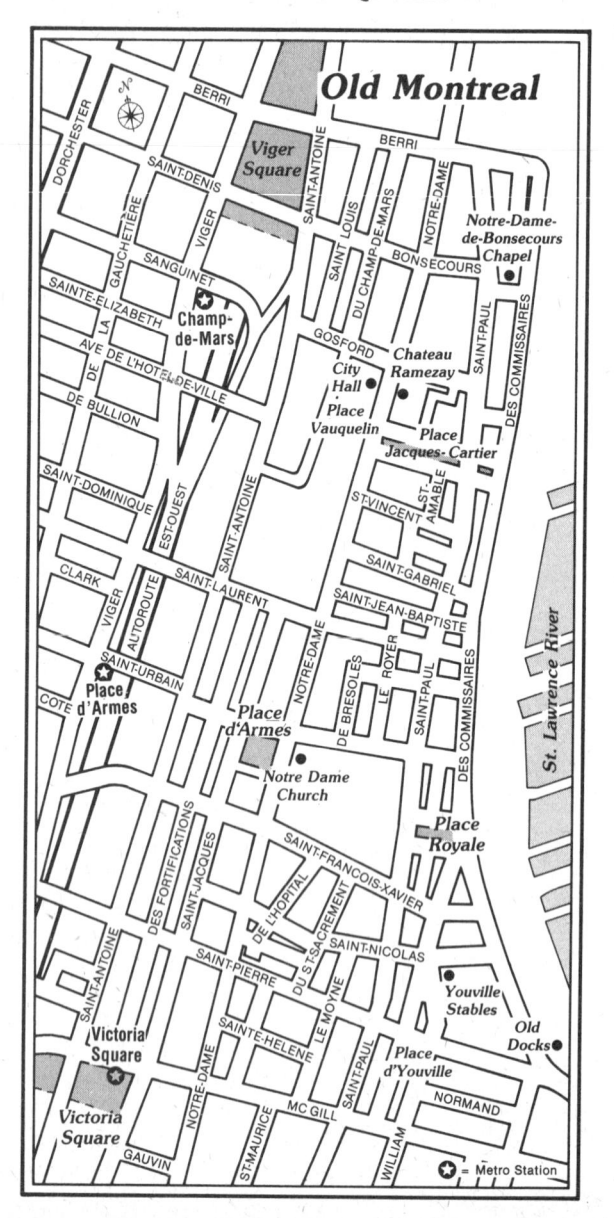

MONTREAL

CIDEM-Tourisme (155 Notre-Dame Est) where you write, call, or visit for tourist information (871–1595).

Maison du Calvet. 400 St-Paul Est, corner of Bonsecours (845–4596). One of the finest examples of domestic architecture of the French regime, with fire walls reaching beyond the roof and all window and door frames of cut stone. Pierre Calvet was a Huguenot merchant and justice of the peace, imprisoned for years for giving information to American general Montgomery. Built around 1725, the house was restored by Ogilvy's department store to commemorate its 100th birthday in 1966. Now an epicurean food shop.

Nelson's Column. Place Jacques-Cartier. British Admiral Lord Horatio Nelson won the battle of Trafalgar in 1805. The column is the oldest existing monument, and predates London's Nelson. He looks down over a lively scene, including a flower market, strolling musicians, jugglers, artists, and people sipping and dining in outdoor cafes. A charming cobblestoned square, where calèches line up to take you exploring. Before boarding, tour the square, noting plaques on the heritage houses at nos. 433, 404–410, and 407.

Papineau House. 440 Place Bonsecours, in old Montreal. Once belonged to Louis-Joseph Papineau (1786–1871), one of the initiators of the 1837 rebellion against British rule.

Place d'Armes. Between Notre-Dame and St-Jacques, Montreal's old financial district. A detailed tribute to Maisonneuve stands dramatically in the center, marking, some say, the exact spot where the city's founder grappled in mortal combat with the Iroquois chieftain, and won. To the south stands Notre-Dame Basilica, opened in 1829. West of the church is Seminaire de St-Sulpice, established in Montreal in 1685. You will notice the remarkable fine woodwork clock (1710).

Place Royale. The city's oldest landmark, bearing an obelisk declaring that Champlain named the square. Maisonneuve's settlers laid the city's foundations here, erecting the first homes, a fort, a chapel, and a cemetery.

Sir George Étienne-Cartier House. 458 Notre-Dame Est. Run by Parks Canada this is a restored property constructed in 1862. Actually two houses, which the Cartier family lived in successively. Now, you can see one elegantly furnished for the affluent folk like the Etienne-Cartiers. The other contains contemporary exhibitions. May–Sept., daily, 9 A.M.–5 P.M. Sept.–May, Wed.–Sun., 10 A.M.–5 P.M. Free.

Youville Stables. A small and very chic complex, housing boutiques, offices, and Gibby's Steak House, in buildings originally constructed in 1825.

HISTORIC RELIGIOUS SITES. In 1881 Mark Twain noted that in Montreal "you couldn't throw a brick without hitting a church." Indeed, Montreal holds more churches than Rome, with over 450 on the island. Of these 70 percent serve Roman Catholics, and 20 percent are Protestant. Of the remaining religious edifices, four percent are Jewish while six percent serve other faiths.

Because of the city's origins, many historical sites hold Catholic associations, for it was not until 1760, when the French regime ended, that the city's ethnic and religious mosaic started forming. Following are some of the more historically interesting religious sites. Although times open were correct at press time, they are subject to change, so do phone ahead.

Cathedral-Basilica of Mary, Queen of the World and St. James the Greater. Dorchester at Mansfield, opposite the Queen Elizabeth Hotel (866–1661). A replica of St. Peter's Basilica of Rome, built from 1870–1894 by Bishop Ignace Bourget, the city's second bishop. Statues atop the cathedral recall the patron

64 PROVINCE OF QUEBEC

saints of the archdiocese in 1894. Open Tues.–Sun., 7:00 A.M.–about 7:15 P.M. (after recitation of rosary); Mon., 7:00 A.M.–about 8:15 P.M. (after 7:00 P.M. mass).

Christ Church Cathedral. 635 St-Catherine Ouest (879–1996). The Anglican cathedral (1851) is pure Gothic. Note the stained glass, gargoyles and angels, and Coventry Cross, made from nails salvaged from the ruins of Britain's Coventry Cathedral, bombed in 1940.

Church of St. Andrew and St. Paul. Rue Sherbrooke Ouest, at Redpath (3415 Redpath Ave.) (842–3431). Presbyterian, regimental church of the Black Watch (Royal Highland regiment of Canada). Fine stained glass, including two Tiffany windows. Fine Sunday choir. Open for Sunday morning services and by appointment.

Cross atop Mont-Royal. At night, when lit by 158 light bulbs, you can see the cross from 30 miles away. Today's cross stands 100 ft high and weighs 26 tons. Paul de Chomedey, sieur de Maisonneuve, planted the first cross in 1643, in thanks for the settlement's being spared from a Christmas-day flood. Schoolchildren raised $25,000 in 1924 to pay for the present structure.

Grand Séminaire de Montreal. Rue Sherbrooke Ouest at du Fort Street, built on the site where Messieurs de St-Sulpice constructed a fort protecting early settlements from the Iroquois. The twin towers form two of the city's oldest structures.

Grey Nuns' Museum. 1185 rue St-Mathieu (937–9501), at the community's Mother House. Collection includes textiles, embroideries, lace, paintings, and sculptures, mostly from 18th century. Wed.–Sun., 1:30–4:40 P.M. Free. Groups by appointment.

Notre-Dame Basilica. Place d'Armes (849–1070). Noted for art and neo-Gothic architecture. Note double-tiered galleries, three rose stained-glass windows. Huge Cassavant organ. Notre-Dame's museum, entrance at 430 rue St-Sulpice (842–2925) holds religious articles including a small silver statue donated by King Louis XV of France. Church open 9 A.M.–5 P.M. for visitors. Museum, Sat., Sun., 10 A.M.–4:30 P.M.

Notre-Dame de Bon-Secours. 400 rue St-Paul (845–9991). Called "the sailors' church," because it holds the carved ships that sailors left as votive offerings. A small, charming church, with observation tower over the St. Lawrence. Memorable statue of Virgin Mary, arms outstretched to the port. Basement museum shows 58 scenes of life in old Quebec and of Blessed Margeurite de Bourgeoys, who founded the Congregations de Notre-Dame order and the first girls' school (1653). Open Mon.–Sat., 9:30–11:30 A.M., 1:30–4:30 P.M.; Sun., 1:30–4:30 P.M. Admission: adults, 75 cents, children, 25 cents. Via Champ-de-Mars Métro.

St. Joseph's Oratory. 3800 Chemin de la Reine-Marie (Queen Mary Road) (733–8211). Over two million pilgrims visit the world's biggest shrine dedicated to St. Joseph, started in 1904 as a tiny chapel for Brother André, a humble, uneducated doorman, credited with many miraculous cures. Finished in 1967 entirely from public subscription, its massive green copper dome is visible for miles. Highlights include stations of the cross, the original chapel, Brother André's tomb, and two museums, one containing hundreds of crutches from people claiming cures. Oratory open 6:30 A.M.–10 P.M. Ten summer organ concerts, Wed., 8 P.M. $3.50. Boys' choir, Sun., 11 A.M. Museum open daily, 10 A.M.–5 P.M. Admission free. Also, art museum containing religious paintings and artifacts. Donations accepted.

St. Patrick's Church. 460 Blvd. Dorchester Ouest (866–7379). Opened 1847, an era that saw a flood of immigration from Ireland. Neo-Gothic with Roman influences, decorated with Celtic crosses, shamrocks, and lilies.

MONTREAL 65

Séminaire St-Sulpice. On Place d'Armes, next to Notre-Dame Basilica. Built by the Sulpicians in 1685, and is the city's oldest building still standing. Bears the oldest (1710) public clock in North America. The seminary is closed to the public.

La Visitation du Sault-au-Recollet. 1847 Blvd. Gouin Est (388-4050). Montreal's oldest church, 250th anniversary in 1986. Sanctuary and vestry date to 1680; the Louis-XV nave, to 1749. Wood sculpture and gilding at their elaborate best. Daily, 8 A.M.-4:30 P.M.

MUSEUMS AND GALLERIES. Cinématheque Quebecoise. 335 de Maisonneuve Est (842-9763) Canada's main technical film museum. Equipment from mid-19th century. Photographs and drawings from animated films. Free. Movies, $1.50. Mon.-Fri., 12:30-5:30 P.M. Tues.-Thurs., 12:30-8:30 P.M.

David Macdonald Stewart Museum. Old Fort, Île Ste-Hélène (861-6701). Military and household items of 19th century; military maneuvers. May-Sept., daily, 10 A.M.-5 P.M. Sept.-May, Tues.-Sun., same times. Adults, $3; children, $2. Phone first.

The Fur Trade at Lachine Historical Museum, 1255 Saint-Joseph Blvd., corner of 12th Ave. Lachine (637-7433). Take 191 bus from Lionel-Groulx Métro. Sept.-April, Wed.-Sun., 10 A.M.-noon, 1-5 P.M. Mid-May-Sept., daily (except Monday A.M.), 9 A.M.-noon, 1-5:30 P.M. Closed Jan., Feb. Free. Always call first.

McCord Museum. 690 Sherbrooke Ouest (392-4778 weekdays or 392-4774 weekends). Fine collections of artifacts of all principal North American native peoples. Huge totem pole dominates entry. See 19th-century art, costumes, and objects including William Notman photographic archives showing Montreal's past. Wed.-Sun., 11 A.M.-5 P.M. Adults, $1; students, seniors, 25 cents; youth (12-16), 50 cents. Under 12, free. Families, $2.

The Montreal Historical Wax Museum. 3715 Chemin de la Reine-Marie (Queen Mary Road), Montreal, PQ H3V 1A7 (738-5959). Dramatic, colorful, religious scenes, famous people in wax. Daily, 9 A.M.-5:30 P.M. Adults, $4.50; students, seniors, $2.50; children six-12, $1.75.

The Montreal History Centre. 335 Place d'Youville (845-4236). The old fire station depicts Montreal from 17th century to the present. Tues.-Sun., 10 A.M.-3:30 P.M. Adults, $2; seniors, children, $1.

The Montreal Museum of Fine Arts. (MMFA) 1379 rue Sherbrooke Ouest (285-1600). Canada's oldest museum, founded 1860. Quebec's main fine arts museum. Big international collections, world-class exhibitions. (See "Seasonal Events.") Tues.-Sun., 11 A.M.-5 P.M. Thurs., 11 A.M.-9 P.M. Adults, $2; students (16-25 with ID cards), 75 cents, youths, 12-15, 50 cents; children under 12, handicapped, seniors, free; families, $4.

Musée d'Art Contemporain. Cité du Havre (873-2878). Today's art in myriad forms. Library. Phone for opening times.

The Musée d'Art de Saint Laurent. 615 Ste. Croix Blvd., Saint Laurent (747-7367). Quebec's early arts and crafts. Periodic thematic exhibitions, guided tours and concerts. Sun., Tues.-Fri., 11 A.M.-5 P.M. Admission free.

Musée Marc-Aurèle Fortin. 118 St-Pierre (845-6108). One of the few museums dedicated to one person's work, an original, outstanding, impressionist. Tues.-Sun., 11 A.M.-5 P.M. Adults, $2; students, seniors, 75 cents.

Royal Canadian Ordnance Corps Museum. In old chapel, Canadian Forces Base at Longue Pointe, 6560 Hochelaga Est, Building 108 (255-8811 ext. 241). 20 km (12 mi) from downtown. Sherman tank and artillery stand guard over

66 **PROVINCE OF QUEBEC**

collection of Canadian force's memorabilia from pre-Boer War to UN missions. Library. Mon.–Fri., 9 A.M.–3 P.M. Free. Call first.

Saidye Bronfman Centre. 5170 Côte-Ste-Catherine (739-2301). Montreal's liveliest, most controversial and interesting contemporary art often shown here. Vibrant art school, workshops, lecture/discussion programs, theater (see "Stage"). Mon.–Thurs., 9 A.M.–9 P.M. Fri., 9 A.M.–3 P.M. Free.

Sir George Williams Art Galleries. Concordia University, 1455 blvd. de Maisonneuve Ouest (849-5917). Canadian art, exhibitions and permanent collection, and lectures. During academic year.

Universal Museum of Hunting and Wildlife. Camillien-Houde Parkway, Parc Mont-Royal, Box 7, Town of Mount Royal, PQ H3P 3B8 (843-6942). Hunting lodge built on Mont-Royal. May–Sept, Tues.–Sun., 10 A.M.–8 P.M. Oct.–Apr., 10 A.M.–5 P.M. Adults, $2; children, students, seniors, $1; families, $5.

GALLERIES. You will find art galleries and boutiques in many parts of the city, including Old Montreal, Westmount around Victoria Avenue, the St-Denis area, and downtown near the Montreal Museum of Fine Arts. Hours vary with exhibits. Many close Sun., Mon. Long-established galleries include: *Canadian Guild of Crafts,* 2025 rue Peel (849-6091). Nonprofit, handicrafts, art, especially Eskimo art. *Continental Gallery Inc.,* 1450 rue Drummond (842-1072). *Dominion Gallery,* 1438 rue Sherbrooke Ouest (845-7833). *Eskimo Art,* 1434 rue Sherbrooke ouest (844-4080) devoted exclusively to Eskimo art. *Walter Klinkhoff Gallery,* 1200 rue Sherbrooke Ouest (288-7306, 288-5972). *Elca London,* rue 1616 Sherbrooke ouest (931-3646). *Verre d'Art,* 1518 rue Sherbrooke Ouest (932-3896). Art glass. *Theo Waddington,* 1504 rue Sherbrooke Ouest (933-3653).

ARTS AND ENTERTAINMENT. Montrealers support arts and culture with enthusiasm and sophistication. (For fine arts see "Museums.") Montreal's English daily, the *Gazette,* lists art, entertainment, lectures, and auditions on Saturday. For tickets call your local Ticketron outlet or Ticketron in Montreal, 300 Léo Parizeau, 5th Floor, Montreal, PQ H2W 2N1 (288-3651). Ticket arrangements vary with show.

The main performing arts complex, *Place des Arts (PdA),* 175 Ste-Catherine Est, Montreal, PQ H2X 1K8 (842-2112), holds three concert halls. Salle Wilfrid Pelletier seats 3,000. Théâtre Maisonneuve is a traditional 1,300-seat theater, and Théâtre Port-Royal seats 800. Salle Wilfrid Pelletier presents major visiting performing groups and the Orchestre Symphonique de Montreal (OSM). All three present plays, recitals, ballet, and other performances. Prices range from $10–$45 (average, $20). Box office, Mon.–Sat., noon–9 P.M. Place des Arts' Sunday programs start at 11 A.M. (box office opens 10:30 A.M.) Nov.–May, at $1.50 for lectures with slides; $1.25 for *Sons et brioches,* ("sounds and buns"), plus $1.50 for light breakfast *(brioches et café).* These miniconcerts are suitable for children. In summer Basilica Notre-Dame in Old Montreal holds Mozart concerts. (See "Seasonal Events.")

MUSIC. *Orchestre Symphonique de Montreal* stars at PdA twice most weeks in the October–May subscription concert season. Tickets at $11–$25 available one month ahead through the box office only. Occasionally tickets available same night. PdA also hosts the McGill Chamber Orchestra (935-4955). *Pollock Concert Hall,* 555 Sherbrooke Ouest, Montreal, PQ H3A 3E3 (392-8224), attached to McGill University, offers classical, light classical, and chamber

MONTREAL

music, often free. Arrive early. *Opéra de Montreal* (842–2112). Produces four operas each winter at PdA. Seats cost $15–$45.

DANCE. Several dance groups perform in the city, including *Les Grands Ballets Canadiens,* 4816 rue Rivard (849–8638) and *Les Ballets Jazz,* at PdA.

Traditional folk dancing. During the summer, folk-dance societies give free performances in city parks. Join them with or without a partner. Call tourist information centers for details. Ethnic folk dancing continues all winter. For instance, Quebec folk dancers meet the third Saturday each month, 8:30 P.M., 4805 ave. Christophe-Colombe (598–8295). Year-round, about 1,500 people dance western-style with the Montreal Area Square Dance Association, Box 906, Pointe Claire-Dorval (744–5036). You can do-si-do at clubs for singles, golden-agers, and couples.

STAGE. Montreal hosts two permanent English theaters, some 10 French theaters, and, occasionally, Yiddish, German, and Hungarian, plus visiting groups, all listed in the *Gazette,* as well as *En Ville,* and *Montreal Scope,* distributed free by many hotels and tourist information centers.

English theaters: *Centaur.* 453 St-François-Xavier (288–3161). Often new plays and experimental theater, Sept.–June, two stages, in original Montreal Stock Exchange Building, Old Montreal. *Saidye Bronfman Centre,* 5170 Chemin de la Côte-Ste-Catherine (739–2301). Reopened fall 1986, revamped and rebuilt, offers exciting program of international theater Sept.–June. The Saidye's Yiddish Theatre group performs plays by leading Jewish writers, directed by founder Dora Wasserman. (Other English-language theater listed under "Dinner theaters.")

French theaters: *Théâtre Denise Pelletier,* 4353 Ste-Catherine Est (253–9874). *Théâtre de Quat'Sous,* 100 ave. des Pins Est (845–7278). *Théâtre du Nouveau Monde,* 84 Ste-Catherine Ouest (861–0563). *Théâtre du Rideau Vert,* 4664 St-Denis (845–0267).

Dinner theaters: Elegant dinner productions renewed interest in Montreal's English theater. Combinations of theater and/or dinner at various prices, ranging from about $12 for the show-only to around $40 for show, dinner (without wine, tips, or tax), parking. Enthusiasts find this a great excuse to dress up and enjoy a night on the town. Note that drinks usually cost about $4.50.

Arthur's Café baroque. Queen Elizabeth Hotel, 900 Blvd. Dorchester Ouest (861–3511). Elegant setting for light suppers and drinks. Musical comedies in French and English, operettas, and leading jazz musicians in jam sessions. Closed Mon., Tues. Cover, Wed.–Sun., $8; Sat., $10.

Le Festin du Gouverneur. In the old fort at Île Ste-Hélène (879–1141). Summer only. Great for groups. Enjoy light operatic airs beautifully rendered. A merry 17th-century frolic in the military barracks mess hall, where copious food comes second to the entertainment. Around $30, including half-liter of wine. Reservations necessary.

Hôtel Méridien. Complexe Desjardins (285–1450). Billed as "after-dinner theater," features light comedy, mainly in English, and special productions like the recent "back to the tango," soirées.

La Diligence. 7385 Blvd. Décarie (731–7771). Thurs.–Sun. Two dinner theaters plus a restaurant. Light musical comedies and plays in English, name entertainment—Eartha Kitt, Al Martino. Prices: $20–$45, depending on show.

Le Caf'Conc. Hôtel Château Champlain, 1050 de la Gauchetière ouest (878–9000). Las Vegas-style Parisienne cabaret, with lots of oo-la-la.

Puzzles Scene. Hôtel du Parc, 333 Prince Arthur (288–3733). Light comedy in English.

PROVINCE OF QUEBEC

FILMS. Montreal is a major center for film events like the *Montreal World Film Festival,* held late August at Le Parisien, rue Ste-Catherine Ouest. Write to Suite 109, 1455 Blvd. de Maisonneuve Ouest, Montreal, PQ H3G 1M8 (848–3883). In October you will find *Montreal's International Festival of New Cinema and Video* at Cinéma Parallèle, organized from 3724 Blvd. St-Laurent, Montreal, PQ H2X 2V8 (843–4725 or 843–4711).

ACCOMMODATIONS. The city continually hosts international conferences, so hotels must meet the organizers' high standards. You will find motels near Dorval airport and at entrances to the city's main arteries. Unless otherwise noted, establishments accept American Express, MasterCard, and Visa. You can call free to most hotels. Before calling long-distance (514 area code), check 800–514–555–1212 for toll-free numbers. All hotel people speak English, French, and often other languages.

Always ask about packages, particularly for weekend visits Nov.–May. Some deluxe hotels offer two nights and three days, including two full breakfasts, for $75–$110, based on double occupancy, subject to availability

Price categories, based on double occupancy without meals, run as follows: *Super Deluxe,* over $175; *Deluxe,* $130–$175; *Expensive,* $90–$130; *Moderate,* $70–$90; *Inexpensive,* $70 and less. All deluxe hotels offer super-deluxe floors and many expensive hotels hold deluxe accommodations.

Super Deluxe

L'Hôtel Ritz-Carlton. 1228 Sherbrooke Ouest, Montreal, PQ H3G 1H6 (514–842–4212). 241 rooms. On fashionable rue Sherbrooke. Five-star hotel.

Le Quatre Saisons (The Four Seasons). 1050 Sherbrooke Ouest, Montreal, PQ H4A 1R6 (514–284–1110). 302 rooms. Elegant, spacious, well-appointed. Fine cuisine, trendy music bar. Fashionable area.

Deluxe–Super deluxe

Bonaventure-Hilton International. Place Bonaventure, Montreal, PQ H5A 1E4 (514–878–2332). 400 rooms. Unusual luxury hotel atop convention facilities, with rooftop outdoor heated pool used even in subzero weather (swimmers wear bathing caps in winter), sauna, health club, parking. Resort atmosphere with gardens. Fine restaurants, entertainment.

Centre Sheraton Montreal. 1201 Blvd. Dorchester Ouest, Montreal, PQ H3B 2L7 (514–878–2000). 827 rooms. Elegant new hotel, 40 suites, indoor pool, entertainment.

Château Champlain. (CP Hotels), Place du Canada, Montreal, PQ H3B 4C9 (514–878–9000). 614 rooms. Gorgeous hotel overlooking park. Free health club with pool, saunas, whirlpool, exercise area, for guests only. Attractions/services include boutiques, movie theaters, fine dining, entertainment.

Hôtel du Parc. 3625 ave. du Parc, Montreal, PQ H2X 3P8 (514–288–6666). 455 rooms. Nightly live music in Puzzles (except Sun.), three cinemas. Adjoining Nautilus health club, includes squash, tennis, gyms, pool, saunas, whirlpools, steam baths.

Hôtel de la Montagne. 1430 de la Montagne, Montreal, PQ H3G 1Z5 (514–288–5656). 132 rooms. Baroque, trendy, action-packed, entertainment, disco, fine cuisine, summer pool.

L'Hôtel Méridien. Place Desjardins, Montreal, PQ H5B 1E5 (514–285–1450). 601 rooms. Business center, pool, sauna, babysitting, opposite PdA. Over shopping plaza. Dinner theater. Direct underground walkway to convention center.

MONTREAL

Le Reine Elizabeth (The Queen Elizabeth). 900 Blvd. Dorchester Ouest, Montreal, PQ H3B 4A5 (514–861–3511). CN hotel, 1,070 rooms. Directly linked to underground city. Valet parking, boutiques, health studio, fine restaurants, including *The Beaver Club*, entertainment.

Expensive

Château de l'Aéroport. Box 60, Aéroport Internationale de Montreal, Mirabel, PQ J7N 1A2 (514–476–1611). CP hotel. Next to Mirabel International Airport. 365 rooms. Pool, sauna, whirlpool, two squash courts, luxury hotel/resort atmosphere. Dining rooms.

Holiday Inns. (800–465–4329). The following expensive Holiday Inns offer air-conditioning, parking, indoor pools, saunas, boutiques, meeting rooms, dining rooms, and cafes. **Downtown Holiday Inn Centre-Ville.** 420 Sherbrooke Ouest, Montreal, PQ H3A 1B4 (514–842–6111). 486 rooms. *L'hôtel Place Dupuis.* downtown, 1415 St-Hubert, Montreal, PQ H2L 3Y9 (514–842–4881). 359 rooms. Pool, sauna. *Le Richelieu, Est.* 505 Sherbrooke est, Montreal, PQ H2L 1K2 (514–842–8581).

Le Grand Hôtel. 777 University, Montreal, PQ H3C 3Z7 (514–879–1370 or 800–361–8155). 730 rooms. Former Hyatt-Regency; near Old Montreal, Stock Exchange. Spa, steam bath, indoor pool, aerobic dance classes. Revolving rooftop restaurant with top-40 quartet, dinner-dancing.

Le Shangrila Hôtel de Luxe. Peel and Sherbrooke, Montreal, PQ H3A 1W7 (514–288–4141 or 800–361–7791). 200-room luxury hotel with Oriental atmosphere in downtown shopping area, near McGill University. Restaurants, bars.

Montreal Airport Hilton International. 12,505 Côte-de-Liesse, Dorval, PQ H9P 1B7 (514–631–2411). 483 rooms. Free shuttle to and from Dorval Airport, two minutes away. Executive floor, health club, indoor/outdoor pool, summer garden bar. Dining, entertainment.

Ruby Foo's Hôtel. 7655 Blvd. Décarie, Montreal, PQ H4P 2H2 (514–731–7701 or 800–361–5419). 118 rooms. Weekly rates.

Moderate

Holiday Inns. (800–465–4329). Moderate Holiday Inns in Montreal also offer air-conditioning, parking, indoor pools, saunas, boutiques, meeting rooms, dining rooms, and cafes. *Le Seville.* 4545 Côte-Vertu, Ouest, Ville St. Laurent, PQ H4S 1C8 (514–731–7582). 92 rooms. Free limo service 7 A.M.–11 P.M. from Dorval Airport, 5 km (3 mi) away. *Le Seigneurie.* 7300 Côte-de-Liesse, Montreal, PQ H4T 1E7 (514–731–7751). 199 rooms. *Le Longueuil.* 999 de Sérigny, Longueuil, PQ J4K 2T1 (514–670–3030). South shore, facing Montreal and St. Lawrence River. *Holiday Inn Pointe Claire.* 6700 Trans-Canada Highway, Pointe Claire, PQ H9R 1C2 (514–697–7110). 300 rooms. In West Island, 11 km (7 mi) from Dorval Airport. Ample outdoor parking for bus, trailers.

Hôtel Château Versailles. 1659 Sherbrooke Ouest, Montreal, PQ H3H 1E3 (933–3611). 70 rooms. Fine, European-style hotel run by same family for over past 25 years. Handsome Edwardian décor on quiet section of elegant Sherbrooke. Special weekend rates October–May. Do reserve.

Hôtel Maritime. 1155 rue Guy, Montreal, PQ H3H 2K5 (932–1411). 214 rooms. Outdoor terrace restaurant, indoor pool, sundeck, sidewalk bar with entertainment. Cheerful service.

Ramada Inns. *Ramada Airport.* 6600 Côte-de-Liesse, St-Laurent, PQ 2 H4T 1E3 (514–737–7811 or 342–2262). 212 rooms, indoor pool, patio. *Ramada Inn Centre-Ville.* 1005 rue Guy, Montreal, PQ H3H 2K4 (514–866–4611 or 800–228–3344). 205 rooms downtown. Outdoor pool, sauna, exercise rooms, piano bar, restaurants. *Ramada Inn Parc Olympique.* 5500 Sherbrooke Est, Montreal,

PQ H1N 1A1 (514-256-9011). 236 rooms. Near Olympic Games site, stadium. Semi-Olympic-size pool, nightclub.

Inexpensive

Le Sherbourg. 475 Sherbrooke Ouest, Montreal, PQ H3A 2L9 (514-842-3961 or 800-361-4973). 200 rooms. Near McGill University. Pool, saunas.

Le Royal Roussillon. 1610 rue St-Hubert, Montreal, PQ H2L 3Z3 (514-849-3214). 104 rooms.

Château de l'Argoat. 524 Sherbrooke Est, Montreal. PQ H2L 1K1 (514-842-2046). Family-run, 35 rooms, near Latin Quarter, Métro, Voyageur bus terminal. Popular with Europeans. Rooms with bath, under $40.

BED AND BREAKFAST. B&Bs prove increasingly popular with out-of-towners who appreciate meeting Montrealers in their own homes. $25-$40 for singles, and $30-$50 for doubles. Deposit required with reservation, usually refundable if cancellation received seven days before arrival. Reservation bureaus include: *Montreal Bed & Breakfast*, 4912 Victoria, Montreal, PQ H3W 2N1 (514-738-9410), which also covers the Laurentians and Eastern Townships; *Downtown Bed & Breakfast–Montrealers at Home*, 3458 ave. Laval, Montreal, PQ (514-289-9749); *Bed & Breakfast de Chez-nous*, 5386 ave. Brodeur, Montreal, PQ H4A 1J3 (514-485-1252); and *Monique Côté*, 5151 Côte St-Antoine, Montreal, PQ H4A 1P1 (514-484-7802).

YS AND YOUTH HOSTELS. Montreal's youth hostel downtown: **l'Auberge de jeunesse de Montreal.** 3541 Aylmer, Montreal, PQ H2X 2B9 (514-843-3317). Members, $8 nightly, nonmembers, $10. L'Auberge sleeps 108 people in rooms—reserved for men or women only—with three to eight beds.

YWCA. 1355 Blvd. Dorchester Ouest. Montreal, PQ H3G 1T3 (514-866-9941). Women residents only. Men may use cafeteria. Overnight singles, $19-$28; doubles, $34-$38. Choose room only, room with sink, or room with private bath. Reserve during summer. Oct.–May, stay seven nights, pay for six. Cafeteria open 7:30 A.M.–8:30 P.M. Pool, sauna, whirlpool, fitness classes, $6 extra daily.

YMCA. 1450 rue Stanley, Montreal, PQ H3A 2W6 (514-849-8393). Accepts women as well as men. Book at least two days in advance. Women must book seven days ahead—there are fewer rooms with shower (at $27.50) for women. Anyone staying summer weekends must book a week ahead. Men's room rates: $24.75 (no shower)–$40 for single, and $45 double. Add $8 per person up to five people, with full bathrooms.

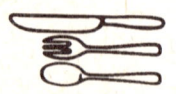

RESTAURANTS. Montrealers study restaurants with the same enthusiasm with which some people follow sports. You will find the latest scores kept by Bee Maguire in *Montreal* magazine; by Helen Rochester, and periodically, Ashok Chandwani in Friday's *Gazette* and Saturday's *TV Times*, a *Gazette* insert.

Of Montreal's over 2,000 restaurants, it is hard to pick a dud. Following is a brief selection arranged according to type of food and price. The price categories, based on the cost of a full meal for one person, without tip, tax, or wine, are: *Super Deluxe*, over $40; *Deluxe*, $30-$40; *Expensive*, $20-$30; *Moderate*, $12-$20; *Inexpensive*, less than $12. Price ranges, however, are hard to pin

MONTREAL

down, since you can dine at almost moderate prices in many restaurants by taking the table d'hôte, or go super deluxe on the à la carte items, particularly in the hotel dining rooms. *Tables d'hôte*—daily specials—usually cover three courses: soup or hors d'oeuvre, main course, and dessert. Coffee is usually extra. Unless otherwise noted, some or all major credit cards are accepted.

Chinese

Deluxe

Ruby Foo's. 7815 blvd. Décarie (737-3377). Seats 700. French and Chinese-style food comes from separate kitchens. Table d'hôte lunches, $8.95. Mon.-Sat., 11;30 A.M.-11:30 P.M.; Sun., 11:00 A.M.-10:30 P.M.

Expensive–Deluxe

Abacus II. 2144 Mackay (933-8444). Spicy Szechuan and Hunan fare served in swish decor that draws beautiful, well-heeled folk. Tues.-Sat., noon-3 P.M., 6 P.M.-midnight. Closed Mon.

Inexpensive–Moderate

La Maison Kam Fung. 1008 Clark (866-4016). Over 700 seats. Gold, red, and black Chinese-dragon décor. At lunchtime dim-sum waitresses sing out names of dishes served from wagons they wheel between the tables. Pick mini-portions from over 100 delicacies, at $1.50-$2 each. No dim sum evenings. Full dinner, $10-$20. Dim sum, Mon.-Sat., 11 A.M.-3 P.M., Sun., 10 A.M.-3:30 P.M. Dinner, Mon.-Sat., 3 P.M.-midnight; Sun., 3:30-midnight.

Inexpensive

You will find many other low-priced Chinese restaurants—such as *Le Jardin Lung Fung,* 1071 rue St-Urbain, (879-0622), and *Fung Shing Restaurant,* 1102 blvd. St-Laurent (866-0469), where full meals cost under $12—in Chinatown, which extends roughly from east and west of Bleury to blvd. St-Laurent, south from blvd. Dorchester to Lagauchetière. No credit cards.

French and Belgian

Deluxe–Super Deluxe

Les Chenêts. 2075 Bishop (844-1842). Possibly the city's most expensive restaurant, with the biggest wine cellar. French classics. *Diner gastronomique* for two at $155 includes half-bottle white wine with fish course, a whole bottle of red with the meat. Table d'hôte lunches, $6.50. Mon.-Fri., noon-11 P.M. Sat., Sun., 5:30-11 P.M.

Expensive–Deluxe

See also below, under "Hotel Dining Rooms."
Chez la Mère Michel. 1209 Guy (934-0473). Business clientele appreciates the rustic French provincial décor, well-appointed cellar, traditional (and some new) French dishes. Liquor license. Tues.-Fri., 11:30 A.M.-2:30 P.M., 5:30-10:30 P.M. Mon. and Sat., 5:30-10:30 P.M. Closed Sun.
La Chamade. 1453 Bélanger Est (727-7040). Least expensive of the fine owner-chef restaurants. Liquor license. Tues.-Fri., noon-2 P.M. Tues.-Sat., 6-10 P.M. Closed Sun., Mon.
Le St-Amable. 188 rue St-Amable (866-3471). In old fieldstone house, Old Montreal. Classic French. Big on flambéing. Business lunches. Liquor license. Mon.-Fri., noon-11 P.M. Sat., Sun., 6-11 P.M.

La Marée. 404 Place Jacques-Cartier (861-8126). Next to St-Amable, also in a heritage fieldstone house. Classic French, like cherries jubilee. Liquor license. Mon.–Fri., noon–3 P.M.; daily 6–11:30 P.M.

Le Fadeau. 423 St-Claude (878-3959). Comfortable old Norman-style house, often brilliant nouvelle cuisine. Often rated tops. Gourmet samplings of many specialties, at $40 per person. Liquor license. Mon.–Fri., noon–3 P.M., 5:30–11:30 P.M. Sat., Sun., 6–11 P.M.

Les Halles. 1450 Crescent (844-2328). Montreal's Establishment loves the glossy décor, perfect textures of fish and lamb. Business lunches. Liquor license. Mon.–Fri., 11 A.M.–11 P.M., Sat., 5–11 P.M. Closed Sun.

La Picholette. 1020 St-Denis (843-8502). Divine Victorian house. Food to die for. Honest. Business lunches, Mon.–Fri. Liquor license. Mon.–Fri., 11:30 A.M.–2:30 P.M.; 5:30–11:30 P.M. Sat., 5:30–11:30 P.M. Closed Sun.

Moderate–Expensive

Le Petit Havre. 443 St. Vincent (861-0581). Long-standing Old Montreal favorite. Daily, 11 A.M.–3 P.M., 5–11 P.M. Closed for lunch Sat., Sun., Sept.–May.

Le Caveau. 2063 rue Victoria (844-1624). Note this Victoria stands downtown, near McGill. Reliable, comfortable, aimiable, and affordable. Liquor license. Open Mon.–Fri, 7:30 A.M.–11 P.M. Sat., noon–midnight; Sun., 4 P.M.–midnight.

L'Express. 2927 St-Denis (845-5333). Quintessential modern bistro. Noisy, bright, lots of mirrors; everyone in overdrive. Wonderful cakes, cheese, nouvelle cuisine. Low wine markup. Dinners under $20. Mon.–Sat., 8A.M.–2A.M.; Sun., 2 P.M.–midnight.

L'Odéon. 4806 ave. Parc (273-4088). Bistro imported from Brussels. Perhaps the city's best bistro cuisine. Liquor license. Tues.–Sun., 6:30–11:30 P.M. Bar open till 1 A.M.

Inexpensive–Moderate

La Duchesse Anne. 6390 rue St-Hubert (273-4352). Métro Beaubien, northeast shopping area. Genuine wafer-thin crêpes from Brittany. French country-inn décor. Liquor license. Tues.-Fri., 11:30 A.M.-3 P.M.; Tues., Wed., Sun., 5–9 P.M.; Thurs.–Sat., 5–10:30 P.M. Closed Mon.

Le Paris. 1812 Ste-Catherine Ouest (937-4898). Good little French restaurant. Fresh market produce only. Liquor license. Open Mon.–Sat., noon–3 P.M.; 5–10 P.M.

Le P'tit Port. 1813 Ste-Catherine Ouest (932-6556). Fish and seafood. Bring wine. Tues.-Fri., noon–10:30 P.M. Sat. 5–10:30 P.M.

Restaurant Julien. 1191 Union Ave. (871-1581). Near downtown hotels, shops. Pretty pink and white décor. Nouvelle cuisine. Liquor license. Mon–Fri., 11:30 A.M.–10:30 P.M. Sat. 6–10:30 P.M. Closed Sun.

Greek

You will find many Greek restaurants dotted throughout the city, most in the pedestrian mall around Prince Arthur. Many favorites in traditionally Greek avenue du Parc area.

Moderate-Expensive

Molivos. 4859 ave. du Parc (271-5354). Seafood by the pound, extras à la carte. Dinner about $10–$30. Liquor license. Daily, 11 A.M.–3 P.M., 5 A.M.

Milos. 5357 ave. du Parc (272-3522). Shrimp, fried squid, and charcoal-broiled fish flown in from New York, four-pound lobsters, soft-shell crabs. A

MONTREAL

la carte. Dinner about $20. Liquor license. Daily, 11 A.M.–3 P.M., 5 P.M.–1 A.M.

Hotel Dining Rooms

You will find some of the most elegant dining (mostly French) in Montreal's fine hotels. They vie jealously to keep their clientele on the premises by offering soft background music (sometimes harp or piano), fine and often innovative cuisine, and service at competitive prices. Dinners are in the *Expensive–Super Deluxe* range. Popular Sunday brunches (reservations necessary) cost around $20; children usually half price. All hold liquor licenses and accept credit cards. The selection includes:

The Beaver Club. The Queen Elizabeth, 900 blvd. Dorchester Ouest (861-3511). Local lions dine among fur-trade artifacts, as they did at the original 18th-century club. Sunday brunch, $19, two sittings, 11:30, 1:30. Open daily from 12 A.M.–3 P.M.; 6–11 P.M.

Café de Paris. L'Hôtel Ritz-CArlton, 1228 Sherbrooke Ouest (842-4212). Classical French food and service. Pianist.

Le Castillon. Bonaventure-Hilton International, Place Bonaventure (878-2332). Unusual 17th-century French castle décor, overlooking rooftop garden. Business lunch, Mon.–Fri., $10.50–$25. Dinner, $25 and up. Sunday brunch. Sun.–Fri. from 11:30 A.M.–2:30 P.M., 6–11:30 P.M. Sat., 6–11:30 P.M.

Lutétia. Hotel de la Montagne, 1430 de la Montagne (288-5656). Baroque mezzanine restaurant overlooks cabaret, piano bar, and lots of action. Sunday brunch. Mon.–Sat., 7–11:30 A.M.; noon–3 P.M.; 6–11:30 P.M. Sun. 11:30 A.M.–3 P.M.

Le Neufchâtel. Château Champlain, Place du Canada (878-9000). Elegant country *château* décor. Harp. A la carte dinner, $35. House wine. Mon.–Sat., 6–10 P.M. Closed Sun. Sun. brunch at rooftop L'Escapade, 11:30 A.M.–2:30 P.M.

Le Point de Vue. Centre Sheraton, 1201 Dorchester Ouest, (878-2000). Harpist. Mon.–Sat., 6–10:30 P.M. Closed Sun.

Le Restaurant. Le Quatre Saisons, 1050 Sherbrooke Ouest (284-1110). A la carte dinner $20–$30. "Alternative cuisine" available for people monitoring calorie, cholesterol, and sodium intake. Daily, 7 A.M.–11 P.M.

Indian

Moderate

Le Taj. 2077 Stanley (845-9015). Elegant. Attracts well-dressed people. Tandoori dishes and north Indian fare. Main dishes, $8.95–$15. Table d'hôte, $16. Buffet lunch, Mon.–Fri. $8. Liquor license. Daily, 11:30 A.M.–2:30 P.M., Sun.–Thurs., 5–11 P.M. Closes midnight Fri., Sat.

Inexpensive–Moderate

New Delhi. 5014 Ave. du Parc (279–0339). Authentic northern Indian. Liquor license. Mon.–Fri., 11:30 A.M.–2 P.M., 5–11 P.M. Sat., Sun., 5 P.M.–midnight.

New Punjab. 4026A Ste- Catherine Ouest (932–9440). New family-run restaurant holds much promise. Liquor license. Daily, 11 A.M.–11 P.M.

New Woodlands. 1241 rue Guy (933–1553). Real south Indian vegetarian fare, plus meat and fish curries. Try masala dosa, big, crisp, and lacy crêpes. Soup and a main course average $10. Liquor license. Summer, daily, 11 A.M.–11 P.M. Winter, 11:30 A.M.–3 P.M., 5–11 P.M.

Italian

Moderate–Expensive

La Sila. 2040 St-Denis (844–5083). Draws rave reviews for ambiance, service, and innovative fare. Liquor license. Dinner only, Mon.–Sat. 5:30–11 P.M. Closed Sun.

Lo Stivale d'Oro. 2150 Mountain St. (844–8714). Critics heap praise on this warm and romantic echo of southern Italy. Table d'hôte $12–$24. Liquor license. Mon.–Fri., 11:30 A.M.–3 P.M., 5 P.M.–midnight; Sat., 5 P.M.–1 A.M. Closed Sun.

Restaurant Baci. 2095 McGill College Avenue (288–7901). Opened in 1985, and worth watching. Pianist plays evenings from Wed.–Sat. Table d'hôte, $10–$17. Mon.–Sat., 11 A.M.–midnight; Sat., 5:30 P.M.–midnight. Closed Sun.

Inexpensive–Moderate

Le Piémontais. 1145A de Bullion (861–8122). Lively and sympatico little downstairs ristorante. Before 8 P.M., complete meals with dessert and coffee, $8.25–$18.50. Liquor license. Mon.–Fri., 11 A.M.–midnight; Sat. 5 P.M.–midnight. Closed Sun.

Japanese

Expensive

Benihana. 7965 Decarie Blvd. (731–8205). Kamikazi chefs entertain with flying knives. Liquor license. Mon.–Fri., noon–11 P.M. Sat., Sun., 5–11 P.M.

Katsura. 2170 de la Montagne St. (849–1172). The city's first and best all-round Japanese restaurant, run by Prince Hotel/restaurant group. Liquor license. Mon.–Fri., 11:30 A.M.–2:30 P.M. Mon.–Thurs., 5:30–10:30 P.M. Fri., Sat., 4:30–11:30 P.M. Sun., 5:30–9:30 P.M.

Sakura Gardens. 2153 Crescent St. (288–9122). Simple décor, but great fresh sushi. Liquor license. Mon.–Fri., 11:30 A.M.–2:30 P.M., 5:30–10:30 P.M. Sat., 5:30–11 P.M. Sun., 5:30–11 P.M.

Deli and Jewish-Style

Vaad Hair, 5491 Victoria Ave., Westmount (739–6363). Supplies lists of true kosher restaurants.

Inexpensive

Balkans & Lennox. 359 ave. du President Kennedy (845–9494). Unpretentious décor, motherly service. Small, kosher-style. Main dishes from $3.25. Full meals, $6–$7. Mon.–Sat., 6 A.M.–8 P.M. Closed Sun.

Beauty's. 93 ave. Mont-Royal Ouest (849–8883). New York diner atmosphere. Wholesome breakfast food all day. Big for Sunday brunch. No liquor license. Mon.–Fri., 7 A.M.–5 P.M. or 7 P.M., depending on demand. Sat., 7 A.M.–5 P.M. Sun., 8 A.M.–5 P.M. July-August, closed Sun. No credit cards.

Ben's. 990 blvd. de Maisonneuve Ouest (844–1001). Serves smoked meat. Open Sun.–Thurs., 7 A.M.–4 A.M.; Fri., Sat., 7 A.M.–5 A.M.

Brisket's. 2055 Bishop (843–3650). Ice-cream-parlor décor in cozy downtown house. One of Montreal's claims to culinary fame rests on smoked meat. Here they cure their own. Classic smoked-meat sandwiches, $3.50. Draft beer.

MONTREAL 75

Cherry coke. Friendly service. Liquor license. Sun.–Wed., 11 A.M.–10 P.M. Thurs.–Sat., 11 A.M.–11 P.M. in winter, and until 1 A.M. in summer.

Main St. Lawrence Steak House Delicatessen. 3864 blvd. St-Laurent (843–5689). Home-cured smoked meat. Main courses from $3.25. A la carte steaks from $10.25, *tout garni.* No liquor license. Never closes.

Schwartz's Montreal Hebrew Delicatessen. 3895 blvd. St-Laurent (842–4813). Lunch-counter style. Montreal smoked meat cured here. $10.50 rib-steak dinner, including coffee, tops the price list. Deli sandwiches under $3. No liquor license. Sun.–Thurs., 9 A.M.–12:45 A.M.; Fri., 9 A.M.–1:45 A.M.; Sat., 9 A.M.–2:45 A.M. No credit cards.

Middle-Eastern/North African

Inexpensive

La Medina. 3464 St-Denis (282-0359). Moroccan *salon* with brass tables, cushion-covered *banquettes.* Authentic Moroccan couscous, brochettes, desserts. Table d'hôte, $15; main dishes under $10. Liquor license. Interesting Moroccan wines. Daily, 5:30 P.M.–midnight.

Steak Houses

Moderate–Expensive

Gibby's. 298 Place d'Youville (282–1837). 200-year-old house in Old Montreal. Consistently fine fare. Liquor license. Four-course business lunch, $7.50–$10. Noon–3:30 P.M. A la carte main courses $14–$25. Daily noon to midnight.

Moishe's Steak House. 3961 blvd. St-Laurent (845–3509). Steak dinners, $25. Business lunches, $10–13. Sun.–Fri., 11:45 A.M.–10:45 P.M. Sat., 11:45 A.M.–11:45 P.M.

Quebec

Expensive

Les Filles du Roy. 415 Bonsecours (849–3535). Features Quebec cooking in traditional Quebec décor. Mon.-Sun., 11.30 A.M.–midnight; Sat., 11.30 A.M.–1 A.M.

Pâtisseries

In case you have a *pâtisserie* attack, here are three treatment centers, offering divine pastry and coffee. None hold liquor licenses or accept credit cards. Count on spending a minimum of $2 for coffee and a real-butter croissant. Opening hours vary. *Au Duc de Lorraine,* 5002 Côte-des-Neiges (731–4128). Closed Mon., Rockland Shopping Centre, Town of Mont-Royal (731–8229). Closed Sun. *LeNôtre,* 1500 Laurier Ouest (270–2702). Closed Mon. *Pâtisserie de Nancy,* 5655 Monkland (482–3030). Closed Mon.

Vegetarian

Inexpensive

Le Commensal. 2115 St-Denis (845–2627) and 680 Ste-Catherine Ouest (871–1480). Inventive veggie fare, sold by weight, so salads cost less than curried rice. Main dishes, $5–$7. You can bring wine to the St-Denis cafe, which opens daily 11:30 A.M.–4 A.M. The Ste-Catherine outlet, which holds a liquor license, opens daily from 11:40 A.M.–midnight.

LIQUOR LAWS. In Montreal, as in the rest of Quebec, a person must be 18 to buy or drink alcoholic beverages. Most restaurants either hold liquor licenses or allow you to bring your own bottle (byob). Restaurants that allow byobs usually display a sign marked: "Apportez votre vin." They supply glasses and corkscrews *(tires-bouchon)*. You can buy imported wines and spirits through provincial government outlets, marked "Société des alcools." Maison des vins, near Place Ville-Marie shopping center's Mansfield Street entrance, holds the best vintages. You can buy locally bottled beer and wine (some of the wine is imported in bulk) at grocery stores and handy stores, or *dépanneurs.* All the big hotels hold liquor licenses.

NIGHTLIFE AND BARS. The big hotels all offer entertainment, from full-fledged cabarets and dinner theater (see "Arts and Entertainment") to dancing to live music between shows by recording artists (*Le Portage,* Bonaventure-Hilton International, Place Bonaventure, 878–2332) and piano bars. Many bars feature happy hours, 5–7 P.M., offering free nibbles. For instance, the *Ritz-Carlton,* 1228 Sherbrooke Ouest (842–4212), holds a ground-floor bar *(très élégant),* with pianist in evening dress, where you nibble on smoked salmon. The most soigné gentlefolk trip the light fantastic on the Ritz' tiny dance floor. You will find a boggling assortment of bars and nightlife in five main areas: first, the trendy, traditionally Anglophone (but really cosmopolitan) Bishop/Crescent streets—no jeans here; second, the Latin Quarter of rue St-Denis above Ste-Catherine as far north as rue Rachel; third, the Laurier Boulevard/St-Laurent area; fourth, the newly awakening (and "in") avenue Parc/St-Joseph quarter; fifth, rue Prince Arthur at Boulevard St-Laurent.

Closing times change without notice. Call for particulars on current acts and hours. Drinks cost about $4.50 for liquor; $3 for local beer and wine. Few downtown *boîtes* allow jeans, most other areas accept "clean jeans"—no rags or tatters, bare feet, or general scruffiness, male or female.

L'Air du Temps, 191 St-Paul Ouest (842–2003). Victorian, with lace and petit point, winding staircase, wood paneling, in this well-established jazz bar offering fine groups and soloists. Imported Paris Métro car provides intimate corners for private conversations. $5 cover.

Le Belmont. 4483 St-Laurent (845–8443). Big with 24–35 age group. Nightly, 8:30 P.M.–3 A.M. Lineups Fri., Sat. Dancing, bar. No cover.

Biddles'. 2060 Aylmer (842–8656). Montreal's annual Jazz Festival attracts the world's greats, but many live and work here, namely, bassist Charlie Biddles' trio, with pianist Oliver Jones, and guest. Great ribs-and-chicken. Biddle and Jones play 10:30 P.M. Other live music earlier. No cover. $6 minimum Sat., Sun. Catch Biddle and Jones 5–9 P.M. Wed.–Fri. at the *Voyageur Lounge,* Queen Elizabeth Hotel, 900 Blvd. Dorchester Ouest, (861–3511).

Business Bar. 3500 St-Laurent at Milton. Alternative disco, like basement parking garage, all cement *au naturel* except for red doors. Holds 300 people.

MONTREAL

Our own dear Queen would not like it, but the 20-35-year-olds do. Clean jeans acceptable. Cover $3.

Casablanca Supper Club. 3964 St-Denis (844-0561). Jazz and a Bogey décor. No cover. Open at noon. Live pianist 5 P.M.

The Cock'n Bull. 1944 Ste-Catherine Ouest (933-4556). British-style pub, with good fare. Double Diamond and Guinness beer on draft.

Club de Danse Ira Murray, Enrg. 3981 St-Laurent (842-4761). The Laflèches learned to dance from Arthur Murray's brother, Ira. For $2.50 you get coffee and foxtrot, rhumba, waltz, and chacha, Sat., from 9 P.M. Closed July/Aug. Rusty? Then come at 7:30 P.M. for lessons, $2.50 each or $25 for 10 ("never a contract"). No liquor served.

Du Côté de Chez Swann. 57 Prince Arthur (844-1019). Fri., Sat. meet the young crowd—ages 18-35. Weekdays, average age rises. Clean jeans acceptable. Three-floor bar, discos, one with dance floor for 250 people, stage. Quiet area, too. Daily, 5 P.M.-3 A.M. Cover $3.

Les Foufounes Eléctriques. 97 Ste-Catherine Ouest (845-4584). At "The Electric Bums," new wave "alternative" disco/stand-up bar. Wear whatever here. Stage, room for 300. Black walls glow in black light. Mix of go-go, tango, poetry readings, theater, mime, magic, action painting, and latest sound. Most avant-garde bar in town. Not for faint-hearted. 5 P.M.-3 A.M. Cover charge varies with events.

Le Grand Café. 1720 St-Denis (849-6955). Downstairs, restaurant. Upstairs, live talent, including pianists, jazz, comedians. Tues.-Sat., from 9 P.M. Last set at 2:15 A.M. Cover charge.

Grumpy's. 1242 Bishop (downtown) (866-9010). Sedate pub with warm atmosphere, mainly well-dressed, over-35 crowd. Mon.-Fri., noon-2:30 A.M. Sat., Sun., 8 P.M.-2:30 A.M.

Lux. 5229 St-Laurent (271-9272). Extraordinary bar-restaurant-tobacconist (exotic Turkish and Egyptian brands), and newsstand. Every kind of magazine you could possibly want. Wine by glass; dazzling tubular décor with grillwork. Like a Parisian "drogstore," never closes.

The Old Dublin Pub. 1219A University (861-4448). Irish, British beer on tap—Guinness, Tartan Bitter, Bass Ale, Harp Lager. Live entertainment, darts, sing-songs. Mon.-Sat., 11:30 A.M.-3 A.M.

Puzzles' Bar. Hotel du Parc, 333 Prince Arthur Ouest (288-3733). Big, comfortable arm chairs, many plants, live jazz. Tues.-Sun., 9 P.M.-2 A.M. No cover.

La Ricane. 177 Bernard Ouest (279-3977). Neighborhood bar serves bargain food *la bouffe*, Scrabble, Go, backgammon. Montreal Storytellers hold forth in English alternate Tuesdays. Irish music some nights, Sat. night jazz. Minimum, cover $5. Daily, 9:30 A.M.-3 A.M.

Shibumi. 5345 St-Laurent (271-5712). Jazz bar, with newest videos, jam sessions Tues.-Thurs.; guest stars Fri., Sat. Opens 9 P.M. Music starts 10 P.M. No cover.

Spectrum de Montreal. 318 Ste-Catherine Ouest (861-5851). A former movie theater with seats replaced by tables, chairs, and bar, holds 1,000 people who pay about $16 for latest rock, jazz, pop *spéctacles*. Opens 8 P.M. for 9 P.M. show; sometimes second show around 10:30 P.M. Closes about midnight. Giant screen for latest music videos.

Thursday's. 1449 Crescent (849-5634). Lots of action at this giant stand-up bar. Vast disco downstairs always lively. The Queen would love the décor, but the oo-la-la might bowl 'er over.

Woody's Pub. 1234 Bishop (395-8118). Tiny dance floor. Young crowd. Upstairs, The Comedy Nest showcases stand-up comics. Shows Thurs., 9 P.M.; Fri., Sat., 9 P.M., 11 P.M.; Sun., 8 P.M.

PROVINCE OF QUEBEC

Yellow-Door Café. 3625 Aylmer (392-6742). Old-style coffee house (no liquor) in student ghetto. Grateful folksingers who started here—like Jesse Winchester, Sneezy Waters—return for gigs.

SOUTHERN QUEBEC

The Garden of Quebec

by
David Dunbar

David Dunbar is a Montreal author who writes about travel for such publications as Travel & Leisure, Reader's Digest, *the* Toronto Globe and Mail *and the* Boston Globe *and for CBC Radio. He is a member of the Society of American Travel Writers.*

This scenic corner of Quebec between the St. Lawrence River and the Appalachian uplands of the northern United States consists of three distinct regions. The Richelieu/South Shore area south and west of Montreal embraces the rich farmland of the St. Lawrence Valley. East of the Yamaska River, this flat terrain rises up in the rumpled hills of L'Estrie, famed for its skiing and sparkling lakes. And south of the St. Lawrence, along the Chaudière River, lies the gently rolling landscape of Maple Country.

Although L'Estrie usually claims the title "Garden of Quebec," the nickname could apply to the entire area. Blessed with Quebec's mildest climate (which is not saying much), this region is nevertheless intensely cultivated. The fertile soil along the Châteauguay River supports Canada's greatest concentration of dairy farms. Cheese, mushrooms, apples, livestock, and ducks are just a few of L'Estrie's agricultural products. The maple groves along the Chaudière River yield most of Canada's syrup.

Towns and villages in southern Quebec are steeped in a long and colorful history which in some places goes back to the late 1600s. Some of the farms along the Richelieu were established in the days of Louis XIV. (Some Quebec farmers still pay land rent under contracts drawn up in the 17th century.) The townships of L'Estrie were founded by Loyalists fleeing the American Revolution. And many of the picturesque villages along the St. Lawrence in Maple Country date from the days when New France included not only present-day Quebec, but also territory north to Hudson Bay, west to the Rockies, and south to the Gulf of Mexico.

Richelieu/South Shore

Flowing from Lake Champlain north to the St. Lawrence, the Richelieu River was often a corridor of conflict in Quebec's early history. Samuel de Champlain, the Father of New France, canoed upriver in 1609 to battle the Iroquois. In 1760 British troops went the opposite direction to attack the French. In 1776, and again in 1812, Americans used the river as a highway of invasion. The Rebellion of 1837, when French-Canadian *Patriotes* tried to overthrow the British, also rocked the banks of the Richelieu.

Today pleasure craft, not warships, navigate this historic river. Cruises usually begin at the provincial marina in Sorel, where the Richelieu joins the St. Lawrence. Sorel also boasts an 18th-century park called Carré Royal, which retains its original Union Jack design, and a nearby open-air market where produce is sold in summer.

Farther south (upstream), the Rebellion of 1837 is remembered with a statue of a *Patriote* in St-Denis and with a stone monument in nearby St-Charles-sur-Richelieu, where the uprising began. There are also guided heritage tours of St-Denis's elegant stone houses, which stand in the shadow of the twin spires of a church built in 1796.

Mont-St-Hilaire refers to one of the most attractive towns in the region, as well as a nearby mountain, one of eight Monteregian Hills that rise from the surrounding farmlands. Nature lovers follow trails through the mountain's peaceful woods, once part of the Gault Estate and now owned by Montreal's McGill University.

Chambly's location at the head of rapids that vault into a deep basin on the Richelieu made the town a strategic military crossroads in the 18th and 19th centuries. A massive stone fort built by the French in

1711 has been partially restored as part of a national historic park. Near the fort, an interpretive center in a lock station house explains the workings of the Chambly Canal, constructed in the 1840s.

Farther south, at Fort Lennox National Historic Park on Île-aux-Noix (accessible by ferry), an officer in period uniform explains how the fortifications were built by the British in 1783 to guard against an American invasion. The barracks, commissary, guardhouse, officers' quarters, and canteen are restored.

Giraffes, zebras, lions, hyenas, elephants, and tigers wander freely in Parc Safari Africain in Hemmingford, southwest of Fort Lennox. Visitors drive their cars along a five-mile (nine-kilometer) road through the park to view the exotic wildlife. There are also magic shows, an enchanted forest for children, and Canada's only House of Reptiles.

To the east, more than a hundred apple orchards carpet the lower slopes of Mont Rougemont. Roadside stands in the village of Rougemont sell local apple varieties, as well as honey, maple syrup, and homemade bread. An interpretive center explains how orchards are nurtured, and how apple juice and cider are made.

L'Estrie

This region has many of the attractive qualities of New England—covered bridges, village greens, white church steeples, welcoming country inns, and quiet backroads winding past fields and farms. L'Estrie comes by these characteristics honestly: the area was settled by Loyalists fleeing north after the War of Independence.

The gateway to the region is the eclectic town of Granby, an industrial city with a dozen European fountains, including a 3,200-year-old Greek fountain on Leclerc Boulevard and a Roman fountain in Pelletier Park. Granby also has a car museum with Canada's finest collection of antique autos and an outstanding zoo. An international song festival in October and a gastronomic festival in September highlight the town's social season.

Nearby Mont Bromont is equipped for night skiing, which makes an impressive spectacle for motorists driving along Highway 10 on a winter's evening. The 18-hole golf course, one of the finest in the region, remains popular even in winter—for its cross-country ski trails.

Farther east, Mont Orford dominates the western part of Mont Orford Provincial Park. Almost 20 ski slopes wind through the woods on its southern face; a chairlift whisks skiers in winter and sightseers in summer to the summit of the 738-meter (2,400-foot) peak. For the past 30 summers some 300 students have come to the Orford Arts Center to study and perform classical music. The center also welcomes artisans—potters, painters, sculptors, lacemakers—who organize art exhibitions throughout the summer.

Another appealing aspect of L'Estrie is its cluster of sparkling lakes, with their strange mixture of euphonious Indian names (Massawippi,

Memphrémagog, Mégantic) and harsher English designations (Brome, Brompton, Stukely).

You can enjoy Memphrémagog's "beautiful waters" (the meaning of its Indian name) on the cruise boat *L'Aventure*. One of the highlights of the trip is the abbey of St-Benoit-du-Lac, which sends a slender bell tower up above the trees like a Disneyland castle. Built on a wooded peninsula in 1912 by the Benedictines, the abbey is home to some 60 monks who produce all their own food. They sell apples from their orchards as well as distinctive cheeses: Ermite, St-Benoit, and ricotta.

After the Civil War, nearby Lac-Massawippi became a favorite summer haunt of wealthy Southerners, who rusticated in the cool North without the annoyance of Yankees. Several of the homes they built here have been converted into gracious inns, including the Manoir Hovey and the Hatley Inn. North Hatley, at the northern end of the lake, still attracts visitors with its antique shops and the region's only English-language theater productions, at a converted barn called The Piggery.

The August milk festival in Coaticook, to the southeast, is a reminder that L'Estrie is one of Quebec's most productive dairy regions. The festival fun includes a fashion show in which bovine beauties model the latest in agricultural haute couture. The Coaticook River Gorge is threaded with hiking trails and spanned by a covered bridge.

Cookshire to the north is best known for its annual bread festival, when the June air around town is scented with the rich aroma of fresh-baked loaves. Visitors come to watch the townswomen prepare traditional family recipes and bake the bread in outdoor ovens, and admire Cookshire's fine 19th-century buildings.

Sherbrooke, the unofficial capital of L'Estrie, was founded by Loyalists in the 1790s. Local greenhouses turn out 50,000 annuals each year; some 15,000 grace a park near the Renaissance-style courthouse and another 25,000 form an abstract design along rue King Ouest, the main drag. The University of Sherbrooke's arts center offers a full range of cultural activities.

Maple Country

The region gets its name (French: *Pays-de-L'Érable*) from its 4,000 maple groves—the greatest concentration of maples in the world. In spring sap from tapped trees is processed at sugar shacks tucked back in the hills. This is a time for celebration, when "sugaring-off" parties at these *cabanes à sucre* combine huge meals featuring maple syrup and other delicacies of the season and music and dancing.

The Chaudière River flows through the heart of Maple Country, rising in Lac-Mégantic (renowned for landlocked salmon and a legendary lake monster), meandering past lake-dotted Parc Frontenac, and finally joining the St. Lawrence near Quebec City. The principal town here is St-Joseph-de-Beauce, a flourishing farming and artistic community. Rich clay deposits nearby are transformed on the potter's wheel into useful and beautiful works of art at an artists' cooperative called

SOUTHERN QUEBEC

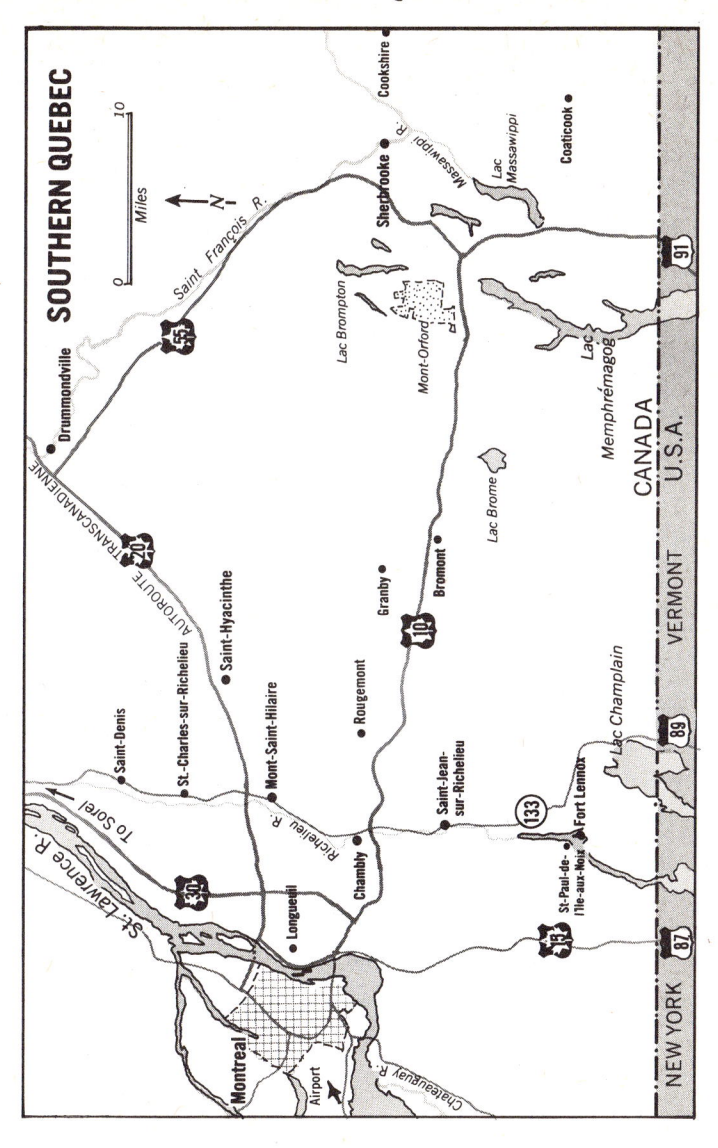

La Ceramique de Beauce. A visit to St-Joseph should also include the convent of the Sisters of Charity, which houses the Maison des Artisans, and the Marius Barbeau Museum, named for a folklorist who preserved traditional French-Canadian songs.

Along the St. Lawrence shore, seigneurial villages dominated by parish churches and stately manors evoke an earlier era. In Beaumont a restored 160-year-old flour mill still grinds grain. Farther downstream, the Montmagny tourist information center is in a manor house built in 1768. In spring and fall, Montmagny skies darken with migrating white geese and mallards. A ferry takes visitors to bird sanctuaries on Île-aux-Grues and Île-aux-Oies in the St. Lawrence.

In nearby St-Jean-Port-Joli, the three Bourgault brothers—Médard, André, and Jean-Julien—opened a wood-carving studio in 1928 and revived a traditional Quebec craft. They trained other carvers and sold their works to travelers passing through the small town. Today St-Jean-Port-Joli is known as the wood-carving capital of Quebec, and its reputation extends all over North America.

The work of the Bourgault brothers graces the parish church, built in 1779, and the house of Médard, now open to visitors. Many of the 50 studios in town also welcome guests. Other artisans in St-Jean produce beautiful copper-enamel art and jewelry, woven fabrics and works in leather and metal.

PRACTICAL INFORMATION FOR
SOUTHERN QUEBEC

WHEN TO GO. This is a four-season destination, but the best times to visit are June–Aug., when the weather is warm and the numerous lakes are busy with watersports enthusiasts, and during the ski season from Dec.-Mar. There are long stretches in what passes for spring and autumn here when it is too warm to ski and too cold to swim. The least interesting times to visit are Apr., after the maple syrup season has ended, and from late Oct.–mid-Dec., after the display of fall foliage and before the ski season.

HOW TO GET THERE. The most convenient way to get to this region, and then to get around it, is to drive. If you do not want to drive to the province, consider flying to Montreal and renting a car. (See *Montreal*, "How to Get Around.")

By Car. Highway 15 south from Montreal gives access route to the Richelieu region. Autoroute des Cantons-de-l'Est (Highway 10) whisks motorists between Montreal and L'Estrie, and Highway 20 (the Quebec section of the Trans-Canada Highway) connects Maple Country with Montreal and Quebec City.

The main routes from the U.S. are Interstate 87 from New York north through Richelieu country to Montreal. Interstate 89 on the Vermont side of Lake Champlain follows basically the same route. Interstate 91 farther east

SOUTHERN QUEBEC 85

connects in L'Estrie with Highway 55, which in turn leads to the Autoroute des Cantons-de-l'Est.

By Bus. *Voyageur* (514–842–2281 or 418–524–4692) has daily service from Montreal and Quebec City to more than 70 towns and cities in southern Quebec. The problem is getting around once you arrive in the region. Intertown service tends to be infrequent.

By Train. *VIA Rail* offers daily passenger service to several communities in southern Quebec, and *CN Rail* has a commuter train connection between Montreal and Mont-Saint-Hilaire. For schedules, call VIA Rail at 514–871–1331 in Montreal or 418–692–3940 in Quebec City.

TOURIST INFORMATION. Regional tourist bureaus are open year-round: *Region de Richelieu/Rive Sud* (South Shore), 1564 rue Bourgogne, Chambly, PQ J3L 1Y7 (514–658–4232). For lodging reservations in the region, call 800–361–3614; the *Association Touristique de l'Estrie,* 2883 rue King Ouest, Suite 200, Sherbrooke, PQ J1L 1C6 (819–566–7404); and the *Association Touristique du Pays-de-l'Erable* (Maple Country), 800 autoroute 20, Bernières, PQ G0S 1C01 (418–831–4411).

TELEPHONES. The area code is 514 for the Richelieu/South Shore region and in L'Estrie east to Lake Memphrémagog. Farther east in L'Estrie the area code is 819. For local directory information, dial 411. For free long-distance information, dial 1–(area code)–555–1212. Calls from pay phones are 25 cents, and there is no time limit. For credit card calls and collect calls, dial 0 first, then the area code and number. When the operator comes on the line, give your credit card number or the name of the person to whom you wish to charge the call.

EMERGENCY TELEPHONE NUMBERS. 911 is the emergency number for the police, fire department, ambulances, paramedics, and any other emergency.

HOW TO GET AROUND. By Bus. The major carrier is *Voyageur* (see *How to Get There*), but less-than-frequent service between small centers makes intraregional travel difficult.

By Rental Car. Driving is the preferred method of transportation, but renting in Quebec is expensive. The region is served by such major firms as *Hertz* (514–842–8537 in Montreal or 800–268–1311); *Avis* (514–866–7906 or 800–268–0303); *Budget* (514–866–7675 or 800–268–8900); and *Tilden* (514–878–2771 in Montreal or 514–842–9445 for out-of-town reservations). A mid-size car costs about $45 a day to rent, or $175 a week. Insurance is approximately $8 a day or $40 a week. *Rent-a-Wreck* (514–871–1166 in Montreal or 800–268–1430) has lower prices, starting at $9 a day or $90 a week for a mid-size car; insurance is $7 a day or $40 a week.

HINTS TO MOTORISTS. Most foreign driving permits are valid in the province. Seat belts are mandatory for drivers and all passengers over the age of five. Quebec's auto insurance premiums are the highest in Canada and no wonder, given the province's exuberant driving style. Drive defensively, especially on Highway 15, the Quebec continuation of Interstate 89 from Vermont. It includes a section with not two, not four, but three lanes. The center lane is used for passing—in both directions.

If you drift across the U.S. border while exploring back-roads, make sure you report to the nearest American border station. There are heavy penalties for not reporting.

For information on road conditions year-round, phone 418-643-6830 in Quebec City and 514-873-4121 in Montreal. Environment Canada also provides weather forecasts by calling 514-636-3284.

HINTS TO HANDICAPPED TRAVELERS. The Quebec Ministry of Tourism publishes an annual accommodation guide which identifies establishments equipped with facilities for handicapped travelers. The tourism ministry also distributes the booklet *Accès Tourisme,* published by the nonprofit group, KEROUL. The guide, which costs $3 and is in French only, lists local and regional organizations that provide tours and assistance to handicapped travelers in Quebec. To order a copy, write KEROUL, 4545 ave. Pierre-de-Coubertin, 1000, Succursale M, Montreal, PQ H1V 3R2 (514-252-3104).

SEASONAL EVENTS. June. *Le festival du pain (Bread Festival).* Held the first weekend of the month, this Cookshire celebration features a crafts fair, displays of weirdly shaped bread "fantasies," and a bread-slicing contest. *Festival de la fraise* (Strawberry Festival). A three-day celebration in late June of Sainte-Madelaine's most important crop.

July. *Fête du Lac des Nations.* This Sherbrooke celebration in mid-July features fireworks and concerts. *Lake Memphrémagog Swimathon.* An annual 50-kilometer (30-mile) event held the third weekend in July. Contestants take the plunge at dawn in Newport, Vermont, and finish up about nine hours later in Magog at the northern end of the lake.

August. *Expo-Sherbrooke.* A century-old agricultural fair during the second week of August. *The Milk Festival.* Highlights of this Coaticook fest include milk-drinking and yogurt-eating contests, and a dairy-cow fashion show. *Stanstead County Agricultural Fair.* Horse shows are the big draw at this fair in Ayer's Cliff. *Festival de Montgolfières du Haut-Richelieu (Hot Air Balloon Festival).* Dozens of brightly colored hot-air balloons float over the Quebec countryside at this four-day event.

September. *Festival gastronomique.* Chefs at Granby's finest restaurants present special menus during the ten-day culinary extravaganza. *Festival de la pomme (Apple Festival).* Rougemont's 15-day celebration of the glorious apple. *Festival des Couleurs de Magog.* The fall foliage stars; also, balloon rides, crafts fairs, and lots of corn on the cob.

TOURS. *Valley Cycle Tours,* based in Ottawa (613-233-0268) conducts four-day, four-night "Gourmet Tours" in L'Estrie, with first-class meals and rooms at the area's best inns. The cost is about $600 per person, including breakfasts and dinners.

The Manoir Hovey, the Hatley Inn, and the Ripplecove Inn—all along the western shore of Lake Massawippi—offer a six-day inn-to-inn *skiing package* called Skiwippi. You stay two nights at each inn, and ski to the others; hotel staff transports your car and luggage. The cost is $420 per person, double

SOUTHERN QUEBEC

occupancy, including breakfasts and dinners. See "Accommodations" for phone numbers of the inns.

SIGHTSEEING CRUISES. The cruise boat *L'Aventure* leaves the dock at Magog daily in summer for 2½-hour trips on Lake Memphrémagog. In addition, *L'Aventure II* makes eight-hour, round-trip excursions to Newport, Vermont, at the southern end of the lake. Information: 819-843-8068.

Farther east on Lake Massawippi, the *Ripplecove Inn* in Ayer's Cliff (see "Accommodations") offers two-hour "cocktail cruises" Wed. and Sun. The trip on the 20-passenger vessel, which is equipped with a bar, costs about $6.

Cruises on the *MV Fort St-Jean II* from St-Jean include a tour of islands in the St. Lawrence River off Sorel, as well as a moonlight trip up the Richelieu River. Write Les Croisières Richelieu, Inc., 68 St-Maurice, St-Jean, PQ J3B 3Y5 (514-347-5394).

PARKS AND GARDENS. Cowansville Nature Center. Church and McKinnon streets, Cowansville, PQ J2K 1T4 (514-263-5615). Rental of canoes, kayaks, sailboards, sailboats, and pedal boats. Open dawn-dusk, late June-Labor Day. Free.
Farfadet Ecology Center. 3755 Chemin Erskin, Franklin-Centre, PQ J0S 1E0 (514-827-2952). Nature trails, cycling paths, horseback riding courses. By reservation. Admission varies with activity.
Mont-Saint-Hilaire Nature Center. 422 rue des Moulins, Saint-Hilaire, PQ H3G 4S6 (514-467-1755). Hiking, nature trails, bird watching. Nature interpretation pavilion. Daily, dawn-dusk. Admission to nature pavilion: adults, $1; children 6-12 and seniors, 50 cents; children six and under, free.

ZOOS. Parc Safari Africain in Hemmingford (514-454-3668) has one of the largest collections of wildlife in Canada. Roads wind through this 162-hectare park (400 acres), where elephants, giraffes, lions, and zebras can be seen from the comfort and safety of your own car. Open daily, mid-May-Labor Day, 10 A.M.-4 or 5 P.M. More than 1,300 animals representing some 300 species are at the **Granby Zoo** (514-372-9113). Open daily, mid-May-mid-Oct., 10 A.M.-7 P.M.

PROVINCIAL PARKS. Parc de Frontenac. RR 3, St-Daniel, PQ G6G 5R7 (418-422-2144). On Lac-St-François. 31 campsites. Fishing, hunting, swimming, sailing. Chalets for rent. **Parc des Îles-de-Boucherville.** 55 Île-Ste-Marguerite, Boucherville, PQ J4B 5E6 (514-873-2843). Located on islands in the St. Lawrence River. Cycling paths, hiking trails, guided nature walks, canoeing, fishing, and ice fishing. **Parc du Mont-Orford.** CP 146, Magog, PQ J1X 3W7 (819-843-6233). Chairlift rides in summer; 18-hole golf course, camping with 333 sites on Lake Stukely, cross-country and downhill skiing (artificial snow). **Parc du Mont-St-Bruno.** 330 Chemin des 25, St-Bruno, PQ J3V 4P6 (514-653-7544). The park covers most of the mountain. Hiking, fishing, cross-country skiing, and nature center. **Parc de la Yamaska.** 8e rang Est, RR 2, Granby, PQ J2G 8C7 (514-372-3204). Swimming, windsurfing, hiking, and skiing.

PROVINCE OF QUEBEC

HUNTING. Wild boar is the most unusual quarry hereabouts. If you want to try bagging a boar with a bow and arrow or crossbow, visit the Sanglier de l'Estrie ranch near Ste-Edwidge. Call 819-849-2025 for details.

FARM VACATIONS. The Fédération des Agricotours du Quebec offers farm vacations throughout the region. Quebec Agricotours, 1415 rue Jarry Est, Montreal, PQ H2E 2Z7 (514-374-3546). The same organization also has listings of the region's *cabanes à sucre* (sugar shacks) holding sugaring-off parties in spring.

PARTICIPANT SPORTS. Downhill and cross-country skiing are the most popular sports here. The best downhill runs are in L'Estrie: Mont Orford, Bromont, Owl's Head, Mont Glen, and Mont Sutton. These hills have vertical drops of 1,300–1,800 feet. A five-day lift ticket, good for any of the mountains, costs $79. Most of these resorts also have groomed cross-country trails.

In Maple Country, Mont Original offers seven runs on an 820-foot vertical drop.

For more information on skiing in Quebec, phone toll free from the eastern U.S., 800-443-7000, and from Ontario, New Brunswick, and Prince Edward Island, 800-361-6490. For up-to-date ski conditions from mid-Nov.–mid-Apr., phone 800-363-3624.

You can also write for information: *Quebec Skiing . . . à la Française,* Tourisme Quebec, CP 20,000, Quebec City, PQ G1K 7X2.

SPECTATOR SPORTS. Granby hosts the *Labatt Grand Prix* in late July. Events include a Formula 2000 race and a Kelly American Challenge race. There is also an airshow, a midway, and helicopter rides. A weekend pass costs about $15 for standing room and $35 for a reserved grandstand seat.

North America's biggest *speedboat regatta,* held on Lac-St-François near Salaberry-de-Valleyfield in early July, attracts about 200 competitors from all over the continent.

MUSEUMS. Canadian Railway Museum. 122 rue St. Pierre, St. Constant (514-632-2410). North America's finest collection of railway memorabilia includes Canada's last working steam locomotive. Daily, 9 A.M.–5 P.M., late Apr.–late Oct. Adults, $3; students 13–17, $2; children 6–12, $1.50; children under six, free.

Granby Car Museum. 288 rue Bourget, Granby, PQ J2G 1E7 (514-372-4433). A 1929 Rolls and a 1903 Holsman are among sixty vehicles displayed here. Daily, May-Oct. May, 10 A.M.–5:00 P.M.; June–Aug., 9:00 A.M.–7:00 P.M.; Sept.-Oct., 10:00 A.M.-5:00 P.M. Adults: $4; 16 and under, $1.

Bernier Maritime Museum. 55 rue des Pionniers, L'Islet-sur-Mer, PQ G0R 2B0 (418-247-5001). This collection honors the town's 300-year tradition of seafarers, especially Capt. Joseph-Elzear Bernier, whose northern voyages established Canada's presence in the high Arctic. Artifacts, model ships, restored icebreaker. Daily 8:30 A.M.–8:00 P.M. June-Sept.; 8:30 A.M.-4:30 P.M. Sept.-June. Adults, $2.25; children, 75 cents; family, $5.50.

SOUTHERN QUEBEC

MUSIC. Evening concerts of classical music are performed at the Orford Arts Center in Mount Orford Provincial Park Friday to Sunday from late June to the end of August. Tickets are about $10. Student concerts on Wednesdays cost $5. Outdoor Sunday dinner concerts amid the pines cost $10.

Summer pop and rock concerts are held at the Théâtre Le Vieux Clocher (819-847-0470) in Magog. North Hatley's The Piggery (819-842-2191) presents special Monday night concerts of classical and jazz artists. In Sherbrooke students from the Orford Arts Center give free concerts of classical music in various downtown parks throughout the summer. Check the tourist information center at 48 rue Depot (819-821-5863) for the time and location.

STAGE. Theater cruises. An unusual arrangement combines a French play with dinner and a cruise on the Richelieu River, from June through August. Total cost: $24. For reservations, phone the *Théâtre du Chenal-du-Moine* (514-743-8446). Another nautical-theatrical combination is the stage aboard a riverboat docked at *St-Marc-sur-Richelieu*. French comedies are offered June through August, with dinner-theater packages available with the nearby Auberge Handfield. Phone 514-584-2226 for reservations.

Summer theater. Ticket prices for summer theater in L'Estrie range from $7–$15. The only remaining English-language productions in the entire province, outside the Montreal area, are at a playhouse in North Hatley called *The Piggery* (819-842-2191). Three productions are usually mounted from June to August in this former pig barn.

The *Cultural Center of Sherbrooke* (819-821-7744) offers comedies in French, July to August. In Deauville, southwest of Sherbrooke, French comedies are staged at *Théâtre du Thé des Bois* (819-864-9569 or 564-3144).

In nearby Eastman, the *Théâtre de la Marjolaine* (819-297-2860 in Eastman; 514-845-0917 in Montreal) mounts a single production, usually a comedy, June through August. The only *dinner theater* in L'Estrie is in Bromont at L'Auberge Bromont, where comedies are performed Thursday to Sunday, from late June to early September. Dinner and the play cost about $20; the play, without dinner, costs about $10. For reservations, phone 800-363-5530.

ACCOMMODATIONS. Quebec's tourism ministry rates more than 2,000 places annually for both accommodations and cuisine, using a system of lilies for lodging and forks for dining. Accommodation ranges from one lily (basic comfort) to five lilies (outstanding comfort). The quality of dinner in the main dining room ranges from one fork (satisfactory) to four forks (excellent). In the list below double-occupancy lodgings are categorized as follows: *Deluxe,* $75–$125; *Expensive,* $50–$75; *Moderate,* $35–$50; *Inexpensive,* $35 and less.

RICHELIEU/SOUTH SHORE

Deluxe

Hostellerie Les Trois Tilleuls. 290 Chemin du Prince, St-Marc-sur-Richelieu, PQ J0L 2E0 (514-584-2231). Luxurious inn overlooking the Richelieu River, appointed with Quebec antiques and such modern amenities as Jacuzzis.

PROVINCE OF QUEBEC

One of five Quebec hostelries in France's prestigious Relais et Châteaux chain. Five lilies; four forks.

Expensive

Auberge Handfield. 555 Chemin du Prince, St-Marc-Sur-Richelieu, PQ J0L 2E0 (514–584–2226). Half-hour south of Montreal on the Richelieu River. Four restored farmhouses on the grounds contain a total of 32 guest rooms; furnished with early Canadian pine antiques. Three lilies; three forks.

Auberge The Willow Place. 208 Main Road, Hudson, PQ J0P 1A0 (514–458–7006). This cozy, eight-room inn 30 minutes west of Montreal has a fine site overlooking Lake of Two Mountains. The bar has the ambience of an old English pub; excellent food. Two lilies; three forks.

Moderate

Auberge de la Rive. 165 Chemin Ste-Anne, Sorel, PQ J3P 6J7 (514–742–5691). 73 rooms. Four lilies; two forks.

Motel Beloeil. 4200 rue Bernard Pilon, St-Mathieu-de-Beloeil, PQ J3G 2C9 (514–467–1373). Near Mont-St-Hilaire nature sanctuary. Two lilies.

Inexpensive

Motel Frontière. Route 133, Philipsburg, PQ J0J 1N0 (514–248–4265). Just this side of the border. Two lilies.

Motel Domaine Guerin. 37 Chemin Noel, St-Bernard-de-Lacolle, PQ J0J 1V0 (514–246–3004). Seven rooms. Near Parc Safari Africain at Hemmingford. Two lilies.

L'ESTRIE

Deluxe

Auberge Hatley Inn. Box 330, North Hatley, PQ J0B 2C0 (819–842–2325). Originally built in 1903 as a summer retreat for a southern gentleman, this outstanding inn has the finest dining in the region. Chef Guy Bohec is a member of Quebec's prize-winning gastronomic team. Three lilies; four forks.

Auberge Lac Brome. 400 Chemin Lakeside, Foster, PQ J0E 1R0 (514–243–5755). European ski-lodge atmosphere in 29-room inn. Cross-country and downhill skiing nearby. Windsurfing and sailing on Lake Brome in summer. Two lilies; two forks.

Hotel Ripplecove Inn. Box 246, Ayer's Cliff, PQ J0B 1C0 (819–838–4296). 11 rooms in main inn, plus seven housekeeping cottages. On the shore of Lake Massawippi, surrounded by century-old white pines. Three lilies; three forks.

Le Manoir Hovey. Box 60, North Hatley, PQ J0B 2C0 (819–842–2421). This replica of George Washington's Mount Vernon was built at the turn of the century by an Atlanta businessman. The elegant appointments and first-rate cuisine make this one of the region's finest inns. Cross-country skiing, downhill nearby. Windsurfing, pedalboats, canoes, tennis, and hiking in summer. Extensive frontage on Lake Massawippi. Three lilies; three forks.

Expensive

Hotel Domaine St-Laurent. Box 180, Chemin Cochran, Compton, PQ J0B 1L0 (800–567–3420 or 819–835–5464). This rambling Tudor inn, formerly a girls' school, has 80 rooms and suites. Villas on the grounds add another 100 rooms. Indoor pool, sauna, gymnasium, tennis, cross-country ski trails. Three lilies; three forks.

Hotel Le Président. 3535 rue King Ouest, Sherbrooke, PQ J1L 1P8 (800–361-6162 or 819-563-2941). Indoor pool, free parking, TV. Five lilies; three forks.

Moderate

Motel L'Ermitage. 1888 rue King Ouest, Sherbrooke, PQ J1J 2E2 (819-569-5551). Outdoor pool. Three lilies.

Motel Panorama. 3284 rue Laval, Lac-Mégantic, PQ G6B 1A4 (819-583-2110). Excellent food, TV, 37 rooms. Three lilies; two forks.

Inexpensive

Hotel-Motel Horizon. Chemin Mont-Sutton, Sutton, PQ J0E 2K0 (514-538-3212). Near Sutton ski area. Indoor pool, TV. Three lilies.

Hotel Stratford. 175 ave. Centrale Nord, Stratford, PQ G0Y 1P0 (819-443-2636). Near Parc de Frontenac. One lily.

MAPLE COUNTRY

Moderate

Auberge Benedict Arnold. 18255 Route Kennedy, St-Georges, PQ G5Y 5C4 (418-228-5558). New England-style inn with 43 rooms, health club, sauna, outdoor pool. Four lilies; three forks.

Auberge du Faubourg. 280 ave. de Gaspé Ouest, St-Jean-Port-Joli, PQ G0R 3G0 (418-598-6455). Nearly 100 rooms, TV, outdoor pool. Three lilies; two forks.

Auberge Manoir de Tilly. 3854 Chemin de Tilly, St-Antoine-de-Tilly, PQ G0S 2C0 (418-477-2407). Lodgings in 1786 manor house. Antique furnishings, delicious cuisine, including a Lac-St-Jean-style tortière made with strips of rabbit and pork. Outdoor pool. Two lilies; three forks.

Hôtel Le Manoir. Lac-Etchemin, PQ G0R 1S0 (418-625-2101). Resort-style lodgings. Disco, lakefront, five kilometers (three miles) from downhill skiing. Two lilies; one fork.

Manoir des Erables. 220 rue du Manoir, Montmagny, PQ G5V 1G5 (418-248-0100). This outstanding inn, destroyed by fire in 1982, has arisen from the ashes to take its rightful place as one of the Relais et Châteaux chain. Excellent cuisine. Three lilies; four forks.

Inexpensive

Auberge des Dunes. rue Principale, St-Antoine-de-L'Isle-aux-Grues, PQ G0R 1P0 (418-248-0129). A nine-room inn on an island in the St. Lawrence River, prime hunting grounds for white geese, mallards, and teal. Two lilies; two forks.

Motel La Paysanne. 497 Route 132, L'Islet-sur-Mer, PQ G0R 2B0 (418-247-7276). Free parking, TV. Two lilies.

RESTAURANTS. Some of the best restaurants in the region are at country inns like Les Trois Tilleuls and the Hatley Inn. Check "Accommodations" for their Quebec government dining ratings (one to four forks). The following is a selection of the rest of the best. Restaurants are listed according to the price of a complete dinner for one (drinks, wine, tip, and tax not included): *Deluxe,* $25–$30; *Expensive,* $20–$25; *Moderate,* $12.50–$20; and *Inexpensive,* under $12.50.

92　PROVINCE OF QUEBEC

La Métairie. Chemin Malenfant, Dunham, PQ J0E 1M0 (514-295-2141). Traditional Quebec cuisine, especially boar, goose, rabbit, and lamb dishes. In summer dinner is served outdoors amid the landscaped grounds. 6:00–11:00 P.M. Closed Mon.

La Vieille Maison, Chemin Raymond, Eastman, PQ J0E 1P0 (514-297-2288). This restaurant in an elegant Victorian manor specializes in French and Italian cuisine. May-Sept., 5:00–11:00 P.M. Closed Mon.

Restaurant Rive Gauche. 1810 blvd. Richelieu, Beloeil, PQ J3G 4S4 (514-467-4650). Outstanding French cuisine along the banks of the Richelieu. Daily from noon, and Sat and Sun from 5:00 P.M. Closed Mon.

Tournant de la Rivière. Autoroute 10, Exit 22, Carignan, (514-658-7372). Housed in an old farmhouse, this exquisite restaurant features fanciful nouvelle cuisine by chef Jacques Robert. Open 6:30–9:00 P.M. for dinner; closed Sun. and Mon.

Moderate

Auberge de l'Etoile. 1133 rue Principale Ouest, Magog, PQ J1X 2B8 (819-843-6521). One of the region's best. Specialty of the house is Brome Lake duckling, prepared by chef Bernard Leroy. Daily, 7:00 A.M.-11:00 P.M.

Au p'tit sabot. 1410 rue King Ouest, Sherbrooke, PQ J1J 2C2 (819-563-0262). Specialty: Quebec wild boar prepared by award-winning chef, Sylvio Clement. 11:30 A.M.-2:00 P.M., 5:00-10:00 P.M. Closed Sun.

Aux Chutes de Richelieu. 486 1ere rue, Richelieu (514-658-6689). As its name suggests, the restaurant in this century-old house faces rapids on the Richelieu in a charming setting. Italian specialties. 11:30 A.M.-11:00 P.M. Sun.-Fri., 5:00–11:00 P.M. Sat.

Inexpensive

Auberge Glen Sutton. RR 4, Glen Sutton J0E 1X0 (514-538-2000). The only restaurant hereabouts serving Mexican food. Wed.–Sun., 4:00–9:30 P.M.

Le Vieux Kitzbuhel. 505 blvd. Perron, Île Perrot (514-453-5521). Austrian cuisine served in an old stone mansion overlooking Lac-St-Louis. 11:00 A.M. -11:00 P.M. Closed Mon. in summer; closed Mon.-Wed. in winter.

Petite Europe. Route 243, Mansonville, PQ J0E 1X0 (514-292-3523). Central European cuisine served in a stylish chalet. Open daily, 5–9 P.M.

NIGHTLIFE. Compared to Montreal and Quebec City, this region is rather sedate. In winter most of the nightlife revolves around après ski activities at the large resorts. The **Oui Ski Bar** at Mont Orford (819-843-4200) features sing-alongs around the piano bar. After a long day on the slopes, though, many people find relaxing with a hot drink in front of a roaring fireplace is all the excitement they can handle. The **Knolton Pub** in Knolton (514-243-6862) attracts a young lively crowd in all seasons with its partying atmosphere and inexpensive beer. One of Sherbrooke's hottest nightspots is **Chez Rene,** a lively disco at 66 rue Meadow (819-8744).

BAS-ST-LAURENT, THE GASPÉ PENINSULA, AND THE MAGDALEN ISLANDS

by
Pauline Guetta

The three tourist regions covered in this chapter make up a richly varied area. Bas-St-Laurent ("Lower St. Lawrence") runs along the southern shore of the St. Lawrence from La Pocatiere north past Rimouski to the Gaspé. (We often refer to the region by its initials—BSL—in this chapter). The Gaspé Peninsula lies at the extreme southeast corner of the province and offers the traveler spectacular scenery, including the famous "pierced rock" off Percé. The Magdalen Islands (Îles-de-la-Madeleine) are an archipelago in the Gulf of St. Lawrence.

Bas-St-Laurent

Towns and villages in this region hug the road along the river (Route 132) that leads on, clear around the Gaspé coast. The BSL's rich farm land rolls to the edge of the broad river. You'll find the land scattered with old manor houses, covered bridges, and villages first settled by French colonists three hundred years ago. You'll want to stop off in towns like St-Jean Port-Joli, where artisans set lifelike wooden sculptures of people and animals outside their workshops. At Trois-Pistoles, you can take whale-watching cruises. In the river near the shore, you'll notice lines of stakes holding nets that form the time-honored means of trapping eel and sturgeon, which the local people smoke to perfection in their own smoke-houses, and serve as hors d'oeuvre. Villages and towns bear mellifluous old Indian names: Kamouraska, Témiscouata, Rimouski, Cacouna, and Pohénégamook, where you can stay, summer or winter, at the nature center. BSL's ski season lasts from December to April, with February and March especially recommended. All along Route 132, and particularly in the BSL, you'll see wayside crosses, many of them masterpieces of religious sculpture, and solid old churches, rich with carving and gold leaf, which you may visit by appointment.

In the BSL as in the Gaspé, local tourist officials help you find outfitters and guides to fish and hunt large and small game. Both regions offer summer and winter camping, boat trips, golf, swimming, and nature study. Stop at an inn by the islands of Bic (Îles du Bic), which dropped from heaven, they say, when the angel in charge of off-shore lands came to the end of the day with too many islands left over. Bic's also renowned as the home of the world's largest colony of eider ducks.

The Gaspé Peninsula

The largest colony of gannets in the world summers on the Gaspé's Bonaventure Island, off Percé. Windsurfers and sailors enjoy the breezes around the Gaspé; there are windsurfing marathons in Baie des Chaleurs (at Carleton) each summer. "Gaspé" is the name of the town at peninsula's tip as well as the name most Anglophones give to the region. The region's most famous sight is the huge fossil-embedded rock off the town of Percé that the sea pierced ("a percé") thousands of years ago. Geologically, the peninsula is one of the oldest lands on earth, although only recently inhabited. A vast, mainly uninhabited forest covers the hilly hinterland. The Gaspé features four major national parks, Port Daniel, Forillon, Causapscal, and Gaspé Park, covering a total of 2,292 square kilometers (885 square miles).

Small fishing and farming villages ring the 270-kilometer (150-mile) Route 132 that hugs the dramatic coastline. The region boasts Quebec's longest ski season and highest peaks. For instance, Ste-Anne-des-

BAS-ST-LAURENT/GASPÉ PENINSULA

Monts offers the only heli-skiing east of the Rockies, with deep powder, open bowl and glade skiing clear into June on peaks that rise to 823 meters (2,700 feet). Other centers operate from mid-November to May.

The Gaspé was on Jacques Cartier's itinerary—he first stepped ashore in North America in the town of Gaspé—but Vikings, Basques, and Portuguese fisher folk came long before. You'll find the area's history told in countless towns along the way. Acadians, displaced by the British from New Brunswick in 1755, settled in Bonaventure. Paspébiac still has a gunpowder shed built in the 1770s to help defend the Gaspé from American ships. United Empire Loyalists settled New Carlisle in 1784. Fishing magnates from the Channel Islands Jersey and Guernsey dominated the peninsula's business until fairly recently, as you'll see at the museum in Gaspé town.

Townspeople in some the Gaspé areas speak mainly English, but most *Gaspésiens* speak slightly Acadian-accented French.

The Magdalen Islands

Acadian accents, strongly laced with sea-faring terms, are even more pronounced on the *Îles-de-la-Madeleine,* where some 13,000 Madelinots, most descended from the Acadians, live on 12 islands. About 700 people of Scots ancestry live on two of the islands. The two main villages are Havre-aux-Maisons and Cap-aux-Meules, with populations of about 2,300 and 1,500 respectively. Birds far outnumber people. The over 200 species of birds nesting on the islands, include great blue herons, cormorants, terns and puffins.

You'll find the Magdalens a marvellously unspoiled chain of 12 islands, each a little different from the next, mainly linked by sandbars along 100 kilometers (62 miles) in the Gulf of St. Lawrence. Island holidays celebrate the simple pleasures of sun, sea, shelling, hiking, biking, sailing, windsurfing, boating, and fishing, along with enjoying well-prepared seafood with a bottle of wine at a pleasant inn or café. The Gulf Stream warms the sea here, so that well into September swimming is as comfortable as on the south side of Cape Cod or Prince Edward Island. Three hundred kilometers (185 miles) of sandy beaches, dramatic red capes and cliffs chiselled by a relentless ocean ring the islands.

PRACTICAL INFORMATION FOR BAS-ST-LAURENT, THE GASPÉ PENINSULA, AND THE MAGDALEN ISLANDS

WHEN TO GO. All hotels, restaurants, museums and sight-seeing facilities operate fully in summer (mid-June–Labor Day). Even though many facilities tail off in September, fall proves great to view the foliage throughout the Gaspé and BSL regions. The Magdalens, warmed by the Gulf Stream, usually enjoy summer weather until well into September. Hunting and fishing enthusiasts can enjoy their sports in late fall (be sure to check the legal seasons). Skiing lasts from mid-Nov. to May or even June in the Gaspé, and from Dec. to May in BSL, where you'll find Feb.–Mar. best for skiing. You can set up winter camping through the regional tourist offices in Gaspé and BSL. People who sail appreciate the steady winds off the Gaspé and Magdalens, but they can also get locked in by fog.

In the Gaspé and Magdalens, summer (July–Aug.) days have average highs of 70°F, lows of 52°F. Winter's temperatures average 3–23°F in Feb. Early in March, you can visit the ice floes around the Magdalens to see and photograph the new seal pups, or "white coats." The regional tourist office makes all arrangements.

The BSL in summer averages 72°F, with Aug. often the best month. In July and Aug., fend off biting black flies in the woods with insect repellant. Light breezes discourage flies and mosquitoes from shore areas. Winter temperatures in the BSL average 5–10°F in Feb. Roads are well maintained.

HOW TO GET THERE. By plane. *Québecair* (514–363–3890; in the Magdalens, 418–969–2764; from elsewhere in Quebec, 800–361–0200) flies daily all year from Montreal to Havre-aux-Maisons in the Magdalens. The flight stops briefly at Mont-Joli in BSL and the town of Gaspé at the tip of the Gaspé Peninsula. June to Sept., Québecair runs two daily flights, some also stopping briefly at Quebec City and Baie-Comeau. If you book more than 14 days in advance Québecair gives a 50 percent discount on the fare.

By train. *VIA Rail* (514–871–1331; in the U.S., contact Amtrak) runs two trains daily, from Montreal to Gaspé. The ride takes 16 hours each way, stopping at towns through BSL including Rivière-du-Loup, Rimouski, and Mont-Joli. It takes the route through the Matapédia Valley to Carleton, Bonaventure, Chandler, and Percé. You can board or disembark at any of these towns, providing you are correctly ticketed.

By Bus. *Voyageur Bus* schedules at least three buses daily from Montreal to Rivière-du-Loup all year. Express buses take six hours. The express bus from Rivière-du-Loup to Rimouski takes 80 minutes. The two daily express buses from Rimouski to Percé in the Gaspé take eight hours. Voyageur serves most towns and villages in both regions.

By car. Scenic Route 132 follows the shore line along the St. Lawrence and continues all around the Gaspé. The faster Highway 20 runs east from Montreal

BAS-ST-LAURENT/GASPÉ PENINSULA

to Cacouna in the BSL. From New Brunswick, follow the Trans-Canada Highway to route 185. To drive to the Magdalens from Montreal, take highway 20 to Rivière-du-Loup. Then follow Highway 185 to Edmunston, New Brunswick, and Highway 2, which connects with routes 15 and 16 to Cap Tourmentine. A 45-minute ferry crossing to Borden, Prince Edward Island, connects you to Highway 1 to Charlottetown, and Highway 2 to Souris. From there, the ferry crosses to the Magdalens in five hours.

By Boat. From Charlevoix to Bas-St-Laurent, the 75-minute ferry from St. Siméon to Rivière-du-Loup runs from May to January (see *Charlevoix* chapter for details). Information: 418–862–9545/5094. The ferry from Souris to Cap-aux-Meules, Magdalen Islands, leaves daily at 2 P.M. You cannot reserve from Souris, but you should reserve seven days ahead for the return trip. Write: Cooperative de Transport Maritime et Aerien (CTMA) Géerard LeBlanc, Box 245, Cap-aux-Meules, Magdalen Islands, PQ G0B 1B0 (Souris, 902–687–2181; Capaux-Meules, 418–986–4264/2213). You can also take the *M.V. Madeleine*, a cargo freighter with room for 12 passengers and 25 cars. For information on this two-day voyage from Montreal, contact the tourist information office at Cap-aux-Meules (see "Tourist Information").

TOURIST INFORMATION. To enjoy the region to the fullest, write to the three regions's tourist information offices. Each will send you the regional guidebook, plus information on national parks and wildlife centers like Bonaventure Island in the Gaspé and the islands of Bic. They also supply lists of hunting and fishing outfitters, camp grounds, ski and other winter activity centers, and any other special information you need. During the summer you'll find tourist information kiosks at frequent intervals along Route 132. For all regions, contact *Tourisme Quebec* (See *Facts at Your Fingertips*).

Bas-St-Laurent Regional Tourist Association, 506 rue Lafontaine, 3e étage, Rivière-du-Loup, PQ G5R 3C4 (418–867–3015). To reserve accommodation, call 800–463–1318.

Gaspésie Regional Tourist Information Office, 337 route de la Mer, Ste-Flavie, PQ G0C 2L0 (418–775–2223). Open Mon.–Fri., 8.30 A.M.–noon, 1 P.M.–5 P.M.

Iles-de-la-Madeleine Tourist Association, CP 1028, Cap-aux-Meules, PQ G0B 1B0 (418–986–5462). In summer, for reservations, call 800–463–5840. A tourist office functions in summer near the wharf at Cap-aux-Meules (418–986–2245).

TELEPHONES AND EMERGENCY NUMBERS. The area code for all three regions is 418. Local phone calls cost 25 cents. Dial 411 for local information. Elsewhere, dial 418–555–1212. To dial long distance from any region, dial 1 before the area code. Dial 0 before the area code for operator assistance on credit card and long-distance calls.

For all emergencies in the three regions, dial 0, or call the provincial police (*Sûreté du Quebec,* or *SQ*) in Rimouski at 418–723–1122. The duty officer will direct you to the correct local number.

Coast Guard/sea rescue: 800–463–4393.

Hospitals: *Centre Hospitalier Régional de Rimouski,* 150 ave. Rouleau, Rimouski (724–8574). *Hôpital Hôtel Dieu de Rivière-du-Loup,* 75 rue St-Henri, Rivière-du-Loup (862–8261).

Îles-de-la-Madeleine: *police,* 986–2555; *ambulance,* 986–2612; *hospital,* 986–2121; *Canadian coastguard,* 986–5333.

Members of AAA/CAA can call 800–366–HELP to request names of recommended garages in all regions.

PROVINCE OF QUEBEC

HOW TO GET AROUND. In summer, cars form the best transport. Preferably, plan to fly in and book a rental car. Winter road conditions in some areas vary greatly, and you should follow advice from your innkeeper or the local tourist office. For instance, route 132 on the north side of the Gaspé hugs the coast so tightly that winter waves can tear sections away. Some years, winds sweep snow-drifts across shore roads along the Lower St. Lawrence, and fog sweeps over the Magdalens. These problems do not arise during summer or fall, when you can easily make the spectacular 270-km (150-mi.) tour of the Gaspé. Trains and Voyageur buses run all year in the Gaspé and Lower St. Lawrence regions. Buses prove particularly reliable, whatever the weather (see "How to Get There"). A ferry links Île d'Entrée with the other Magdalens.

From the Airports. You'll find taxis waiting. Limousine service from Mont-Joli to Rimouski, costs approximately $7 for the half-hour ride. Or ask your innkeeper to have a car meet you.

By Bus. There are no local public buses, but *Voyageur* serves many small towns at least once daily in the Gaspé and Lower St. Lawrence (See "How to Get There.")

Rental Cars. *Budget* (Canada, 800–268–8900; U.S., 800–527–0700) and *Tilden* (Ontario and Quebec, 800–361–5334) serves airports in the three regions. Tilden also rents four-wheel drive vehicles, recommended for May–Dec. driving. *Avis* (Canada, 800–268–2310; U.S., 800–331–2112).

On the Magdalens, you'll find *Budget* (418–969–4209), *Tilden* (418–969–2590), and *Viabec* (418–969–2588) all at the airport at Havre-aux-Maisons.

By Bike. Cycling is well accepted on the Magdalens, where you can rent bikes through the tourist office or bring your own.

TOURS AND SPECIAL INTEREST SIGHTSEEING.
By Bus. Several companies offer two-four-day tours of the Lower St. Lawrence and Gaspé regions from Montreal and Quebec City. Contact the regional tourist offices for details about the tours, which vary from season to season. *Service d'Autobus Madeliniens* (986–2845) organizes island mini-bus tours. Reserve at tourist kiosk on Cap-aux-Meules main street in July, August. Adults, $15; children 7–14 $10; under seven, free. Other months, phone the bus company to reserve.

By Plane. Book in advance for year-round *Icarus Flying Service* at the Magdalen Islands (418–968–2271). Three-passenger plane, about $100 an hour. You can see all the islands in one hour. Larger aircraft take nine passengers at about $500 an hour. Book through tourist office. For an exciting plane/helicopter trip, inquire about early March seal-pup, or "white-coat," photo-safaris. Helicopter rides to the Magdalen ice floes cost $300 per person; the two or three-day package costs around $600 per person. It includes air transportation from Montreal or Quebec City, and overnight accommodation.

For a bird's view of the BSL, contact aeroclubs in Rimouski and Rivière-du-Loup through the regional tourist office.

By Boat. Trois-Pistoles in BSL forms a major center for whale-watching from late July to Sept. Call 851–3099 or the tourist office. Advanced arrangements are necessary. From the Gaspé, you can go out on fishing boats or for jaunts around the coast from towns including Percé, Carleton, and Gaspé. Ask the tourist offices in all regions about sightseeing by boat.

In the Magdalens, July-mid-Sept., the good ship *Tony* (986–2245) leaves Cap-aux-Meules daily at 9 A.M. to see the red cliffs of Gros-Cap and Havre-aux-Meules. The *Tony* returns in time to take you to Île-d'Entrée, leaving you two

BAS-ST-LAURENT/GASPÉ PENINSULA

hours to explore this island of 170 English-speaking people of Scottish descent. At 3 P.M. the *Tony* takes you for a three-hour fishing trip. You can make reservations at the tourist kiosk (986–2245).

HINTS TO MOTORISTS. Motorists should experience no trouble driving in these regions from May to Oct. From Nov. to May, snow-tires (or heavy-treaded all-year tires) are essential. You should also carry a good supply of windshield-washer fluid (available at all gas stations) and, if you plan any winter driving off beaten tracks, a shovel and clip-on chains. The speed limit on Route 132 is 60 kmh (37.2 mph). Seat belts here, as elsewhere in Quebec, are obligatory. Reduce risk of accidents by driving with headlights on at all times. Members of *AAA* or *CAA* can call 800–366–HELP for the names of recommended garages.

HINTS FOR HANDICAPPED. The three main regional tourist offices supply regional guide books clearly showing facilities fully and partially accessible by wheelchair. The offices also hold lists of organizations that set up regional bus tours, in specially adapted buses, from Montreal and Quebec as well as lists of bus and minibus companies whose vehicles can take wheelchairs. Volunteers sometimes register with the tourist offices to accompany handicapped people to some areas.

NATIONAL AND PROVINCIAL PARKS AND RESERVES. Baldwin Wildlife Reserve. CP 551, Ste-Anne-des-Monts, PQ G0E 2G0 (418–392–5388 763–3039). There are two entrances, one on Route 299 at New Richmond and one on Route 132 in Ste-Anne-des-Monts. Fishing by the day with rented boats on lake. Opens early June. There are four cottages on lake, with four beds in each, some with shared showers (about $44). Make reservations through the ministere du Loisir, de la Chasse, et de la Peche, Reservations and Information, CP 8888, Quebec City, PQ G1K 7W3 (418–890–5349).

Bic. 337 rue Moreault, Rimouski, PQ G5L 1P4 (418–722–3779). This river area 10 miles west of Rimouski is being developed for observation of birds, fish, and other wildlife and plants. There are 70 rooms at the inn Vieux Manoir du Français (418–736–4345) and 249 campsites with all modern facilities, including convenience store.

Cap-Chat Wildlife Reserve. 263 rue St-Jérôme, Matane, PQ G4W 3A7 (418–562–3700). Picnicking and camping at 24 sites, at Ruisseau Islet, 14 km (9 mi.) south of Cap-Chat. In the fall, there is hunting for moose, whitetail deer, and small-game hunting.

Chic-Chocs Wildlife Reserve. CP 551, Ste-Anne-des-Monts, PQ G0E 2G0 (418–763–3039, 763–3301). Reception center at 96 blvd. Ste-Anne-des-Mont ouest, on Route 132. The park adjoins Parc de la Gaspesie. Its deep valleys and rugged peaks over 1,000 m (3,280 ft.) high, form part of the Appalachians. Open, early June–Labor Day. Winter camping season, mid Dec.–mid Jan.; Mar.–Apr. Mont-St-Pierre Campsites has 163 sites for camping with modern conveniences (e.g., a pool) or wilderness camping.

Forillon National Park. Parks Canada, District of Gaspé, 2 Morin St., Box 1220, Gaspé, PQ G0C 1R0 (418–368–5505). Off Route 132 in the village of Cap-aux-Os, 20 mi. from the town of Gaspé. 240 sq. km (150 sq. mil) on the hilly peninsula opposite the town of Gaspé are devoted to nature trails, camping, walking, cycling, and skin diving. From the hiking trails you can see many large and small wild animals and even spot seals basking on rocks off shore. There is an interpretation center on Route 132 near Cap-des-Rosiers, with exhibits, films, and slide shows. Open late June–mid Sept., Mon.–Sat., 9 A.M.–5 P.M.; Sun., 10 A.M.–6 P.M. Entrance fee: $3 per day per person. Season pass: $10.

Île-Bonaventure. This 5-mi. long island off the coast at Percé is a bird sanctuary, with the largest, most accessible colony of gannets in the world—also cormorants, gulls, and petrels. Boats leave regularly all summer long, from the Cold Storage Plant, rue du Quai, in Percé. Contact *Les Bateliers de Percé,* Inc., Box 278, Percé, PQ G0C 2L0 (418–782–2974). The fare is about $9 for adults, half price for children. The hiking trails are open early June–Labor Day, 8 A.M. –5 P.M. No overnight accommodations. Snack bar and picnic area.

Jardins de Métis (Métis Gardens). Route 132, Grand-Métis (418–775–2221). Forty-acre garden with over 2,500 species of flowers and shrubs, most of them seldom grown in these climes, in gardens developed by Elsie Reford, niece of Baron Mount Stephen, first president of Canadian Pacific Railway. Gardens open early June–mid Sept., 8:30 A.M.–8 P.M. Guided tour of 30-room villa (small admission fee), mid June–Labor Day, 11:30 A.M.–8 P.M. Picnic area with parking fee. Dining room, snack bar, bar; handicraft boutique.

Matane Wildlife Reserve. 257 ave. St-Jerome, Matane, PQ G4W 3A7 (418–562–3700). The John Reception Center is 40 km (25 mi.) from Matane Route, 195 (418–224–3345). Wildlife observation on lake and from trails and moors. Fishing. Cottages and campsites, picnic areas.

Parc de la Gaspésie. CP 551, Ste-Anne-des-Monts, PQ G0E 2G0 (418–763–3039/3301). The reception center is at 96 rue Ste-Anne-des-Monts. 802 sq. km (500 sq. mi.) on the Gaspé Peninsula, with caribou sanctuary, winter and summer camping, nature interpretation center, hiking, canoeing, sailing, and cross-country skiing. You can stay or dine at *Gîte du Mont-Albert,* with its excellent dining room, run by the Quebec Government. Fishing by the day, with pre-season reservations or with cottage, camp, inn, reservations.

Percé Wildlife Interpretation Center. 1.5 km (1 mi.) west of Percé on Chemin Irish via Route des Falls, opposite Bonaventure Island (418–782–2240). Films, slides, and wildlife and botanical displays show how the ocean and land effect one another. Nature hikes. At low tide (be sure to check times), you can walk to *Rocher Percé* ("pierced rock"), the massive, fossil-encrusted rock that rises straight from the sea.

Rimouski Reserve. See "Bic" for mailing address. 48 km (30 mi.) south of Rimouski on Route 232. Picnic area, nature interpretation, campsites, cottages, lodge. No hunting or fishing.

CAMPING AND PICNICKING. Throughout the Gaspé, you'll see signs, *"Halte routière,"* (resting place), usually featuring an attractive view and picnic tables. Some include children's swings and amusements and monitors who show the children some of the area's features, such as sea birds or the local beach.

You can camp at many of the parks listed above. Unless otherwise noted, campgrounds are all open from the first Sat. in June through Labor Day. For more information, contact Parks Canada, District of Gaspé, 2 Morin St., Box 1220, Gaspé, PQ G0C 1R0 (418–368–5505), or the ministère du Loisir, de la Chasse, et de la Pêche, Communications Service 92 deuxième rue ouest, Rimouski, PQ G5L 8B3 (418–722–3830). There are also two dozen *privately run* campgrounds. A selection is listed here.

BAS-ST-LAURENT/GASPÉ PENINSULA 101

MAGDALEN ISLANDS. Base de Plein Air Maritime des Iles. CP 59, Grande-Entrée, Îles-de-la-Madeleine, PQ G0B 1H0 (418–985–2833). 31 camps for tents; 7 for trailers. Activities include canoing, windsurfing, deep-sea fishing, shelling, hiking, children's activities, evening activities. Also chalet for 54 people, including family groups of 2–4 and 2 dormitories with bunk beds for groups or single travelers. Cafeteria. Rates, about $10–$12.

PERCÉ. Baie Percé Campsites. CP 310, Percé, PQ G0C 1G0 (418–782–2846). Off-season: SEPAQ, 1650 rue Louis-Jette, Quebec City, PQ G1S 2W3 (418–643–4875). Situated right in Percé (on Route 132), near Île Bonaventure sanctuary. 140 units, some with hookups.

ST-ALEXANDRE. Camping Municipal. St-Alexandre, PQ G0L 2G0 (418–862–8241). Access from routes 20 and 507. 150 campsites, about $8–$10. 20 showers. Most modern conveniences.
  Camping St-Alexandre. c/o Mme. Lise Desjardins, St-Germain, PQ G0L 3G0 (418–862–8241). 55 sites. Swim in river. Flush toilets. Campfire. Community centre.
  KOA Rivière-du-Loup. St-Alexandre, PQ G0L 2G0 (418–495–2196). Access via routes 20 and 488. 89 campsites, about $12–$16 for four people, plus $1.25 for each additional person. All modern conveniences, most sites with flush toilets. Campfire. Swimming in rivers. Eight showers. Next to nature reserve.

HUNTING AND FISHING. To hunt in the reserves (but not the parks), permits are required. You may *also* need to hunt with recognized outfitters. Complete lists available through Tourisme-Quebec (see *Facts at Your Fingertips*). Outfitters run comfortable lodges, and provide knowledgeable guides. Game includes moose, whitetail deer, black bear, grouse, partridge, hare, rabbits, snipe, geese and ducks. Efficient roads serve nearly all the regions, and you can also arrange with outfitters to fly into less accessible areas.

Fish include walleyes (doré), smallmouth bass, lake trout, speckled trout, rainbow trout, Quebec red trout, and the king of game fish, Atlantic salmon. Salmon season varies slightly with site, but averages mid June–late Aug. You need a permit to fish in fresh water. Salmon permits cost over $40 per season; other fish, about $30. You may drop a line off any convenient spot into the sea without a permit.

Fishing and hunting permits are available from the ministère du Loisir, de la Chasse, et de la Pêche (see *Facts at Your Fingertips*) as well as from authorized agents (e.g., sports shops) and on the site (but check by phone with the site first). You should try to make reservations before early March. Some farmers in the BSL invite visitors to their trout ponds. For some of the reserves and parks where you can fish and hunt, see "National and Provincial Parks and Reserves" and the list below.

  Matane River Wildlife Reserve. Same address as the Matane Wildlife Reserve, above. Salmon fishing by the day, without reservations, in two sectors. Note that you can observe the salmon's upstream run from the migration channel in midtown Matane.
  Matapédia River Wildlife Reserve. Causapscal, Matapédia. Route 132. Write Jardins de Métis, CP 242, Mont-Joli, PQ G5H 3L1 (418–865–2080, 775–2221). Salmon fishing by the day. Guides and canoes available.

PROVINCE OF QUEBEC

Ste-Anne River. CP 551, Ste-Anne-des-Monts. PQ G0E 2G0. 763-3039/3301. Salmon fishing by the day. Reserve at least 48 hours ahead by calling 418-890-5310 in Quebec City.

St-Jean River Wildlife Reserve. St-Jean-de-Gaspésie. Contact: 11 rue de la Cathédrale, Gaspé, PQ G0C 1R0 (418-368-3444). For salmon fishing downstream, you must reserve at least 48 hours ahead. Upstream you can stay at St-Jean Lodge and fish from a canoe or wade, following rotation system to give all a chance. During fishing season (early June–late Aug.) rates run from $975 to $2,800 for three-four days. Rates include the fishing access right, use of a canoe, services of a guide, meals. Reserve early.

Outfitters

Outfitters, who arrange hunting, fishing for visitors from outside Quebec, a range of rustic accommodations, and family vacations, include:

Club Lechasseur, Inc. 1900 Blvd. Gaboury, Mont-Joli, PQ G5C 3L1. (418-775-3655). Seven lakes, 12 km (7 mi.) of trails, 196 sq. km (122 sq. mi.). Speckled trout, Atlantic salmon, deer, moose bear, duck, hare, ruffed grouse.

Territoire Chasse et Pêche du Mont-Carmel, Enr. 24 rue Fortier, St-Pacôme (Kamouraska), PQ G0L 3X0 (418-852-2680). Five lakes, 30 km (19 mi.) of trail, 62 sq. km (39 sq. mi.). Speckled trout, moose, deer, bear, woodcock, hare, ruffed grouse.

PARTICIPANT SPORTS. You can hike, jog, walk and swim in the parks listed separately. You can cycle on the Magdalen Islands, either by bringing your own bike or renting when you arrive at Havre-aux-Maisons visitors' information kiosk. You can practice all winter sports, including downhill (Alpine) and cross-country (Nordic) skiing, snow shoeing, toboganning and skating in most parks. Every town and village maintains its skating rinks for ice hockey and recreational skating all winter.

Skiing. Chic-Choc Mountain Range, 90-min. drive (about 80 km, 50 mi.) from Mont-Joli airport. Write: CP 10, Cap-Chat, PQ G0J 1E0 (418-786-2134/5366). You reach the top of Mont Logan (vertical drop, 823 m, 2,700 ft) via helicopter. Guides lead groups of intermediate and expert skiers down trails as long as 4.8 km (3 mi.). Accumulations of up to 6 m (20 ft.) of snow. Deep, light, untracked powder in Mar. and early Apr. Hard granular spring surfaces (corn snow) from mid Apr. to end of May, with occasional snow-falls in Apr. Cost of helicopter skiing per day, including guides and lunch, $230. At Ste-Anne-des-Monts, ski lodges and motels offer pool, dining, recreation and social activities, in packages starting at $45 per person per day for double, including two meals, tax and services.

Station de ski Val-d'Irène. Ste-Irène, PQ G0J 2P0 (418-629-3450; mid Oct.–mid April, 800-463-9080). Twelve slopes with 3 ski lifts; altitude, 691 m (2,267 ft.); vertical drop, 274 m (898 ft.). 30 km (19 mi.) of well-maintained Nordic ski trails, with heated warm-up cabins. Equipment rental. Snowshoeing, sleigh-rides, near horse-riding farm.

Parc du Mont-Comi Ski Centre. Parc du Mont-Comi, R.R. #1, St-Donat-de-Rimouski, PQ G0K 1L0 (418-739-4858). Long ski season, Nov.–May. Altitude 573 m. 18 slopes, four lifts, extensive Nordic trails. All natural snow.

Golf. Most of the golf courses in the Gaspé and BSL are nine-holers. There are three public 18-hole golf courses off route 132 in BSL. All rent electric carts, have dining rooms and putting greens. They are: *Club de golf de Bic,* Chemin du Golf (418-736-5744). Par 72. *Club de golf de Rivière-du-Loup,* route 132

(862–7745). Par 72. *Club de golf des Saules,* 261 rue des Saules (724–2295). Par 62. You'll find similar amenities at the dozen courses on the Gaspé. Eleven are nine-holers, including *Terrain de Golfe de Carleton,* at Carleton, Blvd. Perron, Carleton (364–7073). At Métis Beach, the *Club de Golfe Boule Rock,* is off Route 132 (936–3407), mailing address: Rte. 132, Métis-Sur-Mer, G0J 1S0.

Horseback Riding. Ranch des Montagnards Auclair, Témiscouata, PQ G0L 1A0 (418–899–2863). Winter and summer riding and camping. Moonlight rides. Sleigh rides in winter. Very popular, so reserve at least a month ahead. Prices run from about $12 an hour to $55 for a day's riding (9 A.M.–4.30 P.M.). You can spend the weekend (for over $200), Fri. afternoon–Sun. afternoon, either returning to the central camp or taking longer trails to comfortable cabins. All meals provided. Longer stays possible. Bring your sleeping bag.

Windsurfing, is popular on lakes in parks, and around the shore of the three regions. For instance, you can windsurf in Rimouski Wildlife Reserve on Kedwick Lakes, at Matane, Percé Bay, and Bonaventure. Each year, late in July, Carleton in the Gaspé forms the the center for three–four days of windsurfing and catamaron racing. High point is windsurfing race from Carleton beach to Île aux Herons, eight miles away, and return. Contact Festivoile, Carleton, PQ G0C 1J0 (418–364–3251). On the Magdalen Islands, contact Centre Nautique de l'Istorlet at CP 249, Havre-Aubert, Îles-de-la-Madeleine, PQ G0B I5O (418–937–5266). Season runs mid June–end of August.

MUSEUMS AND HISTORIC SITES. Over the last 15 years, people in the Gaspé and BSL established countless small museums dedicated to the region's original pioneers, their work, and everyday lives. Pioneering days seem not so far away in these areas, as you'll realize when local guides show you the region's treasures. Every village holds a fine church—rarely, alas, open to visitors. In the BSL, watch for old mills ("moulins"), and covered bridges, such as the one at St-Onésime 5 km (3 mi.) southeast of Kamouraska's church on route de l'Eglise. Due to budget cuts, many guide and interpretation projects have been dropped, although the sites are usually open, so do phone ahead before contemplating a long drive.

Bas-St-Laurent

ANDRÉVILLE. Here, the region's oldest church dates from 1806. The group of small offshore islands is named "the pilgrims."

CABANO. Fort Ingall, Société de Cabano (418–854–2052). Route 232, 2 km (1.24 mi.) from route 185. The original British fort of 1839–42 was partially reconstructed in 1973. Open mid June–mid Sept., Tues.–Thurs., 9.30 A.M.–5.30 P.M.; Fri.–Sun. 9.30 A.M.–7.30 P.M. Adults, $1.25; children, 75 cents.

CACOUNA. St-Georges' Church and Presbytery. 455 route de l'Eglise (418–862–4338). Louis-Thomas Berlinguet designed this fieldstone church, finished in 1848. You may visit the church (not the presbytery) daily, 9 A.M.–7.30 P.M.

Grand-Portage Trail. Originally the fur-traders' main link between Quebec City and Halifax, this was later a postal and military route during the British régime. Today, you can retrace part of the historic trail from Route 132 by taking Route 291 from Rivière-du-Loup 64 km (40 mi.) to Cabano on Lake Témiscouata, then follow 232 along the river another 36 km (22 mi.) to Rivière-

Bleue and return the roughly 64 km (40 mi.) to Route 132 via Route 289. The circuit totals roughly 164 km (102 mi.).

KAMOURASKA. *Kamouraska,* an Algonquin Indian word, means "where bullrushes fringe the water." Kamouraska includes the principal village of Kamouraska and the area surrounding it along Route 132, from La Pocatière to Notre-Dame-du-Portage. You'll notice many unusually arched eaves, typical of the "Kamouraska house." Interesting sites in Kamouraska village include the church (1914); the old court house (1888), built like a French château; the old schooner "Goélette Monical," tied up at dock; and the Langlais house (1750), on Route 132, one km (0.62 mi.) west of the village, at Rang du Cap. Only this four-chimneyed stone house survived an attack by British troops in 1759. The movie "Kamouraska," which starred Geneviève Bujold, used many exterior shots of the house. Closed to the public.

Moulin Paradis. route de l'Eglise, Kamouraska (418–492–5365). Two turbines once powered this flour mill, built in 1804. Open daily, mid May–mid Sept., 9 A.M.–5 P.M. Groups must make reservations. Contributions appreciated.

Musée de Kamouraska. 69 ave. Morel (418–492–3144). The old convent houses antique furniture and tools used for local fishing, farming, and taxidermists. Knowledgeable local people at reception and in museum explain artifacts if asked. Site is local artisans' boutique. Open daily, late June–Labor Day, 11 A.M.–5 P.M. Guided tours: adults, $1.50; children, 75 cents.

LA POCATIÈRE. Musée Francois-Pilote. 100 Quatriéme Ave. (418–856–3145). Devoted to local agriculture, natural science, and regional history. Mon.–Sat., 9 A.M.–5 P.M.; Sun., 1 P.M.–5 P.M. Closed Sat., Oct.–May. Adults, $2; children, $1.

POINTE-AU-PÈRE. Sanctuaire Ste-Anne. rue du Sanctuaire, (418–723–2962). Groups of pilgrims visit this sanctuary dedicated to Quebec's patron saint (and mother of the Virgin Mary), Ste. Anne, particularly from July 17–26. Daily, 8.30 A.M.–7.30 P.M. All welcome, but groups should make reservations. Free.

RIMOUSKI. Musée Régional de Rimouski. 35 St-Germain Ouest (418–724–2272). The old church houses work by traditional and contemporary artists. Sept.–late June, Wed-Fri., 1 P.M.–5 P.M.; Sat.–Sun., 1 P.M.–9 P.M. Late June–end of Aug., daily, 9 A.M.–noon, 1 P.M.–5 P.M., 7–10 P.M. Adults, $1; children and seniors, 50 cents.

La Maison Lamontagne. 707 blvd. du Rivage, Rimouski-Est, (418–722–3737). One of Quebec's last half-timbered houses holds antique furniture and archeological artifacts. Open daily, late June–Labor Day, 10 A.M.–5 P.M. Guided tours. Free admission.

Musée de la Mer de Rimouski. 1034, rue du Phare, Pointe-au-Père (418–724–6214). From rue Père Nouvel (off Route 132), turn towards river onto du Phare ("lighthouse road"). Marine museum, with exhibitions and interpretation of regional history and marine life including descriptions of salt-marsh formation and marine ecology.

RIVIÈRE-BLEUE. Musée Domaine du Pionnier. 46 rue St-Joseph, (418–893–2052). Collection of everyday objects related to the municipality's history. June–Oct., Tues.–Sat., 1–6 P.M. Adults, $2; children, 75 cents.

BAS-ST-LAURENT/GASPÉ PENINSULA

RIVIÈRE-DU-LOUP. Musée du Bas-St-Laurent. 300 rue St-Pierre, (418–862–7547). Modern art by local and international artists. Tues.–Fri., 10 A.M.–noon, 1–5 P.M. Sat.–Sun., 1–5 P.M. Late June 24–early Sept., daily, 10 A.M.–5 P.M. Adults, $1; children, 50 cents.

ST-LOUIS-DU-HA! HA! Centre d'Interprétation Scientifique du Temiscouata. Chemin Bellevue (418–854–2172). 5 km (3 mi.) west of village whose name comes from happy marriage of French saint's name and Algonquin word. The Indian *hexcuewaska* means "something unexpected." Small science museum includes telescope for observing sky far from city lights; slide shows, lectures, films. Daily, 9 A.M.–noon. Admission, $2.

STE-LUCE. Thomas Baillargé designed the *church* (1840), notable for its unusual stained glass depicting biblical and historical scenes, such as Jacques Cartier erecting the cross at Gaspé.
Moulin Banal du Ruisseau la Loutre. 134 route du Fleuve ouest (418–739–3916). Tourist information center, with historical exhibits, in old communal mill. Picnic area. Mid June–Labor Day, 9 A.M.–9 P.M. Free.

The Gaspé Peninsula

NOUVELLE. Miguasha Park. 6 km (4 mi.) south-west of Nouvelle (418–794–2475, 752–2211). Nature interpretation center. Exhibition of fish and other species. Fossils of many extinct species of fish, such as horny-scaled fish and rare air-breathers. One-hour tour of fossil site daily, except when it rains. June 1–Sept. 15, 9 A.M.–5 P.M. Free.
Ristigouche Museum and National Historic Park. edge of Ristigouche Indian reserve, Route 132, Pointe-à-la-Croix, P.Q. G0C 1L0. 788–5676. About 25 km (15 mi.) west of Nouvelle on Baie des Chaleurs. Battle of Ristigouche Interpretation Centre tells story of the summer of 1760, when the French scuttled three ships in Ristigouche estuary rather than surrender them to the British. The silt preserved the frigate *Machault* until 1960, when archeologists salvaged vestiges, including many everyday items the crew used. Audio-visual effects, in French and English, help you relive the era from an observation terrace. Open daily, early June–Labor Day. Free.

GASPÉ. Musée de Gaspé Museum. 80 blvd. Gaspé (418–368–5710). 2 km (1.4 mi.) north of town on route 132, next to the Jacques Cartier monument. Temporary and permanent exhibitions of art and collections showing the area's history. Open daily, late June–Labor Day, 9 A.M.–7 P.M.; Labor Day–late June, Mon.–Fri., 9 A.M.–5 P.M.; Sun., 2–5 P.M. Families $3.75; adults, $1.50; under 17, $75 cents.

GALLERIES. Throughout the Gaspé Peninsula and Bas-St-Laurent you'll find many galleries and boutiques offering local art and handicrafts. Many are open only from mid June to Sept. The following is a brief selection:

Bas-St-Laurent

LA POCATIÈRE. Galerie d'Art Berthe Khazoom. 504 Quatrième Ave. (418-856-1162). Permanent exhibition by well-known Quebec artists. Mon.-Fri., 1 P.M.-7 P.M., or by appointment. All welcome, but groups please reserve.

RIMOUSKI. Galerie Basque. 1402 blvd. St-Germain ouest, Rimouski. Works by leading Quebec artists. Lectures on art and the art market. Summer hours, Mon.-Sat., 10 A.M.-noon; 1-5 P.M. Rest of the year, 1-5 P.M., plus Thurs. and Fri., 7-9 P.M. Free.

RIVIÈRE-DU-LOUP. Atelier des arts du Grand-Portage: La Tourbière. 152 rue Fraser (418-862-4262). Artists often work in this old barn/workshop/meeting center. Open mid June-Labor Day, 10 A.M.-10 P.M.
  Centre artisinal et communautaire. 407 rue Lafontaine, Riviere-du-Loup (418-862-8141). Thirty local crafts people exhibit and sell their work here. Some work in upstairs gallery. Summer, Mon-Sat., 10:30 A.M.-5 P.M., 7-9 P.M. Winter, Mon.-Sat. 1 P.M.-5 P.M. Thurs.-Fri., 7-9 P.M. All welcome, but groups (40 maximum) must reserve.

ST-SIMON. La Fascine. 27 rue Principale (418-738-2867). Boutique specializes in locally designed clothes, in natural, locally made fibres.

The Gaspé Peninsula

AMQUI. Le Tournassin. 11A rue St-Benoit (418-629-4568). Open daily in summer; in winter for exhibitions and by appointment only.

CARLETON. Gallerie du Vieux Couvent. 778 blvd. Perron, (418-364-3123). Art gallery, open all year.

PERCÉ. Centre d'Art de Percé. 126 rue Principale (Route 132) (418-782-5025). Local artists run this center housing boutiques, art gallery, and a small theater for summer stock and concerts. Open daily in summer.

ACCOMMODATIONS. You'll have no trouble finding the inn, motel or hotel to suit your budget. All three regions offer a wide variety of accommodation, often at lower prices than comparable values elsewhere in Quebec

Two home-grown Quebec chains prove particularly interesting. Members of both groups retain their independance, but pool ideas, standards and reservation facilities. Many of Quebec's finest hotels belong to the *Hôte* (meaning "your host") group, including Percé's Hotel/Motel La Normandie, Motel Les Trois Soeurs, and Carleton's Baie Bleue Motel, all in the Gaspé.

Five small old-style inns (and six restaurants) in the BSL and the Gaspé belong to *La Barouche* ("the old wagon"). Their double rooms average $35. Write to the BSL tourist office for the Barouche pamphlet.

The Quebec government inspects and rates all hotels using a system of zero to five lilies for comfort, and zero to four forks for cuisine. (See *Facts at Your*

BAS-ST-LAURENT/GASPÉ PENINSULA

Fingertips for details.) Reservations are essential in these areas. Some accommodations open only seasonally, i.e. approximately from mid June to Sept.

Price categories often overlap when hotels offer several types of rooms. Prices drop sharply in many hotels from Labor Day to mid-June. Do ask about "packages" that include rooms with meals, or with interesting activities, like golf, boat trips, whale-watching. Categories, based on the price for a double room for one night in full season, are: *Deluxe,* over $70; *Expensive,* $50–$70; *Moderate,* $30–$59; and *Inexpensive,* under $30.

Bas-St-Laurent

ANDRÉVILLE. Manoir St-André et Chalets. *Inexpensive.* Route 132, Andréville, P.Q. G0L 2H0 (418–493–2982). Pretty old house and modest but adequate cabins. Remarkable home-smoked eel, sturgeon, and salmon, plus local specialties. Tiny dining room. In quiet village on shore. One lily, one fork.

BIC. Auberge Le Vieux Manoir du Francais. *Inexpensive–Moderate.* Route 132, Bic, P.Q. G0L 1B0 (418–736–4345). 12 rooms, 2 lilies, 2 forks. Seasonal. Near Bic islands with large colonies of eider ducks. No credit cards.

NOTRE-DAME-DU-PORTAGE. Auberge sur Mer et Motels. *Moderate–Expensive.* 363 route du Fleuve, Notre-Dame-du-Portage P.Q. G0L 1Y0 (418–862–3636). Seasonal. Some kitchenettes. On shoreline. 51 rooms. 3 lilies, 1 fork.
Auberge du Portage et Motels. *Moderate–Expensive.* 671, route du Fleuve, Notre-Dame-du-Portage, P.Q. G0L 1Y0 (418–862–3601). Seasonal. 45 rooms. On shoreline. Outdoor pool.

DÉGELIS. Auberge Marie-Blanc et Motels. *Inexpensive–Moderate.* 1112 rue Commercial sud, Degelis, P.Q. G0L 1X0 (899–6747). 23 rooms, 2 lilies for comfort, 3 forks for good dining, with regional fare.

RIMOUSKI. Auberge des Gouverneurs. *Deluxe.* 155 blvd. Réné Lepage est, Rimouski, P.Q. G5L 1P2 (418–723–4422). Part of Quebec luxury hotel chain. Rates 5 lilies for 165 rooms; two forks.
Hôtel St-Louis. *Expensive.* 214 rue St-Edmond, Rimouski, P.Q. G5L 7B7 (418–724–6944). A grand, older hotel that rates 3 lilies for 85 comfortable rooms, 3 forks for fine dining.

RIVIÈRE-DU-LOUP. Motel Lévesque. *Expensive.* 171 rue Fraser, Riviére-du-Loup, P.Q. G5R 1E2 (418–862–6927). Highest rated establishment in the area, with a bouquet of 6 lilies for comfort, and 4 forks, for excellent dining for the region. 64 rooms. Outdoor pool.
Auberge Ste-Luce et Chalets. *Inexpensive–Moderate.* 52 rue Bord du Fleuve, Ste-Luce, P.Q. G0K 1P0 (418–739–4955). Seasonal. 2 lilies for the 29 rooms, 2 forks.

The Gaspé Peninsula

CARLETON. Baie Bleue. *Expensive–Deluxe.* Route 132, Carleton, P.Q. G0C 1J0 (418–364–3355, 800–361–6162). Part of Hôte, the Quebec chain of 36 quality motels and hotels run by individual innkeepers. 85 motel units, heated

PROVINCE OF QUEBEC

outdoor pool, sandy beach, near golf, tennis, fishing, hiking, windsurfing. Rates bunch of 5 lilies, 4 forks for dining room.

PASPÉBIAC. Auberge du Parc. *Moderate–Expensive.* C.P. 40, Paspébiac, P.Q. G0C 2K0 (418–752–3355). Seasonal. Near tennis, historic building, artists' colony. On beach. Motel units, and inn with magnificent old staircase, fine views. 3 lilies, 2 forks.

PERCÉ. La Normandie. *Expensive–Deluxe.* CP 129, Perce, PQ G0C 1L0 (418–782–2112). 30 modern and comfortable units, all overlooking the great pierced rock. Beach. Fine dining, with 3 forks for gourmet cuisine, 4 lilies for well-appointed rooms.

Magdelen Islands

You can rent a house, cabin or small cottage. Do book well in advance for July. Weekly rentals run from $250 to $350. You can also rent rooms nightly or by the week in private homes, some with breakfast, for between $20 and $35 for two people. In all cases, write to the regional tourist office for complete lists with prices.

CAP-AUX-MEULES. Motel Bellevue. *Expensive.* 40 rue Principale, Cap-aux-Meules, Îles-de-la-Madeleine, PQ G0B 1B0 (418–986–4477). 28 rooms, 3 lilies.
Hôtel-Motel Château Madelinot. *Expensive.* Route 199, Cap-aux-Meules, Îles-de-la-Madeleine, PQ G0B 1B0 (418–986–3695). 40 rooms, 4 lilies, kitchenettes, beach, accessible to handicapped travelers.
Auberge La Jetee. *Moderate.* 153 rue Principale, Cap-aux-Meules, Îles-de-la-Madeleine, PQ G0B 1B0 (418–986–4446). 10 rooms, 2 lilies, 2 forks.

GROS-CAP. Motel L'Archipel. *Moderate.* Route 199, Gros-Cap, Îles-de-la-Madeleine, PQ G0B 1A0 (418–986–3050). 10 rooms, 2 lilies, kitchenettes, beach.

HAVRES-AUX-MAISONS. Motel des Iles. *Moderate.* Route 199, Havre-aux-Maisons, Iles-del-la-Madeleine, PQ G0B 1K0 (418–989–2931). 28 rooms, 2 lilies, kitchenettes, beach.
Motel Theriault. *Moderate.* Dune du Sud, Havre-aux-Maisons, Îles-de-la-Madeleine, PQ G0B 1K0 (418–969–2955). 20 rooms, 4 lilies, 1 fork.
Hotel au Vieux Convent. *Inexpensive.* Route 199, Havre-aux-Maisons, Îles-de-la-Madeleine, PQ G0B 1K0 (418–969–2283). 10 rooms, 1 lily, beach.

Youth Hostels

Youth hostels in these regions open mainly June–Sept. Overnight stays cost from $6 to $10.

BAS-ST-LAURENT. Auberge de Rimouski. 186 rue Rouleau, Rimouski, P.Q. G5L 5S9 (418–724–9595). 40 beds. **Mont St-Pierre.** Auberge les Vagues, 84 rue Cloutier (route 132), Mont St-Pierre, P.Q. G0E 1V0 (418–797–2851). 60 beds. **St-Jean Port-Joli.** 101 rue de Gaspé est, St-Jean Port-Joli, P.Q. G0R 3G0 (418–598–9500). 58 beds.

BAS-ST-LAURENT/GASPÉ PENINSULA 109

THE GASPÉ PENINSULA. Cap-Oso. 2090 blvd. Grande Grève, C.P. 278, Forillon, P.Q. G0E 1J0 (418–892–5153). 53 beds. Open June–Oct. **Auberge de Matane,** 354 rue d'Amours, Matane, PQ G4W 2X9 (418–562–2836). 31 beds. Open all year. Cross-country skiing, ice-fishing.

MAGDALEN ISLANDS. Auberge de la Baie des Iles. C.P. 279, Havre-aux-Maisons, Iles-de-la-Madeleine, G0B 1K0 (418–969–4286). 58 beds.

RESTAURANTS. The waters around the three regions yield the main specialties, but you'll also find local lamb, rabbit and chicken, as well as beef. BSL specialties include smoked eel, sturgeon and salmon, often cured in the hotel or restaurant's own smoke house, and a fine local crab called *Rimouscrabe*. In the Gaspé, you'll discover all kinds of fresh fish and delicacies like cods' tongues, lobster, and tiny, tender Matane shrimp (particularly during the Matane Shrimp Festival in June). Restaurant prices generally come slightly higher on the Gaspé, partly because the season is short. You'll find good value at the hotels listed, such as at *La Normandie* in Percé. The Magdalen Islands offer clams, mussels, lobster, snow crab, scallops, sole, cod and mackerel ... among other fish. Most of the Islands' dozen restaurants open from May to Oct., offering specialties like *pot-en-pot*, a sea-food pie, and wonderful lobster. Average price for a full meal is around $10. You can bring your own wine to some spots. In all regions, you can't go wrong if you check the list of hotels, and note the number of forks the government awards for good cuisine.

The hotel and inn restaurant categories usually approximate the overnight stays: at most moderate inns, you'll pay only moderate meal prices. The regional tourist offices can also give you lists of interesting restaurants along the way. In restaurants, as in hotels, categories often overlap, since you can usually choose a table d'hôte in a lower price category than the à la carte fare. *Deluxe,* over $27; *Expensive,* $22–$27; *Moderate,* $15–$22; *Inexpensive,* under $15. "Summer season," means the establishment closes from Labor Day or shortly after until mid June. All hold liquor licenses unless otherwise mentioned. In the Gaspé and BSL all accept American Express, Master Card, and Visa, unless otherwise noted. No credit card information available for Magdalen Islands.

Bas-St-Laurent

RIMOUSKI. Crèperie Bretonne. *Inexpensive–Moderate.* 124 rue St-Germain est (418–722–4544). Local crab, called "Rimouscrabe," paper-thin French pancakes, grilled meats, sea-food. Reservations.

L'Imprévu. *Inexpensive–Moderate.* 73 rue St-Germain (418–723–7337). The famous "Rimouscrabe" served here in pastas, flambée, even on pizza from the woodburning oven. Do reserve.

RIVIÈRE-DU-LOUP. Le St-Patrice. *Inexpensive–Moderate.* 169 rue Fraser (418–862–9895). Regional lamb cooked on a spit, the local fish soup *(bouillabaisse)*, and many sea-food dishes.

ST-JEAN PORT-JOLI. La Roche à Veillon. *Inexpensive.* On route 132 (418–598–3061). Inexpensive, hearty, Quebec fare like meat pies *(tourtières)*, beans and pea soup. La Roche also puts on summer theater and concerts by popular singers, in French. Summer only.

The Gaspé Peninsula

CARLETON. Le Vivier. *Inexpensive–Moderate.* Route du Quai off route 132 (418-364-7595). Fresh lobster and salad bar.

PERCÉ. Bleu, Blanc, Rouge. *Expensive–Deluxe.* Route 132. 782-2142. Established in the 'forties by Madame Boulanger, now run by one of her daughters, this family hotel/motel/restaurant is renowned for its homespun decor and light, honest hand with fish, seafood and lamb . . . and desserts. Full dinners at around $30.

L'Auberge Gargantua. *Expensive–Deluxe.* 222 route des Falls (418-782-2852). One of the area's most celebrated restaurants, for the faithful clientèle and the inventive, sometimes quixotic character of owner Pierre Péresse. Péresse supervises everything, from the chefs, the garden, and the taxi that brings him fresh crab daily to the semitame bear that comes around for hand-outs. The restaurant, on top of a mountain, overlooks forest and hills on one side and the wide bay of Percé on the other. Péresse's cuisine is remarkably good, the helpings generous: whole fishes, entire tureens of soup per table. Vast wine cellar. Open mid May–late Sept. Reservations essential. No credit cards.

Magdalen Islands

CAP-AUX-MEULES. La Table des Roy. *Moderate–Expensive.* Lavernière. (418-986-3004). Some say this is one of Quebec's best restaurants. It serves mostly seafood, including lobster pie *(feuilleté de homaurd au coulis de poireaux)* and mussels. Good wine cellar. Open Tues.–Sun. Reservations essential.

La Maison de la Couline. *Moderate.* (418-937-5765). Traditional Madelinian cuisine, including sea-food pies, *(Pot-en-Pot).* Bring your wine. Reservations essential.

HAVRE-AUBERT. Café de la Grave. *Inexpensive.* (418-937-5765). Café-restaurant in an old general store. Good for inexpensive snacks, cakes, coffee.

HAVRE-AUX-MAISONS. Le P'tit Café. *Inexpensive.* (418-969-2736). Lobster and crab club sandwiches. Seafood, steaks.

QUEBEC CITY

by
Janet Kask

Janet Kask has worked in Montreal for more than two decades as a journalist and broadcaster for the Canadian Broadcasting Corporation, the Canadian Press news agency, and for many magazines and newspapers.

This jewel of a city perched high on a cliff overlooking the St. Lawrence River is so rich with charm, history, and natural beauty it is an experience not to be missed if you are planning to tour the province. Quebec City is the birthplace of French colonial North America. The explorer Jacques Cartier first set foot here in 1535, beginning a chain of events that would last three centuries and eventually lead to the founding of Canada. The old, walled city is so full of architectural treasures—many dating back to the 17th century—that UNESCO recently declared it a site of "outstanding universal value," ranking with Egypt's pyramids and India's Taj Mahal.

PROVINCE OF QUEBEC

Quebec's history is inextricably tied to its strategic position high above the juncture of two rivers—the St. Lawrence and the St. Charles. ("Kebec" is an Algonquin name for "place where the river narrows.") Its value as a military fortress was first realized by the founder of New France, Samuel de Champlain, who began building the early settlement in 1608. Champlain built Fort St-Louis in 1620, at the highest point of the cliff known as Cap Diamant. The Compte de Frontenac took over the colony's administration in 1672 and started building the walls after the British navy demanded his surrender in 1690. (Frontenac reportedly told an emissary from British Admiral William Phipps who demanded the city's surrender, "My answer will come from the mouths of my cannons.")

These early defense systems would be rebuilt and improved several times during the next two centuries, resulting in the walled fortress that earned Quebec the name the "Gibraltar of North America."

The fortress defended the colony against the British until Quebec fell to General James Wolfe in 1759, and later against the Americans who made several attempts to capture the stronghold. (In a first American takeover attempt, the Kirk brothers sailed from Boston in the 17th century. They took the town, but failed to hold it.) In 1775 the British colonial army defeated General Richard Montgomery and Colonel Benedict Arnold of the American army when they attacked during a New Year's Eve blizzard. During the War of 1812 American armies from Vermont and New York state attacked Quebec again. To ward off further American invasions, the British built the Citadel, the giant star-shaped bunker on Cap Diamant.

Residents still call Quebec a "military town." The historic Citadel is headquarters of Canada's Royal 22nd Regiment known by their English nickname as the "Vandoos" (*Vingt-Deuxieme,* or 22nd) who served in the Korean and two world wars and helped defeat the German army at the famous battle of Vimy Ridge during the First World War. Another Canadian Army base is in Valcartier, just north of Quebec.

Religion was central to the colonists' lives and played a vital role in the settlement of Quebec. In the early 17th century religious orders—the Jesuits and Recollet (Franciscan) fathers and orders of Augustine and Ursuline nuns among others—established hospitals, churches, and centers of learning. Sister Marie de l'Incarnation and Madame de la Peltrie founded the first school for girls in North America. François-Xavier de Montmorency Laval was named bishop of the diocese extending to the Pacific and the Gulf of Mexico. He founded the Séminaire de Quebec which eventually became Laval University. The colonists completed what is now the oldest standing cathedral in North America—Notre Dame de la Victoire—in 1678.

In the meantime, the town became a thriving center of trade and commerce. Fur trading was the major activity in the community Champlain had settled. Eventually, fishing, logging, and shipbuilding flourished. The suburb of Lauzon across the St. Lawrence has one of

QUEBEC CITY

the world's largest shipyards. A major port today, Quebec exports Canadian grain and imports general cargo from around the world.

Today the biggest employer in Quebec, the provincial capital, is the government. The 30,000 civil servants who live and work here make up the bulk of its labor force. Many also work in the city's hospitals and educational institutions.

As a seat of government since its beginnings, the city's political traditions run strong and deep. Politics are as important to Quebecers as hockey and good food, and the fine art of rhetoric can be watched when the National Assembly sits from March to June and from September to December.

With a population of 500,000, Quebec has all the advantages of a middle-sized city, including manageable traffic and easy access to the countryside. Natives are proud of the fact that beautiful Laurentian lakes and mountains and some of the finest ski slopes and trails anywhere are only a 20-minute drive from downtown.

The term *joie de vivre* has been used to death to describe Quebecers' legendary love for a good time, but the ambiance of lively talk, laughter, and general enjoyment is indeed a fact of life here—and it is infectious. Walk down the Grande Allée any summer evening—or winter evening, for that matter—and you will hear it drifting out of the dozens of bars, bistros, and discotheques.

While Quebec is indisputably and proudly French-speaking, most natives—especially those in the tourism business—also speak English. Many British, Scottish, and Irish soldiers married into French-speaking families. Their influence is unmistakable in the jigs, reels, and ballads of Quebec's folk culture. In fact, Quebecers will tell you they speak three languages—French, English, and hospitality.

Exploring Quebec City

There is so much to do and see in Quebec and vicinity, it is best to line up your sightseeing priorities before you set out. To get an idea of the layout—and some hard-to-match panoramic views—you might start with a bird's-eye approach from one of the newer high-rise towers with observation points. Three of the best are Loews Le Concorde hotel's 27th floor revolving restaurant, l'Astral; the Quebec Hilton International; and the "Anima G" (31st floor) of Government Building G. Also highly recommended for a completely different look at the cliff-top fortress is the one General Wolfe studied in detail before his history-making assault—from the city of Levis across the St. Lawrence or from the river itself. (For a spectacular view of the entire St. Lawrence Valley, try the gondola ride at Parc Mont Ste-Anne east of Quebec.)

Canada's destiny was shaped on the famous battlefield, the Plains of Abraham, now a national historic park. The image of General James Wolfe and his army of 4,500 men crossing the St. Lawrence and scaling the cliffs under the Plains on the moonless night of 13 September 1759

PROVINCE OF QUEBEC

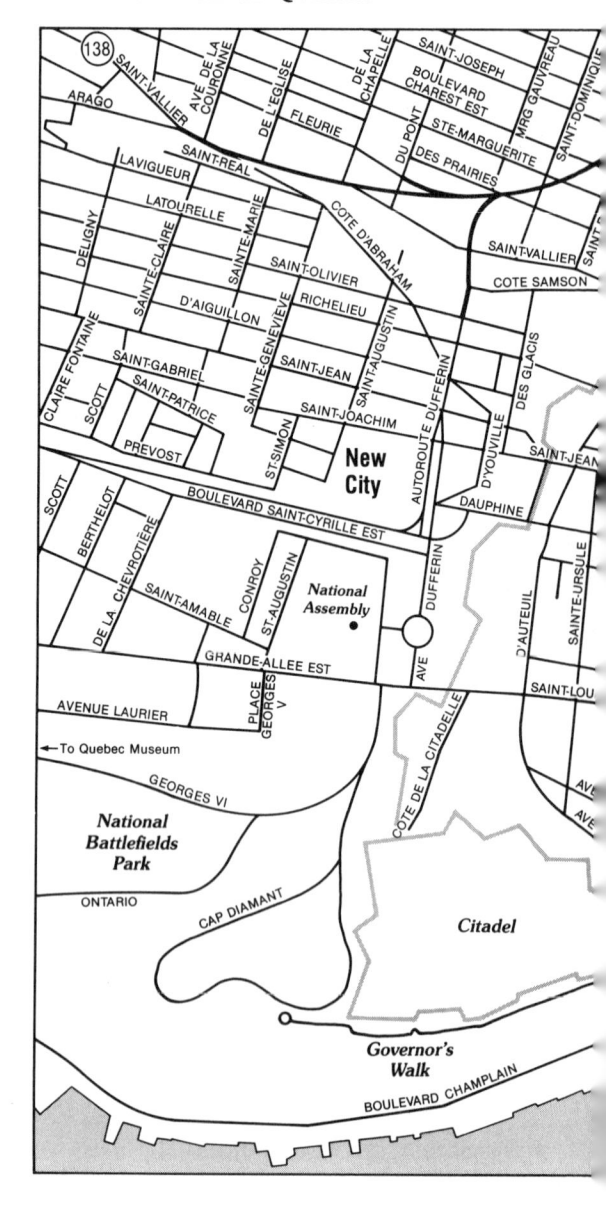

QUEBEC CITY 115

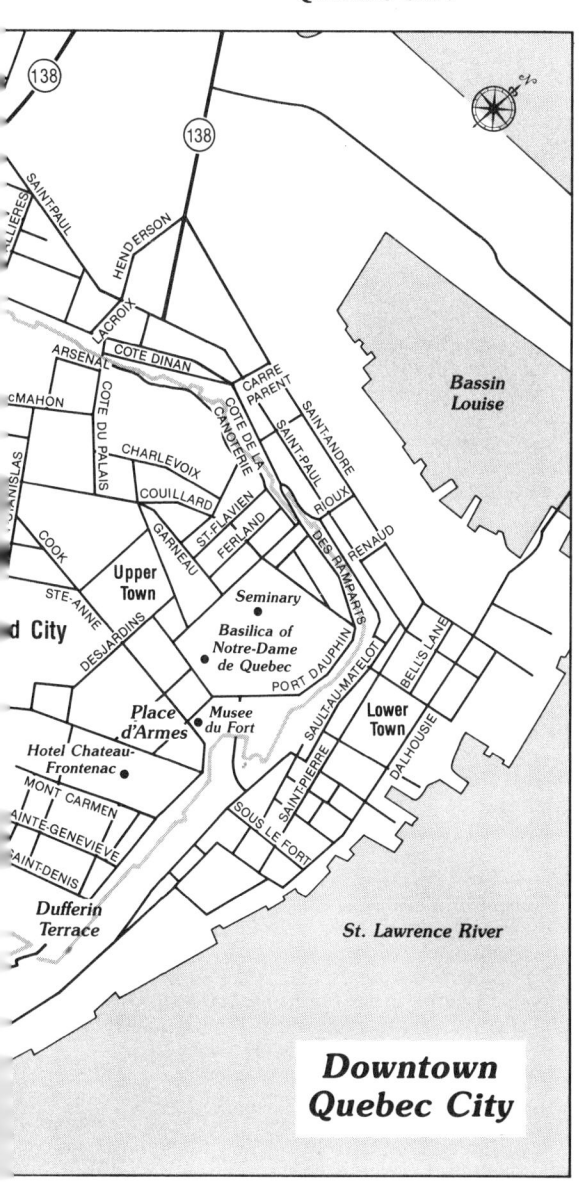

Downtown Quebec City

lives in the memory of every Canadian schoolchild. Both generals Wolfe and the Marquis de Montcalm died heroes' deaths in the battle along with 2,000 soldiers. The Citadel, Martello Towers, and other fortifications built to protect the city from American invasions are part of the remarkable fortifications system in the park.

Just outside the walled city is Quebec's modern face with high-rise hotels and government buildings blending with architecture of the past. The Grande Allée, the main thoroughfare leading to the old city and flanked by mansions once owned by the rich and famous, is now the center of cafe society and nightlife with its lively strip of sidewalk restaurants and bars. On the left (as you enter the city) the Grande Allée borders a complex of new government buildings, including Edifice (Building) G and the fortresslike Edifice H, where the Premier's office is located (not open to the public). Among the new additions stands the stately, 19th-century Hotel du Parlement, seat of the provincial government, and Le Pigeonnier ("Pigeonhole") square, where the city's pigeon population earns a Good Housekeeping award for sticking to its specially built "pigeon condos."

Le Grande Théâtre on St. Cryrille Street, home of major theatrical events here, was designed by architect Victor Prus as a project honoring Canada's 1967 Centennial. A huge (and controversial) three-part mural called "Death, Space, and Liberty" by Spanish-born artist Jordi Bonet—Quebec's answer to Mexican muralist Diego Rivera—stands in the main foyer.

Entering the old, walled city—the only one in America north of Mexico—is like entering a time warp. The walls and great, arched gates lead you to a world so different (at least by North American standards) you may wonder if you have not strayed into a movie set by mistake. Extremely proud of their heritage, Quebecers have taken great care to preserve literally dozens of buildings, battle sites, and monuments, some dating back to the 17th century. The result is a charming blend of winding, cobblestone streets and old houses reminiscent of vintage European cities and towns.

Old Quebec's location on a steep hill gives it a "split-level" character, dividing it into *Haute Ville* (Upper Town), the colonial era's residential area, and *Bas Ville* (Lower Town), center of commerce and shipping. In Haute Ville Monsigneur Laval, first Biship of Quebec, established the Séminaire de Quebec. Central meeting place for the community was Place d'Armes, the square where early military marches and drills took place. Today street musicians and jugglers turn the square into an open air theater in summer. Leading from rue Sainte-Anne bordering the square is rue du Trésor, a narrow lane where the colonial treasury house *(trésor)* once stood. Today artists sell their work there.

Probably the most photographed building in Canada, the Chateau Frontenac, a massive, green-turreted castle, dominates the city. American architect Bruce Price designed the classy CPR (Canadian Pacific Railway) hotel where Queen Elizabeth and Madame Chiang Kai-shek, among many other dignitaries, have stayed. During the Second World

QUEBEC CITY

War, U.S. president Franklin Delano Roosevelt met here with British Prime Minister Winston Churchill.

Built in 1838 by Lord Durham, named after Lord Dufferin, Dufferin Terrace has to be one of the world's most elegant and well-kept boardwalks with its pergola bandstand, green railings, and magnificent view of the St. Lawrence and Lower Town. Linking the Terrace with Place d'Armes is *Promenade des Gouverneurs* (Governors' Walk). The Terrace sits above *Cap Diamant* (Cape Diamond, so named, the story goes, because Jacques Cartier thought the quartz he discovered there was diamonds), site of the original Fort St. Louis.

An elevator (called *funiculaire*) travels up and down the steep cliffs between Dufferin Terrace and Bas Ville. The stouthearted can make the same trip on the fabled "Breakneck Steps"—named by intrepid American tourists who climbed them and survived—which scale the cliffs. At the bottom is Place Royale, a multimillion dollar Quebec government restoration project of 17th- and 18th-century buildings standing on the site where Champlain first settled. In the same area, local artists restored Champlain Village, now an artists' cooperative where some of the province's finest handicrafts can be found.

Île d'Orléans, a lovely island of farmlands and six parishes 16 kilometers (9 miles) east of Quebec via Route 138, was one of New France's earliest settlements. Here you can visit more old houses, churches, and museums and pick your own strawberries (watch for *"Cueillez vos fraises"* signs) and apples in season.

The Montmorency Falls *(Chutes Montmorency)* are further along on route 138. This gorgeous 83-meter (272 feet) waterfall (one and a half times as high as Niagara Falls) is well worth the journey. In winter it forms a giant ice cone called the "sugar loaf." General Wolfe lost the Battle of Montmorency here in July 1759.

Sainte-Anne-de-Beaupré is also on route 138, 40 kilometers (24 miles) east of Quebec. A million pilgrims visit this tribute to Sainte Anne, mother of the Virgin Mary, each year. Colonial sailors caught in a devastating storm prayed to Sainte Anne and were saved, according to popular lore. They set up the original shrine at the site where they reached land. Dominated by the giant romanesque basilica, the shrine is North America's largest.

Sainte-Foy, a suburb just north of Old Quebec is the site of the Quebec Aquarium and Université Laval, North America's oldest French-language university. Founded by Monsigneur Laval in 1663 as the Séminaire de Quebec, it has one of Canada's largest, most modern sports complexes including a speed-skating arena.

On route 369, 7 kilometers (4 miles) north of Quebec in Loretteville, is Huron Village with a 250-year-old chapel, old manuscripts, a giant tepee, and liturgical museum. The Arouanne museum recounts the evolution of the tribe, which moved to the spot from southern Ontario in the 1600s to be near their French allies.

PRACTICAL INFORMATION FOR QUEBEC CITY

WHEN TO GO. Because it is so visually unusual and rich with historical interest and fine cuisine, Quebec City offers fascinating entertainment any time of year. Each season features its own stunning color scheme, giving the city several totally different personalities.

Most tourists favor summer, as balmy-to-warm weather brings everyone outside to enjoy the city's many parks, street festivals, and sidewalk cafes. Cooling breezes generally keep heat and humidity in check.

Quebec's annual Summer Festival held the first two weeks in July features a dazzling variety of concerts, stage shows, and other special events including many special children's activities. Take a jacket or wrap, as evenings, especially in early and late summer, can be chilly.

Nature lays on a stunning show of second-to-none fall foliage, beginning early in September and peaking around mid-October. You will never forget the sight of Quebec's many copper rooftops turned pale green with age against the brilliant golds, reds, and blues of the trees, sky, and water. Fewer tourists and nippy-but-invigorating temperatures make fall an ideal time for walking or *calèche* (horse and carriage) tours through the city's many charming streets.

Winter, while often extremely chilly—(2°-20° Fahrenheit is an average Jan. temperature), has its own special beauty here. The combination of sparkling fresh snowfalls and clear blue skies, or rose sunsets, turns the old, walled city into a scene from Grimm's fairy tales.

Excellent ski facilities within minutes of the downtown area make winter a perfect visiting time for downhill and cross-country enthusiasts. Because snow is most plentiful in December when it averages 74 cm (30 in.), skiers find Christmas holidays ideal for a Quebec adventure. Peak ski season is late Dec.–first week of Jan. and Feb.–early Mar. Many hotels offer reasonable ski packages, reduced during off-season.

The city's renowned Winter Carnival lasts ten days in early Feb. and features dozens of unusual events, parades, gala balls, and a giant ice-sculpture competition.

A note of caution: Because of temperature extremes—from the cold outdoors to sometimes overheated indoors—layers of clothing are advised in winter. Natives wear lots of fur, and you will realize why when icy winds blow across some of the higher areas of the city. But a shirt or blouse, jacket, and topcoat give you the freedom to peel when necessary. Good leather boots should be avoided as salt and slush puddles on streets and sidewalks will ruin them in no time. Wear something warm and waterproof.

HOW TO GET THERE. Quebec City can be reached by land, air, or sea, by all the conventional means of transport. Founded as a trading center, the city continues to flourish as a major Canadian port and plays host to cruise and cargo ships alike.

By Plane. Quebec's International Airport in suburban Ste-Foy, 19 km (12 mi) from downtown Quebec, was enlarged and remodeled in 1984 to accommodate 490 passengers per hour and 350 takeoffs and landings daily. It handles regular service to Canadian and U.S. cities via *Air Canada, Quebecair, Quebec*

QUEBEC CITY 119

Aviation, and *Nordair.* Air Canada flies regularly from Quebec to Montreal, New Orleans, Baton Rouge, Houston, Dallas, Austin, Halifax, London, Ontario, Edmonton, Calgary, Brussels, and Paris.

By Bus. *Voyageur, Inc.* provides hourly service daily between Montreal and Quebec from 6 A.M.–9 P.M. and regular service between Quebec and several other centers from two terminals: Downtown terminal, 225 Charest Blvd. Est (418-524-4692), and Ste-Foy terminal, 2700 Laurier Blvd., Ste-Foy.

By Train. *VIA Rail* travels daily to and from Montreal to Quebec's recently renovated 19th-century CPR (Canadian Pacific Railway) station, Gare du Palais, 450 rue St-Paul (418-524-6452) and suburban Ste-Foy, 3255 Chemin de la Gare, (418-692-3940).

By Car. Several well-maintained highways and expressways lead to Quebec City. From Montreal, highways 40 and 138 will take you on a liesurely route through Trois-Rivières and several picturesque villages. Superhighway 401 from Toronto continues into Hwy. 20 to Quebec—about 3½ hours from Montreal. U.S. highways 87 in New York, 89 in Vermont, and 91 in New Hampshire connect with Hwy. 10—Quebec's Eastern Townships Autoroute—which also joins with Hwy. 20. From Maine motorists may take highways 201, 173, and 73 to Quebec, or a longer riverside route via Hwy. 95 to highways 1, 2, and 185, joining with highway 20 at Rivière du Loup, northeast of Quebec. Hwy. 175 joins Quebec with Chicoutimi to the north. Hwy. 138, a stunning drive along the north shore of the St. Lawrence, travels eastward to Baie Comeau and Sept-Îles.

By Boat. Quebec offers docking facilities and complete services for boaters. Call Société du Port de Quebec (418-648-3645) or write to Ports Canada, 150 Dalhousie, Box 2268, Quebec, PQ G1K 7P7.

TOURIST INFORMATION. You will find an excellent selection of information at one of two major tourism centers in downtown Quebec. *Tourisme Quebec* at 12 rue Ste-Anne (418-643-2280 or 800-443-7000) Office is open daily June–Aug., 8:30 A.M.–8:30 P.M. Sept.–May daily, 9 A.M.–5 P.M. Or write to CP 20,000, Quebec, PQ G1K 7X2. The *Quebec Urban Community Tourism and Convention Bureau,* 60 rue d'Auteuil, Quebec, PQ G1R 4C4 (418-692-2471) is open daily, early June–Labor Day, 8:30 A.M.–8 P.M. April and May, Sept. and Oct., Mon.–Fri., 8:30 A.M.–5:30 P.M. Nov.–April, 8:30 A.M.–5 P.M.

To find out what is going on daily while you are there, check out the city's two daily, French-language newspapers, *Le Journal de Quebec* (A.M.) and *Le Soleil* (P.M.). The English-language *Chronicle Telegraph* appears on Wednesdays. Other sources of information in English are CKMI-TV, Channel 5, and radio station McCBVE, 104.7 FM (6 A.M.–1 A.M.).

TELEPHONES. The area code for Quebec is 418. Cost of a local call is 25 cents, with no time limit. Dial 411 for information, 0 for bilingual operator assistance, and 418-555-1212 for information from elsewhere. Dial 0 before the area code for direct-dial, credit, or collect calls and 1 before the area code for long distance calls from Quebec.

EMERGENCY TELEPHONE NUMBERS. *City police* (691-6123); *provincial police* (623-6262); *24-hour emergency medical service* (687-9915); *Health-info* (648-2626); *Hôtel-Dieu Hospital* (694-5042); *Jeffrey Hale Hospital* (683-4471); *emergency dental service,* Mon.–Fri., 8 A.M.-5 P.M. (653-5412); *24-hour poison*

PROVINCE OF QUEBEC

center (656–8090); *pharmacy,* daily until 2 A.M., 4266 Charlesbourg Ave. (623–1571); *24-hour maritime search and rescue* (872–2859); *air search and rescue* (800–267–7270); *road conditions* (643–6830); *Tel-Aide,* for depression (683–2153); *drug-abuse clinic* (525–4304); *Alcoholics Anonymous* (529–0015); *24-hour weather* (872–2859).

HOW TO GET AROUND. From the airport. The Quebec Airport is 19 km (12 mi) from downtown. Taxis, available just outside the airport exit near the baggage claim, cost around $15 and an airport bus leaving every two hours and stopping at major hotels is $6.75 for the 20-minute trip to downtown Quebec.

By Bus. *Quebec Urban Community Transit* buses run regularly every 15–20 minutes in town and cost $1.20 (exact change) for adults, 65 cents for children. For information, call 627–2511.

By Taxi. Drop rate is $1.50 and 70 cent per kilometer thereafter. Taxi companies are listed in the yellow pages. Among them are: *Taxi Quebec,* 975 8th Ave. (522–2001), and *Taxi Coop de Quebec,* 302 3rd Ave. (525–5191).

By Rental Car. Car rentals are reasonable, with special weekend rates averaging $30–$35. Insurance costs about $10 daily. Quebec is served by the major firms including *Avis* (airport, 872–2861; downtown, 523–0041); *Budget* (airport, 872–9885; downtown, 692–3660; toll-free, 800–268–8970); *Hertz* (airport, 871–1571; downtown, 694–1224; toll-free 800–268–1311); *Holiday* (downtown, 667–0129; Ste-Foy, 656–1411); *Rent-A-Wreck* (683–2333); *Tilden* (airport, 871–1224; downtown, 694–1727); *Sears* (Ste-Foy, 694–1685).

HINTS TO MOTORISTS. Quebec's highway and road signs are in French only, and not always as explicitly marked as they might be, particularly on expressways entering cities. It is a good idea to map out exactly where you want to go in advance, carefully noting highway numbers and street names. Winter driving can be hazardous for the uninitiated. Use good snow tires, drive slowly when roads are icy, and keep plenty of windshield wiping fluid on hand, especially for highway driving. For road conditions, call 643–6830.

Since Quebec is relatively small as cities go (pop. 500,000), traffic is easier to deal with than in most major metropolitan centers. However, during high tourist seasons the narrow, winding streets in the old city can become congested and parking can be difficult. Rush hour starts about 4 P.M. Walking is the best way to see the old city, as most tourist attractions are concentrated in a small area.

Parking is not allowed on many streets in the old city, though about 4,000 parking spaces are available, mostly in lots. Métro parking lots, marked with a green "P," charge average daily rates of about $5, $2 on weekends. Some hotels offer special deals on downtown parking lots. (Provincial and municipal tourist bureaus provide a city map showing where these lots are.) Private lots like the Chateau Frontenac's ($1.98 for the first half hour and up) can be expensive. Parking meters on larger thoroughfares cost 25 cents per half hour to 25 cents an hour, depending on location.

QUEBEC CITY

HINTS TO HANDICAPPED TRAVELERS. The Quebec Urban Community's publication *Access to Métro Quebec* has a comprehensive list of stores, tourist attractions, restaurants, and lodging with special facilities for handicapped travelers. Write in advance or pick up a copy at the Quebec Urban Community Tourism and Convention Bureau, 60 rue d'Auteuil, Quebec, PQ G1R 4C4 (418–692–2471). Most street corners have wheelchair ramps and strictly enforced parking for the disabled marked with blue and white wheelchair signs. Kéroul, 4545 Pierre Coubertin or CP 1,000, Succursale M, Montreal, PQ H1V 3R2 (514–252–3104) lists special tours, as well as orthopedic centers, for the disabled.

WINTER CARNIVAL. Renowned as the world's biggest winter carnival, Quebec's version of the pre-Lenten Mardi Gras festival is an anti-February-blues bash without rival. The ten-day event usually beginning the first week in February has become famous for its celebration of snow and ice, phenomena the natives here take pride in transforming into everything from giant sculptures to a spine-chilling luge run. The festival turns this city of 17th-century châteaus and fortresses into a magical snow-covered Disney world complete with a 26-m-(85 ft.)-tall ice castle, a queen and six duchesses, parades, and gala balls. Founded 32 years ago by a group of local businessmen to "beat the winter blues," the event now draws as many as 1½ million tourists and features more than 100 indoor and outdoor events including concerts, special exhibitions, and nightly dances.

Among the major highlights is the ice-sculpture competition on Place du Palais. Created by local artists and others from as far afield as Mexico and Switzerland, the massive works of art are judged by the Carnival's host, "Bonhomme Carnaval," a huge snowman dressed in the traditional red tuque and woven belt of Quebec's early "habitants." (Another dazzling sculpture competition on rue Ste-Therese in Lower Town features work by local residents.) Bonhomme opens the festival with a command to laugh and make merry, crowns the snow queen, leads two parades of costumed revelers, presides over balls, and awards prizes for athletic events. He might also pick up an unhappy-looking citizen and lock him or her in a prisoner's cell at the ice palace for a few minutes' gentle reprimand.

The carnival's conventional athletic events range from hockey tournaments and speed-skating marathons to provincial swimming, raquetball, and volleyball competitions. More unusual competitions include torch and acrobatic skiing, dogsled racing, and the famous international canoe race across the St. Lawrence in which participants do battle with large chunks of floating ice.

Caution: The carnival's unofficial stimulant is a walloping brew of raw alcohol and wine known as "Caribou," traditionally sipped from the top of a cane to "ward off the cold." The impact of this grog when unjudiciously consumed can result in side effects ranging from acute memory lapses to a night in the emergency ward—or jail. Forewarned is forearmed.

Accommodations in major hotels, the YWCA, and youth hostels are generally booked solid at least a month in advance, though last-minute vacancies are often available in suburban inns, motels, and bed-and-breakfast arrangements in private homes. (Major hotels often raise their rates as high as 30 percent during the Carnival.) If you are willing to rough it with your own towel and sleeping bag, you can stay in a downtown church basement for $7.50. A lodging committee on duty around the clock during the event matches visitors with accommodations, usually within four hours. Call (418) 524–8441 for information. For further details, write to the Carnival's head office at 290 rue Joly, Quebec, PQ G1L 4T8 (418-626-3716).

SUMMER FESTIVAL. With the same native talent for putting on a good show, Quebec celebrates its high tourist season with a summer festival par excellence—billed as the "largest Francophone cultural event in North America." During the festivities held the first two weeks of July, visitors are treated to what seems like an endless program of music, dance, and theater—much of it outdoors and free—guaranteed to entertain travelers of all ages. For more information write or call Quebec Summer Festival, 26 rue Ste-Pierre, Box 24, Succursale B, Quebec, PQ G1K 7A1 (418-692-4540). This period is extremely popular for summer vacationers. Advance planning for accommodations or campsites is advised.

OTHER SEASONAL EVENTS. Late January. *Quebec International Bonspiel.* Quebec curling clubs. Six-day International curling tournament (688-1225). **February.** *International Pee-Wee Hockey Tournament.* Quebec Coliseum, Exposition Park. For 10-12-year-olds from Canada, the U.S., and Europe. Lasts ten days (656-3372). **Mid-April.** *International Book Fair.* Centre Municipal des congrès de Quebec, Place Quebec (658-1974). **July 26.** *Feast of Ste-Anne.* Ste-Anne-de-Beaupré Basilica. Torchlight parade (827-3781). **End of July–early August.** *Quebec handicraft exhibition and sale.* Jardins de l'hôtel de ville (City Hall) (694-0260). **End of August–early September.** *Agricultural Fair.* Parc de l'Exposition. The province's biggest. Also trade and industrial show. Lasts two weeks (694-0260). **Early December.** Salon des artisans de Quebec *(Quebec Crafts Show)* Centre municipale des congrès de Quebec, Place Quebec. Lasts 15 days (694-0260).

TOURS AND SPECIAL-INTEREST SIGHTSEEING.
Bus. *Gray Line* (627-9226) offers guided tours of Quebec City, Montmorency Falls, Ste-Anne-de-Beaupré, Île d'Orléans, and combination city tours and harbor cruises. Prices range from about $11–$16 for adults, half that for children. City tours run year-round, others from May–Oct., or June–Labor Day, depending on tour. Other bus lines with competitive prices and similar tours are: *Maple Leaf Sightseeing Tours* (653-4460); *Contact-Quebec,* which also offers fall foliage tours (692-2801); *Old Quebec Tours* (872-9226); *Orbitour* (692-1223); *Visite touristique de Quebec* (653-9722). *Visites Touristiques Fleur-de-Lys* (658-9635).

Boat. St. Lawrence cruises—including moonlight cruises of Quebec harbor—are offered by *Quebec Maritimes Excursions* (692-1678) and *M/V Louis Jolliet* (692-1159). The *Quebec-Levis ferry* (692-0550) takes 15 minutes and runs every half hour. For whale-watching excursions (July-Oct.) contact the *Société Linnéene du Quebec* (653-8186) or *Lower St. Lawrence Tourist Assoc.* (867-1272).

By Antique Car. *Les Tours d'Antan Inc.,* 396 Principale, St-Étienne, Lévis, PQ G0S 2L0 (831-1678).

By Calèche—horse and carriage—rides cost about $30 (667-9029).

By Plane. *Air Citadelle* (hydroplane) (872-9963); *Quebec Aviation* (872-1200).

By Train. *Le Tortillard du St-Laurent* offers charming excursions through Charlevoix county, but the future of this service is in doubt. (648-1566 or 800-463-5232).

QUEBEC CITY

By Foot. *L.L.M. Tours,* 2216 Chemin du Foulon, Sillery, PQ G1T 1X4 (658-4799).

PARKS AND GARDENS. Quebec City has many lovely parks and public squares both inside and outside the walls of Haute Ville. For information on **Artillery Park** and **Battlefields Park,** see *"Historic Sites and Houses."*

Bois-de-Coulonge. Grande Allée Ouest and Holland St. A summer theater now stands on the grounds of this former seigneurial domain and mansion of lieutenant governors since Confederation. Lieutenant Governor Paul Comptois died in the fire that destroyed the mansion in 1966. Open 24 hours. Free.

Cartier-Brébeuf Park. 175 rue de l'Espinay (648-4038). Operated by Parks Canada, this extensive green space was named after Canada's discoverer Jacques Cartier, who spent the winter of 1535-6 at the site, and Father Jean de Brébeuf, a founder of the Jesuit Order in New France. Special features are a replica of Cartier's flagship La Grande Hermine, guided tours, and an information center explaining Cartier's voyages. The park offers picnic sites, canoeing skating, cross-country skiing, cycling paths, and calèche rides. May 14–Labor Day, Tues.-Sun., 9:30 A.M.–5 P.M. Sept.–May, visitors center only, Mon.–Fri., 10 A.M.–4 P.M. Closed Christmas–New Year's Day. Free.

Joan of Arc Park. Laurier Ave. and Place Montcalm. A statue of the 15th-century heroine on horseback dominates this park belonging to the Battlefields Park Commission. French formal gardens surround the statue and square. Open 24 hours. Free.

Le Jardin des Gouverneurs. Behind the Château Frontenac. Outdoor theater and dance take place in the park in summer. A statue of generals James Wolfe and the Marquis de Montcalm honors both heroes.

Montmorency Park. East of Quebec via the Montmorency-Dufferin Autoroute (440), Autoroute de la Capitale (40), and Hwy 138, this recreation spot faces the spectacular Montmorency Falls. Several picnic areas provide beautiful scenic views. The Natural Stairway Park nearby has nature paths and trails along the Montmorency River. June–Labor Day, 8:30 A.M.–8:00 P.M.

Parc des Braves. Between Chemin Ste-Foy and Cote Franklin. Also part of the national Battlefields Park, the square commemorates the battle of Ste-Foy between François, duc de Levis and General James Murray in 1760. The "Monument des Braves" honors French soldiers who died in battle. Open 24 hours. Free.

Van den Hende Gardens. Between blvd. Hochelaga and Autoroute du Vallon, Ste-Foy (656-3333). Developed by prominent horticulturist Roger Van den Hende, this 15-acre botanical garden belongs to the Laval University Faculty of Agriculture and features some 2,500 species of plants. Open June–Sept. Free.

ZOOS. The Quebec Zoological Gardens. 8191 ave. du Zoo, Charlesbourg (643-2310). On the bank of the Du-Berger River seven miles north of Quebec on route 73, the zoo specializes in native Canadian fauna but features exotic species too. More than 900 species of birds and several hundred mammals live in the 30 developed acres of the 90-acre woodland site. (There is a "petting zoo" for youngsters.) Mid May–mid June, 10 A.M.-6 P.M. daily; mid June–early Sept., 10 A.M.–7 P.M. daily; rest of year, 10 A.M.–5 P.M. daily. Adults, about $3; much less for children; family rates.

The Quebec Aquarium. 1675 du Parc, Ste-Foy (643-5023). This modern circular building stands on a cliff overlooking the St. Lawrence in Aquarium

Park, a terraced woodland offering spectacular views of the river and countryside. The aquarium features native and foreign saltwater species, marine mammals, and reptiles, as well as nature films. Cafeteria is open year-round, picnic tables from mid-May to Sept. Seals' feeding time is 10:15 A.M. and 3:15 P.M. Daily from 9:00 A.M.–5 P.M. May 15–Labor day until 7 P.M. Adults, $2, children, 50 cents. Half price, mid-Oct.–mid-May.

PROVINCIAL PARKS. Quebec's wilderness parks are second to none in natural beauty and large enough to thoroughly escape the wear and tear of daily urban living. The following provincial parks and federal wildlife reserve are all within easy driving distance of Quebec City.

Cap Tourmente. (694-4042). Route 138, 46 km (28 mi) east of Quebec. The thousands of greater snow geese migrating here each spring and fall have made this beautifully maintained federal wildlife reserve famous. Boarded sidewalks through the tidal marshlands give birdwatchers a passage to the great, white mass of bird life, which peaks in mid-October. The park's 5,000 acres of mud flats and forest shelter many species of plants and animals. Naturalists on hand and information center explain wildlife to visitors. Open May-Oct. Free.

Laurentides Park. (848-2422). This vast expanse of lakes, rivers, and forests 48 km (29 mi) north of Quebec on route 175 includes a wildlife reserve as well as *Parc des Grands Jardins* and *Parc de la Jacques-Cartier* (see below). It offers camping, canoeing, mountain climbing, 42 km (26 mi) of ski trails, waxing room, snowshoeing, snack bar, equipment rentals, cottage rentals. Limited hunting and fishing (speckled trout) in season. Free.

Parc de la Jacques-Cartier. (848-2422, 848-3169, or 622-4444). In Laurentides Park. Magnificent scenery in the Jacques-Cartier River valley offers camping, mountain climbing, hiking trails, shelter rentals, fishing, canoeing, nature tours, and information centers. Open year-round. Free.

Parc des Grands Jardins. (622-4444). In Laurentides Park, on route 138, 120 km (74 mi) east of Quebec City. Same facilities as Jacques-Cartier Park. Open year-round.

Parc du Mont-Ste-Anne. (826-2323 or 827-4561; ski conditions, 827-4579). Located 40 km (25 mi.) east of Quebec on highways 138 and 360, this splendid recreation area has just about every amenity a nature lover could dream of, including a gondola ride to the top of the mountain with a spectacular view of the St. Lawrence Valley. It also features a 1.2 km (¾ mi) fitness trail, a 4.3 km (2.6 mi.) jogging trail, and a 6.4 km (4 mi.) cycling trail maintained and patroled daily, June 21-Sept. 2, and after Sept. 2 every Sat. and Sun. until the first snowfall. From mid-December–end of March, cross-country skiers and snowshoers enjoy 80 kilometers of ski trails, waxing room, snowshoeing, snack bar, and equipment rentals. Ski lifts and jumps for alpine skiers from end of Nov.–early May, depending on conditions. An 18-hole golf course open May 1–Oct. 30. For campers, 166 campsites for trailers, trailer tents, and tents open June 21–Sept. 2. Also available are laundry rooms, a community room, grocery store, service station, ice, and firewood. Rates, $7–$12 daily, depending on site. Special rates for those 65 and over.

CAMPING. Besides the government-operated campgrounds listed in the provincial parks section, the Quebec City area has some 16 private campgrounds to accommodate tents, trailers, and campers. Rates range from $8 per night per person for an unserviced campsite to $16 for a serviced site with washrooms, showers, and electricity. Many have lakefront or other

QUEBEC CITY 125

swimming facilities. For detailed information on private and government-operated campgrounds, write to ministère du Loisir, de la Chasse, et de la Pêche, Information and Reservations Service, CP 8888, Quebec, PQ G1K 7W3 (890–5349, 418–890–5349, or 800–462–5349).

PARTICIPANT SPORTS. Sports enthusiasts can enjoy anything from snowshoeing to windsurfing in the Quebec region, though alpine and cross-country skiing are the main attractions here. *Village des Sports,* 1869 blvd. Valcartier, Valcartier, route 371 north of Quebec, (844–2212) offers a complete range of sports activities including roller-skating, cycling, horseshoe throwing, volleyball, badminton, trampoline, waterfall and water slides (summer), toboggan slides and lifts, cross-country skiing and snowshoeing, rubber tube sliding, and skating paths (winter).

Curling. *Club de curling Jacques-Cartier* (643–4431); *Club de curling Etchemin* (839–9067); *Club de curling Victoria* (656–0403).

Cycling, jogging. *Battlefields Park* and *Parc du Mont-Ste-Anne,* among others, have extensive cycling and jogging paths. (See "Parks and Gardens" and "Provincial Parks.")

Golf. Quebec and suburban centers offer 18 golf courses, several open to the public. Reservations (including clubs and motorized carts) during summer months are essential and members generally book weekends well in advance. Closest to downtown Quebec is *Club de Golf Métropolitain,* 1575 ave. Chauveau (872–9292).

Fitness centers. *Pavillon d'Éducation physique et des Sports,* campus universitaire, Université Laval (694–7224); *YWCA,* 855 ave. Holland (656–2155); *En Forme,* 330 rue Ste-Hélène (529–1329); *Fitness 2,000,* 3 Place du Quebec (525–9909).

Horseback Riding. *Ranch El Paso,* 24 blvd. du Lac, Ste-Brigitte-de-Laval (825–2630); *Ranch JJ,* 506 rue Jobin, Lac-St-Charles (849–8986); *Centre d'équitation Le Paddock,* 8622 ave. Royale, Château-Richer (824–3351).

Jogging. Battlefields Park and Parc du Mont Ste-Anne, among others, have extensive jogging paths. (See "Parks and Gardens" and "Provincial Parks.")

Racquet sports. Tennis attire required at all clubs. Reserve in advance and bring your own equipment, as racquets are not always available. *Club de Tennis & Squash Montcalm Inc.,* 901 blvd. Champlain (687–1250); *Club Tennisport Inc.,* 4200 blvd. Hamel, Ancienne Lorette, (872–0111); *Raquetball Laurentien Inc.,* 5050 blvd. Hamel Ouest, Ste-Foy, (871–5051).

Downhill skiing. Five major ski centers within 40 km (25 mi) of Quebec, including Mont St-Anne, site of several World Cup international ski competitions (see "Provincial Parks") offer lifts, jumps, and extensive trails for downhill and cross-country skiing. Downhill: *Mont-Ste-Anne,* Beaupré (827–4561); *Le Relais,* 1085 blvd. du Lac, Lac Beauport (849–3073); *Mont-St-Castin-Les Neiges,* 82 Tour du Lac, Lac Beauport (849–6776); *Ski Stoneham,* 1420 ave. Hibou, Stoneham (848–2411); *Mont-Hibou,* 825 ave. Hibou, Stoneham, (848–3283).

Cross-country skiing. *Centre l'Éperon,* 06 Tour du Lac, Lac Beauport (849–2778), *Le Saisonnier,* 78 Chemin du Brûlé, Lac Beauport (849–2821); *Club Mont Tourbillon,* Club Ook-Pic Inc., 55 Montée du Golf, Charlesbourg (849–4418); *Manoir du Lac Delage,* 40 ave. du Lac, Lac Delage (848–2551); *Camp Mercier,* Stoneham (848–2422); *Centre Le Refuge,* 1186 rue Emond, St-Adolphe, (848–3329); *Cap Rouge,* Centre de ski de fond, 4473 rue St-Félix, Cap Rouge (653–9381); *Parc Mont-Ste-Anne* (827–4561).

PROVINCE OF QUEBEC

Skibus: A special municipal bus service (627–2511) leaves from downtown Quebec and Ste-Foy daily (except Christmas and New Year's Day), Dec. 21–Jan. 5, and weekends through the end of March, for Lac Beauport, Stoneham, and Mont-Ste-Anne. $2.50.

Sailing. *Vieux Port de Quebec,* rue Abraham Martin (692–0043); *Parc nautique Levy,* 205 rue St-Laurent (833–9421). *Yacht Club de Quebec,* 1061 blvd. Champlain (681–4617); *Marina de la Chaudière,* Chemin du Bac (839–7939).

Ice-skating. *Château Frontenac,* St. Charles River.

SPECTATOR SPORTS. Hockey is the abiding passion here, and Quebec is proud of its own *Nordiques.* The National Hockey League team's fancy skating can be seen at home games during the season at Le Colisée de Quebec, parc de l'Exposition, 2205 ave. du Colisée (694–7110), Sept.–May. During the summer you can watch harness racing at the Hippodrome de Quebec, also at the parc de l'Exposition, (524–5283).

BEACHES. While picnicking and sunbathing in the many parks along the St. Lawrence is ideal for scenery buffs, swimming in the river is not recommended. Try dipping in a cool Laurentian lake for a memorable experience. Lakes St. Joseph, Sergent, Sept-Îles and Beauport located 20–40 km. (12–24 mi) north and northwest of Quebec have public beaches (some with entrance fees), camping, walks, sailing, inns, and restaurants. Provincial parks have many excellent free swimming beaches.

CHILDREN'S ACTIVITIES. During the *Winter Carnival,* special children's theater, clown shows, and sports events take place at Place de La Famille in Le Vieux Port. For details call 626–3716. During the summer, at *Artillery Park,* 2 rue d'Auteuil, youngsters take part in military drills, dressing up in uniforms of the colonial French and British armies. For information on this as well as films on Canada's history and guided tours, call 691–4205. *Parc National Historique,* 100 rue St-André, has reproductions of 19th-century ships and buildings, and it is free.

HISTORIC SITES AND HOUSES. It would be hard to find another area on the continent that boasts more historic sites and houses than Quebec City and its neighboring suburbs. (The towns of Charlesbourg, Neuville, and Beauport have restored entire districts' 17th- and 18th-century homes.) Following are some of the major attractions.

Artillery Park. 2 rue d'Auteuil (691–4205). Part of the city's fortification system, the defense complex in the park includes 20 buildings ordered built after the fall of Louisbourg in 1745. First acting as headquarters for the French garrison, the buildings were taken over by the British in 1759. The garrison played an important role in the city's defense system during the American seige of Quebec in 1775–76. A cartridge factory on the site produced munitions for the Canadian army from 1880–1972 when restoration began. Visitors reception and interpretation center provides slide shows, guided tours. July, Aug. Daily except Monday, 10 A.M.–5 P.M. Free.

Battlefields Park. Between Grande Allée and Champlain Blvd. Also known as the Plains of Abraham, this 250-acre expanse of green on a cliff overlooking

QUEBEC CITY

the St. Lawrence is a national historic preserve. A free 20-minute guided bus tour (June-Sept.) with 13 stops includes an exhibition center with slide show explaining historic battles and three of the city's four Martello towers. Picnic areas, jogging, and bicycle paths. Free parking on Montcalm Ave. Open 24 hours. For group reservations and other information call 648-3506.

Cathedral of the Holy Trinity. 31 rue Desjardins (691-2193). The first Anglican cathedral built outside the British Isles.

Château Frontenac. Inaugurated in 1893 and completed in 1925 when a central tower was added, the grand CPR hotel was designed by American architect Bruce Price. Prime Minister Mackenzie King invited Sir Winston Churchill and Franklin Delano Roosevelt for two historic conferences in 1943-1944.

The Citadel. Battlefields Park. (694-3563). The bunker on Cap Diamant, called the "largest set of fortifications in North America still occupied by troops" (Canada's Royal 22nd Regiment), includes 25 buildings. The Musée militaire (regimental museum) in the complex has military exhibits from the 17th to 20th centuries. Museum tours are part of Citadel guided tours. Changing of the Guard, mid-June-Labor Day, daily at 10 A.M., weather permitting. Beating the Retreat, June 23-Labor Day, Tues., Thurs., Sat., Sun., 7 P.M., weather permitting. Cannon firings from Prince of Wales bastion daily at noon and 9:30 P.M. Adults $2.25, children $1.

Fortifications. 2 rue d'Auteuil (648-4206 or 7016) The history of Old Quebec's fortifications is recounted on guided tours leaving from the Poudrière de l'Esplanade (Esplanade Powder House). The 4.6 km (3 mi) walls are a National Historic Park. May-Sept., 10 A.M.-5 P.M. Free.

Gare du Palais. 450 rue St. Paul (524-6452). This splendid 19th-century train station was renovated and reopened recently by popular demand, after a decade of disuse. Future plans include an "Intermodal" station for buses and trains.

Hôtel du Parlement. (643-7239). The seat of Quebec's government, the National Assembly was designed in French Renaissance style by Eugene Étienne-Taché and built between 1877-86. Life-sized solid bronze statues of Quebec heroes stand at various points on the building's front wall, and Taché wrote "Je me souviens" ("I remember")—later to become a nationalist motto—above the front door. (The motto was a response to disparaging remarks about French-speaking Quebecers by Lord Durham, author of the famous Durham Report describing the life and administration of Upper and Lower Canada. Durham called them a "singularly ignorant peasantry," among other things.) Bilingual guided tours last 30 minutes. Sept.-June, weekdays 9 A.M.-9 P.M., weekends 9 A.M.-5 P.M. Free. Parking in lots near government buildings G and H.

Krieghoff House. 115 Grande-Allée Ouest. Cornelius Krieghoff, one of Canada's best-known landscape artists, settled in Quebec in 1852. The Amsterdam-born painter married a Quebecer and lived in this house for several years.

Martello Towers. Battlefields Park (648-3506). The British erected four Martello towers after the American War of Independence. Three of the four towers still stand. Exhibit at Martello Tower No. 2, corner of rue Taché and rue Laurier; daily, 10 A.M.-8 P.M., Wednesday, noon-8 P.M. Exhibition center on towers, Martello Tower No. 4, rue Lavigueur; daily, 11:30 A.M.-6 P.M. Wednesday, noon-6 P.M. Free.

Notre Dame Basilica. 16 rue Buade (692-2533). The original basilica was built in 1647, on the site of Champlain's original Notre Dame-de-la-Recouvrance church built in 1633 and destroyed by fire in 1640. Partially destroyed during seige of Quebec in 1750, it was rebuilt from 1768-71.

Montcalm Monument. Built jointly by France and Canada to commemorate Louis-Joseph Montcalm, commander of the troops in New France.

128 PROVINCE OF QUEBEC

Place-Royale. A multimillion dollar renovation project by the Quebec government, the original site of Champlain's settlement is now a group of restored 17th- and 18th-century buildings, called the "largest concentration" of houses from this period in North America. Some 2,000 years before Champlain's arrival, Amerindians lived on the site. Several houses are open to the public. Others are shops and restaurants. Among notable buildings are Notre-Dame-des-Victoires church, built in 1688, Maison Chevalier, and Îlot la Cetière—archaeological remains of Champlain's settlement. Visitors information center is at La Maison Soumandre, 29 rue Notre Dame (643–6631). Free.

St. Louis Gate. Corner of rue d'Auteuil and rue St. Louis. Originally built in 1693, the gate was demolished and rebuilt several times. Architecture is the same as the original.

Le Vieux-Port. 36½ rue St-Pierre (692–0043). Currently being restored by a $100-million federal government restoration project. Plans for the 72 acres of parkland on the site of Quebec's original port include a Museum of Civilization now under construction, a theater and several parks. Open to visitors. Group tours by reservation.

The Wolfe Monument. Wolfe Ave., just off Grande Allée Ouest. Erected on the spot where General James Wolfe died. His 4,500 British troops won the battle of the Plains of Abraham after having lost the Battle of Montmorency in the summer of 1759.

MUSEUMS AND GALLERIES. Quebec and its suburbs are a museum buff's paradise, with literally dozens of exhibits, with everything from historical to contemporary art galleries. What follows is only a sampling.

Centre d'Artisinat Amerindien et Inuit. 17 rue Desjardins (392–3056). Amerindian and Inuit art.

Christorama. 7450 blvd. Ste-Anne, Château-Richer. Route 138, Ste-Anne-de-Beaupré. A giant mural of Christ's life by artist Albert Gilles. Open daily, 8 A.M.–8 P.M. Free.

L'Empire de Madame Belley. 24 Côte de la Fabrique (692–4579). Madame Belley, a designer, clairvoyant, and eccentric, lived from 1905 to 1980 and made a name for herself by creating and wearing extravagant clothes. Her remarkable collection drew record-breaking crowds when shown at the Musée du Quebec in 1971. The exhibit is billed as the biggest private costume museum in Canada. Daily tours for groups with reservations in summer, Thurs.-Sun., 1–5 P.M. in winter. Adults $3, students and over 65, $2.50, children under 12 with adult, free.

Galerie du Musée. 24 blvd. Champlain (643–7975). Contemporary art featuring Quebec and foreign artists, in historic Amiot and Langlois houses. Mid April–Sept., daily, 11 A.M.–6 P.M. Sept.–mid April closed Mon., Tues. Open Wed., Sat., Sun., 11 A.M.–6 P.M. Thurs., Fri., 11 A.M.–9 P.M. Free.

Maison Chevalier. 60 Marche Champlain, Place Royale. Early Canadian furniture and art. Open year-round. Closed Mon. Free.

Musée de cire. 22 rue Ste-Anne (692–2289). Canadian and American historical figures. May 15-Labor Day, 9 A.M.-8:30 P.M.; winter, weekdays 10 A.M.–5 P.M. Adults $2, students, $1, children 75 cents, over 65, $1.50.

Musée du Fort. 10 rue Ste-Anne (692–2175). A sound and light show reenacting the Battle of the Plains of Abraham on a 450-square-foot model of 18th-century Quebec. Bilingual narration. Hours 10 A.M.–5 P.M. (Sun, opens at noon). Closed Dec. 1-20. Adults, $2.75; students, $1.50; children under 6 free.

Musée de l'Hôtel Dieu. 32 rue Charlevoix (692–2289). Monastery of Augustine nuns. Early colonial art and implements. Daily, 9–11 A.M., 2–5 P.M.

QUEBEC CITY

Musée du Quebec. Battlefields Park (643–4103, 643–2150). Built in 1933. Commemorates 300th anniversary of founding of Quebec. Permanent collections of sculpture, paintings, antique furniture and Quebec folk art, visiting collections of Canadian and foreign art. Daily, 9:15 A.M.–4:15 P.M. Wed. until 11 P.M. Guided tours arranged by reservation.

Musée du Séminaire de Quebec. 9 rue de l'Universite (692–2843). Permananent collections of Quebec, European, and Oriental art, scientific instruments, stamps, and currency. May 1–Oct. 31, daily 10 A.M.–4 P.M. Sunday, 10 A.M.–5 P.M. Nov. 1–April 30, daily 11:00 A.M.–4 P.M. Sundays, 11 A.M.–5 P.M. Closed Mon. Adults, $2; students and over 65, $1; family, $5. Children 12 and under free.

Musée des Ursulines. 12 rue Donnaconna (694–0694). Furniture and silverware from the 17th and 18th centuries. Centre Marie-de-L'Incarnation, near the museum, exhibits objects belonging to the founder of the convent and girls' school. Open all year, Tues.–Sat., 9:30 A.M.–noon, 1:30–5 P.M. Sun., noon–5:30 P.M. Closed Mon. Adults, $1; students, 50 cents; children, 25 cents.

Voûtes du Palais. 1033 rue des Prairies (694–6092 or 694–6285). Underground vaults. Information center. Tues.–Sun., 12:30–5 P.M. Guided tours, groups only. Free.

ARTS AND ENTERTAINMENT. Music, dance, and opera. *Le Grande Théâtre de Québec,* 269 blvd. St-Cyrille (643–8131) is Quebec's theatrical pièce de résistance. (See "Exploring Quebec" for more background.) It is the home of Canada's oldest symphony orchestra (the Quebec Symphony Orchestra). Leading artists perform in the Salle Louis-Fréchette. Other concert halls are *Bibliothèque Gabrielle-Roy,* 350 rue St-Joseph (some free concerts); *Colisée* (Coliseum), Parc de l'Exposition, 2205 ave du Colisée (694–7110); *l'Institut canadien* 37 rue Ste-Angèle (692–2135) (some free concerts); *le Palais Montcalm,* 995 place D'Youville (670–9011); *La Salle Albert Rousseau,* CÉGEP Ste-Foy, 2410 Chemin Ste-Foy (659–6710); *Théâtre de la Bordée,* 1091½ rue St-Jean (694–9631); and *Théâtre Le Petit Champlain,* 68 rue Petit Champlain (692–4398). Check papers for details.

Theater: *Grande Théâtre,* Salle Octave-Crémazie; *Salle Albert-Rousseau* and *Théâtre de la Bordée* (see above); *Théâtre de la Cité Universitaire,* Université Laval, Cité Universitaire, Ste-Foy (656–3333). **Summer theaters.** *Théâtre du Bois-de-Coulonge,* rue St-Louis, Sillery, (681–4679, 681–0088 in summer, 692–3041 off-season); *L'Anglicane,* 33 rue Wolfe, Levis (833–8831); *Théâtre La Fenière,* 1500 de la Fenière, Ancienne-Lorette (872–1424, summer, 651–3218 off-season); *Théâtre de l'Île,* 342 rue Galendor, St-Pierre, Île d'Orléans (878–3581); *Théâtre Paul-Hébert,* 1451 ave. Royale, Île d'Orléans (829–2202, summer, 523–2163, off-season); *Implanthéâtre,* 2 rue Crémazie, (529–2183). Remember, most but not all productions are in French.

Film. Repertory: *La Boîte à films,* 1044 3 ave. (524–3144), $3.50, $2 over 65 and under 14; *Cartier,* 1019 rue Cartier (525–9340), shows films in English; $3.50, $2 over 65 and under 14; *Clap,* 2360 Chemin Ste-Foy, (653–3750), $3.75, $2 over 50 and under 14. Films usually in French, sometimes with English subtitles.

ACCOMMODATIONS. Because tourism is a major industry here, Quebec City's large variety of hotels, motels, tourist homes, and inns offer a total of 8,000 rooms and at a broad range of prices. During high tourist seasons—May-Sept. and the Winter Carnival in February—reservations are advised. Prices listed here are for May-Oct. While rates in larger hotels and motels

PROVINCE OF QUEBEC

generally stay the same all year, smaller establishments often lower their rates $10–$20 from Nov.-April. During Winter Carnival, however, rates often go up as much as 30 percent above those listed here. Categories, based on double occupancy rates, are as follows: *Deluxe,* $140–$200; *Expensive* $100–$140; *Moderate,* $75–$100; *Inexpensive,* under $75. For a complete listing of accommodations in the Quebec City region, write to the Quebec City Region Tourism and Convention Bureau, 60 rue d'Auteuil, Quebec, PQ G1R 4C4 (692-2471).

Deluxe

Château Frontenac. 1 rue des Carrières, Quebec, PQ G1R 4P5 (418–692–3861). 527 rooms (some only expensive). One of oldest luxury hotels in Canada, parking, sauna, air-conditioning, antique furniture in public rooms, excellent restaurants.

Loews le Concorde. 1225 Place Montcalm, Quebec, PQ G1R 4W6 (418–647–2222 or 800–463–5256). 413 rooms, overlooking Battlefields Park, panoramic views of city and countryside, indoor and outdoor pools (indoor pool is in another building), sauna, restaurants including rotating l'Astral on 27th floor, room service. Interesting modern architecture.

Expensive

Auberge des Gouverneurs. 690 blvd. St-Cyrille, Quebec, PQ G1R 5A8 (418–647–1717 or 800–463–2820). 379 rooms, parking, sauna, dining room, coffee shop, outdoor pool.

Hilton International Quebec. 3 Place Quebec, Quebec, PQ G1K 7M9 (418–647–2411 or 800–361–7171). Next to the Parliament Buildings, just outside the walls. 564 rooms, some *deluxe,* free parking, indoor and outdoor pools, good restaurants.

Moderate

Auberge des Gouverneurs. 3030 blvd. Laurier, Ste-Foy, PQ G1V 2M5 (418–651–3030 or 800–463–2820). 318 rooms, moderate to expensive, free parking, air-conditioning, dining room, coffee shop, outdoor pool.

Auberge Quality Inn. 3115 blvd. Laurier, Ste-Foy, PQ G1W 1R8 (418–658–5120 or 800–228–5151). 204 rooms, some *expensive,* free parking, air-conditioning, dining room, outdoor pool, kitchenettes.

Auberge du Trésor. 20 rue Ste-Anne, Quebec, PQ G1R 3X2 (418–694–1876). 21 rooms, some *inexpensive,* parking, air-conditioning, downtown location.

Auberge Ramada Inn. 1200 rue de LaVigerie, Ste-Foy, Quebec, PQ G1W 3W5 (418–651–2440). 100 rooms, some *expensive,* free parking, air-conditioning, dining room, coffee shop, outdoor pool.

Auberge Universel Wandlyn. 2955 blvd. Laurier, Ste-Foy, PQ G1V 2M2 (418–653–8721). 140 rooms, air-conditioning, dining room, indoor pool.

Best Western Hotel Aristocrate. 3100 Chemin St-Louis, Ste-Foy, PQ G1W 1R8 (418–653–2841 or 800–528–1234). 97 rooms, free parking, air-conditioning, dining room, outdoor pool.

Château Bonne-Entente. 3400 Chemin Ste-Foy, Ste-Foy, Quebec, PQ G1X 1S6 (418–653–5221). 102 rooms, free parking, air-conditioning, outdoor pool.

Holiday Inn. 395 rue de la Couronne, Quebec, PQ G1K 7X4 (418–647–2611). 233 rooms, free parking, dining room, coffee shop, indoor pool.

Holiday Inn. 3225 rue Hochelaga, Ste-Foy, PQ G1V 4A8 (418–653–4901). 349 rooms, some *expensive,* free parking, air-conditioning, outdoor pool.

Hôtel Clarendon. 57 rue Ste-Anne, Quebec, PQ G1R 3X4 (418–692–2480). 93 rooms, moderate to expensive, downtown location, parking, excellent restaurant.

QUEBEC CITY

Maison Au Jardin du Gouverneur. 16 rue Mont-Carmel, Quebec, PQ G1R 4A3 (418–692–1704). 17 rooms, parking, air-conditioning.

Manoir des Remparts. 3½ rue des Remparts, Quebec, PQ G1R 3R4 (418–692–2056). 39 rooms, parking.

Inexpensive

Auberge du Boulevard Laurier. 3125 blvd. Laurier, Ste-Foy, Quebec, PQ G1W 3Z6 (418–653–7221). 93 rooms, some *moderate,* free parking, air-conditioning, outdoor pool.

Château de la Terasse. 6 Place Terrace Dufferin, Quebec, PQ G1R 4N5 (418–694–9472). 18 rooms, parking, kitchenettes, excellent view.

Château Grande Allée. 601 Grande Allée, Quebec, PQ G1R 2K4 (418–522–2007). 21 rooms, free parking, kitchenettes.

Hôtel Château Laurier. 695 Grande Allée, Quebec, PQ G1R 2K4 (418–522–8108 or 800–463–5256). 55 rooms, inexpensive to moderate, air-conditioning, central location.

Hôtel le Manoir d'Auteuil. 49 rue d'Auteuil, Quebec, PQ G1R 4C2 (418–694–1173). 17 rooms, some *moderate,* parking.

Hôtel Le St-Laurent. 3135 chemin St-Louis, Ste-Foy, PQ G1W 1R9 (418–653–4941 or 800–463–4752). Free parking, air-conditioning, outdoor pool.

Motel le Voyageur Laurentian. 2250 blvd. Ste-Anne, Quebec, PQ G1J 1Y2 (418–661–7701). 62 rooms, free parking, air-conditioning, outdoor pool.

BED AND BREAKFAST. For homes away from home at reasonable prices, contact one of the following: *Bed and Breakfast-Bonjour Quebec,* 395 blvd. Monaco, Quebec, PQ G1P 3J3 (418–527–1465); *Bed and Breakfast in Old Quebec,* contact François Begin, 300 rue Champlain, Quebec, PQ G1K 4J2 (418–525–9826, ext. 8711); *Gite Quebec,* 3729 ave. Le Corbusier, Ste-Foy, PQ G1W 4R8 (418–651–1860); *Hebergement Bed & Breakfast Quebec,* 72 rue Ste-Ursule, Suite 103, Quebec, PQ F1R 4E8 (418–692–2801). Rates average between $40–$50 per night for two people. For farmhouse bed and breakfast and family farm vacations, contact *Vacances-Familles/Agrigotours,* 1661 ave. du Parc, Ste-Foy, PQ G1W 3Z3 (418–658–0576).

YS AND HOSTELS. Quebec has one Y and several youth hostels. The *YWCA* at 855 ave. Holland, Quebec, PQ G1S 3S5 (418–656–2155) has rooms for men and women, Sept.-May.; women only, May-Sept. Prices are $30 for two people, $20 for one. Reasonable cafeteria meals: breakfast, 7–9 A.M., $2; dinner, 5–6:30 P.M., $3.25; weekend brunch, 9 A.M.-1 P.M., $3.25.

The city's largest hostel, *Centre international de séjour,* 19 rue Ste-Ursule, Quebec, PQ G1R 4E1 (418–694–0755) has 200 beds and charges International Youth Hostel members $10 per night, nonmembers $11.25, for bed, bedding, and breakfast. Open all year. Membership costs $18 per year.

Others in similar price range are *Auberge de la Paix,* 31 rue Couillard, Quebec, PQ G1R 3T4, near Château Frontenac, May-Oct., 50 beds (418–694–0735); *Auberge de la Haute-Ville,* 1190 Claire-Fontaine, Quebec, PQ G1R 3B3 (418–525–9233); and *La Belle Étoile,* 1100 de la Chevrotière, Quebec, PQ G1R 3J5 (418–525–5874).

PROVINCE OF QUEBEC

RESTAURANTS. The main problem with eating in Quebec is deciding where. True to the French culture, Quebecers consider fine cuisine a matter of honor. The city's 300 restaurants give it the distinction of having more eateries per capita than any other city in the country. You can find just about any kind of food to suit your palate—from Vietnamese to hamburger chain. But the specialties here are French and continental cuisine. Seafood is also favored and deliciously prepared. Try the thin, Breton-style pancakes filled with cheese, ham, or fruit at a *crêperie*. Or the *tourtière* (meat pie) Lac St.-Jean for a sampling of native cuisine. Inexpensive home-style fare can be found at one of the city's many *brasseries*—Quebec's version of the British pub.

The fashionable dinner hour here is around 8 P.M. To avoid disappointment it is best to reserve, especially on weekends and during high tourist seasons. Casual dress is generally acceptable, though jackets and ties are de rigueur in some of the more expensive spots. (Phone first to be sure, or go prepared.) A 12–15 percent tip is considered correct. Meals above $3.25 are taxed 9 percent.

Restaurants are listed according to the price of a complete dinner not including drinks, tax, and tip. *Super Deluxe,* $30 and up; *Deluxe,* $25–$30; *Expensive,* $20–$25; *Moderate,* $12–$20; *Inexpensive,* under $12. (Note: Many restaurants with expensive dinners offer affordable lunches. Menus are generally posted outside.) Unless otherwise noted, restaurants take some or all major credit cards.

Super Deluxe

Le Champlain. Château Frontenac, 1 rue des Carrières (692-3861). Waiters dressed in 16th-century attire, elegant décor, and a chamber orchestra combined with good food and a first-rate wine cellar guarantee a memorable eating experience. French cuisine. Lunch and dinner.

Clarendon Hotel. 57 rue Ste-Anne (692-2480). Provincial government hotel inspectors give the main dining room in this elegant vintage hotel a "four-fork" (top) rating. Continental cuisine. Breakfast, lunch, and dinner daily.

Le Croquembroche. Quebec Hilton. 3 Place Quebec (647-2411). Reputed to offer the city's best hotel cuisine. French. Lunch and dinner daily.

A la table de Serge Bruyère. 1200 rue St-Jean (694-0618). Food critics say this restaurant specializing in nouvelle cuisine is second to none in the city. Reservations essential. Dinner. AE.

Deluxe

L'Astral. Hôtel Loews le Concorde, 1225 Place Montcalm (747-2222). Definitely worth the trip for a stunning view of the city—especially under night lights—from the hotel's 27th floor. The revolving restaurant slowly turns as you dine so you do not miss anything. Piano bar. Continental, French cuisine. Excellent table d'hôte (full course) meal for $20.00. A la carte is deluxe. Lunch and dinner.

Café de la Paix. 44 rue Desjardins (692-1430). Elaborate French cuisine, seafood in an intimate Parisian atmosphere. Lunch *(expensive)* and dinner.

La Chaumière. 22 rue Couillard (692-2051). Fine French cuisine in an 18th-century house. Dinner, Tues.-Sat. only.

Le Marie Clarisse. 12 rue Petit-Champlain (692-0857). Seafood, nouvelle cuisine, warm atmosphere, excellent fare. Lunch (moderate–expensive) and dinner. AE.

QUEBEC CITY

Expensive

Chalet Suisse. 32 rue Ste-Anne (694–1320). Specializes in such Swiss standards as fondue and raclette, which the owners introduced to Quebec some 30 years ago. This 12-room complex in three beautifully renovated houses is best known as the favored hangout of politicians and journalists. April-Oct., lunch *(moderate)* and dinner daily. Nov.-March, dinner daily. No credit cards.

Le Deauville. 300 blvd. Laurier, Ste-Foy (658-3644). Friendly atmosphere, good steaks and seafood. Lunch and dinner.

Le Paris-Brest. 590 Grande Allée Est (529–2243). Top-rated continental cuisine. Lunch and dinner.

Chez Umberto. 770 rue de l'Alverne (527–4442). Good Italian food for connoisseurs. Intimate setting. Lunch *(moderate)* and dinner.

Moderate

Aux Anciens Canadiens. 34 rue St-Louis (692–1627 or 694–0253). Authentic Quebec dishes in La Maison Jacquet, one of the city's oldest houses, built in 1675 and later the home of prominent 19th-century novelist Philippe-Aubert de Gaspé—best known for his novel *Aux Anciens Canadiens*. Good full-course lunch available for $6; dinner is *moderate-expensive*. Reservations recommended.

Anse-aux-barques. 28 blvd. Champlain (692-4674). Excellent fresh seafood, grills, shipboard décor. Lunch and dinner.

Le Biarritz. 136 rue Ste-Anne (692–1430). Simple continental cuisine at good prices. Specializes in Basque dishes. Bohemian atmosphere. Lunch and dinner. MC.

Restaurant Café Buade. 31 rue Buade. (692–3909). Canadian and French cuisine. Breakfast, lunch, and dinner.

Restaurant d'Europe. 27 rue St-Angèle (692–3835). Excellent French and Italian cuisine. Lunch and dinner daily.

Restaurant Gambrinus. 25 rue du Fort (692–5144). Italian food and seafood specialties in a lovely dining room with carved wood and plants.

Chez Guido. 75 rue Ste-Anne (692–3856 or 692–3857). French and Italian cuisine. Lunch and dinner.

Wong's. 19 rue Buade (692–2409). Good quality Chinese food and attractive decor. Lunch and dinner.

Inexpensive

La Boîte a spaghetti. 22 côte de la Fabrique (692–4199). Exactly what the name promises and more, with several varieties to choose from. Higher priced dishes are especially tasty. Lunch and dinner.

Au Petit Coin Breton. 655 Grande Allée Est (525-6904). Breton-style pancakes. Open 10 A.M.–11 P.M.

NIGHTLIFE AND BARS. Quebec has plenty to offer in this department, whether it be throbbing discos or intimate *boites à chansons*—small nightclubs with singing or musical acts. The Grande Allée just outside the city gates is the action center, with its two-block strip of bars, outdoor cafes, and discotheques. The Old City tends to specialize more in piano bars and jazz clubs. Natives say much of the local population moves to the bars and discos of suburban Ste-Foy in winter. Cover charges are not the rule in night spots here. (The price of your drinks generally covers entertainment.) For specific shows, consult the two daily newspapers, *Le Soleil* or *Le Journal de Quebec*.

PROVINCE OF QUEBEC

Discos. *Disco le Cabaret,* Hôtel Loews le Concorde, 1225 Place Montcalm (647-2222) is the "in" dance scene. You cannot get near it on a Saturday night unless you arrive sometime before 9. Wear a jacket and tie (natty dressers come here to see and be seen). Also in the chic and trendy category is *Disco l'Eden,* Quebec Hilton, 3 Place Quebec (647-2411). Others are: *Le Beaugarte,* 2590 blvd. Laurier, Ste-Foy (651-5000); *Chez Dagobert* (disco-rock), 600 Grande Allée Est (522-0393); *Chez Rasputine* (waiters dressed as monks), 2960 blvd. Laurier, Ste-Foy (659-4318); and *Disco-bar Vendredi 13* (Friday the 13th), 1018 rue St-Jean (694-0611).

Ballroom and folk dancing. *Soirée de Danse Moderne et Canadienne,* 155 blvd. Charest Est (647-5858). Sat., 8 P.M., orchestra. Admission $3.

Jazz. Tops in this category is the *Hôtel Clarendon's* elegant *bar l'Emprise* 57 rue Ste-Anne (692-2480), where the art deco is genuine. Quality performers make early arrival a must on weekends. Others are *Bar le Jazzé,* 19 rue St-Pierre, Place Royale (694-1244); *Bar Élite,* 54 rue Couillard (692-1204); *L'Air du temps,* 191 St. Paul ouest, (842-2003).

Bars. *Bar La Bourgeoise L.M. Inc.* 5930 ave. Charlesbourg (623-4996). Orchestra on weekends; *Bar LaGrande* 1114 Cartier (529-9767). Piano bar daily; *Bar-Spectacles Ainsi-Soit-Il,* 1135 Cartier (522-5370); *Saint-Charles Bar Spectacles.* 545 1 ave. (647-1777). Progressive rock shows Thurs.-Sun.

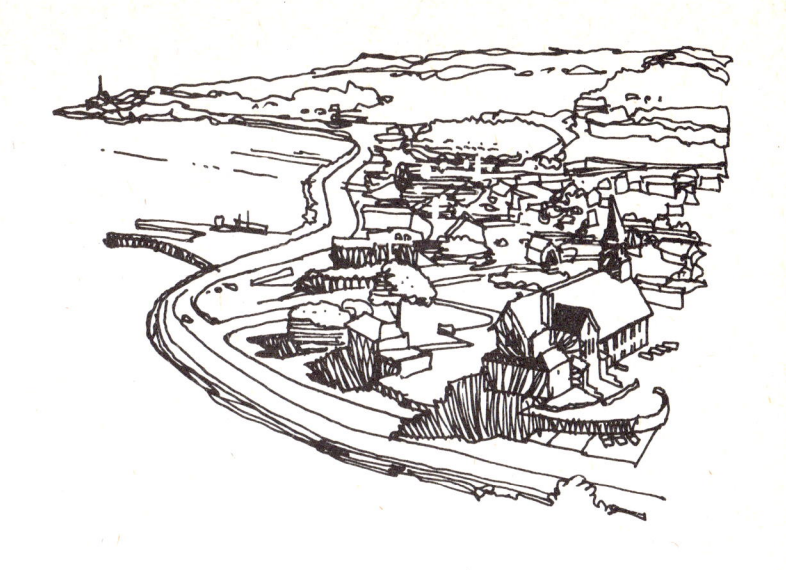

CHARLEVOIX

by
Pauline Guetta

Charlevoix stretches along the St. Lawrence River's north shore east of Quebec City from Ste-Anne-de-Beaupré to the Saguenay River. Millions of years ago, ice ages that affected all eastern Canada molded Charlevoix's hills, sculpted rocky cliffs (at Les Palissades), and left glacial deposits (near Clermont, at Lac-Nairn). An ice age that missed a large segment of Charlevoix, left vestiges of plant life from preglacial times, including rare natural bonsai (dwarf) trees. Some 350 million years ago a meteorite's impact marked an entire valley with concentric circles like a pebble dropped in a pond, and raised Mont des Eboulements.

The name Charlevoix (pronounced, approximately, "Shar-le-vwah") comes from New France's first historian, a Jesuit father. Explorer Jacques Cartier landed in 1535. The first colonists arrived from France during the 17th century. They built up a thriving shipbuilding industry which lasted until fairly recently, specializing in the schooners *(go-*

élettes) that hauled everything from logs to lobsters up and down the coast in the days before trailer trucks. You will see abandoned goélettes on many beaches.

Today, you will find Charlevoix a land of long, rolling mountains rising from the sea; a succession of valleys, plateaus, and cliffs, cut by waterfalls, brooks, and streams. The roads wind into villages of picturesque old houses and huge tin-roofed churches. Farming, fishing, logging, and tourism form the region's main industries.

The region starts 33 kilometers (20 miles) east of Quebec City, at Ste-Anne-de-Beaupré. Each year over a million pilgrims come to the region's most famous religious site, Ste-Anne de Beaupré Basilica, dedicated to Quebec's patron saint, the Virgin Mary's mother. (See *Quebec City* chapter.) Outside the nearby town of Beaupré, you can visit the park and waterfall at "Grand canyon des chutes Sainte-Anne."

Only eight kilometers (five miles) further on, in October and May you will find a multigaggle of 100,000 greater snow geese at the Cap Tourmente wildlife preserve and nature interpretation center. In May ducks, herons, swallows, and red-winged blackbirds nest in the many ponds. (See *Quebec City* chapter). Other parts of the region offer whale-watching cruises. You can sometimes spot seals, whales, and dolphins from ferries and on land. Bring those binoculars!

Active hikers, cyclists, joggers, campers, skiers of all types, and snowshoers, as well as walkers and painters, all enjoy the region's three main ski areas. They include Parc du Mont-Ste-Anne, on the World Cup downhill ski circuit; Mont Grand Fonds, with a vertical drop of 335 meters (1,000 feet), 13 slopes, and 135 kilometers (84 miles) of cross-country trails; and three-peaked Le Massif, including the province's highest vertical drop (800 meters, 500 feet). Here, you bus 30 minutes to the top, and a guide leads you down through powder snow.

Baie-St-Paul, Charlevoix's earliest settlement (1628) after Beaupré, proves popular with hang gliders and artists. You will find artists and artisans working in old *habitant* houses. (Habitants were early settlers —farmers—of French origin.) Here, the high hills circle a wide plain holding the village beside the sea. Many of Quebec's greatest landscape artists portray the area, as you will see at the art center, June to September. At town-center you will find Maison Otis, a stone house built in 1858, housing what many describe as the area's finest inn/ restaurant.

At Baie-St-Paul, choose between the open, scenic coastal drive (Route 362) or the faster (and also lovely) Route 138 to Pointe-au-Pic, La Malbaie, and Cap-à-l'Aigle. This section of Route 362 provides memorable views of rolling hills—green, white, or ablaze with fiery tones, depending on the season—meeting the broad expanse of the "sea," as people call the St. Lawrence estuary.

A secondary road leads sharply down into St-Joseph-de-la-Rive, with its line of old houses hugging the mountain base on the narrow shore road. Here, you discover peaceful inns and restaurants, like l'Auberge Sous les Pins ("under the pines"). Nearby Papeterie St-Gilles

CHARLEVOIX

produces unusual handcrafted stationery, using a 17th-century process. A small museum commemorates the days of the St-Lawrence goélettes.

You take the ferry from St. Joseph to Île aux Coudres, the island where Jacques Cartier's men gathered hazel nuts *(les coudres)* in 1535. Since then, the island produced many a goélette, and former captains now run several small inns. Larger inns feature folk-dancing evenings. Many visitors like to cycle the 16-kilometer (10-mile) circuit around the island, visiting inns, a windmill, an old schooner, and boutiques selling paintings and local handicrafts like household linens.

Returning to the mainland, you will discover more small villages, each with a unique point of interest linked to its past. Les Eboulements, for instance, is named after a rock slide following a massive quake back in 1663. Cap-aux-Oies forms a stopover point for migrating geese. Ste-Irénée holds a summer music, dance, and arts colony, which gives exhibitions, concerts, and musical Sunday brunches *sur la terrace.*

Continuing on Route 362, you will come to one of the most elegant and historically interesting resorts in all Quebec. La Malbaie was known as Murray Bay in an earlier era when wealthy Anglophones summered there and in the neighboring villages of Pointe-au-Pic and Cap-à-l'Aigle.

The regional museum—Musée Laure-Conan—traces its history as a vacation spot in a series of exhibits and is developing an excellent collection of local paintings and folk art.

Once called "the summer White House," this area became popular with both American and Canadian politicians in the late 1800s. Ottawa Liberals and Washington Republicans often partied decorously through the summer with members of the Quebec judiciary.

American civil governor of the Philippines William Howard Taft built the first of three summer residences in Pointe-au-Pic in 1894. He became the 27th United States president in 1908, then Chief Justice in 1921. Local residents still fondly remember the Tafts, and the parties they threw in their elegant summer homes. Interestingly, local people refer to Americans, like all English-speaking people, as "Les Anglais."

Now many Taft-era homes serve handsomely as inns and hotels, guaranteeing you an old-fashioned coddling with extras like breakfast in bed, whirlpool baths, gourmet meals, and free rides to the ski centers in winter. Many serve lunch and dinner to nonresidents, so you can tour the area going from one gourmet's delight to the next. The cuisine, as elsewhere in Quebec, is genuine French, rather than a hybrid invented for North Americans.

The road, the views, and the villages continue all the way up to Baie-Ste-Catherine, at the mouth of the Saguenay fjord. Pretty Port-au-Persil harbors a small, inexpensive inn of the same name, founded by the Taft's former head cook.

Perhaps you will continue on to Tadoussac, at the mouth of the Saguenay (see section on the Saguenay region), or take the ferry over the Lower St. Lawrence *(Bas St-Laurent).* With any luck you might see

PROVINCE OF QUEBEC

whales and seals, and you are sure to see many sea birds on the 90-minute crossing.

PRACTICAL INFORMATION FOR CHARLEVOIX

WHEN TO GO. Although Charlevoix is a year-round tourist area, with most ski slopes open from mid-November to May, and many inns and hotels open all year, you will find three main seasons best for traveling and visiting: winter, from Christmas to mid-April; summer, from mid-June to Labor Day; and fall, September and October. July and August daytime temperatures can rise to 85°F, dropping after sunset so that you need a sweater or light blazer for evening wear. After Labor day, many inns, museums, and galleries close, the water is usually too chilly for swimming, and most whales head for other climes . . . but the blazing colors of autumn maple trees make fall one of best times to visit Charlevoix.

HOW TO GET THERE. By Plane. You can fly to Quebec City and then travel to Charlevoix by bus or car (La Malbaie is about a two-hour drive). From Quebec City, *Les Ailes de Charlevoix,* 400 Chemin Ste-Madeleine, St-Irénée, PQ (418–439–3927) flies to Charlevoix Airport in St. Irénée three times a week.

By Bus. *Voyageur* serves all towns along Highway 138 with fast, reliable service in all weather, with a minimum of three buses daily.

By Ferry. Green and white signs marked *"Traversier"* depict a ferry boat steaming away from dock. The free, 15-min. ferry from St. Joseph-de-la-Rive to Île aux Coudres runs hourly in summer and three-four times a day in winter. (Information: 438–2743). The 75-min. ferry from St-Simeon to Rivière-du-Loup runs from early Apr. to the end of Dec. Cars, over $15; adults, about $7; less for children and seniors. Information: St-Siméon, 418–638–2856; Rivière-du-Loup, 418–862–5094; management, 418–862–9545. The 15-min. ferry from Baie-Ste-Catherine to Tadoussac departs regularly all day long, year-round. Information, 418–235–4395.

By Car. As it leads east, the Trans-Canada Highway 401 becomes Autoroute 40 at Montreal, and 138 after Trois-Rivières. Route 20, along the south shore, is faster. At Quebec City, cross to the north shore to take 138 east *(est)*. From Baie-St-Paul, you can reach La Malbaie (Murray Bay) either through the forest on 138, or along the scenic coastal Route 362, which merges with 138 in La Malbaie.

TOURIST INFORMATION. Before leaving, write for copious information, including an 80-page illustrated tour guide: *Association Touristique de Charlevoix,* CP 417, La Malbaie, PQ G0T 1J0. Or, contact *Tourisme Quebec* (see *Facts at Your Fingertips*). All year, you can call or visit the regional tourist office at 136 blvd. de Comporté, La Malbaie, PQ G0T 1J0 (418–665–4454). Mon–Fri., 8.30 A.M.–noon, 1 P.M.–4.30 P.M. In addition, you will find tourist information kiosks (look for the big question mark signs on maps and roads), open from 9 A.M.–9 P.M. from mid-June to Labor Day at: Ste-Anne-de-

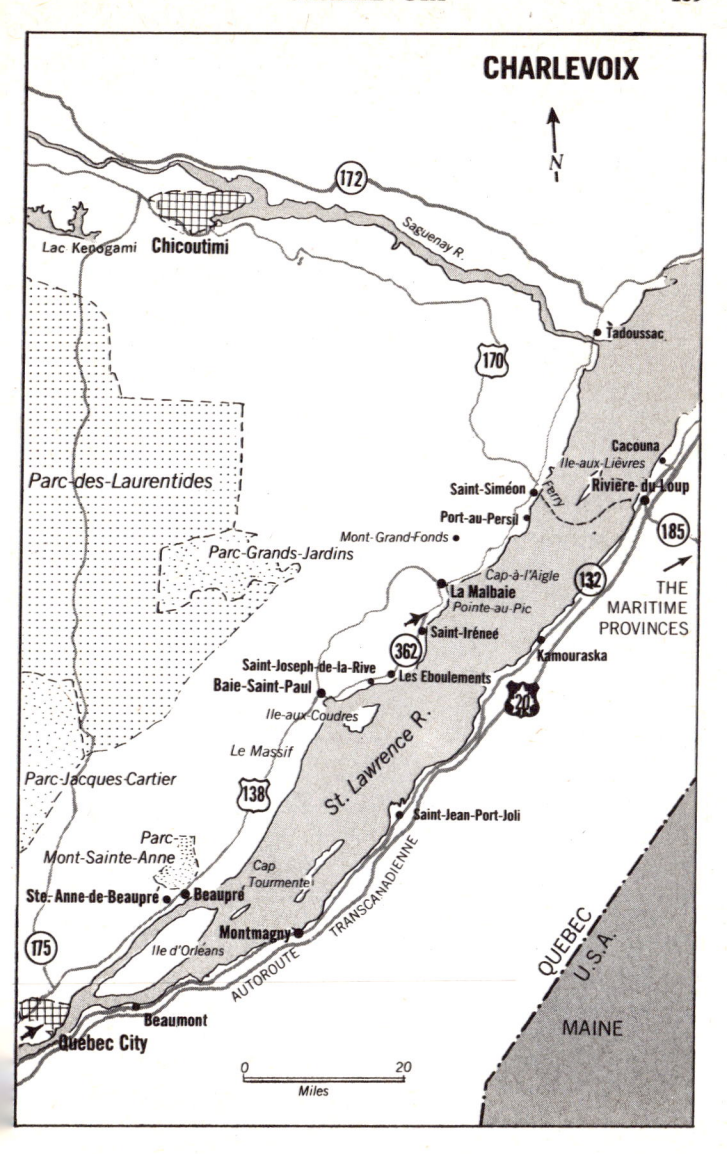

CHARLEVOIX

PROVINCE OF QUEBEC

Beaupré, Route 138; Baie-St-Paul, Route 138 and Centre d'Art; Île aux Coudres, St-Bernard-sur-Mer; La Malbaie, Route 138 (665–3162); Pointe-au-Pic, Manoir Richelieu; St-Siméon, Route 138; Baie Ste-Catherine, and Route 138. The information clerk can help you reserve lodgings.

TELEPHONES. The area code for Charlevoix is 418. Local phone calls cost 25 cents, with no time limit. In Charlevoix dial 411 for information; from elsewhere, dial 418–555–1212. To dial long-distance from Charlevoix, dial 1 before the area code. Dial 0 before the area code for operator assistance on credit card and long-distance calls.

EMERGENCY TELEPHONE NUMBERS. Police Provincial *(Sûreté du Quebec*—SQ) and Municipal—M: Ste-Anne-de-Beaupré, M: 872–3212; SQ: 827–4545; Baie-St-Paul, M: 435–2857; SQ: 435–2012; La Malbaie, M: 665–2515; SQ: 665–6473; Clermont, M: 439–3355.

Ambulance Services. Ste-Anne-de-Beaupré, 827–4514. Baie-St-Paul, 435–2303. Île aux Coudres, 438–2393. Clermont, 439–2828. La Malbaie, 665–3774. Other localities, 800–463–4742.

Health Services. Centre hospitalier de Charlevoix, 74, blvd. Fafard, Baie-St-Paul, 435–5150. Centre hospitalier St-Joseph, 303 rue St-Etienne, LaMalbaie, 665–3711. Clinique médicale, 347 rue St-Laurent, St-Siméon, 638–2404. Santé communautaire, Île aux Coudres, 10 rue Royale Ouest, St-Bernard-sur-Mer, 438–2788. Clinique médicale régionale, 10103 ave. Royale, Ste-Anne-de-Beaupré 827–4511.

Poison Center. Centre hospitalier de l'Université Laval, Quebec City, 656–8090. **Sea Rescue.** Sea rescue services, all localities, 800–463–4393.

HOW TO GET AROUND. Your first choice, especially in summer, should be to rent a car or bring your own. *Voyageur* buses serve the region all year round. Main *car rentals* in the area include: *Avis Rent-a-Car,* 800–268–2310; *Budget-Rent-a-Car,* 800–268–8900, and, for a local bargain, *Tilden,* 800–361–5334. (These are Canadian toll-free numbers.)

From the Airport. You will probably find several taxis waiting at Charlevoix airport, or pick up the special phone for a direct line to the dispatcher. When reserving at your inn or hotel, ask for a taxi to meet you. *Budget* rents cars at the airport. Call their La Galbaie office: 418–665–3333.

HINTS TO MOTORISTS. Route 138 is kept very well cleared of snow in winter. Route 362 may have some snow and ice, but is usually passable with care—and the drive is spectacular. For winter driving hints and list of speed limits, see *Facts at Your Fingertips.* Parking is free in most areas. You can reach *AAA* and *CAA* (653–2602) Mon.–Fri., 9 A.M.–5 P.M. Members of AAA/CAA can call 800–336–HELP for the names of recommended garages.

HINTS TO HANDICAPPED TRAVELERS. The region's "Tourist Guide," available through the tourism offices, marks all sites accessible for partially and fully handicapped people. The area in and around Ste-Anne-de-Beaupré is particularly geared to handicapped people. You will find special

CHARLEVOIX

ramps and other facilities. Volunteer aides—*Aides de Ste-Anne*—wearing dark shirts and arm bands, help people move from one place to another. Information kiosks give full details. *Autobus Charlevoix,* in Ste-Agnés, near La Malbaie, (439-3372), has minibuses for handicapped people. Contact them through the regional tourist office.

SEASONAL EVENTS. February. La Clermontaine, Winter Carnival, tournaments and games, fancy skating exhibitions, and dances. First two weeks of February at the Clermont Arena (439-3773). **March.** *Les Frolics du mont Grand Fonds.* Ski competition, outdoor meals, and activities. Two days in late March, at Mont Grand Fonds in La Malbaie (452-4405). **May.** *Festival du capelan.* Capelin-fishing festival. Contests and social activities, early in May for seven days, at St-Irénée (435-3250). *Le Tour de la baie.* An official 21-km (13 mi.) marathon (435-6237).

June. *Festival d'été.* Summer art festival, with folksingers, actors, street musicians, and activities. Two days, at Petite-Rivière-St-François (632-5964). Golf tournament at Murray Bay Golf Club, La Malbaie (665-4454). *Festival du papier.* Paper festival, in Clermont, the pulp and paper manufacturing center (439-2090). *Festival des moustiques.* Various cultural and social activities in Notre-Dame-des-Monts (439-3382/2840).

July. *Festival Champenois.* Cultural, social, and sports activities in St-Fidèle (434-2486). *Smelt festival* (Festival de l'éperlan). Fishing competitions, social activities for eight days in St-Siméon (638-2465/2242). *Canoe races.* Racing down Rivière du Gouffre, from Route 138 bridge to Leclerc Highway bridge in Baie-St-Paul (435-6237). *Festival du Béluga.* Shows, parade, sports, and social activities for three days. Baie-Ste-Catherine (237-4242).

August. *Festival hippique.* Provincial horse-racing competitions and social activities. Parc du Gouffre in Baie-St-Paul (635-2259). Early August, fancy dress balls for children and adults, theater, Manoir Richelieu, Pointe-au-Pic (665-4411). *Golf tournament.* Omnium de Charlevoix, two days, at Manoir Richelieu in Pointe-au-Pic, (665-3047).

TOURS AND SPECIAL-INTEREST SIGHTSEEING. Sightseeing-bus companies offer tours of the area's main points of interest for groups only. Please book through the regional tourist office at least seven days ahead. *L.G. Dufour,* La Malbaie (665-3967); *Richard Audet,* St-Irénée (452-3261 or 439-3987); *Louis-Marie Gagnon,* Île aux Coudres (438-2834); *Autobus Ménard,* Baie-St-Paul (435-2303).

By plane. You can rent a plane (with pilot) from Les Ailes de Charlevoix. Call 439-3927/3429.

Calèches. Rent a horse and carriage from Ranch la Balade, La Malbaie (439-3430) or Pointe-au-Pic (665-3703); Centre équestran (Equestrian Center) Louise Dubois et François Desjardins, St-Hilarion (457-3224).

Whale-watching Cruises. While you can sometimes see whales from the shore or the St-Simeon ferry, special cruises are the best way to spot the world's largest mammals. Some 10 different whale species come to the St. Lawrence estuary, ranging from white belugas that stay year-round to 140-ton blue whales who arrive late in July. Marine biologists from Montreal's *Zoological Society* accompany four popular weekend trips from Montreal, one each in July, Sept., two in Aug., with two overnights at Tadoussac. Contact Zoological Society at 2055 Peel, Montreal, PQ H3A 1V4 (514-845-8317, between 10 A.M. and noon). From Baie-Ste-Catherine, the *Société Linéene St-Laurent,* 1675 du Parc (Québec

Aquarium), Ste-Foy, PQ G1W 4S3 (418–653–8186) sets out whale watching from July 28 to Oct. 8. You'll find a private company, *Croisières Navimex Canada, Inc.,* at 126 rue St-Pierre, Quebec City, PQ G1K 4A7 (418–692–4643). Three-to six-hour cruises leave from Baie-Ste-Catherine, (418–237–4274) and cost about $35–$60 for adults, half that for children.

Film site. In summer, visit the film sites for the French CBC-TV series, *Le Temps d'une Paix* ("a peaceful time"), the story of Charlevoix in bygone days. Accessible from routes 362 and 138, buildings stand in six spots on the cape from Baie-St-Paul to La Malbaie. You can drive by the old houses, working sheepfolds and farm buildings, an old sawmill, a church, train station and smithy. There are free visits to the smithy near Les Eboulements (route 362 and Rang Ste-Catherine). Each person pays $1 to tour the working water-powered sawmill, at 444 rang St-Joseph, St-Irénée (452–3367), where you may obtain a map showing the sites.

PARKS (including parks, nature reserves, educational centers, and outdoor recreation centers). **Centre écologique de Port-au-Saumon.** Route 138, St-Fidèle, PQ G0T 1T0 (434–2209). Hike the nature trails, swim in the river, skate, snowshoe, cross-country ski. Snack bar.

Centre éducatif forestier Les Palissades. Route 170, St-Siméon, PQ G0T 1X0 (638–2442 or 665–3721 in winter). Forest education center. About 13 km (8 mi) inland from St-Siméon. A network of hiking trails from two to nearly five km long, across cliffs rising to 300-m (984-ft), through the forest and alongside a lake. No camping, but picnic and parking areas. June–Oct., 9 A.M.–5 P.M. Free.

Centre de plein air La Tourmente. On Route 138, west of St-Tite-des-Caps, at 101 rue de la Montagne, St-Tite-des-Caps, P.Q. G0A 4J0 (823–2424). In summer obstacle courses, nature interpretation center (see *Quebec City* chapter for details on snow geese who come here), hiking, archery, swimming, picnic area, fishing. In winter skating, snowshoeing and cross-country skiing. Overnight accommodation, camping, and snack bar.

Parc des Grands-Jardins. via St-Urbain, Route 381 (846–2218, 622–4444 or 800–462–5349). An immense nature preserve where you will find the taiga—flora and fauna typical of Quebec's far north, including typical Arctic vegetation and caribou. Take the 2.5-km (1.6-mi) ecological trail to the top of Swan Lake Mountain (Mont-du-Lac-des-Cygnes). In summer canoeing, rock climbing, hiking, picnic area, fishing. In winter snowshoeing and cross-country skiing. Camping and cottage facilities available.

Parc du Mont-Ste-Anne. CP 400, Beaupré, P.Q. G0A 1E0 (827–4561). Accessible from routes 40, 138, and 360. A vast year-round vacation area. Extensive downhill facilities of all kinds, since Ste-Anne's forms part of the World Cup circuit. You can also ski cross-country, snowshoe, camp, golf, cycle, hike, and jog. Cottages for extended visits. See also "Participant Sports."

Reserve nationale de faune du Cap-Tourmente. St-Joachim, P.Q. G0A 3X0 (827–3776). Accessible from Route 138. You can follow the nature trails and hike, but this park's main attraction is the hundreds of greater snow geese who arrive here each fall.

CHARLEVOIX 143

CAMPING. Charlevoix has two provincial and over a dozen private campgrounds, all with flush toilets. Write to the regional tourist office for further information. Two private camps belong to the Quebec Camping Grounds Association. **Le Genevrier**, near Baie-St-Paul (435–6520), off Route 138, offers 256 campsites, and charges about $12 daily. **Camp des Chutes Fraser**, at Rivière Malbaie, (665–2151), off Route 138, has 102 sites available, and charges about $11 daily. The two government campgrounds are **Lac Arthabasca**, at Parc des Grands-Jardins, (848–2422), off Route 381, with 24 sites, which charges about $8 a night (no hookups for water or electricity, no showers), and **Parc du Mont-Ste-Anne**, at Beaupré, (826–2323), off Route 360, with 166 sites, and 110 hookups each for electricity and water.

HUNTING AND FISHING. Since time immemorial people have hunted large and small game, and found exciting fishing in this region. Today you can fish for speckled trout, red trout, salmon, capelin, and smelt. Provided you hold a license, you can hunt black bear, moose, hare, partridge, ducks, and geese. You will find a wide choice of outfitters, offering all or some of the following: small-game hunting, fishing, trapping, and accommodations. You can also fish in ponds and pools on about nine Charlevoix farms. Seven of them welcome you year-round, with ice fishing in winter, and all charge by the pound for the fish you catch. You can phone ahead for this type of fishing, otherwise, do reserve well in advance for fishing and hunting. See *Facts at Your Fingertips* for more information on hunting and fishing regulations.

Salmon fishing. Fish for Atlantic salmon in beautiful surroundings at Rivière du Gouffre, between Baie-St-Paul and Notre-Dame-des-Monts, only an hour's drive from Quebec City. Write: Association de conservation de la Vallée du Gouffre, 929 rue St-Edouard Sud, St-Urbain, PQ G0A 4K0 (639–2907). Reception center at the junction of routes 138 and 381. Accommodations available in private homes. June 24–Aug. 31, 6 A.M.–9 P.M. It costs about $10 a day to fish sections of the river with unlimited numbers of fellow anglers and about $25 to fish sections limited to six anglers.

SKIING. Powder snow, deep and fluffy, never fails the area, which annually receives over 200 inches from mid-Nov. clear into Apr. With mechanical snowmakers, the season extends to May. All areas offer special packages that include skiing and accommodations.

You will find three main downhill and three cross-country ski areas in Charlevoix, although many people clip on their cross-country skis all around Île aux Coudres and in the region's many pastures.

Le Massif. Route 138 (435–3593), rises vertically higher than any other mountain in Quebec, 762 m (2,500 ft), making the longest run 4,487 m (14,720 ft). With ten slopes, 400 to 600 cm (averaging around 225 in) of powder snow each year, and no lifts, it is a skiers' paradise, but not for novices. A 30-min. bus takes you to the top. Slopes are not groomed, and a guide must accompany you the 30-odd minutes down, for Alpine or Télémark skiing. Two trails turn through the woods, ending within 100 ft of the St. Lawrence River at Petite-Rivière-St-François. For four bus rides, the guide, and lunch, you pay about $32. For cross-country skiing and snowshoeing, Le Massif offers 35 km (21.7 mi) of trails ranging from easy to "quite difficult." Facilities include a snack bar, equipment rentals, and a waxing room.

PROVINCE OF QUEBEC

Mont Grand-Fonds. 1000 Chemin des Loisirs, La Malbaie (665-4405), rises 335 m (1,200 ft) behind La Malbaie. Three lifts give you a choice of 13 slopes, the longest running 2,353 m (7,710 ft). Pick wooded trails or moguled runs down to the log buildings that form the base lodge. Snowshoeing and cross-country ski facilities include 135 km (83.7 mi) of trails; heated relay stations, restaurant, baby-sitting, a snack bar, equipment rentals, and a waxing room.

Parc du Mont-Ste-Anne. See *Quebec City*.

SUMMER SPORTS. Boating and Sailing. Several marinas offer space for visiting craft. The largest is Port de refuge de Cap-à-l'Aigle, 10 Route du Quai (665-3698) with a dock depth of 4.5 m (15 ft). Facilities include a watchman's services, a repair shop, gas, diesel, electricity, drinking water, toilets, showers, food supplies, ice, and a snack bar. You will find other marinas at St-Siméon, Beaupré, Baie-Ste-Catherine, St-Joseph-de-la-Rive; Baie-St-Paul and St-Bernard-sur-Mer.

Golf. Four golf courses welcome all visitors at anytime. You can rent clubs and electric carts at each, and dine on site. Putting greens at each. *Golf du Parc du Mont-Ste-Anne (MLCP),* Route 360, Beaupré (827-4561). One 18-hole course, 6,139 m (20,136 ft). Par 72. *Golf municipal de Baie-St-Paul,* 40 Route de l'Equerre, Baie-St-Paul. 435-2117. Nine holes; 2,792 m. (9,160 ft). Par 36. *Murray Bay Golf Club,* 1013 rue St-Etienne, La Malbaie (665-2494). One nine-hole, par 35. One 18-hole course, 5,166 m (17,000 ft). Par 68. Putting green, practice range. *Club de golf du Manoir Richelieu,* 19 rang, Terrebonne, Pointe-au-Pic (665-3703). One 18-hole, 5,587 m (18,325 ft). Par 70.

Riding. You can ride horses at three main centers. *Ranch Jean-Baptiste Martel,* 2123 ave. Royale, St-Ferréol-les-Neiges, (826-2520). Summer and winter riding, sleigh rides, and tours lasting more than one day. *Ranch Le Cavalier,* 1337 blvd. Monseigneur de Laval, Baie-St-Paul (435-3253). Summer riding. Sleigh rides. *Ranch Le Corral,* 126 rang Terrebonne, CP 553, Pointe-au-Pic (665-6835). Summer riding, tours lasting more than one day.

Swimming. Local people call the St. Lawrence River *"la mer"* ("the sea") not just because of its size, but because the water's salty here in the estuary. You will find cool bathing on sandy beaches in many spots, including St-Joseph-de-la-Rive, Cap-aux-Ouies (Les Eboulements), St-Irénée, Baie-St-Paul (rue Ste-Anne), and St-Siméon, and you can swim in lakes and rivers in public parks.

MUSEUMS AND SPECIAL BUILDINGS. Centre d'Initiation à l'Histoire des Goélettes du Saint-Laurent Inc., 116 Chemin des Coudriers, La Baleine, Île aux Coudres, PQ G0A 2A0 (438-2734). Theme exhibit on schooners features "The master carpenter, a craftsman." Slide show, guided tour of schooner. Mid-May–mid-June, daily, 9 A.M.–7 P.M., mid-June - early Sept., 9 A.M. - 7 P.M.; early Sept. - mid-Oct., Sat., Sun. 9 A.M. - 7 P.M. Adults, $2; seniors, $2; children, 50 cents. The schooner has no facilities for handicapped people.

Domaine Forget. 398 Chemin les Bains, St-Irénée, PQ G0T 1V0 (452-3233). The Forget's former summer estate perches high above the river. A nonprofit summer arts center, the Domaine presents summer concerts plus musical brunches Sun. on the terrace. Expositions of paintings, tapestries, and drawings, June 24 - Labor Day, noon - 6 P.M. Guided tours. Free.

Exposition Maritime. St-Joseph-de-la-Rive, PQ G0A 3Y0 (635-2803). Maritime museum in the old shipyard shows navigation equipment, radar, telegraph, and other instruments. Photographs show construction of a schooner. Slide

CHARLEVOIX

show of life on board. June–Sept., daily, 11 A.M. - 6 P.M. Off season, groups only, by reservation. Adults, $1; children, 50 cents. Buses, 75 cents per person.

Maison Leclerc. 114 rue Principale, La Baleine, Île aux Coudres, PQ G0A 2A0 (438–2217). Local antiques shown in one of island's earliest houses (1750). Summer, 11 A.M. - dusk. Adults, $1; groups, 75 cents per person.

Manoir de Sales-Laterrière. 159 rue Principale, Les Eboulements, PQ G0A 2M0 (635–2666). Owned by Brothers of the Sacred Heart, the manor house, communal mill and outbuildings, demonstrate daily life in the seignorial system. Free tours of mill (1790) above waterfall. All are welcome, but groups must make reservations.

Mills. The area includes many old mills—carding mills, sawmills, and flour mills *(moulins),* including Moulins Desgagnés, Chemin du Moulin, St-Louis-de-l'Île aux Coudres (438–2231), on Île aux Coudres. The two mills date from the early 1900s. The conical roof on the stone-towered windmill turns to set the sails windward. The Desgagnés watermill works with a lock system supplying the paddle wheel. Restored, they both hold handicrafts and models. Mid-June-early Sept. 9:30 A.M. - 6 P.M. Adults, $2; children, 50 cents.

Musée du patrimoine (heritage museum). 67 rang St-Laurent, Baie-St-Paul, PQ G0A 1B0 (435–5336). Charlevoix's oldest (1721) wooden house. The walls are built from squared logs dovetailed together on a stone foundation. Antique exhibit. Reserve for tour, $1.

Musée du Phonographe à cylindres (cylinder phonograph museum). 9812 ave. Royale, Ste-Anne-de-Beaupré (827–5367). Over 100 old phonographs and records, well preserved and restored. June - Sept., daily, 10 A.M. - 10 P.M., Oct. - May, daily, 10 A.M. - 8 P.M. Adults, $2; students, seniors, $1.50; children, $1; groups, $1.50 per person.

Musée Les Voitures d'Eau (schooner museum). 203 Chemin des Coudriers, St-Louis-de-l'Île aux Coudres, Île aux Coudres, PQ G0A 1X0 (438–2208/2936). Inshore navigation on the St. Lawrence. Tour of schooner. Nautical equipment. No facilities on the schooner for handicapped people. June - Sept., 8:30 A.M.- 7 P.M.; $4 per person.

Musée Régional Laure-Conan. 30 rue Patrick-Morgan, La Malbaie, PQ G0T 1J0 (665–4411). The Victorian Room shows furniture belonging to Quebec's first woman novelist, Laure Conan, (1845–1924). Permanent and temporary exhibits of local art and artifacts. The museum won awards for "Charlevoix: Two hundred years as a resort area," an exposition well worth seeing, although frequently on loan elsewhere.

ART. From the 17th century, settlers constructed their buildings on hillsides, with workshops or stores at ground level and living quarters upstairs. Latter-day artists and artisans follow the tradition, as you'll see from many of the over 50 boutiques, galleries, handicraft stores, and workshops operating throughout Charlevoix. You'll find a notable workshop is the pottery at Port-au-Persil, on Route 138 (638–2349). The *Centre d'Art Baie-St-Paul,* 4 blvd. Fafard (435–3681), works to advance the visual arts and holds special exhibits in the summer with an annual symposium or festival in Aug. The town also has a number of galleries, shops, and studios.

ACCOMMODATIONS. Charlevoix has built up a great clientele of inn-goers, who in turn encourage innkeepers to keep improving on their "product" and service. Competition among innkeepers proves keen, as all Charlevoix's hotels vie for regular clients from Quebec City, as well as for travelers' dollars. The provincial government rates all inns and and hotels, awarding up to five lilies for comfort, and four forks for cuisine, ambiance, and service. See *Facts at Your Fingertips* for details.

Reservations are essential. Many establishments quote prices according to the Modified American Plan, for a room with breakfast and evening dinner. One inn often has rooms in several price categories so check when you phone, write, or go through your travel agent, to book. Always ask about special packages, such as golf weeks, whale watching, tennis, skiing, and lower rates Sept.-May. Price categories cover high season (May–Labor Day), room only, double occupancy: *Super Deluxe,* over $120; *Deluxe,* $100–$120; *Expensive,* $80–$100; *Moderate,* $55–$80; *Inexpensive,* under $55. Following is a sampling of the area's nearly 100 hotels, motels, and inns.

BAIE-ST-PAUL. Maison Otis. *Expensive-Deluxe.* 23 rue St-Jean-Baptiste, Baie-St-Paul, PQ G0A 1B0 (418–435–2255). Many rate this one of the region's best. The old stone house in a picturesque village proves a romantic setting for fine nouvelle cuisine dishes, all market-fresh. Lunch on the terrace in summer only. Gourmet dinners. The 42 well-appointed rooms (some with whirlpool baths, fireplaces, antique furniture), garnered four lilies. Three forks for cuisine. The inn is across the street from several galleries and only a block or two from the art center.

Motel La Brinde. *Moderate.* 896 blvd. Monseigneur de Laval, Baie-St-Paul, PQ G0A 1B0 (418–435–3910). European French cuisine, dinner only. 18 rooms, three lilies, one fork.

CAP-A-L'AIGLE. Auberge des Peupliers. *Deluxe–Super Deluxe.* 381 rue St-Raphael, Cap-a-l'Aigle, La Malbaie, PQ G0T 1B0 (418–665–4423). Charming old farmhouse with original antiques, beautiful dining room, genuine Quebec fare from owner's family recipes. New section features very comfortable rooms. 21 rooms, four lilies, three forks.

Auberge la Pinsonnière. *Deluxe–Super Deluxe.* 124 rue St-Raphael, Cap-a-l'Aigle, La Malbaie, PQ G0T 1B0 (418–665–4431). Swimming pool, private beach, view over the St. Lawrence and back across the bay to Pointe-au-Pic. Classical music in rooms. Highest government rating both for the comfort of its 24 rooms (five lilies) and cuisine (four-R forks).

LES EBOULEMENTS. Auberge de Nos Aieux et Motels. *Inexpensive–Moderate.* 183, Route 362, Les Eboulements, PQ G0A 2M0 (635–2483). *Nos Aieux* means "our forefathers." This is an exceptionally lovely village. Partial access for handicapped people. 42 rooms. Three lilies for comfort, one fork.

ÎLE AUX COUDRES. Auberge la Coudrière. *Moderate–Expensive.* 244 rue Principale, Île aux Coudres, PQ G0A 2A0 (418–438–2838). Typical Quebec fare, folk dancing. Seasonal. Three lilies for its 43 rooms. Two forks.

Auberge les Voitures d'Eau et Motels. *Moderate–Expensive.* 214 rue Principale Ouest, Île aux Coudres, PQ G0A 1X0 (418–438–2208). Typical Quebec fare. Seasonal. Three lilies for 46 rooms. Two forks.

CHARLEVOIX

Hôtel Cap aux Pierres et Motels. *Moderate–Expensive.* 220 rue Principale, Île aux Coudres, PQ G0A 2A0 (418–438–2711 or 800–361–6162). Pool, tennis, traditional Quebec fare, folk dancing. Seasonal. Four lilies, 86 rooms. Two forks.

Hôtel La Roche Pleureuse et Motels. *Moderate–Expensive.* 238 rue Principale, Île aux Coudres, PQ G0A 2A0 (418–438–2232). Pool, tennis. Typical Quebec fare. Folk dancing, entertainment. Seasonal. Four lilies for its 90 rooms. Two forks. No credit cards.

Hôtel Motel du Capitaine. *Moderate–Expensive.* 131 Chemin des Coudriers, Île aux Coudres, PQ G0A 2A0 (418–438–2242). Seasonal. Two lilies, 22 rooms. Two forks.

Hôtel St-Bernard. *Inexpensive–Moderate.* 36 rue Royale Ouest, Île aux Coudres, PQ G0A 1X0 (418–438–2261). One lily for its 14 rooms. Reasonably priced Quebec fare. No credit cards.

LA MALBAIE. (See also Cap-à-l'Aigle and Pointe-au-Pic.) **Manoir Charlevoix.** *Moderate–Expensive.* 1030 rue St-Etienne, La Malbaie, PQ G0T 1J0 (418–665–4413). Fine old pine-paneled hotel perched on rocks. European French cuisine (three forks). 42 rooms (three lilies);

POINTE-AU-PIC. Auberge des Falaises. *Expensive–Deluxe.* 18 blvd. des Falaises, Pointe-au-Pic, La Malbaie, PQ G0T 1M0 (418–665–3731). A most romantic dining room and terrace overlooking the bay. Nine-course gourmet dinners in winter. Nouvelle cuisine with local produce, lamb, smelts, rabbit (three forks). 12 rooms (four lilies).

Manoir Richelieu. *Expensive-Deluxe.* 181 ave. Richelieu, Pointe-au-Pic, La Malbaie, PQ G0T 1M0 (418–482–2862). Biggest hotel in the region, a remnant of the days when rich visitors arrived by the "white boats." Several dining rooms, entertainment, golf, tennis, swimming pools. 344 rooms, four lilies, two forks.

Auberge des Trois Canards et Motels. *Expensive–Deluxe.* 49 Côte Bellevue, Pointe-au-Pic, La Malbaie, PQ G0T 1M0 (418–665–3761). Pleasantly rustic. Swimming pool. 38 rooms, three lilies, three forks.

Auberge les Sources. *Expensive–Deluxe.* 8 ave. des Pins, Pointe-au-Pic, La Malbaie, PQ G0T 1M0 (418–665–6952). Fine old Taft-era house overlooking water. European French cuisine. 20 rooms, four lilies, Two forks.

Auberge au Petit Berger. *Expensive–Deluxe.* 1 Côte Bellevue, Pointe-au-Pic, La Malbaie, PQ G0T 1M0 (418–665–4428). The "little sheepfold," is actually several old houses turned into very comfortable rooms, some with whirlpool baths. Special packages for tennis players, golfers. 20 rooms, three lilies, three forks.

Auberge la Petite Marmite. *Moderate.* 63 rue Principale, Pointe-au-Pic, La Malbaie, PQ G0T 1M0 (418–665–3583). Small seven-room inn, two lilies, two forks.

ST-IRÉNÉE. Auberge les Sablons. *Inexpensive–Moderate.* 223 blvd. Les Bains, St-Irénée, PQ G0T 1V0 (418–452–3594). Gorgeous site for big old house overlooking sea, beach. One lily for comfort (ten rooms). Not open long enough for fork-rating.

ST-JOSEPH-DE-LA-RIVE. Auberge la Perdriole. *Expensive.* 278 rue Principale, St-Joseph-de-la-Rive, PQ G0A 3Y0 (418–635–2435). On main road through village. One lily for comfort (14 rooms), but three forks for good cuisine and wine cellar. No lunch.

Hotel-Motel Castel de la Rive. *Moderate–Inexpensive.* 280 Chemin du Quai, St-Joseph-de-la-Rive, PA G0A 3Y0 (418–635–2846). 21 rooms, one lily, one fork. All fresh regional produce. Outdoor pool.

BED AND BREAKFAST. Maison Donohue. *Expensive–Deluxe.* 145 rue Principale, Pointe-au-Pic, La Malbaie, PQ G0T 1M0 (418–665–4377). In the Victorian former home of a pulp and paper magnate. Some huge rooms. Outdoor pool. Seasonal.

Maison Larochelle. *Inexpensive–Moderate.* 68 rue Principale, Pointe-au-Pic, La Malbaie, PQ G0T 1M0 (418–665–6633). Graceful house from Taft-era. No credit cards.

YOUTH HOSTEL. Auberge de jeunesse **Le Balcon Vert.** Route 362, Rivière-du-Gouffre, Baie-St-Paul, PQ G0A 3Y0 (418–435–4720). Low-cost overnight stays, mainly for young people, from June to Sept. The hostel accepts no credit cards.

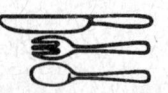

RESTAURANTS. In Charlevoix, you dine best in the inns, manors, and hotels, although you can find many good, inexpensive snack bars and cafes for light repasts. Regional fare includes a unique bean soup, made with a local legume called *gourgane,* fresh seafood of all kinds, locally raised fresh lamb, rabbit, Quebec meat pies *(tourtières),* and desserts like sugar pie, which tastes somewhat like an English treacle tart or an American pecan pie without the pecans. Most dining rooms open from about noon to 2:30 or 3 P.M., and from 5:30 or 6 P.M.–8:30 or 9 P.M. Reservations are essential, so check times when you call to reserve. Price categories for a complete dinner for one (not including beverage, tax, or tip) at the inns listed in the previous section are: *Super Deluxe,* over $35; *Deluxe,* $24–$35; *Expensive,* $18–$23; *Moderate,* $8–$18; and *Inexpensive,* under $8. Because most restaurants offer *table d'hôte*—complete meals, usually with hors d'oeuvre or soup, a main dish, and dessert—the prices often range through two categories. All the hotels hold liquor licenses, so do not bring your own wine.

A good restaurant not associated with an inn, and so not listed above, is: **Le Mouton Noir.** *Moderate–Inexpensive.* rue du Quai, Baie-St-Paul (435–3075). Open 11 A.M.–9 P.M. daily. Charlevoix specialties, wild-rabbit pie, veal scallop, lamb, and homemade Merguez sausages. No credit cards.

NIGHTLIFE AND ENTERTAINMENT. You will find that dining out is the region's principal form of entertainment, but there are also bars and nightclubs in the big hotels like *Manoir Richelieu,* and classical music concerts at *Domaine Forget* throughout the summer (398 Chemin les Bains, St-Irénée, 452-3233). *Maison Otis'* popular Bistro, 23 rue St-Jean-Baptiste, Baie-St-Paul (435–2255), hosts some of the best-known *chansonniers* (popular singers) from Quebec and Montreal, in a genuine wine cellar with four-foot-thick stone walls. Still, you may want nothing more than to relax in the lounge of your auberge after a splendid dinner in its dining room.

French **summer-stock** comes alive at *Manoir Richelieu,* 181 ave. Richelieu, Pointe-au-Pic (665–3703); and *Hôtel Cap-aux-Pierres,* (438–2208) 220 rue Principale, La Baleine, on Île aux Coudres.

The four large hotels on Île aux Coudres also host **folk dancing**—with the waiters and waitresses doubling as dancers (see "Accommodations.").

THE LAURENTIANS AND THE OTTAWA VALLEY

by
Bernadette Cahill

Born in Glasgow, Scotland, Bernadette Cahill has lived in Dublin, Ireland, and Vancouver, Canada, and now lives in Montreal. She is a free-lance writer covering many subjects but specializing in writing for business periodicals.

Some regions of the world are lying in wait to give new life to expressions that have lost their meaning through time and overuse. Such is the case with the area of Quebec northwest of Montreal. The phrase "pretty as a picture" might have been made for the Laurentians and the Ottawa Valley (French, *Laurentides* and *Outaouais,* pronounced "oot-away"). Abundantly beautiful all year with lakes, rivers, and trees aplenty, spectacular scenery lies there, ready to be framed by the cam-

LAURENTIANS-OTTAWA VALLEY

era's lens or captured on canvas with the artist's brush. Well developed for tourists, with numerous world-class resorts that cater to the most expensive tastes, nestling at lakesides among woods and mountains, it is the embodiment of the description, "playground of the rich."

At the same time, "Montreal's backyard" or "the capital's playground" are equally apt expressions because the facilities available cater to all budgets. And if all this were not enough, it could even be claimed that this is one place in the world where you can really capture the meaning of the expression "as old as the hills," for the Laurentians are among the oldest mountains in the world, possessing the same atmosphere of peace and tranquility that comes with many an old age.

The Laurentians and the Ottawa Valley are adjacent to each other in the territory to the northwest of Montreal. Bounded on the southeast by Lac-des-Deux-Montagnes and Milles-Îles River, on the southwest by the Ottawa River, the region extends to La Vérendrye Wildlife Reserve in the northwest and Parc du Mont-Tremblant and the de Lanaudière region in the northeast. Although essentially one unit geographically because the ancient hills of the Canadian Shield rise up virtually from the Ottawa River's edge, it is comprised of two of Quebec province's official tourist regions: because the two parts have had very different histories. The Laurentians, a highly exploited resort area, the best developed in the whole of Canada, owes its growth to the vision and encouragement of a 19th-century priest, Curé Labelle, who saw the potential of the mountains and lakes—where farming had limited possibilities—as a recreation area.

The Ottawa Valley, by contrast, has not been so systematically exploited. There is quite a contrast, therefore, between the two parts of this region, the Ottawa Valley being more a charming land for gentle exploration, while the Laurentians are for the holidaymaker serious about the business of recreation.

The Ottawa River, wrote Montreal writer Hugh MacLennan in *Seven Rivers of Canada*, is Canada's unknown river: this despite its central role in the early development of the country. Its route, and those of nearby water systems, enabled early European explorers, from the 17th century on, to penetrate by canoe and portage right to the Great Lakes, as the Indians had done centuries before. Its powerful tributaries, such as the Gatineau and the Lièvre, permitted the *coureurs des bois* (fur traders) to bypass Montreal on their journey from Quebec. Its more recent history was tied to forestry after Philomen Wright, an American from Massachusetts, came to the region in 1799, saw the potential of the river and its surrounding forests and decided to exploit the demand created for wood in Europe by the Napoleonic wars by sending timber down the Ottawa to Quebec and then to Europe.

Geologically it appears that the Ottawa was upstaged by the St. Lawrence River many thousands of years ago. Once the Ottawa River was the original drainage system of the Great Lakes, but major upheavals of the earth caused a change in its course and now it is only a tributary of the more important channel. According to official Quebec maps, the headwaters of the Ottawa, considered by many to flow from Lake Temiscaming in the north actually lies in La Vérendrye Wildlife Reserve, making it rival the St. Lawrence in length.

Although often neglected, the river and its valley has been the scene of some important incidents in French Canadian history. Paradoxically, however, although its left bank is situated in French Quebec, it was largely settled by Anglophones and the township layout of the land often reflects these origins. The area known as "La Petite Nation" in the southwest was settled by Francophones and has the familiar French *rang* or longlot pattern of subdivision.

The Laurentian Mountains themselves were formed during the Precambrian Age more than 600 million years ago. Long ages of glacial erosion have left in their wake sweeping valleys, gentle, rounded mountains, and a complicated lacework of lakes and rivers. Mont-Tremblant is the highest and most important mountain in the area.

As Curé Labelle saw 100 years ago, the mountains and waterways create in this region boundless opportunities for recreation. Most of the Laurentian resorts lie between St-Jérome and Ste-Agathe. There is also a busy resort at Mont-Tremblant. In the Ottawa Valley, the Hull-Gatineau and Parc Gatineau area is the most developed for recreation, with other important centers located at Lac-Simon and Lac-Ste-Marie.

The region lends itself both to extended vacations in one location and more widespread exploration. The combination of water- and landscapes makes for pleasant casual touring, while the rich past of the area is an attraction for history buffs. Arts and crafts enthusiasts will also find a number of centers appealing to them.

Water and weather combine to provide a multitude of sporting opportunities, a different one, it would seem, for every week of the year. In summer, the countless lakes are dotted with a rainbow of sails of a flotilla of craft, while the hills echo with the hum of powerboats, their passengers thrilling to the wind in their faces, or their waterskiers being put through their paces. At a "lower tech" pace, swimmers can relax on the innumerable beaches, and pedal- or tour-boat enthusiasts can take a leisurely outing around the resort lakes.

On the rivers, enthusiastic canoeists follow once more the old routes of the *voyageurs* and coureurs des bois, and daredevils forge their determined way on rafts through rapids as the tributaries of the Ottawa tumble off the Canadian Shield.

Off the water, amateurs of horseback riding, tennis, and golf have plenty to gratify their appetites. Many resorts offer competitive packages concentrating on specific sports, while the whole region is a cycling challenge.

In winter, when the landscape turns white, downhill skiing *(ski alpin)*, cross-country skiing *(ski di fond* or *ski randonnée)*, snowshoeing, and skating opportunities abound. Sleigh rides and snowmobile touring afford the less agile the chance to take an equal part in the winter activities. Again, a wide variety of competitively priced packages are available.

LAURENTIANS–OTTAWA VALLEY

As well as being Canada's capital city and situated on the doorstep of metropolitan Montreal, this whole area is also a hunting and fishing paradise within easy reach of major U.S. population centers. Trophy-sized muskies, bass, and walleyes have been won from the Ottawa River, and near-record-sized ouananiche are being fished from Lac-Tremblant. Moose, whitetail deer, black bear, ducks, and Canada geese are only some of the species available for hunting.

PRACTICAL INFORMATION FOR THE LAURENTIANS AND THE OTTAWA VALLEY

WHEN TO GO. This region has the major benefits of a continental climate: when it is summer it feels like summer and when it is winter, snow is guaranteed. Spring and fall have their own attractions, although the colors of fall and the slightly lower temperatures make regulars claim that it is the best time of the year for a visit. July and August, the Christmas–New Year's break, and February and March are the busiest times, with prices structured accordingly. At virtually any other time, prices are lower and the crowds smaller. If there is an off-season in this part of the world, it is often just after Easter until the end of May, or between Thanksgiving and the beginning of December in some of the resorts and smaller establishments. During the summer weekends, the region hums as the whole of Montreal, it seems, foresakes city life and escapes to the great outdoors.

HOW TO GET THERE. By Plane. Major carriers from all U.S. departure points arrive at *Dorval Airport* in Montreal (Transport Canada Information, 514–636–5921), which is southeast of this region. Some cut-price carriers, such as *People's Express* and *Presidential Airways* arrive at *Mirabel Airport* (Transport Canada Information, 514–476–3010) from U.S. departure points like New York and Washington. All other international flights land at Mirabel, which is north of Montreal on the route to the Laurentians.

By Bus. Several express and local *Voyageur* buses (514–842–2281) connect Montreal daily to the main resort centers in the Laurentians and Hull, departing from the terminal at 505 de Maisonneuve Est, at the Berri-de-Montigny Métro station. Rates are from $15 one-way. *Miracar* (514–397–9999) operates a bus from Mirabel Airport to the ski resorts during winter weekends. *Autobus Le Promeneur* (819–425–3096) operates buses between Dorval and various ski resorts on the weekends during the ski season.

By Car. Autoroute 15 from Montreal is the quickest route to Ste-Agathe, via the Laurentian resorts. There it joins up with the older, and more leisurely 117, which passes through all the towns and villages bypassed by 15. 117 continues to the Mont-Tremblant turnoff. Autoroute 640 from the east joins with 117 at Ste-Thérèse for destinations in the Laurentians. It continues to Parc Paul Sauvé, near Oka, where it meets 344 and later 148, following the Ottawa River to Hull and Parc Gatineau and as far north as Rapides-des-Joachims. 158 from exit 39, near St-Antoine on 117, joins 148 after Lachute.

PROVINCE OF QUEBEC

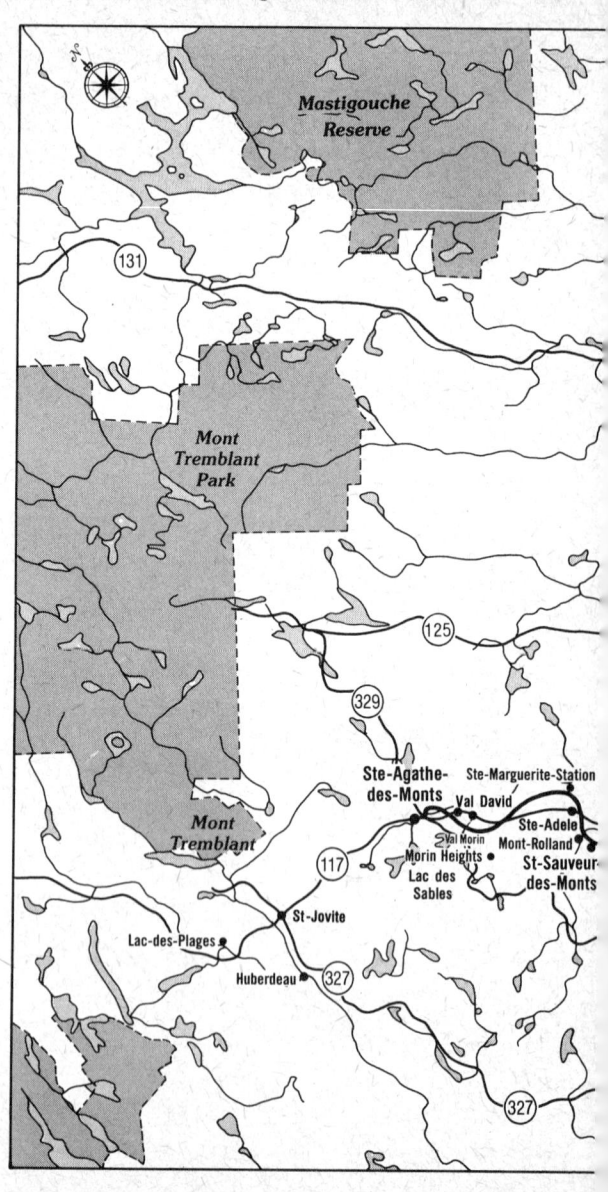

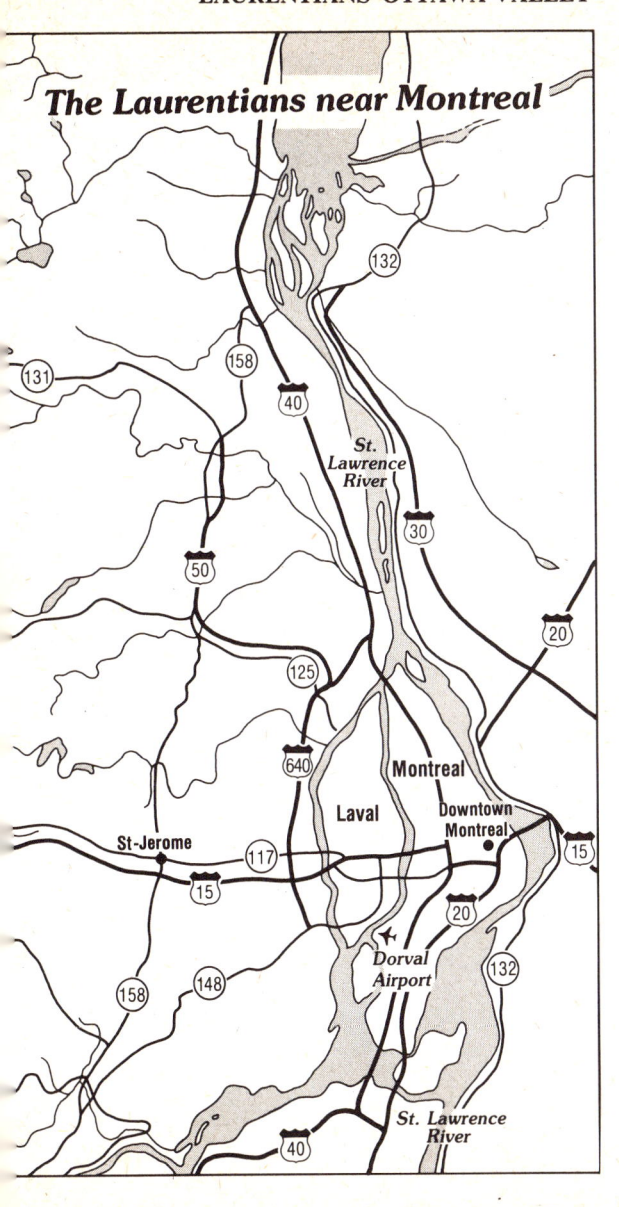

LAURENTIANS–OTTAWA VALLEY

The Laurentians near Montreal

By Cab. Many hotels will make arrangements for guests flying in to the area to be met by a local taxi and driven to their destination. One hotel quotes about $100 for a trip for five passengers from Dorval to near Mont-Tremblant. Check with the hotel when making reservations.

By Train. *VIA Rail's* passenger trains (514–871–1331), which leave five or six times daily from Montreal's Central Station, arrive at the Ottawa Valley's back door: Ottawa, the nation's capital. They connect there with local bus services to Hull. Schedules may vary each season. One-way tickets cost about $20 and reduced prices are available for the round-trip, depending upon the time spent at the destination. Bikes are permitted on the VIA Rail train when there is a baggage car.

TOURIST INFORMATION. A permanent information office provides brochures and other information on the Laurentians: *La Maison du Tourisme de l'Association touristique des Laurentides,* 14 142 rue de Lachapelle, R.R. #1, St-Jérome, PQ J7Z 5T4 (514–436–8532). Summer offices operate at L'Annonciation, Mont-Laurier, Lachute, St-Adolphe d'Howard, Terrebonne, and Val-David.

The tourist region is divided into subregions: *Region des Basses Laurentides,* 301 blvd. Ste-Adele, Ste-Adele, PQ J0R 1L0 (514–229–2921). *Région des Hautes Laurentides,* 190 rue Principale Est, Ste-Agathe-des-Monts, PQ J8C 1K3 (819–326–0457). *Region St-Jovite/Mont-Tremblant,* Junction Route 117 and rue Paquette, CP 605 St-Jovite, PQ J0T 2H0 (819–425–3300). *Région Vallée de St-Sauveur Galeries des Monts,* CP 1710, St-Sauveur-des-Monts, PQ J0R 1R0 (514–227–4661).

For information on the Ottawa Valley, contact *Association touristique de l'Outaouais,* 2,000, Succursale B, Hull, PQ J8X 3Z2 (819–778–2222). Summer offices are in Grand Remous and La Petite Nation. Or, contact *Centre d'accueil touristique à Hull,* 25 rue Laurier, Maison du Citoyen, Rez-de-chaussée, Hull, PQ, J8X 4C8.

Information about outdoor activities is available from *Regroupement loisir Quebec* at 4545 ave Pierre de Coubertin, CP 1000, Succursale M, Montreal, PQ H1V 3R2 (514–252–3000).

The Quebec cyclists' organization, Vélo Quebec publishes a *Guide du Quebec Cyclable* (in French only). This guide, which has maps of the province with different trips superimposed includes itineraries for the Laurentians. It can be obtained at the same address as Regroupement loisir Quebec above for $5, plus 15 percent to cover mail costs.

TELEPHONES. 514 is the area code for the southern Laurentians, and 819 is the code everywhere else in this region. Some 514 numbers are local calls from Montreal and some are long-distance. For the latter, dial 1 plus the number. Dial 411 for all local directory information and from elsewhere dial the area code plus 555–1212. For direct-dial long-distance calls to another area code, dial 1, the area code, and then the number. For any operator-assisted calls, dial 0 before the area code. All local pay-phone calls, which have no time limit, cost 25 cents.

Yellow-page telephone directories for the area are divided into French-language and English-language sections, with the English section at the back.

LAURENTIANS-OTTAWA VALLEY

EMERGENCY TELEPHONE NUMBERS. Emergency numbers for the whole of the region vary according to the locality. To find the local emergency number for the police, fire department, and ambulances anywhere in this region dial 411. Or dial 0 and the operator will connect you with the emergency service required. No money is required.

HOW TO GET AROUND. By Bus. This whole region is served by a network of routes linking the centers. Contact *Voyageur* (514–842–2281 or 819–771–2442) or *Laval Transit* (514–688–6520), which travels to Oka.

By Car. Rentals can be arranged at both airports and in Montreal itself. *Hertz, Budget,* and *Avis* all operate in the region. To ensure a reservation, it is advisable to book in advance during the peak summer months. (See *Montreal* for further information about car rental firms.)

By Bike. Bikes are sometimes permitted at quiet periods on the Canadian National commuter trains (514–871–1331), which depart almost every hour from Montreal's Central Station for Deux-Montagnes, across the Milles-Îles River from the Island of Montreal and on the edge of the Laurentians. This is a good starting point for a cycling tour of the region. One-way tickets cost under $5.

HINTS TO MOTORISTS. Most Quebecers were originally French and their driving style is as hectic as in the Old Country. Many drivers specialize in tailgating, breaking the speed limits, and quicksilver maneuvers, weaving from lane to lane in order to shave a few minutes from the journey. On Friday evenings, all of Montreal seems to exit en masse and head for the hills, and *le retour* on a Sunday evening is particularly hectic. This driving style is at its most highly refined on the Laurentian Autoroute. If it were not essential to keep one's eyes glued to the road, it would be interesting to observe the locals apparently in training for the grand prix circuit, for which they have, in fact, produced some front-runners. Since tolls were abolished here in 1985, there is now nothing to slow down drivers speeding as they approach Montreal. Driving in this part of the world requires more caution and attentiveness than usual.

Off the autoroute, where there are many slower and more circuitous roads, it is enjoyable to drive more slowly in order to enjoy the scenery. Also, these roads require drivers to be alert for the road repairs that spring up all over the place in the summer months after the ravages of the winter frost.

HINTS TO HANDICAPPED TRAVELERS. For preboarding facilities for bus travel, phone Voyageur (514–842–2281 or 819–771–2442) to make arrangements. Some bus companies in the region allow the escort of a visually impaired passenger to travel free of charge. An identification card is usually required. Other companies grant a similar concession to the permanently disabled. Again, identification is required. Wheelchairs are treated as ordinary baggage.

PROVINCE OF QUEBEC

SEASONAL EVENTS. The changing seasons are celebrated with appropriate festivals in different parts of the region. The Ottawa Valley regional capital, Hull, takes part in February in the annual Winter Carnival with Canada's capital, Ottawa, when the cold season is turned to advantage with sculptures, ice slides and every imaginable entertainment. In August it has a summer festival. March sees Ste-Cécile-de-Masham near La Pêche, celebrating the annual tapping of its maple trees with a "sugaring off" festival. Ste-Anne-des-Plaines holds a strawberry festival in July. A brochure containing information on these events can be obtained from *La Société des Festivals Populaires* at the address of Regroupement loisirs Quebec (see "Tourist Information").

TOURS. Guided tours of the *Laurentides Satellite Earth Station*, Weir, Quebec (819-687-3241) near Morin Heights, are available daily 10 A.M. – 4:30 P.M., mid-June to Labor Day and on weekends only between Labor Day and Thanksgiving.

The education service of the province's Ministry of Energy and Resources operates eight *forestry education centers* in the Laurentians, where exhibits explain the business of forestry. Call 819-326-1606 or write the Service at CP 390, St. Faustin, PQ J0T 2G0.

To get up-to-date about the summertime steam train excursions between Ottawa and Wakefield, phone the Ottawa tourist information center (819-778-2222). The trip takes about 1 hour 15 minutes, allowing a few hours to enjoy the recreation facilities at Wakefield. It costs about $8.

PROVINCIAL PARKS. A number of wildlife reserves and provincial parks each with a variety of outdoor activities from nature walks to canoeing are located here. The *Papineau-Labelle Wildlife Reserve (reserve faunique)* and *Parc Gatineau* are two of the most important. "Parcs et Reserves Fauniques du Quebec," available from Quebec Tourisme (see Facts at Your Fingertips, "Tourist Information"), is a comprehensive guide to all the parks and their services.

CAMPING. Many provincial parks allow camping. Specific information can be found in the brochure on parks (see *"Provincial Parks"*). There are also many private campgrounds with a range of hookups, both winter and summer. A comprehensive brochure on campgrounds is available from Quebec tourism (see *Tourist Information*).

Private campgrounds are the way to see the real Quebec lifestyle. Quebecers often reserve a place in a campground for the whole season. Semipermanent villages spring up, gardens are planted, and colored lights strung around individual "homesteads." Campgrounds like this usually have the full range of facilities. They are the places to get to know the locals and lose the kids in safety. Many Quebecers are very religious people and on a Sunday or a holy day, everything can stop for a religious service at the poolside, so check schedules carefully.

Grounds with a large number of their hookups reserved for the season are clearly marked in the Quebec camping guide.

LAURENTIANS-OTTAWA VALLEY

FISHING AND HUNTING. Many professional outfitters are located in this area, particularly in the northern Laurentians. Grand Remous is a major center of outfitters for hunting in La Vérendrye Wildlife Reserve. Outfitters often rent out summer cottages to families vacationing in the region. Province of Quebec hunting and fishing guides can be obtained from Tourisme Quebec. The *Quebec Outfitters' Association* produces a comprehensive directory of hunting and fishing and of members and services. Write to the Association at 2900 blvd. St-Martin, Montreal, PQ H7T 2G2 (514–687–0041).

PARTICIPANT SPORTS. Equipment rentals for every type of sport are available at a number of the resorts (see *"Accommodations"*), and in the provincial parks canoes can often be hired (see "Provincial Parks"). *Adventures en Eau Vive*, R.R. #2, chemin Rivière Rouge, Calumet, PQ J0V 1B0 (819–242–6084) is one of many companies operating whitewater rafting trips in this area, which is one of the best in the world for whitewater rafting. Starting in May, prices begin at about $50.

SKIING. With about 30 downhill ski centers receiving plentiful snow during winter, the Laurentians is one of North America's finest ski areas. 2,000 km of well-groomed cross-country ski trails, snowmobile trails, and ice skating rinks complete the Laurentian list of winter activities.

Mont Tremblant. Mont Tremblant, PQ J0T 1Z0 (819–425–8711; snow reports, 514–861–1925). The most important winter sport area in the region, Mont Tremblant is renowned for the best skiing in eastern Canada. The Parc du Mont-Tremblant, named after the mountain, becomes a winter paradise for cross-country and downhill skiing, snowshoeing, and snowmobiling. Mont-Tremblant village is a well-frequented winter resort boasting many fine hotels and restaurants. The road from Mont Tremblant to Montreal connects all the major villages in the region, each a ski center in its own right. Mont Tremblant Reservations, Box 240, Mont Tremblant, PQ, J0T 1Z0 (819–425–8681), is a central reservation service for hotels, chalets, and condominiums.

The Piedmont, Saint-Sauveur-des-Monts, and Mont-Gabriel area is one of the most popular in the Laurentians, packed with hospitable hotels and hostelries. Ski centers with a total of 80 slopes and 32 modern ski lifts are to be found at almost every turn in the road. Sainte-Adele is near 4 downhill ski centers and more than 70 km of cross-country ski trails.

In the Outaouais, Mont-Cascades ski center near the town of Gatineau sports an alpine slide and downhill and cross-country skiing while Gatineau Park near Hull has alpine and there is cross-country skiing at Camp Fortune. Lac Sainte-Marie, located off Route 105 between Hull and Grand Remous, with two mountains almost 400 meters high, 3 double chair lifts and a ski school, is an extremely popular downhill and cross-country skiing center.

CHILDREN'S ACTIVITIES. The most accessible of a number of water slides in the area are those at *Cascades d'eau* (514–227–3353), open seven days a week in the summer, exit 58 from the Laurentian Autoroute. Plans in 1986 are to open the tallest water slide in Canada. Look for the giant tap on the hillside.

PROVINCE OF QUEBEC

Seraphin Village (514–229–4777), at Ste-Adele is a reconstruction of an historic French village open from mid May to mid Oct.

Late in the year, Val-David opens its *Father Christmas Village* (819–322–2146) for children's seasonal entertainment.

Edphy, Suite 102B, 100 blvd. des Prairies, Laval, PQ, H7N 1T5 (819–322–3011). Boasting "the largest number of sports facilities in Quebec," organizes one of the best childrens' camps in the region at Val-Morin. It has adult facilities as well.

HISTORIC SITES AND HOUSES. *Papineau Manor,* a mansion complete with secret passages, built by Louis-Joseph Papineau, one of the 1837 Patriots in the 1840s, can be visited during the summer months at Montebello. In its grounds lie the famous Château Montebello hotel.

The riverside road from Terrebonne to Hull has a number of historic stops. The *Île des Moulins* at Terrebonne, open from early June, has many preserved 17th-century houses. The church at *St-Eustache* was the scene of a showdown between government forces and the Patriots during the 1837 rising. *Carillon* was the site of the battle of Long Sault of May 1660, when a tiny group of men saved New France from a full-scale Indian attack.

A local museum is established in the *Old Carillon Barracks* at the town of that name, a former 17th-century trading post. At *Grenville* the remains of an old military navigation canal constructed in 1819 can be visited.

ACCOMMODATIONS. Resorts, hotels, motels, and inns of all standards and for all budgets abound in this region. Direct price comparisons are difficult because so many packages are offered all year. Many resorts also have a variety of rooms ranging from modest to luxurious, so price shopping can produce real bargains. Activities for all seasons can be found in the resorts, and most other accommodations are situated near ski slopes or lakeside beaches, with equipment rentals available. Summer and winter sport weekends start around $80 and soar from there. Individual establishments will supply information about these packages on request. Categories, (all for two people) are: *Super Deluxe,* $180 and up; *Deluxe,* $130–$180; *Expensive,* $90–$130; *Moderate,* $50–$90; and *Inexpensive,* $50 and below. For an explanation of the province's lily and fork rating system, see *Facts at Your Fingertips.*

GATINEAU. Auberge des Gouverneurs. *Inexpensive–Moderate.* 111 rue Bellehumeur, Gatineau, PQ J8T 6K5 (819–568–5252 or 800–463–2820 from Ontario and Quebec). Pool, sauna, health club.

HUBERDEAU. Auberge Lac-à-la-Loutre (Otter Lake House). *Moderate–Expensive.* Lac-à-la-Loutre, PQ J0T 1G0 (819–687–2767). Lakefront. Boats and pedalos (pedal boats), which can be rented by nonguests if available. Golf locally.

HULL. Hotel Plaza de la Chaudière. *Deluxe–Super Deluxe.* 2 rue Montcalm, Hull, PQ J8X 4B4 (819–778–3880 or 800–567–1991 from Canada only). This region's only "six lily" hotel looks over the river to Parliament Hill in Ottawa. Swimming pool, sauna. Sometimes offers weekend specials from about $60 per

LAURENTIANS-OTTAWA VALLEY 161

night, single or double. Its Châteauneuf Dining Room rates four forks, the best cuisine award in the province.

LAC-DES-PLAGES. Hôtel Mon Chez-Nous. *Inexpensive.* rue Principale, Lac-des-Plages, PQ J0T 1K0 (819-426-2186). Cross-country skiing, lake fishing, skidoo, snowmobile trails, skating nearby, water sports, good beach, organized activities. Five cabins on the lake.

LAC-STE-MARIE. Hotel Mont-Ste-Marie. *Deluxe–Super Deluxe.* Lac-Ste-Marie, PQ J0X 1Z0 (819-467-5200 or 800-567-1255 from Canada only). A four-season resort and conference center about 55 miles from Hull with summer and winter sport facilities. Winter and summer packages available.

LAC-SUPÉRIEUR. Auberge Caribou. *Inexpensive.* Chemin Tour du Lac, Lac-Supérieur, PQ J0T 1P0 (819-688-5201). Good solid winter ski lodge with good food. In summer it becomes a fat farm at thin prices for women only.

MONT-ROLLAND. Auberge Mont-Gabriel. *Expensive–Deluxe.* Autoroute 15, Sortie (Exit) 64, Mont-Rolland, PQ J0R 1G0 (514-861-2852). 1200-acre estate. Tennis, golf, ski week and weekend packages.

MONT-TREMBLANT. Auberge Cuttle's Tremblant Club. *Expensive–Deluxe.* Lac-Tremblant, PQ J0T 1Z0 (819-425-2731). Lakeside. Skiing, tennis, swimming, fishing, golf.
Station Mont-Tremblant Lodge. *Expensive–Deluxe.* Mont-Tremblant, PQ J0T 1Z0 (819-425-8711, 514-861-6165 from Montreal, 800-567-6761 elsewhere). "The only hotel at the foot of the big mountain." Chalets, apartments. All winter sports facilities. Ski schools.
Hôtel-Motel Chalet des Chutes. *Moderate–Expensive.* CP #1, Lac-Tremblant, PQ J0T 1Z0 (819-425-2738). Near lake, waterfalls. Tennis, golf, all skiing locally.
Hôtel-Motel Villa Bellevue. *Moderate–Expensive.* Mont-Tremblant, PQ G0T 1Z0 (819-425-2734 or 800-567-6763 from Ontario, Quebec, and the Maritimes). Lakeside, with all water sports; tennis; skiing.

MONTEBELLO. Le Château Montebello. *Deluxe–Super Deluxe.* 392 rue Nôtre-Dame J0V 1L0 (819-423-6341, 800-268-9420 Canada only), a wonderwork of the Great Depression is a giant, 204-room super luxurious log cabin that attracts politicians and diplomats for their meets. Every possible recreation facility, including hunting and fishing. Golf and skiing packages available.

MORIN HEIGHTS. Auberge Hollandaise. *Inexpensive.* 796 Route St-Adolphe, Morin Heights, PQ J0R 1H0 (514-226-2009). Two lakes nearby for windsurfing, swimming. Cross-country skiing.
Hôtel The Carriage House. *Inexpensive.* Route 329 Nord, 486 route St-Adolphe, Morin Heights, PQ J0R 1H0 (514-226-3031). Lake, windsurfers, canoes for guests, winter sports, cross-country trails.

OTTER LAKE. Motel Bellevue. *Inexpensive.* 68 rue Martineau, Otter Lake, PQ J0X 2P0 (819-453-7035). Skidoo trails nearby.

PROVINCE OF QUEBEC

ST-JOVITE. Gray Rocks Resort. *Deluxe–Super Deluxe.* Box 1000, Lac Ouimet, St-Jovite, PQ J0T 2H0 (819–425–2771, 514–861–0187 from Montreal, or 800–567–6767 from Ontario, Quebec, and the Maritimes). About the oldest of the Laurentian resorts. Extensive landscaped grounds on lakefront. Water sports, children's program, golf, all winter sports. Private airstrip and seaplane anchorage.

ST-SAUVEUR-DES-MONTS. Auberge St-Denis. *Moderate–Expensive.* Box 1229, 61 rue St Denis, St-Sauveur-des-Monts, PQ J0R 1R0 (514–227–4766). All sports available locally.
  Motel Mont-Habitant. *Inexpensive–Moderate.* 12 blvd. des Skieurs, St-Sauveur-des-Monts, PQ J0R 1R0 (514–227–2637, 800–363–3612). On private lake. Some of the 25 rooms have fireplaces. Tennis, water and winter sports.

STE-ADELE. Hotel Le Chanteclerc. *Deluxe–Super Deluxe.* CP 1048, Chemin du Chanteclerc, Ste-Adele, PQ J0R 1L0 (514–229–3555, 800–363–2420 Quebec). Cross-country and downhill skiing, pool, tennis, squash, horseback riding, and golf. Lakeside beach.
  Motel Altitude. *Moderate–Expensive.* CP 1234, Route 117, Ste-Adele, PQ J0R 1L0 (514–229–6616 or 800–363–3683 from Ontario and Quebec). 45 min from Montreal. Near all winter sports. 52 rooms, many with fireplaces. Swimming pools, squash, sauna.

STE-AGATHE-DES-MONTS. Le Manoir d'Ivry. *Inexpensive.* 3800 chemin Renaud, Ste-Agathe-Nord, PQ J8C 2Z8 (819–326–3564). Lakeside, all-season accommodation in a *fin-de-siècle* manor house near Parc Mont-Tremblant. Winter and summer sports and water sports.

STE-AGATHE-SUD. Motel Ste-Agathe. *Inexpensive.* 1000 rue Principale, Ste-Agathe-Sud, PQ J8C 1L6 (819–326–2622). Sports close by.

STE-MARGUERITE-STATION. Hotel Alpine Inn. *Expensive–Deluxe.* Chemin Ste-Marguerite, Ste-Marguerite-Station, PQ J0T 2K0 (514–229–3516 or 800–363–2577 from Quebec only). 104 units, log construction, rooms and cottages. Pools, tennis, golf, winter sports. One hour from Montreal.
  Motel Snowy Owl. 1990 Chemin Ste-Marguerite, Ste-Marguerite-Station, PQ J0R 1L0 (514–228–4645). Lakeside. Pedalos (pedal boats). Other sports at Ste-Adele nearby.

VAL-DAVID. Hôtel La Sapinière. *Deluxe–Super Deluxe.* CP 190, 1244 chemin de la Sapinière, Val-David, PQ, J0T 2N0 819–322–2020, 514–866–8262 from Montreal, or 800–567–6635 from Quebec and Ontario). 70 rooms with private bath. Canoeing, golf, biking, nature trails, tennis, all winter sports, equipment rentals. One of the very best hotels in the whole area.
  Auberge Parkers' Lodge. *Inexpensive–Moderate.* 1340 Chemin Lac-Paquin, Val-David, PQ J0T 2N0 (819–322–2026). Near lake. Cross-country and downhill skiing. Instructors. Swimming, boating, golf nearby.

VAL-MORIN. Auberge Far Hills Inn. *Moderate–Expensive.* Rue Far Hills, Val-Morin, PQ J0T 2R0 (819–322–2014, 514–866–2219, or 800–567–6636 from Canada and eastern U.S.). Principally cross-country. Lakeside, water sports, equipment available for guests, local club for tennis and squash.

LAURENTIANS-OTTAWA VALLEY

WAKEFIELD. Motel Alpengrüss. *Inexpensive.* River Road, Wakefield, PQ J0X 3G0 (819–459–2885). 16 rooms with private bath. Near Gatineau Parc with all summer water sports and fishing. Near downhill and cross-country ski areas.
    Motel Edelweiss. *Inexpensive.* R.R. #2, Route 366 Est, Wakefield, PQ J0X 3G0 (819–459–3052). Lake, tennis, golf, water slide.
    Pension Wunderbar. *Inexpensive.* Box 272, Route 105 Nord, Wakefield, PQ J0X 3G0 (819–459–2471). Rooms and 1-bedroom apartments with fireplace in an Austrian-style chalet. 20 miles from Hull, near Parc Gatineau with all summer water sports and fishing. Near downhill and cross-country ski areas. Very good reports.

BED AND BREAKFAST. Two provincewide networks that organize holidays-with-a-difference in people's homes and other unusual settings are well established in this region. *Vacances-Familles,* 870 est blvd. de Maisonneuve, Suite M16, Montreal, PQ H2L 1Y6 (514–282–9580) offers accommodation in private homes, on farms, in chalets, and schools. *Agricotours du Quebec,* 201 blvd. Crémazie Est, 4eme etage, Montreal, PQ H2M 1L4 (514–873–4182) arranges farm vacations in La Conception, Lac-du-Cerf, Mont-Laurier and Ferme-Neuve.
    Some B&B operations in the region are run by Marian Kahn, who also owns Montreal Bed & Breakfast, 4912 Victoria, Montreal, PQ H3W 2N1 (514–738–9410). Rates are $25–$40 single, $30–$50 double. A reservation and deposit are required.
    Monique Côté, 5151 Côte St Antoine, Montreal, PQ H4A 1P1 (514–484–7802) runs two Laurentian houses that can take four couples. Rates are $50 a night. Her Ste-Marguerite house, which has a fireplace, cook, and maid service, is on a small private lake near tennis, golf, and all sports. A ten-minute drive from the nearest downhill ski center. Cross-country skiing is at the door. Her St Adele house is two blocks from downhill skiing.

RESTAURANTS. Quebecers go to the Laurentians as much for dining as for sports, so renowned is the region for the quality and variety of its cuisine, and it is practically impossible to go wrong in choosing a delightful place to eat—often, also, with inexpensive accommodations attached. *Three- and even four-fork* restaurants are common in many of the hotels listed under *Accommodations.* Prices reflect the intense competition between the chefs, many restaurants offering table d'hôte menus, considerably reducing relatively expensive prices. There is a concentration of excellent restaurants in the range of $40–$50 per person. Restaurants, like accommodations, are very difficult to categorize by price. There is a 9 percent tax on meals. Reservations are always advisable. Categories (based on the price of a meal for one) are: *Super Deluxe,* $80–$100; *Deluxe,* $60–$80; *Expensive,* $40–$60; *Moderate,* $20–$40; and *Inexpensive,* below $20. This, however, is only a very rough guide. A quick check of menus will indicate gastronomic delights at special prices. Unless otherwise noted, the restaurants take some or all major credit cards.

Super Deluxe

    Le Châteauneuf Dining Room. Hotel Plaza de la Chaudière, 2 rue Montcalm, Hull (819–778–3880). First-class French cuisine. Lunch, 12–2 P.M.; dinner, 6:30–11 P.M. Weekdays, D, Sat. 6:30–11 P.M. Closed Sun.
    Hôtel La Sapinière. 1244 chemin de la Sapinière, Val-David (819–322–2020). Classic continental cuisine. Lunch, 12–2 P.M.; dinner, 6:30–8:30 P.M. daily.

PROVINCE OF QUEBEC

Moderate–Expensive

Auberge des Cèdres. 26–305th Ave, Lac-à-l'Achigan, Ste-Hippolyte (514–563–2083). Excellent French cuisine. Des Cèdres' chef is recognized in the trade as one of the best. Dinner, 6 P.M.–midnight, Tues.–Sun. No AE.

Auberge Le Rucher. 2368 rue de l'Église, Val-David (819–322–2507). Excellent French cuisine. Dinner, 5–9 P.M., weekends until 10 P.M. Closed Apr. No AE.

Auberge du Vieux Foyer. 3167 Montée Doncaster, Val-David (819–322–2686). International cuisine. Lunch, 12:30–3 P.M.; dinner, 6–8:30 P.M. Daily, June–Oct. and mid Dec.–Easter. Weekends only the rest of the year.

Chez Girard. 18 rue Principale Ouest, Ste-Agathe (819–326–0922). French cuisine in a small traditional auberge. Lunch, 11:30 A.M.–2:00 P.M.; dinner, 5–9 P.M., Tues.–Sun. No AE.

Eberhard's Chatel Vienna. 6 rue Ste-Lucie, Ste-Agathe (819–326–1485). Viennese and continental cuisine in a lakeside setting. Dinner, 5–11 P.M. Tues.–Fri. Lunch and dinner, noon–11 P.M., Sat. and Sun. Closed Apr. and Nov. No AE.

La Clef des Champs. 875 Chemin Ste-Marguerite, Ste-Marguerite (514–229–2857). Gourmet French cuisine in a family-owned hillside restaurant. Dinner, 5:30–10:30 P.M., Tues.–Sun. and holiday Mon. Closed for vacations after Easter. No AE.

La Table Enchantée. Route 117 nord, Lac Duhamel, St-Jovite (5 km north of St-Jovite). (819–425–7113). Quebec cuisine. Dinner, 5–9 P.M. Tues.–Sun. No AE.

Le Pied du Cochon. 242 rue Montcalm, Hull. (819–777–5808). Small, bistro-style restaurant specializing in French cuisine. Lunch, 12–2 P.M.; dinner, 6–10 P.M. weekdays; dinner, Sat., 6–10 P.M. Closed Sun. and all July.

Le St-Trop. 251 rue Morin, Ste-Adele (514–229–3298). French cuisine in a lakeside setting. Dinner, Wed.–Mon. 7 P.M.–midnight; lunch, 12:30–2:30 P.M. Sun. No AE.

Inexpensive–Moderate

Auberge du Coq de Montagne. Lac Moore, Mont-Tremblant (819–425–3380). Wholesome Italian food from the kitchens of this auberge. Dinner, 5:30–10 P.M. No AE.

COEUR-DU-QUEBEC, DE LANAUDIÈRE, AND PORTNEUF

by
Kathe Lieber

Kathe Lieber is a Montrealer born and bred. She lives in her native city; works as a writer, editor, and translator; and loves to spend her spare time on the back roads of Quebec.

This chapter describes the vast central region between Quebec's two major cities. Coeur-du-Quebec (the heart of the province) includes la Mauricie, the valley of the St. Maurice River; de Lanaudière is the region around Joliette, near Montreal; and Portneuf County is not far from Quebec City. It's here, roughly halfway between the bright lights of Montreal and Quebec City, that visitors can enjoy some of the best outdoor activities in North America, twelve months a year.

For the active, there is skiing, camping, canoeing, riding, hunting, and fishing. And what fishing! In summer there are bass, catfish, pike, perch, and speckled trout; in winter ice fishing for the elusive tommycod, a coveted local delicacy. Less strenuous pursuits include the spring ritual of sugaring-off, bird-watching, blueberry picking, and, of course, sightseeing. This is the region for meandering along tree-lined country roads, picnicking, and admiring the spectacular sites.

National and provincial parks are a big attraction, with thousands of kilometers of wilderness, unspoiled but carefully controlled—you will need a license for hunting or fishing. Wildlife preserves and ZECs (an acronym for the French name, which means controlled environmental zones) attract visitors by the thousands every year.

The cities of the region—Trois-Rivières, Joliette, La Tuque, Shawinigan, and Grand-Mère—make convenient stopping-off points for the visitor en route to discovering the delights of the parks and wildlife preserves. While you will not find many gourmet restaurants or pulsating nightclubs here, you will taste the simpler pleasures of small-town life.

First Stop: De Lanaudière

This is cottage country for many Montrealers, especially around Rawdon and St-Donat, within easy commuting distance of the city. Campsites and year-round recreation centers abound here, with something for everybody (there is even a nudist camp at Chertsey).

Press on to Joliette, and you are in prime tobacco-growing country. Here, you will see field after field of lush green plants, punctuated by little drying huts. Harvest time is August through September. August is also blueberry-picking time in De Lanaudière, and you can pick your own at a number of local farms. The harvest figures prominently in the regional cuisine.

Le Chemin du Roy: The King's Road

Now you are into the heart of the heartland as you travel along the Chemin du Roy, prosaically known as Highway 138, the oldest navigable road in Canada. The road was opened in 1737, and you can still wend your way along its curves today, enjoying the hills, cliffs, and spectacular scenery beside the St. Lawrence.

Ancient (by North American standards, at least) Trois-Rivières is the capital of the region, with a history that predates Champlain's settlement in 1634. This is an industrial town, known primarily for its pulp and paper mills and, in the old days, for its ironworks. The city was ravaged by a massive fire in 1908 which spared a scant dozen buildings from the old regime. The harbor area is currently under renovation; plans call for a complex of boutiques, restaurants, an amphitheater, and a historical interpretation center.

COEUR-DU-QUEBEC

The name of Shawinigan is inextricably linked with Quebec's major export, hydroelectric power, which in turn has fostered the development of the chemical industry. In the spring, visitors flock here to admire the breathtaking beauty of the St. Maurice waterfalls as the thawing icicles hang suspended. Several Hydro plants in the area give guided tours.

Grandmothers and Ear Warmers

Local history and legends are attached to almost every place name in the region. Shawinigan's sister city, the old trading-post town of Grand-Mère, for example, derives its name from a rock resembling an old woman, which the local tribes called Kokomis, meaning grandmother. Another trading post, La Tuque, takes its name from a mountain said to look like the woolen hat Quebecers pull down over their ears in winter.

History, nature, agriculture, and industry—it is all in the friendly, casual Coeur-du-Quebec region. Bring your fishing rod, skis, snowshoes, hunting gear, and especially, your camera. Bienvenue to off-the-beaten-track Quebec!

PRACTICAL INFORMATION FOR COEUR-DU-QUEBEC, DE LANAUDIÈRE, AND PORTNEUF

WHEN TO GO. The region has its beauties in every season, but the timing of your visit will naturally depend upon the sports or events you hope to take in. In winter major highways are cleared quickly and efficiently, but side roads may be impassable for several days after a snowstorm. Photo buffs will want to plan a fall trip to this heavily wooded region, where the leaves are nothing short of magnificent.

HOW TO GET THERE. Your best bet is by car, especially if you are carrying skis or camping equipment. Alternatively, you may prefer to get to Joliette, La Tuque, or Trois-Rivières by public transportation, and rent a car from there.

By Bus. *Voyageur* offers daily service to Joliette, Trois-Rivières, Grand-Mère, Shawinigan, and La Tuque from Montreal (842–2281) and Quebec City (524–4692).

By Train. *VIA Rail* operates a daily train service from Montreal and Quebec City to Trois-Rivières, and regular, but not daily, schedules from Montreal to Joliette, La Tuque, Grand-Mère, and Shawinigan. Trains can be agonizingly slow at times, but train travel does let you soak in the scenery in a way that is

PROVINCE OF QUEBEC

just not possible if you are at the wheel, watching out for exit signs. For train times, call 514–871–1331 in Montreal or 418–692–3940 in Quebec City; from elsewhere, call toll-free, 24 hours a day, 800–361–5390.

By Car. Highway 40 is the fast route from Montreal to Quebec City, but be sure to take the Chemin du Roy (Highway 138) at least part of the way. Since the early settlers who cleared the road had no thought of superhighways, you will find it a pleasant, meandering drive. From Trois-Rivières, Highway 55 will take you on to Shawinigan, and 155 on further still into the hinterland, to the parks and La Tuque.

TOURIST INFORMATION. If you are starting your trip to de Lanaudière or Coeur-du-Quebec from Montreal, be sure to stop by the Tourisme Quebec offices, in the heart of town at 2 Place Ville-Marie. The department publishes a wide variety of brochures on the area in French and English, including detailed pamphlets on snowmobiling, hunting, fishing, and the national and provincial parks of the region. Or you can write for information before you leave home: *Tourisme Quebec,* Ministère du Tourisme, CP 20,000, Quebec City, PQ G1K 7X2 (418–873–2015 from the Montreal area, toll-free from elsewhere in the province, 800–361–5405, or from the eastern U.S., 800–443–7000).

A wide variety of promotional materials on the region is also available from the regional tourist offices: *Tourisme de Lanaudière,* 3647 rue Queen, CP 1210, Rawdon, PQ J0K 1S0 (800–363–2788 from anywhere in the province) and the *Association touristique du Coeur-du-Quebec,* 197 rue Bonaventure, Trois-Rivières, PQ G9A 5M4 (819–375–1222 for lodging reservations).

Year-round tourist offices are also located at 695 de la Station in Shawinigan, 290 St-Joseph in La Tuque, and 3643 rue Queen in Rawdon. If you will be touring the hydroelectric facilities in the region, summer tourist offices are open from June–Aug. on Highway 116 at Arthabaska, and on Highway 132 at 4040 Bécancour Blvd. in Bécancour (Gentilly).

TELEPHONES. The region has three area codes. The parts of de Lanaudière nearest Montreal share the city area code, 514. The code for Trois-Rivières, La Tuque, Shawinigan, and the rest of the Coeur-du-Quebec region is 819. For points north towards Quebec City, the code is 418. If you need directory assistance within the area code, dial 411; to get numbers in other area codes, dial 1-area code-555–1212. To reach another exchange within the same area code, dial 1 and then the seven-digit number. Dial 0 before the area code for credit card, collect, or person-to-person long-distance calls. Operators generally speak both French and English; local telephone calls from a phone booth cost 25 cents.

EMERGENCY TELEPHONE NUMBERS. The *Quebec Provincial Police,* or *Sûreté du Quebec* (819–523–2731 in the Mauricie, and 819–379–7311 in Trois-Rivières); *24-hour poison control* (418–656–8090 in Quebec City); *emergency medical service* (819–376–1616 in Trois-Rivières).

In winter call for *road conditions* (819–375–7334) before you set out: if you get stuck, call the *Canadian Automobile Association* (819–379–9393) during business hours or *Emergency Road Services* (819–379–3838).

COEUR-DU-QUEBEC 169

HOW TO GET AROUND. The heartland of Quebec is a vast region, best traveled by car. The cities in the region are of a manageable size, which makes them fun to explore on foot. In the national and provincial parks, of course, getting around may involve skis, snowshoes, or a canoe.

By Rental Car. The major car rental companies have offices in Trois-Rivières, with some offices in smaller centers. Call before you leave Montreal or Quebec City (see those chapters) to have a car waiting for you.

HINTS TO MOTORISTS. If you are traveling in winter, always call the road conditions number (see "Emergency Telephone Numbers") before you set out. If you are driving your own car, be sure you have heavy snow tires for good traction. "Skid school" or winter defensive-driving techniques can come in handy. If you are renting a car, stop by a hardware store and pick up a shovel and a bag of coarse salt in case you get stuck on the road. And be sure you have warm clothes, a blanket, and perhaps some light provisions (fruit or chocolate) in the car. Chances are you will not need them, but you might as well be prepared for all eventualities.

HINTS TO HANDICAPPED TRAVELERS. In general, access for the handicapped is limited in this area. However, Tourisme Quebec guidebooks to the region do indicate with a small wheelchair symbol whether specific buildings have total or partial access and the accommodations guide shows which hotels or motels are accessible. (See "Tourist Information.")

SEASONAL EVENTS. Seasonal events in the heartland of Quebec are literally that—related to the seasons. Quebecers have long since learned that having four distinct seasons is a big plus—and we glory in all four. Winter means skiing, *bien sûr*, along with snowshoeing, ice fishing, dogsled races, and snowmobiling. With the spring thaw come sugaring-off, and a chance to watch great flocks of ducks and Canada geese head north. In summer Quebecers head for the beaches and lakes, which dot the map of the province. And in fall, with the leaves in full blaze, we savor the joys of Indian summer.

To confirm dates of events and for further information, call 252-3037 before leaving Montreal or 800-361-9013 from anywhere in the province.

January–February. Tommycod *ice fishing* on the Ste-Anne River at La Pérade. Call 418-325-2475 or 800-463-3868.

February. *Festiglace Ice Festival.* Joliette. *Winter carnivals.* St-Donat and St-Côme.

March. *"Jackrabbit" cross-country ski race.*

April. *Maple Sugaring-off Festival.* Plessisville. Call 819-362-3284.

May. *Snorkeling* on the Oureau River between St-Liguori and Crabtree.

June. *Crafts Festival.* Grand-Mère. Call 819-538-6362. *Mattawin Canoe Classic.* 7-km (4-mi) race at St-Michel-des-Saints. *De Lanaudière Summer Festival.* Classical music concerts in the churches, parks, and theaters of Joliette and surrounding area. Call 800-363-2788, or 514-759-7636 from the Montreal region. *Festival de Trois-Rivières.* A 12-day festival of concerts, shows, exhibitions, and crafts. Call 819-374-3521.

July. *Festival du draveur.* Loggers' Festival, with activities relating to lumberjacks and the logging era, Grandes-Piles. Call 819-538-7845.

August. *Tomato Festival* celebrates the harvest with a rally and a Bavarian-style evening, St-Pierre-Les-Becquets. Call 819–263–2877.

September. *La Maurice International Canoe Classic.* A three-day canoe race down the St. Maurice River from La Tuque to Trois-Rivières. Call 819–537–9221. *Trois-Rivières Labatt Grand Prix.* Trois-Rivières. Three days of Atlantic and Can-Am Formula car racing. Call 819–379–9141. *Festival Western de St-Tite,* a Quebec-flavored cowboy carnival, with rodeos, parades, and entertainment, St-Tite. Call 418–365–6606.

October. *Optimist Club Hunting Festival.* La Tuque. A five-day celebration of the hunt, with antler and calling contests, parties, and other events. Call 819–523–2125.

INDUSTRIAL TOURS. Gentilly 2, Shawinigan 2, and La Tuque **Power Stations.** One of Quebec's major exports, thanks to our bountiful natural resources, is hydroelectric power. These Hydro-Quebec power stations are open to visitors seven days a week mid-June–late Aug. Be prepared for an awesome experience as what Hydro-Quebec calls their "energetic" guides take you around the mammoth installations.

Gentilly 2 (819–298–2943, ext. 275) tours daily from 9 A.M.–4 P.M.; Shawinigan 2 (819–537–8327) tours daily at 9:30 and 11 A.M., and 1:30 and 3 P.M.; La Tuque (819–523–8776) tours daily at same times as Shawinigan 2. Admission is free, but children under the age of 14 are not allowed on the tours.

NATIONAL AND PROVINCIAL PARKS. The heart of the heartland of Quebec is the vast system of provincial and national parks. La Mauricie is a national park, administered by the federal government; other parks and reserves in the region are under the jurisdiction of the Quebec Recreation, Fish, and Game Department, which is usually referred to by its French acronym, MLCP. The MLCP has a regional office at 100 rue Laviolette, Trois-Rivières, PQ G9A 5S9 (819–373–4444). For general information and reservations, call 800–462–5349 from anywhere in the province or use the individual numbers listed below for each park.

La Mauricie National Park. CP 758, Shawinigan, PQ G9N 6V9 (819–536–2638). Take exit 217 or 226 from Highway 55. Bounded on two sides by rivers (the St. Maurice and the Mattawin) and dotted with countless lakes, La Mauricie National Park is a favorite with campers, canoeists, and cross-country skiers alike. Logs were floated down the rivers in the park more than a century ago, as evidenced by several old dams and logging camps scattered around the park.

The park contains many wilderness campsites, some with, some without fireplaces, a semiserviced campground, boat rental site, launch ramp, and visitor reception center. Park naturalists are available from June-Sept., presenting a special nature interpretation program for visitors.

This is a magnificent wildlife preserve, but Parks Canada reminds visitors that *we* are the interlopers, not the animal inhabitants. "When a man meets a bear, the bear has the right of way. HE IS AT HOME."

Mastigouche Reserve. CP 450, St-Alexis-des-Monts, PQ J0K 1V0 (819–265–2098). Highways 347 and 349, with access from 7 A.M.–10 P.M. only. The reserve is on the western border of La Mauricie National Park.

In summer (the season is May-Sept.), there is canoeing on the many rivers and lakes within the park, plus canoe camping on Rivière-du-Loup (take your fishing rod) and other tributaries. Hunters and trappers are welcomed in autumn, and chalets are available for weekend stays. Cabins can also be reserved

COEUR-DU-QUEBEC

for ski trekkers from mid-Dec.–end of Mar. Snowmobilers can enjoy 65 km (40 mi) of trails in the park.

Portneuf Wildlife Reserve. Rivière-à-Pierre, Comté de Portneuf, PQ G0A 3A0 (418–323–2028). Entry point at Rivière-à-Pierre and Talbot on Highway 367, closer to Quebec City than the other parks. Access only from 7 A.M.–10 P.M.

Canoeing on Lake Lapeyrère is a big attraction here from May-Sept., as is canoe camping. For river trips each group must have at least two canoes. Trapping and moose and small game hunting take over in the fall. If you come in summer or fall, be sure to stop for a picnic by the waterfall at la Marmite; the picnic area stays open till the end of Oct.

St-Maurice Wildlife Reserve, 605 de la Station, Shawinigan, PQ G9N 1V9 (819–537–6674, Mon.-Fri. only). Highways 55, 155, 109 km (65 mi) north of Trois-Rivières; the last leg of the journey is by ferry from Matawin.

This splendid fish and game reserve north of La Mauricie National Park attracts fans of various sports at different times of the year. Canoe camping enthusiasts and naturalists visit between May and Sept., hunters in the fall, and the big attraction in winter (Dec.-Mar.) is treks for experienced cross-country skiers. Shelters along cross-country trails are furnished with wood stoves and firewood, basic furniture, and beds for up to eight people, and a propane lighting system. Dry toilets and drinking water are available nearby.

CAMPING. There are over 50 campgrounds in the parks and reserves (see "National and Provincial Parks" for information from the MLPC or from the individual parks) plus a network of *bases de plein air* (outdoor sites) and ZECs (controlled environmental zones) throughout the area. Accommodations range from the decidedly rustic to the thoroughly civilized. *Réseau Plein Air,* 4545 Pierre-de-Coubertin, CP 1000, Succursale M, Montreal, PQ H1V 3R2 (252–3007 in Montreal; from elsewhere in the province, 800–361–9202), a specialized central reservation and information service, can supply full details; the *Quebec Camping Association* is at the same address (252–3113 in Montreal or 800–361–3834).

FARM VACATIONS. Ever wished you could really get into the way of life of the area you are visiting? Outside the major cities, *Vacances-Familles/Agricotour* offers visitors country-style B&B accommodations. Overnight and longer stays can be booked through *Vacances-Familles Inc.,* 1415 rue Jarry Est, Montreal, PQ H2E 2Z7 (514–374–3546 or 374–4700).

FISHING AND HUNTING. What is your game? Whitetail deer . . . spruce or ruffed grouse . . . black bear . . . or partridge? Or perhaps you would prefer to combine a hunting trip with angling for smallmouth bass, Atlantic salmon, rainbow trout, or sturgeon. The big ones are biting in the waterways of de Lanaudière and Coeur-du-Quebec.

Fishing and hunting camps operated by experienced outfitters make it all easy for visitors. Nonresidents (anyone who has not lived in Quebec for 12 consecutive months) are required to use the services of outfitters north of the 52nd parallel; even further south, it is a good idea. Ask for the *Outfitters' Association Directory* put out by Tourisme Quebec (see "Tourist Information"), which contains details on all kinds of hunting and fishing packages including travel, accommodations from roughing-it wilderness sites to luxurious lodges, food, boats, and guides. And be sure to get copies of the *Quebec Hunting Guide* and the *Quebec Fishing Guide,* with full details on species found, seasons and limits, taking your catch home, and recommended equipment to bring.

Fishing licenses are available at most sporting goods stores, or from MLPC offices (see "National and Provincial Parks"). You can also pick up your hunting license at the local sporting goods store. If you are going to an outfitting lodge, you will probably be able to get your nonresident permit there, but be sure to mention it when you make arrangements for your trip. If you are planning any migratory-bird shooting, you will need a special permit for woodcock and snipe. Pick one up at the post office.

Winter fishing for pike, walleye, and yellow perch is a specialty of the Coeur-du-Quebec region. No permit is required for tommycod fishing (the season lasts from mid Dec. to mid Feb.).

PARTICIPANT SPORTS. Golf. There are a number of excellent courses in the Trois-Rivières area and the St. Maurice Valley that are open to nonresidents. And you do not have to lug your clubs from home—you can rent them on the spot. Call the *Club de golf du Moulin,* St-Louis-de-France (819-378-2819); the *Club les Vieilles Forges,* Trois-Rivières (819-379-7477); or the *Club de golf Grand-Mère* (819-538-3560) for details and times.

See "National and Provincial Parks" for the places for choice **cross-country skiing** and **snowshoeing.**

SPECTATOR SPORTS. Sept. is the big month for spectator sports. Plan your trip then, and you can cheer on the drivers in the Trois-Rivières *Labatt Grand Prix* as cars careen through the streets of the city at dizzying speeds; call 819-379-9141. The *Western Festival* at St-Tite, touted as an eastern version of the Calgary Stampede, goes on for ten days in mid-Sept.; call 418-365-6606. Also in Sept., the *International Canoe Classic* sees contestants race down the St-Maurice River from La Tuque to Trois-Rivières; call 819-537-9221.

HISTORIC SITES, CHURCHES, AND HOUSES. Batiscan Presbytery. 346 rue Principale. Batiscan, PQ G0X 1A0 (418-362-3051). The quaint farming village of Batiscan, at the confluence of the Batiscan and St. Lawrence rivers, was founded in 1639. The presbytery has been restored, with authentic period furnishings and arts and crafts displays. June–Sept., Tues.–Sun., 9 A.M.–noon and 1–4:30 P.M. $1 per person, seniors, 50 cents.

Les Forges du Saint-Maurice. 10150 blvd. des Forges, Trois-Rivières PQ G9C 1B1 (819-378-1663). The ironworks at Trois-Rivières was Canada's first heavy industry, starting production in 1738. The forge, which employed up to 500 laborers and craftsmen, made Trois-Rivières Canada's first company town, and was considered highly advanced in its first century of operation. It closed down in 1883. In 1973 the site was made a national historic park, where today you can see the master's house, forges, films, models, murals, and artifacts. Mid May–Labor Day, daily 9:30 A.M.–5:30 P.M.; Sept.–mid Oct., Wed.–Sun., 9 A.M.–5 P.M. Guided tours. Free.

Katimavik Handicraft Village. 75 rue St-Laurent, Louiseville, PQ J5V 2L6 (819-228-9422). Tucked behind the church is a small village of five houses chock-full of local handicrafts. You can tour the houses and see craft demonstra-

COEUR-DU-QUEBEC

tions and displays. Handicrafts are also for sale. Open weekends in June and Sept.; daily, late June–Labor Day, 10 A.M.–4 P.M. Free.

Maison Hertel-de-la-Fresnière. 802 rue des Ursulines, Trois-Rivières, PQ G9A 5B5 (819-373-1887). Built in 1695, the house has sturdy firebreak walls and a high roof with several skylights. Today it is a branch of the Maison des vins (liquor store), and exhibits of works by local artists are held regularly. Tues.–Thurs., 9 A.M.–6 P.M., Fri., 9 A.M.–9 P.M., Sat., 9 A.M.–5 P.M. Free.

Manoir Boucher-de-Niverville. 168 rue Bonaventure, Trois-Rivières, PQ G9A 2B1 (819-375-9628). Dating from around 1730, the house bears the name of one of its many owners, Sieur Boucher de Niverville, superintendant of the Abenaki tribe. Today the building houses the local chamber of commerce and tourism office, as well as an exhibit of locally made 18th-century furniture. Open in summer, weekdays, 9 A.M.–8 P.M., Fri. and Sat., noon–5 P.M. Off-season, weekdays, 9 A.M.–5 P.M., Fri. and Sat., noon–5 P.M. Free.

Monastère des Ursulines. 784 des Ursulines, Trois-Rivières, PQ G9A 5B5 (819-375-7922). The Ursulines, settling in Trois-Rivières in 1697, were the first religious congregation to establish themselves in the city. The convent served as a hospital from 1701 to 1886, and was for many years the only hospital between Montreal and Quebec City. The convent museum has a collection of old medical instruments, Indian relics, and religious art. May–Aug., Tues.–Fri., 9 A.M.–5 P.M.; Oct.–Apr., Wed.–Sun., 1:30–5 P.M. Closed in Sept. Reservations required for groups. Free.

Moore Canadiana Village. Chemin Morgan, Rawdon, PQ G0K 1S0 (514-834-4135 or 514-457-6234). Twenty restored buildings include seven houses, a chapel, a general store dating from 1884, and a schoolhouse, circa 1835. Most buildings are authentic, and each is furnished with period artifacts. May–Sept., weekdays and Sun., 1:30–4:30 P.M. Call for reservations. $4 per person.

Tonnancour Mill. 2930 rue Notre-Dame, Pointe-du-Lac, PQ G0X 1Z0 (819-377-3131). Built in 1721 by René Godefroy de Tonnancour, the mill produced flour from locally grown cereals for the benefit of the seigneur. The mill was closed in 1965, but a sawmill added in 1940 remains in operation. Late June–late Oct., Tues.–Sun., 1–7 P.M. $1 per person.

Trois-Rivières Cathedral. 362 rue Bonaventure, Trois-Rivières, PQ G9A 2B3 (819-374-2402). Built in the 1850s, the cathedral is the only Westminster-style church in North America. The steeple was added in 1905, and the 31 stained-glass windows were created by Florentine artist Guido Nunchiori in 1923. Daily, 9–11:30 A.M. and 2:30–4 P.M. Free.

MUSEUMS. Abenakis Museum. Highway 226, Odanak, PQ J0G 1H0 (514-568-2600). The Abenaki tribe was caught in the midst of the conflicts between whites and Indians in New England, and sold into slavery after the Mayflower settlers came to Plymouth in 1620. They fled to New France, where they were granted land around Odanak, a strategic site at the mouth of the St. François River. This museum traces their history in a variety of exhibits. Open early May–late Oct., daily 10 A.M.–5 P.M. Adults, $1.50; students, 75 cents.

Archaeological Museum. 3351 blvd. des Forges, Trois-Rivières, PQ G9A 5H7 (819-376-5229). Part of the Université du Quebec, the museum delves into the creativity of Neanderthal and Cro-Magnon man and the Indian tribes, showing fossils, tools and exhibits highlighting the prehistory of France and the Mauricie and the evolution of our ancestors. Mon.–Fri., 9 A.M.–noon and 2–5 P.M.; Sat., Sun., 1–5 P.M. Free.

Joliette Museum. 145 rue Wilfrid-Corbeil, CP 132, Joliette PQ G6E 3Z3 (514-756-0311). An art museum with a fine collection of Canadian arts, highlighting the work of a number of well-known Quebec artists. You can also see a collection of Quebec religious art and statues from the late Middle Ages and early Renaissance periods. Tues., Thurs., Sat., and Sun. noon–5 P.M. Adults, $1; students and seniors, 25 cents.

Musée du Bûcheron. 780 5e ave., Grandes-Piles, PQ G0X 1H0 (819–538–7895). The lumberjack museum commemorates some of the most colorful episodes in the history of Quebec. You can tour the cookhouse, sleeping quarters, and reconstructed lumber camp, and if you book ahead, they will even cook up a lumberjack-style meal for you. Open weekends only in May; late May–early Nov., daily 6 A.M.–6 P.M. Adults, $3; children, $1.

Musée Pierre Boucher. 853 rue Laviolette, Trois-Rivières, PQ G9A 1V7 (819–373–7816). The permanent collection includes local artifacts and archaelogical finds, home furnishings, blacksmith's tools, and instruments (of torture?) from the old prison. By special appointment, visitors can see a collection of works by painter Rodolphe Duguay, a local artist who died in 1973. Daily 2–4 P.M. and 7–9:30 P.M. Free.

ARTS AND ENTERTAINMENT. Summer theaters run plays in repertory from about St-Jean-Baptiste Day (June 24)–Labor Day. Check local newspapers for listings. Plays will be in French, but comedies and musicals often transcend the language barrier. In Trois-Rivières, call the *Théâtre des Marguerites* (819–377–3223) to see what is playing; in the St-Maurice Valley, try the *Théâtre d'été de la Mauricie* (819–539–5451).

ACCOMMODATIONS. You will find all kinds of hostelries in the region, some rustic, some up to the highest city-slicker standards. As elsewhere in the province, lilies are awarded to indicate the standard of service, and forks for the quality of the food served in hotel restaurants (see *Facts at Your Fingertips*). There is no tax on accommodations in Quebec.

Peak season depends on the area: hunting and fishing seasons are peak season in some regions, summer in others.

Double-occupancy lodgings in the heart of Quebec are classified as follows: *Deluxe,* $80–$100; *Expensive,* $60–$80; *Moderate,* $40–$60; *Inexpensive,* under $40.

BÉCANCOUR (GENTILLY). Motel La Place. *Moderate.* 3735 blvd. Bécancour, Bécancour, PQ G0X 1G0 (819–298–3144). A two-lily rating for the 16 rooms here, all with TV and phones.

Manoir Marie-Victorin. *Inexpensive.* 2340 blvd. Bécancour, Bécancour, PQ G0X 1G0 (819–298–3100). 22 rooms with AC and TV. One lily—basic but satisfactory.

Motel du Manoir Gentilly. *Inexpensive.* 1420 blvd. Bécancour, Bécancour, PQ G0X 1G0 (819–298–2952). 14 rooms, most with TV and kitchenettes. Outdoor pool and tennis courts. A likely choice for families. Two lilies.

DESCHAMBAULT (Chemin du Roy). Auberge du Roy. *Deluxe.* 106 rue St-Laurent, Deschambault, PQ G0A 1S0 (418–286–6958). Off Highway 138, but hard to find—get directions when you reserve. A five-room Victorian inn that has earned three lilies and three forks. Excellent local cuisine; special weekend rates.

COEUR-DU-QUEBEC

GRAND-MÈRE. Auberge Grand-Mère. *Expensive.* 10 6th Ave., Grand-Mère, PQ G9T 2E8 (819-538-8651). A four-lily, three-fork hostelry where you will eat and sleep in comfort. Amenities include AC, phones, and TV in each of the 38 rooms, plus an outdoor pool.
Motel La Rocaille. *Expensive.* 1851 5th Ave., Grand-Mère, PQ G9T 5L3 (819-538-8683). Four lilies, one fork; the 41 rooms here have AC, phones, and TV; sauna on the premises.
Motel Mauricien. *Moderate.* Autoroute 55, exit 223, Grand-Mère, PQ G9N 7M7 (819-539-6451). Facilities include AC, phone, and color TV in each of the 30 rooms; a comfortable place to stay; three lilies.

JOLIETTE. Auberge des Gouverneurs. *Expensive.* 1000 rue Visitation, Joliette, PQ J6E 3Z1 (800-463-2820). One of the 11 comfy Auberge des Gouverneurs inns across the province. Four lilies and three forks make this a likely bet. 40 rooms with AC, phones, color TV. Cross-country ski trails; partial wheelchair access.
Motel Bonsoir. *Moderate.* 120 Club de Golf, Joliette, PQ J6E 2B6 (514-753-4258). The Quebec tourism department gives the Motel Bonsoir three lilies, for above-average comfort. 20 rooms, all with telephone, AC, color TV.
Hôtel Victoria. *Inexpensive.* 544 rue Notre-Dame, Joliette, PQ J6E 3H7 (514-753-5935). 28 rooms, breakfast upon request. No tourism department rating.
Maison St-Louis. *Inexpensive.* 521 rue Notre-Dame, Joliette, PQ J6E 3H6 (514-756-8001). A somewhat basic establishment—one lily—13 rooms, most with TVs.

LA TUQUE. Motel le Gîte. *Expensive.* 1100 blvd. Ducharme, La Tuque, PQ G9X 3C4 (800-361-6162 or 819-523-9501). A 51-room hostelry that boasts three lilies, a one-fork restaurant, rooms with AC, phones, color TV.
Hotel Windsor. *Expensive.* 547 rue Commerciale, La Tuque, PQ G9X 3P5 (819-523-2701). Full-service restaurant plus 48 comfortable rooms with AC, phones, TV.
Hotel Le Castel Blanc. *Inexpensive.* 269 rue St-Joseph, La Tuque, PQ G9X 1K6 (819-523-2172). Comfy budget hotel with 16 rooms, TV in most.
Maison Beaudet. *Inexpensive.* 589 St-Antoine, La Tuque, PQ G9X 2Y8 (819-523-8937). Your basic budget hotel; 14 rooms.

RAWDON. Auberge Rawdon. *Inexpensive.* 3663 rue Queen, Rawdon, PQ J0K 1S0 (514-834-4200). Three lilies, two forks for a cozy inn with a good restaurant on the premises. 22 rooms, cross-country ski trails.
Motel le Tournesol. *Inexpensive.* 315 première Ave., Rawdon, PQ J0K 1S0 (514-834-6656). Ties with the Rawdon Inn at three lilies, two forks. AC and color TV in each of the 14 rooms.

ST. DONAT. Auberge St-Donat (formerly La Réserve). *Expensive.* Lac Ouareau, PQ J0T 2C0 (800-567-6719 or 819-424-2377). The inn has earned its spurs: three lilies for accommodation, two forks for the dining room. 56 rooms with phones and color TV; outdoor pool, sauna, plus cross-country skiing, water sports, and tennis courts.

SHAWINIGAN AND VICINITY. Auberge L'Escapade. *Moderate.* 3383 rue Garnier, Shawinigan, PQ G9N 6R4 (819-539-6911). A recommended—four-lily—inn with 40 rooms; AC, phones, color TV, and a good two-fork restaurant. Partial wheelchair access.

Motel Val Mauricie. *Inexpensive.* 4612 12e Ave., Shawinigan-Sud, PQ G9N 6T5 (819–537–6696). 17 comfortable rooms, all with phones, color TV. No credit cards.

TROIS-RIVIÈRES AND VICINITY. Auberge des Gouverneurs. *Expensive.* 975 rue Hart, Trois-Rivières, PQ G9A 4S3 (800–463–2820 or 819–379–4550). Part of the reliable Auberge des Gouverneurs chain, this comfortable inn has 125 rooms, all with phone, AC, color TV; partial access for the handicapped.

Hotel Le Baron. *Expensive.* 3600 blvd. Royal, Trois-Rivières Ouest, G9A 4M3 (800–268–9411 or 819–379–3232). A full-service hotel-restaurant with a four-lily, two-fork rating. 102 rooms with AC, phones, color TV. Outdoor pool.

Hotel-Motel Penn-Mass. *Expensive.* 303 blvd. Ste-Madeleine, Cap-de-la-Madeleine, PQ G8T 4X8 (819–379–8877). Located in a nearby suburb of Trois-Rivières, the Penn-Mass boasts four lilies, a two-fork restaurant, and 37 rooms with phones, AC, color TV. Partial access for the handicapped.

Motel Complexe Hôtelier Le Sapineau. *Moderate.* 217 rue Thibeau, Cap-de-la-Madeleine, PQ G8T 6X9 (819–375–6482). A comfortable establishment with 24 rooms, all equipped with phones, AC, color TV.

Motel Le Démocrate. *Moderate.* 2070 rue Bellefeuille, Trois-Rivières, PQ G9A 3Y8 (819–378–2881). Phones, AC, color TV in each of the 30 rooms in this two-lily (above-average comfort) hotel.

Motel Ste-Madeleine. *Inexpensive.* 1205 Route 138, Ste-Marthe-du-Cap-de-la-Madeleine, PQ G8T 4J8 (819–376–7804). Nine rooms with TV. One lily.

HOSTELS. La Flotille Youth Hostel, 497 rue Radisson, Trois-Rivières, PQ G9A 2C7 (819–378–8010). Open year-round, La Flotille offers bargain accommodations to young travelers.

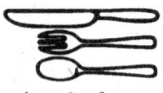

RESTAURANTS. *De Lanaudière and Coeur-du-Quebec* have a wide variety of eating places, from *casse-croûtes* (the ubiquitous snack bar where you can grab a quick sandwich and *frites*—French fries) to Chinese, Greek and, of course, French restaurants. See *Facts at Your Fingertips* for an explanation of the fork ratings awarded by the tourism department, which indicate the degree of dining excellence in the hotel's restaurants. In small towns, the hotel dining room may well be your best bet.

Dress code is generally casual, but no jeans. The more expensive hotel restaurants may require a jacket and tie.

Price categories for a three-course meal for one person, including beverage, tax, and tip, but no wine, are as follows: *Expensive,* $15–$25, and *Moderate,* $8–$14. There is a 10 percent tax on meals over $3.25.

Expensive

Aloha Restaurant. Motel au Noix de Coco, 7531 Notre-Dame, Trois-Rivières Ouest, PQ G9B 1L7 (819–377–3221). Polynesian specialties in cozy surroundings. Reservations required. All credit cards accepted.

L'Accueil. 16600 blvd. Bécancour, Bécancour, PQ G0X 1G0 (819–222–5777). French cuisine in a charmingly rustic setting. Get specific instructions when you call for reservations. Accepts all cards.

COEUR-DU-QUEBEC

Restaurant Chez Claude. Motel Castel des Pres, 5800 blvd. Royal, Trois-Rivières Ouest, PQ G9A 4P2 (819-375-4921). A fine French restaurant with a great local reputation. The tourism department gives it four forks with a special mention. Reservations required. All credit cards.

Moderate

Restaurant La Chaumière. 25 Chemin du Golf, Joliette, PQ J6E 2B5 (514-753-4124). An owner-chef-operated country restaurant that specializes in steaks and such. Get precise instructions when you call for reservations. All credit cards.

NORTHERN QUEBEC

by
Terri Foxman and Rosa Harris-Adler

Terri Foxman is a free-lance researcher and writer in Montreal. Rosa Harris-Adler is a nationally published Canadian free-lance writer.

The scope of territory known as Northern Quebec is vast, wild, and a remarkably picturesque haven for nature lovers and outdoor adventurers. But regarding it as one large area does the territory a disservice. For visitors, it can be divided more practically into four sections: Abitibi-Témiscamingue, Saguenay–Lac-Saint-Jean–Chibougamau, the North Shore, and Nouveau Quebec. Each offers a wide array of unique recreational activities and tourist attractions. In the following pages, each of these regions will be covered in depth. But there are some basic facts to consider before planning your trip that apply to the district as a whole.

The more populated areas of Northern Quebec have a moderate climate that lends itself to outdoor activities—from sailing and swim-

NORTHERN QUEBEC

ming to snowmobiling and ice fishing—all through the year. The northern reaches, however, are for heartier souls; there, the summer season is short and even in mid-July temperatures hover around 11°C (50°F).

Because the region is so vast, traveling by car is one of the best ways to see it. If you plan to motor through the area during the winter months, make sure your car is equipped with an efficient heating and defrosting system and snow or studded tires. You can get information on road conditions by dialing 418-643-6830 in Quebec City; 819-732-3670 in Amos; and 418-549-2966 in Chicoutimi. Even in the northern reaches of Quebec, gas stations are easy to find; many are open 24 hours a day seven days a week.

An abundance of pristine lakes and forests awaits those for whom fishing, hunting, and camping make the ideal holiday. Just a few of the fish and game available include Atlantic salmon, Arctic char, northern pike, sturgeon, caribou, hare, and snow geese. But there are strictly enforced government regulations regarding these activities, and several categories of territories. Fishing is permitted in all parks and wildlife preserves, whereas hunting and trapping are allowed only in some. In addition, some territories have been designated as ZECS (Zone Ecologique Controlée) by the province—zones where wildlife is protected stringently for ecological purposes.

Outfitter establishments will help you get through the maze of regulations; they staff expert guides, provide accommodations, and very often hold exclusive fishing, hunting, and trapping rights within specific territories. The personnel working with outfitter services have years of expertise and familiarity with the terrain, and can ensure the success of your trip. Licenses, required for all fishing and hunting activities in Quebec, are available at most sporting goods stores and through the ministère du Loisir de la Chasse et de la Pêche (see under *Facts at Your Fingertips*).

In addition to a wide range of comfortable hotels and motels in Northern Quebec, you might want to try staying at a Base de Plein Air, literally a fresh air camp, ideal for family vacations. Open year-round, these camps offer pleasant accommodations (usually in cabins), hardy meals, and a welcoming staff. In the majority of cases, everything is included in the price of your stay. Tourisme Quebec can provide lists of these camps.

Not all of the joys of Northern Quebec take place outdoors. Each region has a tradition of fine summer theater, equivalent to summer stock in the United States, mounting French productions annually. Those with a knowledge of the language, or those who merely want to get a flavor of the culture, should contact the relevant regional tourist offices for the schedules.

A colorful tradition in Northern Quebec are the many festivals that take place throughout the year. The most important one here is the Carnaval-Souvenir, which takes place in February in Chicoutimi. Recreating the history of the region, the festival is Northern Quebec's equivalent of Mardi Gras.

Abitibi–Témiscamingue

This region, in northwest Quebec, is a marvel of natural beauty. Although no one knows the exact origin of the Indian name Abitibi, linguists tell us the root of the word means water. And water there is. Every major center is within 10 kilometers (6 miles) of a lake and there are an estimated 100,000 waterways wending their way throughout the area.

Abitibi-Témiscamingue is as rich in history as it is in clear lakes and rugged countryside. In the 17th century when it was first explored, the remarkable abundance of wildlife made it a fur trapper's delight. As early as 1679, French settlers established a trading post on the shores of Lac Témiscamingue to sell their pelts. After 1885 prospectors discovered that the ground in the area had treasures to offer, too. Rich veins of silver, cobalt, copper, and even gold, were unearthed and mines were established. Commerce had come to the region and it was ripe for development.

And then there were the forests. As North America was being settled and towns and villages were springing up, the wealth of lumber in Abitibi-Témiscamingue became yet another valuable commodity. Forestry and mining are still crucial to the region today.

But never has the bustle of industry intruded on the exquisite wilderness that typifies the region. Here, travelers looking to escape into the arms of Mother Nature have come to the right place. Sportsmen in particular will enjoy the wide variety of fish and game. Outdoor enthusiasts can canoe for weeks and never end up in the same waterway twice. Some of the finest camping sites in the country are to be found here, and the hiking, snowshoeing, and snowmobiling trails rival those anywhere else in the world.

Saguenay–Lac-Saint-Jean–Chibougamau

The Saguenay–Lac-Saint-Jean–Chibougamau region of Quebec has it all—history, culture, remote and exquisite vistas, sandy beaches, and exotic fjords. It is a cornucopia of year-round outdoor activities; the summer months are mild and pleasant and ideal for camping and swimming. And with its gourmet-class restaurants and its welcoming residents complementing all the rest, it is a microcosm of all that is special about Quebec.

In 1535 French explorer Jacques Cartier first set foot in this region, which follows the St. Lawrence River's northern bank as far as the estuary of the Saguenay. He was so taken by its natural riches that he dubbed it the Kingdom of Saguenay, a name that does justice to its wild majesty. But it was nearly 300 years before the region could be tamed and tapped sufficiently to attract permanent settlers. *Couriers du bois* (fur traders), miners, and finally businessmen harnessing the enormous

NORTHERN QUEBEC

force of the electric energy generated here have all brought their own histories and vision to the region.

To the east is the vast Manicougan region of Quebec, and to the south is Quebec City and Charlevoix. To the west is Abitibi–Témiscamingue and to the north are the crisp tundras of Nouveau Quebec. This is pure Quebec—a side you will not see in the sophisticated clubs of its big cities—but as vibrant and worldy, in every sense, as a visitor could hope to find.

The North Shore

Stark rock formations and wide expanses of waterways are part of the exquisite backdrop of the St. Lawrence River's North Shore. Fishermen from the Normandy and Breton regions of France, exploring here in the 16th century, must have paused in their boats to marvel at the natural riches they saw before them. But no one was truly equipped or prepared to brave the elements and settle here until the mid-19th century, when the extent of this region's resources became apparent; fur, lumber, and electric energy are the main industries in the region even today.

The North Shore, comprising the regions Manicouagan and Duplessis, meanders from Tadoussac, north toward Baie-Comeau (hometown of Canadian Prime Minister Brian Mulroney), past the magnificent wildlife reserve on Anticosti Island, all the way up to Labrador. Hunting and fishing enthusiasts will be in their element throughout the year here.

Nouveau Quebec

There is something that captures the imagination about the northern reaches of the province, called Nouveau Quebec. Perhaps it is because this is one of the few places left to have a true adventure in North America. In winter, with the magic display of the northern lights as a backdrop, you can camp and explore endlessly, pausing to watch the magnificent herds of caribou as they migrate across the land.

Summer in Nouveau-Quebec is spectacular and bittersweet because of its brevity. There is an explosion of color as blackberry flowers, violet campanulas, and buttercups compete with each other for sheer beauty in the white sunlight. And the skies are filled with the sound of loons, marmettes, and ducks, who like to summer here in the Arctic's cool environs.

The vastness of the region is often underestimated. It covers a full 51 percent of the province and is 28 times as large as the Gaspé. France, Belgium, and Germany could all fit within its boundaries. And yet only about 12,000 people live here—the majority native Inuit and Cree.

The region is best seen with a guide. You can hire an Inuit or Indian guide—many work with outfitting establishments—to take you along snowshoe and hunting trails and give you a sense of the history of a

PRACTICAL INFORMATION FOR ABITIBI-TÉMISCAMINGUE

HOW TO GET THERE AND HOW TO GET AROUND. By Plane. There are regular flights to Val-d'Or and Rouyn-Noranda from Montreal, Quebec City, Toronto, and Ottawa. Major domestic airlines serving the area are *Air Canada, Quebecair,* and *Nordair.* The Rouyn-Noranda Airport is 15 km (9 mi.) southeast of the twin towns. The Val-d'Or Airport is close by at 5 km (3 mi.) from the city. *Air Creebec* (819–824–3494) flies north from Val-d'Or to Matagami, and to James Bay in Nouveau Quebec.

By Bus. *Voyageur* buses run from Montreal to Val-d'Or and Rouyn-Noranda. Voyageur also operates within the region, serving most towns including Amos, Malartic, Témiscaming, and Ville-Marie.

Some of the localities in northwest Quebec have an information service on urban transportation. In Amos call 819–732–5863; in Rouyn, 819–762–0838; and 819–825–4767 in Val-d'Or.

By Train. *VIA Rail* provides limited service to and within the region. There is a train from Montreal to Senneterre. Passengers can then catch a train to Amos or take a bus that is operated by VIA, to Val-d'Or.

By Car. From Montreal and the Laurentians take Route 117; routes 167 and 113 from the Saguenay–Lac-St-Jean–Chibougamau area; from Ontario routes 63, 65, 66, and 101.

The best way to get around is by car. You can rent a car in all major centers and at the airports. For toll-free numbers to make reservations, see *Facts at Your Fingertips.*

TOURIST INFORMATION. The permanent provincial tourism office is *Association Touristique Abitibi-Témiscamingue,* 212 Ave. du Lac, Rouyn, PQ J9X 4N7 (819–762–8181, 800–567–6423 in Quebec). Seasonal tourist offices, June–August, are set up in Val-d'Or, Malartic, Rouyn, LaSarre, Amos, Matagami, Senneterre, Lebel-sur-Quevillon, Notre-Dame-du-Nord, Ville-Marie, Témiscamingue, and the southern entrance to La Vérendrye Wildlife Reserve. Other information sources are: *Office du Tourisme et des Congres du Rouyn-Noranda Regional,* 69 rue Perreault Est, Rouyn, PQ J9X 3C1 (819–762–0447). *Office des Congres et du Tourisme d'Amos-Region Inc.,* 182 première rue Est, Amos, PQ J9T 2G1 (819–732–3250). *Services Touristiques de Val-d'Or,* 1034 3eme Ave., Val-d'Or, PQ J9P 1T6 (819–825–3703).

TELEPHONES AND EMERGENCY NUMBERS. The area code for Abitibi-Témiscamingue is 819. The cost of a telephone call in a pay phone is 25 cents. In the region, dial 411 for information; elsewhere, dial 819–555–1212. In case of an emergency, dial 0 and the operator will help you. In Val-d'Or, call

NORTHERN QUEBEC

the local police at 825-6161; the provincial police at 824-3693. In Rouyn, dial 762-6575 for the local police; 764-3202, for the provincial police.

SEASONAL EVENTS. The Abitibi–Témiscamingue region boasts numerous celebrations—everything from winter carnivals and popular theme festivals to tournaments and wild west rodeos: **February.** *Angier Fish Festival.* Fish tasting, snowmobiling, and dancing are part of the fun here. For information call 819-949-3441. **May.** *Normétal Lumberjack Festival.* Competitions, shows, and dances celebrate the trade of the woodsman. Runs five days at the end of the month. For information, call 819-788-2525/2882. **June.** *The Amos Regatta.* Features canoe races and a treasure hunt. For information, call 819-732-5321/4330. **July.** *Le Tour de l'Abitibi.* An international cycling competition (junior category) with events scheduled in towns along the route. End of the month. For information, call 819-825-5554. *The Ville-Marie International Regatta.* Three days of water sport and fun is part of the summer festival of Lake Témiscamingue. For information, call 819-629-2632. **October.** *The Moose Festival* at the end of the month sees Val-d'Or celebrate the close of the hunting season. For information, call 819-825-8106. **November.** Rouyn plays host to the *Abitibi-Témiscamingue International Film Festival* at the beginning of the month. Many first screenings and North American films are featured. For information, call 819-762-6212.

TOURS AND SPECIAL-INTEREST SIGHTSEEING. Those with an interest in the industries of the area might benefit from the pamphlet *Industrial Tours* available from the regional tourist office (see "Tourist Information").

Covered Bridges. At the beginning of the 20th century, there were over 1,000 covered bridges in Quebec. In the Amos area alone, there are five. Built to prevent deterioration of roads caused by rain and snowfall, these bridges typify an earlier, less technological era. The Abitibi region has the most covered bridges in the province.

Sigma Mines. Route 117, Val-d'Or, PQ J9P 4N8 (819-825-4182). A notable attraction of the area. Guided tours available during the summer months on Thurs. and Fri. at 1:15 P.M.

PROVINCIAL PARKS AND WILDLIFE RESERVES. **La Vérendrye Wildlife Reserve.** Le Domain RR 1, Montcerf, PQ J0W 1N0 (819-435-2216/2541 or 438-2017). If you need the therapeutic powers of fresh air and wilderness, this is the place to visit. This wonderland of natural beauty has over 800 km (500 mi) of shoreline for the outdoor adventurer to discover. Pitch your tent at one of the equipped campgrounds on the site or opt for your own spot. If you do not wish to rough it, you can rent a chalet with kitchen. Full park facilities are available from mid-May–mid-Sept., and there is moose hunting in the fall.

Parc Aiguebelle. 180 blvd. Rideau, Noranda, PQ J9X 1N9 (819-637-5322 or 762-8196). Route 101 from Rouyn-Noranda is the main road to this spectacular park. Fine cross-country skiing, hiking, canoeing, and fishing make this an excellent spot for outdoor enthusiasts. Open year-round. Equipment and services rentable.

PROVINCE OF QUEBEC

CAMPING. This region has over 25 campgrounds, most of them fully equipped. Camping enthusiasts would do well to contact the *Abitibi-Témiscamingue Camping and Caravaning Association,* 280 Place Jacola, Val-d'Or, PQ J9P 5N1 (819–824–9958).

FISHING AND HUNTING. This is prime territory for hunters and fishermen. There are over 100 outfitters in the region, who will guide you to such key spots as Lac-Témiscamingue, La Sarre, Duparquet, Amos, Matagami, Lebel-sur-Quévillon, Senneterre, Louvicourt, Val-d'Or, and Cadillac. Hunters will find fox, bear, moose, rabbit, partridge, duck, and Canada geese; while fisherman can try their luck on any of the thousands of waterways teeming with pike, walleye, sturgeon, bass, and trout. Aside from contacting the provincial Ministry of Tourism, CP 20,000, Quebec City, PQ G1K 7X2, you might also contact the main office of the *Ministère du Loisir, de la Chasse, et de la Pêche,* at CP 22,000, Quebec City, PQ G1K 7X2.

SUMMER SPORTS. Golf. *Club de Golf l'Oiselet d'Amos,* Chemin Saint-Mathieu, CP 334, Amos, PQ J9T 3A7 (819–732–5587). Access by Routes 111 and 109. *Club de Golf Noranda,* Chemin McDonald, CP 446, Noranda, PQ J9X 5B1 (819–762–6252). Access by Route 117. *Club de Golf Val-d'Or,* Île-de-Siscoe, PQ (819–824–4631). Access by Route 111.

WINTER SPORTS. Alpine, Cross-Country Skiing, and Snowshoeing. *Centre-de-Plein-Air Mont-Kanasuta,* Route 117 North, J9X 5C6 (819–762–8107). *Mont-Video,* RR 1, CP Box 1 Barraute, PQ J0Y 1A0 (819–734–2193). *Val-d'Or Ski Centre,* 600 rue 7ème, Val-d'Or, PQ J9P 3P3 (819–825–3060).

Snowmobiling. Snowmobile enthusiasts can enjoy a 420-km (260-mi) trail throughout this region, well serviced in such towns as Amos, Senneterre, and Val-d'Or.

HISTORIC SITES AND HOUSES. Fort Témiscamingue. Box 636, Ville-Marie (819–629–3222). Located 4 km (2.4 mi) south of Ville-Marie in Fort Témiscamingue Historical Park. Remains of trading post built 1720. Exhibition reviving fur-trading era, Amerindian cemetery called "the enchanted forest" for its oddly twisted tree trunks. Guided tours of park. On-site campground. Mid-May–June, Mon.–Fri., 8:30 A.M.–4:30 P.M. End of June–Labor Day, Mon.–Fri., 10 A.M.–6 P.M.; Sat.–Sun., 10 A.M.–8 P.M. Free.

Maison du Colon. 3 rue Notre-Dame-de-Lourdes, Ville-Marie (819–629–3533). Built in 1881, this house is typical of those erected by first settlers of the area. Visits by reservation. Free.

Maison Dumulon. 191 Ave. du Lac, Rouyn (819–764–6404). General store, post office, and family home built in 1924 by Jos Dumulon, first merchant in Rouyn. This restored log cabin houses diverse, temporary exhibitions, a restaurant, handicraft boutique, and a municipal tourist kiosk. Open from end of June–Labor Day; 9 A.M.–9 P.M., daily. The rest of the year only the general store is open; Mon.–Fri., 9 A.M.–5 P.M. Free.

NORTHERN QUEBEC

Village Minier de Bourlamaque. 144A Ave. Perreault, Val-d'Or (819-825-7616). Historic mining village comprised of 80 pinewood houses restored to way original miners lived. House 123 serves as a museum. Open 9 A.M.–9 P.M., daily from end of June–mid-Sept. The rest of the year it is open Mon.–Fri., 9 A.M.–noon, 1–5 P.M. Free.

MUSEUMS. Several centers offer temporary exhibits ranging from regional history to modern works of local artists: **Centre d'Exposition de Rouyn-Noranda.** 425 blvd. du College, Rouyn (819-762-6600). Open daily from 2–5 P.M., 7–10 P.M. **Centre d'Exposition de Val-d'Or.** 600 rue 7ème, Val-d'Or (819-825-0942). Wed.-Fri., Sun., 2–5 P.M., 7:30–8:30 P.M.; Sat., 2–5 P.M. **Galerie du Centre Culturel d'Amos.** 182 rue 1ere Ouest, Amos (819-732-6541). Wed.-Sun., 1:30–5 P.M., 7:30–10 P.M.

Musée Régionale des Mines et des Arts de Malartic. 650 rue de la Paix (819-757-4677). Permanent exhibition, mining theme. Model of a mine shaft open to visitors. Mid-May–mid-Sept., daily 10 A.M.–noon, 1–5 P.M. Rest of year, Wed.-Fri., 10 A.M.–noon, 1–5 P.M.; Sat.-Sun., 1–5 P.M. Adults, $2.50; children over 12, $2; under 12, $1.

ACCOMMODATIONS. A selection of fine lodgings is available in this region, from motels for the budget-minded to deluxe inns. Double-occupancy lodgings in Abitibi-Témiscamingue are categorized as follows: *Deluxe,* $70 and up; *Expensive,* $40–$70; *Moderate,* $25–$40; *Inexpensive,* $25 and under.

AMOS. Le Château d'Amos. *Expensive.* 201 Ave. Authier, Amos, PQ J9T 1W1 (819-732-5386 or toll free in Quebec 800-361-6162). Spacious rooms and superior comfort in the heart of Abitibi region. AC, TV, excellent restaurant, bar, disco.

Motel Chez Tony. *Expensive.* 652 Première Ave. Ouest, Amos, PQ J9T 1V6 (819-732-3228). 24 individual units, AC, TV, bar, disco.

MALARTIC. Motel au Filon d'Or. *Moderate.* 1311 Ave. Royale, Malartic, PQ J0Y 1Z0 (819-757-4377). At the exit of the city, TV, partial accessibility for handicapped.

NORANDA. Hôtel-Motel Noranda. *Moderate–Expensive.* 41 6ème rue, Noranda, PQ J9X 1Y8 (819-762-2341). Hotel less expensive than motel. Located downtown, over 60 rooms, piano bar, three-fork restaurant.

ROUYN. Hôtel Albert. *Moderate.* 84 rue Principale, Rouyn, PQ J9X 5C4 (819-762-3545). On the main street, AC, TV, two-fork restaurant. Hotel of pioneers of mining industry.

TÉMISCAMING. Auberge White Oaks Inn. *Inexpensive–Moderate.* 10 River Road, Témiscaming, PQ J0Z 3R0 (819-627-3363). In middle of city on Ottawa River. Rooms with or without bath, suites, some TV, bar, dining room. Basic comfort.

PROVINCE OF QUEBEC

VAL-D'OR. Auberge des Gouverneurs. *Expensive–Deluxe.* 1001 3ème Ave. Est, Val-d'Or, PQ J9P 1T3 (819–825–5660 or 800–463–2820 from Ontario, Quebec, and the Atlantic Provinces). A luxury hotel at the entrance to the city. AC, TV, dining room, bar, laundry service, boutique, car rental. Near Bourlamaque Mining Village, Sigma Mines, and the airport. Suites available.

Motel L'Escale. *Expensive–Deluxe.* 1100 rue de l'Escale, Val-'Dor, PQ J9P 4G8 (819–824–2711). Superior comfort, spacious rooms, AC, TV, dining room.

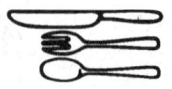

RESTAURANTS. Categories for restaurants in these regions are as follows: *Deluxe,* $25 and up; *Expensive,* $20–$25; *Moderate,* $10–$20; *Inexpensive,* $10 and under. Restaurants are listed according to the price of a complete dinner; drinks, tax, and tip are not included. Unless otherwise noted, the restaurants accept some if not all major credit cards.

AMOS. Château d'Amos. *Moderate.* 201 ave. Authier (819–732–5386). This hotel restaurant was awarded four forks for excellence by the Quebec government. French cuisine. Dinner, Tues.-Sat. Reservations recommended.

ROUYN-NORANDA. Le Caveau. *Moderate–Expensive.* 636 ave. Larivière, Rouyn (819–764–5525). Old Quebec style building makes for quaint, cozy dining. Char-broiled steaks, seafood, Quebec specialties. Summer: lunch, Mon.-Sat.; dinner, Sun.-Sat.; brunch, Sun. Winter: dinner, daily. Reservations recommended.

Le Trianon. *Moderate–Expensive.* 38 rue Gamble Est, Rouyn (819–762–8722). Fine cuisine with excellent service, situated downtown. Homemade pastas and flambées are specialties. Lunch, Mon.-Fri.; dinner, daily. Reservations recommended.

Les Trois Fourchettes. *Moderate–Expensive.* 41 6ème rue, Noranda (819–762–2341). Named for its three-fork government rating for very good dining. In Hôtel-Motel Noranda. Steak, seafood, roast beef specials Sun. Dinner, daily. Reservations recommended.

La Maison Quebecoise. *Inexpensive–Moderate.* 636 Ave. Larivière, Rouyn (819–762–2003). Upstairs from Le Caveau. Features Quebec specialties including tourtière. Outdoor cafe in summer. Breakfast, lunch, and dinner daily.

Le Café-Terrasse. *Inexpensive.* 84 rue Principale, Rouyn (819–763–3545). Good dining in the Hôtel Albert. Canadian food; roast beef, Thurs.; turkey, Sun. Breakfast, lunch, and dinner daily.

VAL-D'OR. L'Aubergine. *Moderate–Deluxe.* 1001 3ème Ave. Est; (819–825–5660). Three-fork dining in Auberge des Gouverneurs hotel. Pine walls and plants create a welcoming atmosphere. French cuisine. Breakfast, lunch, and dinner daily. Table d'hôte during the week, à la carte weekends. Reservations recommended.

La Cale du Navire. *Moderate–Deluxe.* 1504 rue de la Quebecoise (819–825–2122). Designed like the hold of a ship, naturally it specializes in seafood. Lobster tank. Dinner daily. Reservations recommended.

Brasserie La Maison Quebecois. *Inexpensive.* 1504 rue de la Quebecoise (819–825–2122). Less formal dining than La Cale du Navire. Quebec cooking in a rustic setting. Breakfast, lunch, and dinner Mon.–Sat.

PRACTICAL INFORMATION FOR SAGUENAY, LAC-SAINT-JEAN, AND CHIBOUGAMAU

HOW TO GET THERE AND HOW TO GET AROUND. By Plane. *Quebecair* and *Quebec Aviation* (800–463–4004) fly from Montreal to Bagotville (part of Ville de la Baie). Quebecair also flies from Quebec City to Bagotville. The Chibougamau Airport is 15 km (9 mi) southwest of the city; the Bagotville Airport is 8 km (5 mi) west of La Baie and 13 km (8 mi) southeast of Chicoutimi.

By Bus. *Voyageur* (514–842–2281) connects Quebec's major cities with the main towns of the region, including Chicoutimi and Jonquière. Several companies provide interurban service within the region including: *Autocars Fournier*, based in Alma (418–662–5441); *Autobus Jasmin*, based in Jonquière (418–545–2167); and *Autobus Laterrière* in Chicoutimi (418–549–2463). The bus terminal in each center can supply further information on service in the area. For information on citywide transportation, phone 418–662–7414 in Alma; and 418–543–3344 in Chicoutimi and Jonquière.

By Train. *VIA Rail* provides service from Montreal to the Lac-St-Jean area and Chicoutimi. VIA also has package tours, including transportation and accommodation, available year-round. Trips include the Old-Timers' Train to Chicoutimi for the popular winter carnival celebrations in February and whale-watching excursions up the Saguenay in the fall.

By Car. A good network of roads makes it easy to drive to this region from almost anywhere in the province. There are three principal points of entry into this area. Entering through the Saguenay sector on the east, take Route 172 from the North Shore, Route 170 from St-Siméon, and Route 175 from Quebec City, through the Laurentides Wildlife Reserve. To arrive at the Lac-St-Jean sector, travel routes 175 and 169 from Quebec City, Route 155 from the Coeur-du-Quebec through La Tuque, and Route 167 from Chibougamau through the Chibougamau Wildlife Reserve. To enter through the Chibougamau sector in the west, take Route 113 from Abitibi, via Senneterre and Lebel-sur-Quévillon.

The best way to see the many towns and attractions in the region is by car. Here are some auto rental facilities in the area. *Avis* (800–268–2310 in Canada and 800–331–2112 in U.S.); *Budget* (800–268–8900 in Canada and 800–527–0700 in U.S.; for Chibougamau you must call them directly at 418–748–7275; *Tilden* (800–361–5334 in Quebec, Ontario, and the Atlantic Provinces).

TOURIST INFORMATION. The following offices are open year-round: *Association Touristique Saguenay–Lac-St-Jean–Chibougamau*, 198 rue Racine Est, Bureau 200, Chicoutimi, PQ G7H 1R9 (418–543–9778 or 800–463–9651 in Quebec). *Bureau de Tourisme et de Congrès de Chicoutimi*, 300 rue Dubuc, Chicoutimi, PQ G7H 5C8 (418–543–4758). *Office de Tourisme de Ville de la Baie et du Bas-Saguenay*, 491 blvd. de la Grande-Baie, Ville de La Baie, PQ G7B 3C9 (418–544–5850). *Salon du Tourisme et de l'Industrie de Jonquière*, Centre des Congrès, 2665 blvd. du Royaume, Jonquière, PQ G7S 4S9 (418–548–

4004). *Conseil de la Zone Touristique d'Alma et du Lac-St-Jean,* 140 rue Saint-Joseph Sud, Alma, PQ G8B 3R1 (418–662–6501).

Information centers are set up during the summer in Albanel, Dolbeau, Roberval, St-Félicien, Ste-Jeanne-d'Arc, Hébertville, Normandin, Chambord, Petit-Saguenay, St-Bruno, St-Gédéon, and Péribonka.

TELEPHONES AND EMERGENCY NUMBERS. The area code is 819. The cost of a local telephone call is 25 cents. Dial 411 for information within the region; from elsewhere, dial 819–555–1212. In an emergency, dial 0 and the operator will help you. *Police:* 662–3456 in Alma; 549–9440 in Chicoutimi; 542–8111 in Jonquière. *Ambulance:* Ambulance Alma, 662–6483; Ambulance Aubin in Chicoutimi, 543–3331; Ambulance St-Jean in Jonquière, 542–2872.

SEASONAL EVENTS. February. The *Chicoutimi Carnaval-Souvenir* is the largest and most popular festival of the region. Every year Chicoutimi relives the rhythm of bygone eras. Chicoutimians don period costumes for 11 days of nonstop action. Highlights include an operetta, a cancan, concerts, plays, and exhibits. Contact Carnaval-Souvenir du Chicoutimi, 67 rue Jacques-Cartier Ouest, Chicoutimi, PQ G7J 1E9 (418–543–4438). **June.** The *Saguenay Festival* in Ville de la Baie. Program of activities revolving around the heritage of this magnificent region. This may be the northernmost point for body surfing in North America. For information call 418–544–7837. **July.** The *Jonquière Festival,* a five-day party that features costume balls, a parade, and live entertainment, gets the month off to a rousing start for tourists residents alike. For information call 418–542–5896 or 547–3125. **July.** *Western Festival.* The town of Dolbeau relives the colorful days of gunslinging and attracts over 50,000 people a year in the bargain. An on-site western village houses a rodeo stadium, ranch, barn, saloon, and theater. For information call 418–276–1838/0984. **July.** *Eight Days of Fun* and the *International Lac-St-Jean Swimming Meet.* These two events in Roberval run side-by-side. A week of eight action-packed days lead up to this renowned international endurance competition that attracts the best swimmers in the world. For information call 418–275–2851. **August.** The *Blueberry Festival.* The blueberry is king in this area and is celebrated in this festival in Mistassini, the heart of blueberry country. Sample the delightful blueberry products for which the region is famous while wandering through the market or taking in the shows mounted for the occasion. For information call 418–276–1241.

SIGHTSEEING CRUISES. Services Maritimes **Piékouagami Inc.** Marina de la Dam-en-Terre, Alma, PQ G8B 5W1 (418–662–6854 or 418–668–6556). Mid-June–mid-Sept., the two-hour cruises offered by this company aboard the M.V. *La Tournée* provide a leisurely way to explore the spectacular Lac-St-Jean lakescape. On Sunday, special tours depart from St-Félicien, Roberval, Péribonka, and St-Gédéon. Fare: about $12; less for students, seniors, and children.

Croisières Marjolaine Inc. Ave. Lafontaine. Mailing address: CP 203 Port de Chicoutimi, PQ G7H 5B7 (418–543–7630). Day-long Saguenay cruises (June–Sept.) are the ideal way to take in the fjord and other magnificent sights such as Cap-Trinite, La Baie des Ha! Ha! and Ste-Rose-du-Nord. Evening cruises are

NORTHERN QUEBEC

also available. Prices range from $10–$24 depending on the tour. Reduced prices for children under 14.

TOURS AND SPECIAL INTEREST SIGHTSEEING.
Centre Astro. 1200 rue de la Friche, Dolbeau, PQ (418-276-0919). Observatory equipped with Newton telescope, museum of natural science and technology, and amphitheater. Mid-June to the end of Aug., 9 A.M.–midnight. Adults, $3; children, $1.50.

Centre Historique Aquatique. 700 blvd. de la Traversée, Roberval, PQ G8H 2N7 (418-275-5550). History, ecology, fauna, and water species of Lac-St-Jean presented via an aquarium, audio-visuals and a fantastic trip through time on board a submarine. Open year-round. From 10 A.M.–10 P.M. in summer. Phone or inquire at tourist office for off-season hours. Adults, $3; children, students, and seniors, $2.

Julac Inc. 453 7ème Ave., Dolbeau, PQ (418-276-4120). Tour the factory and sample the fine blueberry-based aperitif manufactured here. Visits by reservation.

Les Tours Sagamiens Inc. 3460 blvd. St-François, Jonquière, PQ G7X 8L3 (418-547-6645). Professional guided tours in French, English, German, and Spanish of the Lac-St-Jean area.

Trappist Monk Monastery. 255 blvd. des Pères, Mistassini (418-276-5327). For over 70 years the Trappist fathers here have been turning their divine talents to chocolate making, proving there is more to Mistassini than blueberries. The results of their efforts are available to the general public, another reason for visiting this historic monastery.

ZOOS. Le Jardin Zoologique de St-Félicien. 2230 blvd. Onésime-Gagnon, CP 520, PQ G0W 2N0 (418-679-0543). Access via Route 167. Spread over 1,270 acres, this phenomenal natural zoo houses over 2,400 species of animals enclosed in and in their own habitat. There are nature trails and trains to explore this massive, magnificent park. While you are there, enjoy a quick history lesson and visit the replicas of trading posts, jobber and trapper camps, and Amerindian huts. June–Sept., 9 A.M.–5 P.M. Adults, $4.50; children under 13, $1. For nature trail, adults, $3.50; children under 13, $2.

PROVINCIAL PARKS AND WILDLIFE RESERVES.
Chibougamau Wildlife Reserve. 625 blvd. Sauvé, Roberval, PQ G8H 2N4 (418-275-1702). The south entrance at milestone 33 and the north entrance at milestone 178 of Highway 167 will lead you in to a park of rugged, natural beauty. You can rent space in a campsite or a cottage and enjoy canoeing, hunting, and fishing in some of the finest terrain Quebec has to offer. Facilities available May–Oct.

Parc Saguenay, 491 blvd. de la Grande Baie, Ville de la Baie, PQ G7B 2C9 (418-544-7388, 235-4434 or 272-2267). This charming park wends its way from la Baie des Ha! Ha! to the St. Lawrence River and from Ste-Rose-du-Nord to Tadoussac. At the western end is the natural and noble Saguenay fjord whose magnificent capes and towering cliffs are a must-see. Facilities from May–Oct. Nature guides and interpretation service available.

PROVINCE OF QUEBEC

CAMPING. No fewer than 60 campsites dot this region, all of them fully equipped, usually set against a majestic backdrop. Contact the *Saguenay–Lac-St-Jean Camping and Caravaning Association,* 3172 rue Ste-Marie, Jonquière, PQ G7S 1A5 (418–548–8110). See "Provincial Parks and Wildlife Reserves" for more specific information.

FISHING AND HUNTING. Remember that fishing and hunting licenses are required; be sure that you have yours ahead of time or that your outfitter can provide one. There are ten controlled hunting and fishing zones in this region, where, in season, you can hunt for moose and small game, and fish for walleye, pike, and trout—particularly abundant in the Chibougamau area. Aside from contacting the provincial ministry of tourism (see *Facts at Your Fingertips*), you might also contact the main office of the ministère du Loisir, de la Chasse, et de la Pêche (MLCP), at CP 22,000, Quebec City, PQ G1K 7X2.

PARTICIPANT SPORTS. Golf. *Club de Golf de Chicoutimi* (418–549–2018); *Club de Golf Saguenay d'Arvida,* Jonquière (418–548–4235); *Club de Golf de Chibougamau* (418–748–4119).

Alpine Skiing. *Mont Villa Saguenay,* near Alma (418–662–2901); *Mont Fortin,* near Jonquière (418–547–3613); *Le Valinouet,* near Chicoutimi (418–696–1962).

Cross-Country Skiing. *Club de Ski du Fond Saguenay,* near Chicoutimi (Laterrière) (418–678–9633); *Club Les 3 Criques,* at Chambord, on the southern shores of Lac-St-Jean (418–342–5274); *Centre de Plein-Air Obalski,* at Chibougamau (418–748–2071).

Snowmobiling. There is a fine trail here circling Lac-St-Jean totaling 380 km (240 mi) with a panoramic view atop Mont-Vallin, near Jonquière.

HISTORIC SITES. Le Moulin des Pionniers (The Pioneers' Mill). 15 rue des Peupliers, Notre-Dame-de-la-Doré, PQ G0W 2J0 (418–256–3821). Route 167 to Chibougamau, 10 minutes from the zoo. An old hydraulic mill of vital importance to pioneers. Tours are given by guides in period costume. Visit the pioneer house, the mill in operation, observation sites, and art exhibits. June–Sept., 9 A.M.–7 P.M. daily. Adults, $3; students, $1.

La Vielle Pulperie. 300 Dubuc, Chicoutimi, PQ G7J 4M1 (418–543–2729/4758). Contains five buildings of the Chicoutimi Pulp Company built between 1896 and 1923. Historical exhibition, guided tours, films, activities for children, summer theater. Open air cafe on site. Mid-June–Labor Day. Phone for hours. Free.

Village de Val-Jalbert. 625 blvd. Sauvé, Roberval, PQ G8H 2N4 (418–275–3132/1702). In 1927 Val-Jalbert was deserted after the closing of the Quebec Pulp and Paper Mill. Fifty years later it was restored and opened to the public. The old convent, the general store, the artisan boutique, the old mill, and historic houses are just some of the sites. Guided tours, films, restaurants, waterfalls, a hotel, and camping nearby help make this revitalized ghost town a must-see for visitors to the region. May–Sept. Phone for hours and admission fee.

NORTHERN QUEBEC 191

MUSEUMS. Centre National d'Exposition Mont-Jacob. 4160 rue de Vieux Pont, Jonquière, PQ G7X 7W4 (418–542–4516). Accredited by the National Museums of Canada. Artistic, scientific, and historical exhibitions. Open daily; call for hours. Free.

Musée Amérindien de Pointe-Bleue. La Société d'Histoire et d'Archéologie, 407 Amishk, Pointe-Bleue, PQ G0W 2H0 (418–275–4842). Exhibition of objects illustrating history of the Montagnais Amérindians. Guided tours on request. Audiovisual presentations. Mid June–late Sept.; call for hours. Minimal admission.

Musée de l'Automobile de St-Félicien. 2303 blvd. Onésime Gagnon, St-Félicien, PQ (418–679–2756). Route 169 facing the zoo. Features two dozen cars from the years 1917–1930. Open end of May–Labor Day, 7 A.M.–7 P.M. Small admission fee.

Musée du Fjord. 3346 blvd. de la Grande-Baie, La Baie, PQ G7B 1G2 (418–544–7394). Exhibitions of art, science, and history. Regional and national works are on display. Open daily. Small admission fee.

Musée Louis-Hémon. 700 Nationale 169, Péribonka, PQ G0W 2G0 (418–374–2177). Where celebrated French author, Louis Hémon, visited and was inspired to write the classic, *Maria Chapdelaine.* The museum, a monument, houses dating back to 1900, and a miniature village recreate Hémon's stay in Péribonka and the way of life of the first colonists. Open daily, late May–Labor Day. Small admission fee.

Musée du Saguenay–Lac-St-Jean. 534 rue Jacques-Cartier Est, Chicoutimi, PQ G7H 5K3 (418–545–9400). Showcase of art and history of region including furniture, handicrafts, archaelogical pieces of Amerindians and Inuit, sculptures, and paintings. Open year-round. Small admission fee.

ACCOMMODATIONS. Visitors to this region might want to stay in a *base de plein air* (fresh air camp); write to *Tourisme Quebec* for information. The following is a list of more standard accommodations. The categories for this area are: *Deluxe,* $70 and up; *Expensive,* $40–$70; *Moderate,* $25–$40; and *Inexpensive,* $25 and under.

ALMA. Hôtel-Motel Universel. *Expensive.* 1000 blvd. des Cascades, Alma, PQ G8B 3G4 (418–668–5261; reservations from Ontario, Quebec, Atlantic Provinces, and New England: 800–463–4495). Located downtown in the Jacques Gagnon complex; connected to modern mall. AC, TV, piano bar, restaurants, accessible to handicapped.

Motel Cascades. *Moderate.* 140 ave. du Pont Nord, Alma, PQ G8B 5C2 (418–662–6547). Spacious rooms, TV, dining room, panoramic salon-bar, terrace, room service.

Motel Dequen. *Moderate.* 800 ave. du Pont Nord, Alma, PQ G8B 5E9 (418–662–6649). Named in honor of the discoverer of the region, the Reverend Father Jean Dequen. TV.

CHIBOUGAMAU. Hôtel-Motel Chibougamau. *Moderate–Expensive.* 473 3ème rue, Chibougamau, PQ G8P 1N6 (418–748–2669, reservations in Quebec 800–361–6162). Grand comfort at a good price. AC in some of the 70 rooms, TV, piano bar, very good restaurant.

PROVINCE OF QUEBEC

CHICOUTIMI. Auberge des Gouverneurs. *Deluxe.* 1303 blvd. Talbot, Chicoutimi, PQ G7H 4C1 (418–549–6244, reservations from Ontario, Quebec, and Atlantic provinces 800–463–2820). At entry to city, over 150 comfortable and spacious rooms, AC, TV, restaurant, room service, car and limo rental, laundry service, outdoor pool, accessible to handicapped. Near two shopping centers.

Hôtel-Motel Universel. *Expensive.* 250 blvd. des Saguénéens, Chicoutimi, PQ G7H 3A4 (418–545–8326, reservations from Ontario, Quebec, the Maritimes, and New England 800–463–4495). Over 100 luxurious rooms, AC, TV, outdoor pool, restaurant, accessible to handicapped. Next to two shopping centers.

Motel au Parasol. *Moderate.* 1287 blvd. Saguenay Est, Chicoutimi, PQ G7H 5C2 (418–543–7771). Downtown on waterfront, panoramic view of Saguenay and town, some TV, kitchenettes available, outdoor pool, bar, terrace, dining room. Cruises depart from front of motel in summer.

DOLBEAU. Auberge La Diligence. *Expensive.* 414 rue de la Friche, Dolbeau, PQ G8L 2R1 (418–276–6544, reservations in Quebec, 800–361–6162). Over 50 modern rooms, intimate, relaxing atmosphere, AC, TV, piano bar, three-fork restaurant, partial accessibility to handicapped.

JONQUIÈRE Hôtel Rousillon-Saguenay. *Expensive.* 2675 blvd. du Royaume, Jonquière, PQ G7S 5B8 (418–540–3124; in Quebec, 800–361–6162). Modern hotel complex connected to convention center, 160 units, AC, TV, outdoor pool, room service, minibar, piano bar, restaurant, dining room rated four forks for excellence, accessible to handicapped.

Motel Richelieu. *Moderate.* 3075 blvd. du Royaume, Jonquière, PQ G7X 7V3 (418–548–8265). Over 100 rooms, above-average comfort, AC, TV, sauna, piano bar, room service, kitchenettes, partial facilities for handicapped.

MISTASSINI. Motel Chute des Pères. *Moderate–Expensive.* 46 blvd. Panoramique, Mistassini, PQ G0W 2C0 (418–276–1492). In the heart of wild blueberry country, magnificent view of waterfalls; TV, good restaurant, partial facilities for handicapped.

HOSTELS. All youth hostels listed have discounts for members of the international network of Youth Hostels; nonmembers are charged a small additional fee. These establishments are geared to those from 16–30.

Auberge Saguenay. 16 rue Bossé Ouest, Chicoutimi, PQ G7J 1K8 (418–543–5103). A complete roster of holiday activities available including arts and crafts, tennis, swimming, and theater. June 1–Sept. 1. Accommodations under $10. Accessible to handicapped.

Auberge St-Félicien. 2025 blvd. Onésime-Gagnon, St-Félicien, PQ G0W 1N0 (418–679–5555). Near the scenic waterfall at Michel. Windsurfing, tennis, and cycling facilities are all available. June 17–Sept. 15. Under $10.

Auberge Île-du-Repos. StepMonique-de-Honfleur, Lac-St-Jean, PQ G0W, 2T0 (418–347–5649). May 15–Sept. 15. Arts and crafts, tennis, volleyball, nature trails, etc. Under $10. Accessible to handicapped.

NORTHERN QUEBEC

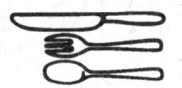

RESTAURANTS. This region offers fare both exotic and hearty. Specialties to ask for include a variation on traditional *tourtière* (meat pie), prize-winning cheddar, and a dried-bean soup, *soupe à la gourgogne*. The superb regional blueberries find their way into numerous desserts and into a local aperitif, DuBleuet. Categories for this area, based on the price of a complete meal but not including beverage, tax, or tip, are: *Deluxe,* $25 and up; *Expensive,* $20–$25; *Moderate,* $10–$20; *Inexpensive,* $10 and under. Space limits coverage to larger centers, although restaurants serving regional treats, fast food, and family meals can be found in smaller towns. Unless otherwise noted, restaurants accept some or all major credit cards.

ALMA. Le Doyen. *Expensive.* 320 rue Collard Ouest (418–662–4201). Located in an old English Colonial house, this award-winning restaurant features regional and nouvelle cuisine. Medaillons, duck, pheasant, and kidneys are some of the foods done up in an original way. Dinner Tues.-Sun. Reservations.

Brasserie Mario Tremblay. *Moderate.* 534 Collard Ouest (418–668–7231). Owned by Canadiens hockey player Mario Tremblay, this spot is popular among locals and tourists. Brochettes, steaks, and plenty of beer. Lunch and dinner, daily.

Salon Panoramique. *Moderate.* 140 ave. du Pont Nord (418–662–6547). In Motel Cascades. Enjoy brochettes and fondues with a great view of the city. Summer terrace. Breakfast and dinner, daily.

Le Paris Match. *Inexpensive.* 505 rue Sacre-Coeur Ouest (418–668–4798). Indoor terrace looking on to the main street. Pizza cooked in a wood-burning oven, steaks, and brochettes. Breakfast and lunch, Mon.–Sat.; dinner, daily.

CHIBOUGAMAU. Le Bon Accueil. *Moderate.* 473 3ème rue (418–748–2669). In Hôtel Chibougamau; three-fork rating from the government. Seafood, fresh fish, steak au poivre, fondue, and brochettes. Breakfast and lunch, Mon.–Fri.; dinner, daily; Sun. brunch. Reservations recommended.

CHICOUTIMI. Restaurant Bar Bonsai. *Moderate–Expensive.* 2195 blvd. Tadoussac (418–545–2333/2342). Something for everyone here. Features Canadian, Chinese, French, and Italian cuisine. Lunch and dinner, daily.

Restaurant Le Deauville. *Inexpensive–Moderate.* 720 blvd. Talbot (418–696–4144). Steak and seafood served up in an intimate atmosphere. Live lobsters. Lunch, Mon.–Fri.; dinner, daily. Reservations recommended.

Café St-Ex. *Inexpensive–Moderate.* 425 rue Racine (418–543–7766). Good food and drink, a glassed-in terrace and lots of plants make this bar-restaurant a popular meeting place. Chicken, steaks, and salads. Lunch and dinner, daily; Brunch Sat.–Sun.

La Butte à l'Équerre. *Inexpensive–Moderate.* 379 Jacques-Cartier Est (418–545–7656). Dine in the warm ambiance of this charming old residence. Crêpes, salads, and tournedos. Try the scallops in wine. Lunch and dinner, daily. Reservations recommended.

Restaurant Chez Georges. *Inexpensive–Moderate.* 433 rue Racine Est (418–543–2875). A 25-year tradition of good eating stands behind this establishment, which has earned a great reputation for service as well as food. Steaks, brochettes, cutlets, chicken, and pasta. Lunch and dinner, daily. Reservations recommended.

DOLBEAU. Le Relais. *Inexpensive.* 414 rue de la Friche (418-276-6544). Cozy couches, elegant linen, and a pink and gray color scheme make for chic and comfortable dining in the Auberge La Diligence. Steaks, seafood, and a Sun.-night buffet. Breakfast, lunch, and dinner every day; brunch Sun.

JONQUIÈRE. Restaurant Amato. *Expensive.* 604 blvd. Harvey (418-542-5479). Owner-chef Mr. Amato runs the show in this intimate eatery. French and Italian cuisine. Ask Amato for suggestions. Dinner, Tues.-Sun. Reservations.
Le Saguenay. *Moderate-Expensive.* 2675 blvd. Royaume (418-548-3124). Gourmet food in elegant surroundings in the Hôtel Rousillon-Saguenay. Awarded four forks for excellence. French and continental dishes included duck à la pêche, lamb, veal kidneys, and Alaska King Crab. Lunch, Mon.-Fri.; dinner daily. Reservations recommended.
Aux Quatres Cents Coups. *Inexpensive.* 338 St-Dominique (418-542-0400). Popular spot, where each dish is named for a film. Try Saguenay specialties; steak or seafood. Breakfast, lunch, and dinner daily.
Margo Lee. *Inexpensive.* 2440 St-Jérôme (418-542-4523). Sip on a tropical drink in this Polynesian-style dining room. All-you-can-eat buffet featuring Chinese, Canadian, and seafood dishes. Lunch and dinner daily. Reservations recommended.

PRACTICAL INFORMATION FOR
THE NORTH SHORE

HOW TO GET THERE AND HOW TO GET AROUND. By Plane. *Air Canada* flies between Montreal and Sept-Îles; *Quebecair* flies from Montreal and Quebec City to Baie-Comeau and Sept-Îles. Within the region Quebecair connects Baie-Comeau, Blanc Sablon, Harrington-Chevery, Havre-St-Pierre, Natashsquan, Port-Menier (Anticosti Island), St-Augustin, and Sept-Îles.

By Bus. *Voyageur* buses run from Montreal and Quebec City to the North Shore, with stops between Tadoussac and Havre-St-Pierre.

By Car. From the Saguenay - Lac-St-Jean - Chibougamau area, follow Route 172 to Tadoussac. From Montreal or Quebec City take Route 138. At Baie-Ste-Catherine there is a ferry across the Saguenay River to Tadoussac. Route 138 then resumes, following the St. Lawrence River until Havre-St-Pierre. There is no automobile route beyond here.

You can rent a car in Baie-Comeau and Sept-Îles, in town or at the airport.

By Boat. There is a ferry service year-round linking Matane to Baie-Comeau and Godbout (418-562-2500 or 418-296-2593). A ferry runs between Trois-Pistoles and Les Escoumins Apr. to Dec. (418-233-2512). From Rimouski, the Fort Mingan connects Sept-Îles to Blanc-Sablon, stopping at many towns and travels to Anticosti Island (418-962-9837 in Sept-Îles; 418-538-3030 in Rimouski).

NORTHERN QUEBEC

TOURIST INFORMATION. There are two permanent government tourist offices in the area. *Association Touristique Régionale Manicouagan,* 872 rue Puyjalon, Box 2366, Baie-Comeau, PQ G5C 2T1 (418–589–5319); and *Association Touristique Régionale de Duplessis, Inc.,* Box 156, Sept-Îles, PQ G4R 4K3 (418–962–0808). From the middle of June to the beginning of Sept. offices are open in Tadoussac (418–235–4292); Baie-Comeau (418–589–4191); Godbout (ferry ticket office); Forestville (418–587–4000); Les Escoumins (418–233–2663); Havre-St-Pierre (418–538–2512).

TELEPHONES AND EMERGENCY NUMBERS. The area code for the North Shore is 418. The cost of a local telephone call is 25 cents. Within the region, dial 411 for information; from elsewhere, dial 418–555–1212. Dial 0 for operator assistance in case of an emergency. In Baie-Comeau the local police are reached at 589–3788; the provincial police at 296–2324. In Sept-Îles dial 962–4415 for local police; 962–9438 for provincial police.

SEASONAL EVENTS. June. *The Mingan Festival,* at Havre-St-Pierre, in the last week of the month, is a good reason to visit the National Park here at this time of year. For information, call 418–538–2761. **July.** *The Provincial Salmon Festival,* in Sacré-Coeur, offers ten days of such activities as bicycle races and amateur talent shows. But the salmon is the true star of this celebration, available in fresh and succulent form at restaurants in the region. For information, call 418–236–4622. **July.** *The All-Been Festival* in Chute-aux-Outardes. Remember to ask how this ten-day party got its name; it is a story in itself. For information, call 418–567–4245. **August.** *The Blue Whale Festival* marks the peak hours of the hottest singles bar for blue whales in North America. Residents here celebrate the congregation of the whales for their mating season with a remarkably diverse roster of activities. For information, call 418–232–6403/6326.

WHALE-WATCHING. The Great Blue Whale, an elegant and mighty creature (arguably the largest animal in the world), populates the waters of the St. Lawrence River throughout the summer months and sighting one is an unusual and dramatic experience for the traveler. There are said to be 1,500 in the region; the best way to see them is on one of the fine cruises organized for this purpose. Height of the season for sightings is July. A number of groups offer cruises for whale sighting. Fares are about $30, less for children.

La Société Écologique des Baleines du St. Laurent, 306 rue de la Rivière, Grandes Bergeronnes, PQ G0T 1G0 (418–232–6294/6666). This group has the definitive story on whale sightings for the area. Departures twice daily June–Sept. aboard Le Rorqual and L'élan des Eaux II.

Hôtel Tadoussac, 165 rue Bord de l'Eau, Tadoussac, PQ G0T 2A0 (418–235–4421 or 800–361–6162 from Quebec, Ontario, and the Atlantic provinces). Tours aboard the Marie-Clarisse depart three times daily.

Crosières à la Baleine et au Saguenay Inc., Marina du Tadoussac, 100 Rue Bordeleau, Tadoussac, PQ G0T 2A0 (418–235–4585). There are four departures a day aboard the Pierre Chauvin May–Oct. Bar and restaurant on board. Saguenay cruises also available.

La Compagnie de la Baie du Tadoussac Enr., 147 Coupe de l'Islets, Tadoussac, PQ G0T 2A0 (418–237–4358 or 235–4372). This pneumatic boat excursion through whale-sighting territory allows the adventurous traveler a chance to see these magnificent creatures up close. Excursions daily. Gear provided.

OTHER SPECIAL-INTEREST TOURS. The **Manic-Outarde Hydro** electric power complex, with five stations stretching from the outskirts of Baie-Comeau inland 200 km (120 mi) is a major feat of engineering, worthy of a visit when you are in the area. One of the dams alone produces 1,290.000 kilowatts and can hold 35 billion cubic meters of water. Daily visits throughout the summer. Contact Hydro-Quebec, 135 rue Comeau, Baie-Comeau, PQ (418–296–7816).

Tourist excursions, 546 Ave. Dequen, Sept-Îles, PQ G4R 2R4 (418–962–1238 or 968–1818). These excursions, run by the city, include a trip to Grande-Basque Island, a tour of the seven islands for which the town is named, puffin sightings, and others. Tickets and reservations at shelter no. 4 of the town park. Prices range from $5–$15 for adults; $3–$8 for children.

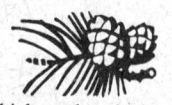

PROVINCIAL AND NATIONAL PARKS AND WILDLIFE RESERVES. Anticosti Island Wildlife Reserve. Port-Menier, Île-d'Anticosti, PQ G0G 2Y0 (418–535–0156/0231). The entire island here is a wildlife haven, which, archaeologists tell us, was inhabited as long as 4,000 years ago. Nowadays, trips here must be planned in advance and the best way to do so would be with the help of an outfitting service. Once your visit is organized, you can hunt—or just observe—white-tail deer, moose, and other species, amidst breathtaking caverns, canyons, coves, and waterfalls. Facilities open throughout the summer and fall. Consult an outfitter for details.

Sept-Îles-Port-Cartier Wildlife Reserve. 818 Ave. Laure, Sept-Îles, PQ G4R 1Y8 (418–766–3211 or 968–1041). Enter through Port-Cartier, 1 km (.6 mi) north of Highway 138. This vast reserve is open for hunting, fishing, camping, canoeing, and for those with nothing more in mind than a picnic and a leisurely stroll. Facilities available June–Sept.

Mingan Archipelago National Park. 1047 rue Dulcinée CP 1180, Havre-St-Pierre, PQ G0G 1P0 (418–538–2512 or 538–3331). This 500-million-year-old group of islands is a testimony to the prevailing power of the elements. The rock formations alone, eerily mimicking modern sculpture, are unique, exquisite and a cherished national treasure. Archaeological digs have turned up vestiges of a French trading post circa 1680 and an ancient burial ground proving that Indians once made their home here. Drop by the information center at Havre-St-Pierre for details on camping permits, facilities, and transportation on park grounds.

CAMPING. The North Shore has over a dozen spectacularly appointed campgrounds. Contact the *North Shore Camping and Caravaning Association,* 36 Ave. de Salaberry, Baie-Comeau, PQ G4Z 1C3 (418–296–5374). See "Provincial and National Parks and Wildlife Reserves" for more specific information.

NORTHERN QUEBEC 197

PARTICIPANT SPORTS. Golf. *Club de Golf de Baie-Comeau* (418-235-4421). *Club de Golf Ste-Marguerite,* near Sept-Îles (418-583-2844). *Club de Golf de Tadoussac* (418-235-4421). **Alpine Skiing.** *Mont Tibasse,* near Baie-Comeau (418-296-4019). *Gallix,* near Sept-Îles (418-766-4372). **Cross-Country Skiing.** *Club les Sakis,* near Tadoussac (418-235-4297). *Base de Plein Air Goélands,* near Port-Cartier (418-766-2346). *Club de Ski du Fond Rapido,* at Lac-Rapido near Sept-Îles (418-968-4011).

HISTORIC SITES AND HOUSES. Chapelle de Tadoussac. Beside the Hotel Tadoussac. The oldest wood chapel in North America (1747). Open from end of June to beginning of Sept., 9 A.M.–9 P.M. There is a minimal admission fee.

Ilets-Jérémie. Ste-Thérèse des Colombiers. Route 138 toward Tadoussac. A pilgrimage site dedicated to Ste-Anne since the 1939 reconstruction of the Jesuit chapel first built there in 1735. Chapel contains pieces from the original. Open to public from end of June to middle of Aug., 9 A.M.–8 P.M.

Maison Chauvin. Tadoussac (418-235-4446). Replica of the first trading post built on the continent in 1600. Open during the summer, daily. Adults, $1; children and students, 50 cents.

Le Phare de Pointe-des-Monts. Pointe-des-Monts, between Godbout and Baie-Trinité (418-939-2332/589-6979). Built in 1830, this lighthouse is testimony to the spectacular maritime heritage of the North Shore. Guided tours peppered with regional history. Daily, 11 A.M.–8 P.M. Free.

MUSEUMS. Musée de Baie-Comeau. 43 Rue Mance, Baie-Comeau, PQ G4Z 2H1 (418-296-9690). Prehistoric artifacts, 18th-century furniture, history of region. June–Dec., 10 A.M.–6 P.M., daily. Jan.–June, Tues.–Fri., 9 A.M.–5 P.M., Sat., 1–5 P.M. Free.

Musée des Sept-Îles. blvd. des Montagnais, Sept-Îles, PQ G4R 4K9 (418-968-2070). Archaeological relics from excavation of old post office, Amerindian art, fauna of region. Guided tours. Mid June–Sept.; Mon.–Fri., 9 A.M.–5 P.M., Sat.–Sun., noon–5 P.M. Regular season, Wed.–Fri., 9 A.M.–noon, 1–5 P.M., Sat., Sun., noon–5 P.M. Free.

ACCOMMODATIONS. This selection of hotels and motels on the North Shore is listed alphabetically by city or town. The price categories, based on the price of a double room, are: *Deluxe,* $70 and up; *Expensive,* $40–$70; *Moderate,* $25–$40; and *Inexpensive,* $25 and under.

BAIE-COMEAU. Hôtel Le Manoir. *Expensive–Deluxe.* 8 rue Cabot, Baie-Comeau, PQ G4Z 1L8 (418-296-3391; reservations in Quebec, 800-361-6162). Sumptuous hotel on a hill overlooking the St. Lawrence; French colonial style. Large and modern rooms, AC, TV, tennis, four forks for excellent cuisine.

Hôtel-Motel La Caravelle. *Expensive.* 202 blvd. Lasalle, Baie-Comeau, PQ G4Z 1S6 (418-296-4986). On a hill with a view of the town and the water. TV, kitchenettes, indoor pool, sauna, whirlpool, bar, dining room. Skiing nearby.

PROVINCE OF QUEBEC

BAIE-COMEAU (HAUTERIVE). Motel Hauterive. *Expensive.* 1145 ave. Nouvelle, Baie-Comeau (Hauterive), PQ G5C 2E3 (418–589–2041). Over 40 rooms of above-average comfort, TV, bar-restaurant, near shopping centers.
  Motel Manic. *Moderate.* 2791 blvd. Laflèche, Baie-Comeau (Hauterive), PQ G5C 1E6 (418–589–3751). Three dozen comfortable rooms, TV, partial facilities for handicapped.

FORESTVILLE. Motel Danube Bleu. *Moderate.* 5 rue Principale, Forestville, PQ G0T 1E0 (418–587–2278). Superior comfort in country surroundings, TV, restaurant, near beaches and sports centers.

ANTICOSTI ISLAND. Auberge de Port-Menier. *Expensive.* Port-Menier, PQ G0G 2Y0 (418–535–0122). View of the bay. Over two dozen rooms, near hunting and fishing; deer wander nearby. Park, TV, dining room. Ten rooms.

LONGUE POINTE DE MINGAN. Motel Gravel. *Expensive.* Route 138, Longue-Pointe, PQ G0G 1V0 (418–949–2992). At the entrance of Mingan Archipelago National Park, TV, dining room. Ten rooms.
  Motel E. Vaillancourt. *Moderate.* Route 138, Longue-Pointe, PQ G0G 1V0 (418–949–2286). Natural setting at entrance to Mingan Archipelago, good comfort in ten rooms, TV, bar, dining room.

PORT CARTIER. Hôtel-Motel Château. *Expensive.* 30 rue Élie Rochefort, Port-Cartier, PQ G5B 1N2 (418–766–3444). Near downtown, over 70 rooms, TV, sauna, bar, restaurant, dining room, partial facilities for handicapped. Near beaches, hunting, and fishing.

SEPT-ILES. Auberge des Gouverneurs. *Deluxe.* 666 blvd. Laure, Sept-Îles, PQ G4R 1X9 (418–962–7071; reservations from Ontario, Quebec, and Atlantic provinces, 800–463–2820). Downtown on main street, over 100 comfortable and spacious rooms, AC, TV, outdoor pool, piano bar, laundry service, car rental, restaurant with two-fork rating, accessible to handicapped.
  Hôtel-Motel Mingan. *Expensive.* 665 blvd. Laure, Sept-Îles, PQ G4R 1X8 (418–968–2121). Central location, above-average comfort, AC, TV, piano bar, good restaurant.
  Hotel Sept-Îles. *Expensive.* 451 rue Arnaud, Sept-Îles, PQ G4R 3B3 (418–962–2581). Picturesque view of the waterfront, promenade in back, rated high for comfort, some AC, TV, good restaurant.

TADOUSSAC. Hôtel Tadoussac. *Deluxe.* 165 rue Bord de l'Eau, Tadoussac, PQ G0T 2A0 (418–235–4421; in Quebec, Ontario, and Atlantic provinces, 800–463–5250). Magnificent red-roofed building nestled against a mountainside, between fresh water and the sea. Used as a location for the film *Hotel New Hampshire.* 149 units, TV, tennis, outdoor pool, excellent restaurant, snack bar, nursery, nine holes of golf, art gallery, Ping-Pong, entertainment, fjord excursions, and whale-watching trips, long sandy beach, accessible to handicapped. American plan.
  Hôtel Georges. *Moderate.* 135 rue du Bateau-Passeur, Tadoussac, PQ G0T 2A0 (418–235–4393). In charming renovated house built in 1838. Varnished wood walls, panoramic view of St. Lawrence, dining room. Swimming, fishing, golf nearby.

NORTHERN QUEBEC

HOSTELS. All youth hostel listings have discounts for members of the international network of Youth Hostels; nonmembers are charged a small additional fee. These establishments are geared to those from 16–30.

Auberge de Pointe Ouest. Île-d'Anticosti, PQ G0G 2Y0 (418–535–0311). On the site of an old lighthouse by the sea, this charming inn offers a panoramic view of the surrounding area. Nature trails and horseback riding available. June 1–Sept. 1. Under $10. Accessible to handicapped.

Auberge de Jeunesse du Sept-Îles. 510 rue Cartier, Sept-Îles, PQ G4R 2T9 (418–962–8180). In the heart of one of the major centers of the North Shore. Open summer months. Under $10.

Maison Majorique. 158 rue Bateau-Passeur, Tadoussac, PQ G0T 2A0 (418–235–4372). A wide range of summer and winter activities available at this popular tourist spot. Under $10. Accessible to handicapped.

RESTAURANTS. The regional specialties are fresh fish and seafood in season. Traditional North American fare is also available. Categories for the restaurants are as follows: *Deluxe*, $25 and up; *Expensive*, $20–$25; *Moderate*, $10–$20; and *Inexpensive*, $10 and under. Prices apply to full course meals excluding tax, liquor, and tip. Unless otherwise noted, all restaurants take some or all major credit cards.

BAIE-COMEAU. Hôtel le Manoir. *Moderate–Expensive.* 8 rue Cabot (418–296–3391). This hotel restaurant received four forks for excellence from the government. Continental cuisine and seafood served in a European-style dining room. Breakfast, lunch, and dinner, daily. Reservations recommended.

Restaurant Boustifaille. *Moderate.* Galeries Baie-Comeau, 300 blvd. de Lasalle (418–296–9800). Relaxing atmosphere, French-style décor. Fondues, brochettes, seafood, pizza. Breakfast and lunch, Mon.–Sat.; dinner, every night.

Les Crêpes du Roy. *Inexpensive.* 600 blvd. Laflèche (418–589–2111). You can see your crêpes cooking. Lunch, Mon.–Sat., dinner, daily.

FORESTVILLE. Brasserie La Brochette d'Or. *Inexpensive–Moderate.* 33 Route 138 (418–587–4060). Beside the shopping center at entrance to Forestville. Filet mignon, brochettes, fondues, Fisherman's Platter. Breakfast, lunch, and dinner, Mon.–Sat.

SEPT-ÎLES Auberge des Gouverneurs. *Moderate–Expensive.* 666 blvd. Laure (418–962–7071). The tranquil and cozy atmosphere of this hotel restaurant attracts both locals and visitors. French and continental cuisine. Seafood from May. Lunch and dinner, daily; brunch Sun. Reservations recommended.

Le Bourguignon. *Moderate–Expensive.* 451 rue Arnaud (418–962–6674). In Hôtel Sept-Îles. Enjoy grilled meats with a splendid view. Breakfast, lunch, and dinner, daily.

Restaurant de l'Hôtel-Motel Mingan. *Moderate–Expensive.* 665 blvd. Laure (418–968–2121). This downtown dining room features seafood, fondues, flambées, brochettes, and a lunchtime buffet. Breakfast, lunch, and dinner. Reservations recommended.

Restaurant le Renaissance. *Moderate–Expensive.* 395 rue Arnaud (418–962–1922). Plants and lots of windows make for pleasant dining. Greek cuisine. Lunch and dinner, daily. Reservations recommended.

TADOUSSAC. Beluga. *Expensive.* 165 rue Bord de l'Eau in the Hôtel Tadoussac (418–235–4421). Three-fork rating by government. The pointed diamond woodwork of this dining room has been labeled a historical monument. Enjoy fresh cod, turbot, and salmon. Breakfast, lunch, and dinner, daily. Reservations recommended.

PRACTICAL INFORMATION FOR NOUVEAU QUEBEC

When planning your trip to Nouveau Quebec, remember that it is impractical and very much not recommended for tourists to attempt traveling on their own to this region. You should seek the assistance of a tour or outfitter organization.

HOW TO GET THERE AND HOW TO GET AROUND. By Plane. The most predominant mode of transportation here is by plane, although some points can be reached by car and train. *Nordair* (800–361–6735 in Quebec) flies to Radisson, Kuujjaraapik, Kuujjuaq (Fort Chimo), and Purtuniq; *Quebecair* flies to Radisson, Sakami, Keyano, Fermont, and Schefferville; call toll-free in Quebec, 800–361–0200. *Air Creebec* (819–825–8355) flies from Val-d'Or to Fort-Rupert, Eastmain, Wemindji, Chisasibi, and Kuujjaraapik. *Air Inuit,* based in Kuujjuaq, (819–964–2914) flies to over a dozen points in Nouveau Quebec.

You can also charter flights to reach hunting and fishing outfitters or to tour the region. Fermont: *Air Caribou* (418–287–3203). Kuujjuaq: *Air Inuit* (819–964–2914), *Johnny May's Air* (819–964–2662). Quebec City: *Quebec Aviation Ltd* (418–872–1200). Montreal: *Air Inuit* (514–636–9445). Val-d'Or: *Air Creebec* (819–824–3494).

By Train. The *Côte-Nord and Labrador Railway* (418–968–7539) runs from Sept-Îles to Fermont and Schefferville.

By Car. The network of roads in the region totals 1620 km (972 mi). However, visitors planning to drive beyond Matagami (northeast of Amos in the Abitibi-Témiscamingue area) must possess a hunting or fishing permit.

If you plan to travel on your own in this region, you must first inform the Sûreté du Quebec (provincial police). To stay overnight you must use the Baie-James municipal campground on the banks of the Rivière Waswanipi, 38 km (23 mi) past Matagami.

TOURIST INFORMATION. There are no manned tourism offices in Nouveau Quebec, and they are not missed because virtually all visitors travel as part of a tour. For information on this region, write to *Tourisme Quebec,* CP 20,000, Quebec City, PQ G1K 7X2.

NORTHERN QUEBEC

TELEPHONES AND EMERGENCY NUMBERS. The area code for the western part of the region is 819, for the eastern part, 418. Calls to James Bay and some of the Inuit areas require operator assistance. *Sûreté du Quebec* (provincial police): Kuujjuaq, 819–964–2823; Kuujjaraapik, 819–929–3260; Fermont, 418–287–5655.

TOURS. Because of the remote nature of this region, organized tours are the only way to visit. There are a wide variety of these to choose from, offering activities ranging from skiing in the high Otish Mountains, the Torngat Mountains—or even at the Nouveau Quebec Crater—to rock climbing in the Torngat, dogsledding in the frozen Ungava, canoeing or kayaking down swift-flowing rivers or photographing exquisite landscapes. Or you can arrange a tour simply to see the incredible man-made wonder of Baie-James, the source of electric power for much of Quebec and the Eastern seaboard. The following agencies organize such tours:

Cépal, 3350 70 St., Jonquière, PQ G78 7W8 (418–547–5728).

Nortour, 310 rue St-Catherine, 3emétage, Montreal, PQ H2X 2A1 (514–875–7400).

Passe Montagne, 2025A Mason, Montreal, PQ H2H 2P7 (514–521–9548).

HUNTING AND FISHING. There is a wide array of fish and game here, ranging from virtually every conceivable species of goose to caribou, loons, Arctic char, salmon, and pike. More than 30 hunting and fishing outfitters equip upwards of 3,000 tourists every year in this area. For a pamphlet on Quebec outfitters, contact the *Quebec Outfitters Association Inc.*, 482 blvd. St-Cyrille Ouest, Quebec City, PQ G1S 1S4 (418–527–1524). Or contact the *Montreal Travel Agency Arctic Adventures*, 8102 TransCanada Highway, St-Laurent, PQ H4S 1R4 (514–332–0880) and they will arrange a trip for you.

MUSEUMS AND GALLERIES. The great attraction here, of course, is the magnificent Cree and Inuit art indigenous to the region. Over two dozen galleries and museums in the region regularly exhibit the beautiful soapstone sculptures and prints for which they are noted. For information on where to buy these traditional arts and crafts, contact Direction Générale des Opérations Nouveau Quebec-Baie James, Ministry of Tourism, 710 Place d'Youville, 3rd floor, Quebec City, PQ G1R 4Y4 (418–643–6820).

ACCOMMODATIONS. Again, most people travel here through tours or with outfitters, so they are not searching out accommodations on their own. Standard accommodations are limited in Nouveau Quebec. Your best bet is to reserve through a travel agent or contact an establishment in advance to get a sense of what you can expect. Also, there are really no **restaurants** for tourists to drop in on. The following is a short list of accommodations. Prices range from under $100 to $150. This is not a cheap place to travel.

INUKJUAK. Motel Inoucdjouac, Inoucdjouac, PQ J0M 1M0 (819–254–8969). Nine rooms.

PROVINCE OF QUEBEC

JAMES BAY. Auberge Radisson, Baie-James (Radisson) PQ J0Y 2X0 (819-638-7201). Over 40 rooms of superior comfort. AC TV, indoor pool, very good restaurant.

KUUJJUAQ (FORT CHIMO). Auberge Kuujjuaq. Fort Chimo, PQ (819-964-2903). 20 comfortable rooms. Located near water.

POVUNGNITUK. Hôtel Povungnituk. Povungnituk, PQ J0M 1P0 (819-988-2817). Seven rooms.

SCHEFFERVILLE. Hôtel Schefferville. 182 rue Montagnais, Schefferville, PQ G0G 2T0 (418-585-2605). 37 large and comfortable rooms. AC, TV, bar, restaurant.

FRENCH-ENGLISH TOURIST VOCABULARY

Daily Expressions

Can anyone here speak English?	Y a-t-il quelqu'un qui parle anglais?
Do you speak English?	Parlez-vous anglais?
Do you understand?	Comprenez-vous?
Don't mention it	Pas de quoi
I beg your pardon	Pardon! (pahrr'dong)
Good morning/day/afternoon	Bonjour
Good evening/night	Bonsoir
Goodbye	Au revoir
How much/many?	Combien?
I don't know	Je ne sais pas
I don't understand	Je ne comprends pas
Yes/No	Oui/Non
Please speak more slowly	Parlez plus lentement, s'il vous plaît
Stop	Arrêtez
Go ahead	Continuez
Come in!	Entrez! (ahn'tray)
Thank you very much	Merci bien
There is, there are	Il y a
Very good/well	Très bien
What is this?	Qu'est-ce que c'est? (kes-kuh-say)
What do you want?	Que voulez-vous?
Please	S'il vous plaît (seevooplay)
I'm sorry	Je regrette
You're welcome	Je vous en prie
What time is it?	Quelle heure est-il?
What is your name?	Comment vous appelez-vous?

Days of the Week

Sunday	Dimanche
Monday	Lundi
Tuesday	Mardi
Wednesday	Mercredi
Thursday	Jeudi
Friday	Vendredi
Saturday	Samedi

Common Questions

Is there . . .
—a bus for . . . ?
—an English interpreter?
—a good hotel at . . . ?
—a good restaurant here?
—a train for . . . ?
Where is . . .
—the airport?
—a bank?
—the bar?
—the bathroom?
—the ticket (booking) office?
—a drugstore?
—the movies (cinema)?
—the cloakroom?
—the lavatory?
—the luggage?
—the museum?
—the police station?
—the post office?
—the railway station?
When . . .
—is lunch?
—is dinner?
—is the first (last) bus?
—is the first (last) train?
—does the theater open?
—will it be ready?
—does the performance begin (end)?
What is . . .
—the fare to . . . ?
—the one-way (round trip) fare?
—the price?
—the price per day? per week?
—the price per kilo? (2.2 pounds)
—the price per meter?
Have you . . .
—a timetable?
—anything ready? (Food)
How often?
How long?

Y a-t-il . . .
—un autobus pour . . . ?
—un interprète anglais?
—un bon hôtel à . . . ?
—un bon restaurant ici?
—un train pour . . . ?
Où est . . .
—l'aéroport?
—une banque?
—le bar?
—la salle de bain?
—le guichet?
—une pharmacie?
—le cinéma?
—le vestiaire?
—le lavabo?
—le bagage?
—le musée?
—le gendarmerie?
—le bureau de poste?
—le gare?
Quand . . .
—le déjeuner est-il servi?
—le diner est-il servi?
—le premier (dernier) autobus part-il?
—le premier (dernier) train part-il?
—ouvre-t-on le théâtre?
—sera-t-il (elle) prêt(e)?
—le séance commence-t-elle (finit-elle)?
Quel est . . .
—le prix du billet à . . . ?
—le prix d'aller (d'aller et retour)?
—le prix?
—le prix par jour? par semaine?
  Combien le kilo?
  Combien le mètre?
Avez-vous . . .
—un indicateur?
—quelque chose de prêt?
Combien de fois?
Combien de temps?

VOCABULARY

Daily Needs

I want . . .
- —my bill
- —to buy
- —cigars, cigarettes
- —a dentist
- —a dictionary
- —a doctor
- —something to drink
- —something to eat
- —some American papers
- —a porter
- —to send a telegram
- —some stamps
- —a taxi
- —to telephone
- —the waiter
- —some beer
- —change for . . .
- —water
- —my key
- —razor blades
- —a road map
- —soap

Je désire . . . Je voudrais . . .
- —l'addition (la note)
- —d'acheter
- —des cigares, cigarettes
- —consulter un dentiste
- —un dictionnaire
- —consulter un médicin
- —prendre quelque chose à boire
- —manger quelque chose
- —des journaux américains
- —un porteur
- —envoyer un tétégramme
- —des timbres
- —un taxi
- —téléphone
- —parler avec le garçon
- —de la bière
- —la monnaie de . . .
- —de l'eau
- —ma clé
- —des lames de rasoir
- —une carte routière
- —due savon

Travel by Car

Stop—*Arrêt*
Go—*Allez*
Left, right—*Gauche, droit*
Straight ahead—*Tout droit*
U-turn—*Demi-tour*
Oil—*Huile*
Bridge—*Pont*
Highway—*Autoroute*
No parking—*Défense de stationner*
Toll—*Péage*

Exact change—*Péage exact*
Near/far—*Près/loin*
Here/there—*Ici/là*
Self-service—*Libre service*
Empty—*Vide*
Full—*Plein*
Lead-free—*Sans plomb*
Gas—*Essence*
Tow zone—*Zone de remorquage*
Exit—*Sortie*

North, south, east, west—*Nord, sud, est, ouest*
Wait for the green light—*Attendez le feu vert*
Car rental company—*Location de voitures*

PROVINCE OF QUEBEC
Menu Translator

Meats (Viandes)

Agneau	Lamb
Jambon	Ham
Bifteck	Steak
Lapin	Rabbit
Boeuf	Beef
Lard	Bacon
Charcuterie	Pork cold cuts
Mouton	Mutton
Châteaubriand	Rump steak
Porc	Pork
Côte	Chop
Rosbif	Roast beef
Entrecôte	Rib steak
Saucisse	Sausage
Gigot d'agneau	Leg of Lamb
Veau	Veal
Gibier	Wild game

Poultry (Volaille)

Canard	Duck
Oie	Goose
Caneton	Duckling
Pintade	Guinea hen
Coq	Young cock
Poulet	Chicken
Faisan	Pheasant

Offal (Abats)

Cervelles	Brains
Langue	Tongue
Foie	Liver
Rognon	Kidney

Fish (Poisson)

Anguille	Eel
Perche	Bass
Maquereau	Mackerel
Saumon	Salmon
Morue	Cod
Truite	Trout

VOCABULARY

Shellfish (Coquillages, Crustaces)

Crevettes	Shrimp
Homard	Lobster
Ecrevisses	Crawfish
Huîtres	Oysters
Escargots	Snails
Langouste	Spiny rock lobster
Fruits de mer	Mixed shellfish
Moules	Mussels
Grenouilles	Frogs' legs
Palourdes	Clams

Vegetables (Légumes)

Aubergine	Eggplant
Epinards	Spinach
Chou	Cabbage
Haricots	Beans
Cresson	Watercress
Haricots verts	Green beans

Desserts (Desserts)

Beignets	Fritters
Glace	Ice cream
Gâteau	Cake
Tarte	Pie

Speak a foreign language in seconds.

Now an amazing space age device makes it possible to speak a foreign language *without* having to learn a foreign language.

Speak French, German, or Spanish.
With the incredible Translator 8000—world's first pocket-size electronic translation machines—you're never at a loss for words in France, Germany, or Spain.

8,000-word brain.
Just punch in the foreign word or phrase, and English appears on the LED display. Or punch in English, and read the foreign equivalent instantly.

Only 4¾" x 2¾", it possesses a fluent 8,000-word vocabulary (4,000 English, 4,000 foreign). A memory key stores up to 16 words; a practice key randomly calls up words for study, self-testing, or game use. And it's also a full-function calculator.

150,000 sold in 18 months.
Manufactured for Langenscheidt by Sharp/Japan, the Translator 8000 comes with a 6-month warranty. It's a valuable aid for business and pleasure travelers, and students. It comes in a handsome leatherette case, and makes a super gift.

Order now with the information below.

To order, send $69.95 plus $3 p&h ($12 for overseas del.) for each unit. Indicate language choice: English/French, English/German, English/Spanish. N.Y. res. add sales tax. MasterCard, Visa, or American Express card users give brand, account number (all digits), expiration date, and signature. SEND TO: Fodor's, Dept. T-8000, 2 Park Ave., New York, NY 10016-5677, U.S.A.

INDEX

Abitibi—Témiscamingue, 180, 182–186
Acadians, 95
Air tours, 98, 122, 141
Air travel, 54, 96, 118–119, 138, 153, 167, 182, 187, 194, 200
  to Quebec from Britain, 3
American Plan (AP), 12
American Revolution, Quebec and, 24, 46, 80, 81, 95, 112
Amusement park, 59
Anticosti Island, 196
Apples and apple cider, 81, 82, 86
Aquariums, 123–124, 189
Arnold, Benedict, 24, 46, 112
Art galleries, 66, 105–106, 145
  of Cree and Inuit art, 201
Austrian restaurant, 92
Automobile racing, 58, 61, 88, 170, 172
Automobiles
  antique-car tour, 122
  hints to motorists, 6–7, 57, 85–86, 99, 120, 140, 157, 169
  metric tire-pressure converter, 18
  travel directions for, 54, 84–85, 96–97, 119, 138, 153, 168, 182, 187, 194, 200
  winter driving, 7, 120, 179

Baie-St-Paul, 136, 146
Ballet, 33, 67
Banking hours, 16
Baseball, 61
Bas-St-Laurent, 94
  art galleries in, 106
  hotels and motels in, 107
  museums and historic sites in, 103–105
  restaurants in, 109
  youth hostel in, 108
Bases de Plein Air, 179
Bed-and-breakfast, 13, 70, 131, 148, 163
Belgian restaurants, 71–72

Bird-watching, 11, 84, 94, 95, 100, 136, 142
Black Watch, 64
Blueberry-based aperitif factory, 189
Boat cruises, 58–59, 80, 87, 98–99, 122, 188–189
  theater, 89
  whale-watching, 141–142, 195–196
Boat travel, 54, 97, 194
Bread festival, 82, 86
British visitors, tips for, 3
Bus tours, 98
Bus travel, 54, 85, 96, 119, 138, 153, 167, 182, 187, 194
Business hours, 16

Calèche rides, 59, 122, 123, 141
Calendars of events
  Charlevoix, 141
  Coeur-du-Quebec, 169–170
  Laurentians-Ottawa Valley, 158
  Montreal, 57–58
  Northern Quebec, 183, 188, 195
  Quebec City, 122
  Southern Quebec, 86
Camping, 8, 9, 99–101, 124–125, 142, 143, 158, 170, 171, 184, 190, 196
Canadian dollars, 15
Canoe races, 121, 141, 170, 172, 183
Canoeing, 87, 123, 124, 142, 170–171, 183, 196, 201
Caribou grog, 121
Carnival, 35–36, 121–122, 141, 158, 169, 179
Cartier, Jacques, 21, 43, 95, 105, 123, 135, 137, 180
Chambly, 80–81
Champlain, Samuel de, 22, 43, 63, 80, 112, 128
Charlevoix, 135–149
  hotels and motels in, 146–148
  map of, 139

INDEX

Charlevoix (continued)
  museums and special buildings in, 144–145
  nightlife in, 148–149
  parks and gardens in, 142
  religious sites in, 136
  restaurants in, 148
  summer sports in, 144
  transportation in, 140
  winter sports in, 39, 142–144
Château de Ramezay, 24, 46, 61
Chateau Frontenac, 116–117, 127
Cheeses, 82
Chemin du Roy, Le, 166
Chicoutimi, 36, 187, 188, 190–193
Children
  Laurentians–Ottawa Valley activities for, 159–160
  Quebec City activities for, 126
  zoo for, 53, 59
Chinese restaurants, 71, 133, 193, 194
Churches and cathedrals, 63–65, 103–105, 112, 117, 127, 172, 173, 197
Civil War, U.S., Quebec and, 46
Climate, 4–5, 20, 53–54, 84, 96, 118, 138, 153, 167
Clothing, 4, 5, 118
Coaticook, 82
Coeur-du-Quebec, 165–177
  historic sites and houses in, 172–173
  hotels and motels in, 174–176
  museums in, 173–174
  religious sites in, 172, 173
  restaurants in, 176–177
  spectator sports in, 172
  summer sports in, 170, 172
  theaters in, 174
  transportation in, 169
  winter sports in, 169–171
Cookshire, 82, 86
Cost of trip, 3–4
Covered bridges, 183
Credit cards, 16
Curling, 60, 125
Currency, 15
Customs and duty, 2, 3
Cycling, 60, 86, 98, 123, 125, 183

Dance, 33, 67, 129, 134
De Lanaudière, 166, 169, 171
  winter sports in, 39–40
Delicatessens, 74–75
Dinner theaters, 67
Discos, 76, 77, 134
Dogsled racing, 121
Dogsledding, 201
Drama, 33, 67, 89, 129, 174
Dufferin Terrace, 117

Eastern Townships. See Southern Quebec
Economy of Quebec, 28–29, 47–48
Emergency numbers. See Telephones
Eskimos (Inuit), 21, 30–31, 181
  museums of, 65, 191
  sculpture of, 34
Estrie, L', 81–82, 88, 90–91
European Plan (EP), 12

Farm vacations, 13–14, 88, 171
Film, 33, 58, 68, 129, 183
  museum of, 65
Fireworks, 57
Fishing, 10–11, 87, 101–102, 124, 142, 143, 159, 171–172, 183, 184, 190, 196, 201
  ice, 143, 169, 172
Flag of Quebec, 1
Flower show, 59
Football, 12, 60
Forest education centers, 142, 158
Forillon National Park, 8, 99–100
Fort Chimo (Kuujjuaq), 200, 202
French language, 6, 26–28, 30, 47, 95
  auto terms in, 7, 205
  number of speakers of, 1
  tourist vocabulary for, 203–207
French restaurants, 71–72, 92, 132, 133, 163–164, 176–177, 186, 193–194, 199

Gaspé Peninsula, 94–95
  art galleries in, 106
  hotels and motels in, 107–108

INDEX

museums and historic sites in, 105
parks and gardens in, 99–100
restaurants in, 110
winter sports in, 40, 102
youth hostel in, 109
Golf, 11, 60, 87, 102–103, 125, 141, 142, 144, 172, 184, 190, 197
Granby, 81, 88
Grand-Portage Trail, 103–104
Greek restaurants, 72–73
Guides, requirement for, 10

Handicapped travelers, 7–8, 57, 86, 99, 121, 140–141, 157, 169
Hang gliding, 136
History of Quebec, 21–28, 43–47, 95, 112
See also National historic sites
Holidays, 16, 58
Horse racing, 141
Horseback riding, 103, 125, 144
Horse-drawn carriages. *See* Calèche rides
Hostels. *See* Youth hostels
Hot air balloons, 86
Hotels and motels, 12–13
tipping in, 15
See also each place
Hull, 158, 160–161
Hunting, 9–10, 87, 88, 99, 101–102, 143, 159, 170–172, 183, 184, 190, 196, 201

Ice hockey, 49, 60, 126
Ice skating, 60, 126, 142
Île aux Coudres, 137, 138, 146–147
Indian restaurants, 73
Indians, 21–22, 30–31, 43, 181
museums of, 65, 117, 173, 191
Inns. *See* Hotels and motels
Italian restaurants, 74, 92, 133, 164, 193, 194

Japanese restaurants, 74
Jazz, 32, 33, 58, 76, 77, 134
Jewish-style restaurants, 74–75

Kuujjuaq (Fort Chimo), 200, 202

La Mauricie National Park, 8, 170
Laurentians, 150–164
hotels and motels in, 160–163
map of, 154–155
restaurants in, 163–164
transportation in, 157
winter sports in, 37–38, 40–41, 159
Laurentides Satellite Earth Station, 158
Lighthouse, 197
Liquor laws, 17, 76
Literature, Canadian, 32
Loggers' and lumberjacks' festivals, 169, 183

Magdalen Islands, 95, 101
hotels in, 108
restaurants in, 110
tours of, 98–99
youth hostel in, 109
Maple Country, 82–84, 88, 91
Maple syrup and sugar, 4, 57, 82, 158, 169
Massif de Petit-Rivière St-François, 39
McGill University, 49, 66, 80
Metric conversion charts, 18
Mexican restaurant, 92
Mime, 58
Mingan Archipelago, 8, 196
Modified American Plan (MAP), 12
Monasteries, 82, 189
Mont Bromont, 39, 81
Mont Orford, 38, 81, 87
Mont Ste-Anne, 39
Mont Tremblant, 159, 161
Montcalm, Marquis de, 23–24, 46, 116, 123, 127
Montmorency Falls, 117
Montreal, 42–78
average temperatures in, 5
Chinatown of, 58
dance in, 33, 67
drama in, 33, 49
exploring, 48–53
film in, 33, 58

INDEX

Montreal (*continued*)
  historic sites and houses in, 61–63
  history of, 22, 24–26, 43–47
  hotels and motels in, 68–70, 73
  map of, 44–45
  map of downtown, 50–51
  map of Métro of, 56
  map of old, 62
  Marathon in, 58
  museums in, 65–66
  music in, 32, 58, 66–67
  nightlife in, 76–78
  parks and gardens in, 59–60
  religious sites in, 63–65
  restaurants in, 14, 70–76
  shopping in, 49, 66
  smoking in, 55
  spectator sports in, 58, 60–61
  summer sports in, 60
  telephones and emergency numbers in, 55
  tourist information in, 54–55
  tours of, 58–59
  transportation in, 55–56
  underground walkways in, 36, 49–52
  winter sports in, 59, 60
Mont-St-Hilaire, 80
Moroccan restaurant, 75
Motorists. *See* Automobiles
Movies. *See* Film
Museums
  antique autos, 81, 88, 191
  art, 65, 66, 104, 105, 128, 129, 137, 173–174, 185
  Barbeau, 84
  costume, 128
  Eskimo (Inuit), 65, 128, 201
  film, 65
  Fortin, 65
  fur trade, 65
  Grey Nuns', 64
  history, 65, 104, 105, 128, 129, 137, 145, 160, 174, 191, 197
  Hémon, 190
  hunting, 60, 66
  Indians, 65, 117, 128, 173, 197, 201
  lumberjack, 174
  maritime, 88, 104, 144–145
  military, 65
  of mills, 145
  mining, 185
  of miraculous cures, 64
  natural history, 105
  Notre-Dame Basilica, 64
  photography, 145
  railway, 88
  St-Lawrence goélettes, 137, 144
  science, 105, 189
  of seignoral system, 145
  snowmobile, 37
  Ursuline, 129, 173
  wax, 65
  See also National historic sites
Music, 31–32, 66–67, 89, 90, 129
  performance center for, 81
  See also Nightlife

National historic sites, 8, 80–81, 105, 127, 172, 184
Nightlife, 76–78, 92, 133–134, 148–149
North Shore, 181, 194–200
Northern lights, 181
Northern Quebec, 178–202
  guides required in, 10
  historic sites and houses in, 184–185, 190, 197
  hotels and motels in, 185–186, 191–192, 197–199, 201–202
  museums in, 185, 191, 197
  restaurants in, 186, 193–194
  summer sports in, 184, 190
  winter sports in, 184, 190, 197
Nouveau Quebec, 181–182, 200–202

Opera, 67, 129
Otish Mountains, 201
Ottawa Valley, 150–164
  historic sites and houses in, 160
  hotels and motels in, 160–163
  restaurants in, 163–164
  transportation in, 157
  winter sports in, 38, 39

INDEX

Owl's Head, 38, 88

Painting. *See* Visual arts
Papineau, Louis Joseph, 25, 26, 63, 160
Parks
  national, 8, 94, 99, 170
  provincial, 8-9, 11, 87, 99-100, 124, 158, 170-171, 183, 189, 196
Passports and identification, 1, 2
Pâtisseries, 75
People of Quebec, 1, 30-31
Percé, 100, 101
Permafrost, 182
Pets, 9, 17-18
Planning your trip, 1
Plâteau Mont-Royal, 52-53
Pointe-au-Pic, 137, 147
Polynesian restaurants, 176, 194
Postage, 17
Power stations, tours of, 170, 196, 201
Pulp and paper mills, 190
Puppetry, 58

Quebec City, 111-134
  Carnival in, 35-36, 121-122
  exploring, 112-117
  film in, 129
  historic sites and houses in, 111, 126-128
  history of, 23-24, 46, 112
  hotels and motels in, 121, 129-131
  map of, 114-115
  museums in, 128-129
  music in, 32, 129
  nightlife in, 133-134
  parks and gardens in, 123
  religious sites in, 112, 117, 127, 128
  restaurants in, 132-133
  spectator sports in, 126
  summer festival in, 122
  summer sports in, 123, 125-126
  telephones and emergency numbers in, 119-120
  transportation in, 120
  winter sports in, 39, 123, 125-126
  zoos and aquarium in, 123-124
Quebec-style restaurants, 34, 75, 92, 109-110, 133, 164, 186, 193

Racquet sports, 125
Rafting, 60, 159
Railway museum, 88
Railway trip, Ottawa-Wakefield, 158
Regattas, 88, 183
Rental cars, 56, 85, 98, 120, 140
Restaurants, 14, 34
  fast food, 34
  provincial rating system for, 13
  tipping in, 15
  See also each place
Richelieu/South Shore area, 80-81, 89-90
Rock climbing, 142, 201
Rodeos, 170, 172
Roman Catholic Church, 23, 24. *See also* Churches and cathedrals
Rougemont, 81
Running and jogging, 58-61, 124, 125, 142

Saguenay–Lac-Saint-Jean–Chibougamau, 180-181, 187-194
Sailing, 126, 144
St-Jean-Port-Joli, 84, 91
St-Joseph-de-Beauce, 82-84
St. Lawrence River, 11, 84, 166
  whale-watching on, 141-142, 195-196
  winter sports near, 39
  See also Charlevoix
Ste-Anne-de-Beaupré, 136
Sculpture. *See* Visual arts
Sept-Îles, 194, 196, 197-199
Shawinigan, 29, 167, 175-176
Sherbrooke, 38, 82, 86, 91, 92
Size of Quebec, 1
Skiing, 11

INDEX

Skiing (*continued*)
  alpine, 38–41, 60, 81, 87, 94–95, 102, 124, 125, 136, 143–144, 159, 190, 197
  cross-country, 37–38, 59, 60, 87, 123–125, 142, 159, 169–171, 183, 190, 197, 201
  heli-, 95
  night, 39, 81
  six-day tour, 86–87
Snorkeling, 169
Snowmobiles, 11–12, 36–37, 171, 183, 190
Snowshoeing, 124, 142, 172, 181
Song festival, 81
Southern Quebec, 79–92
  drama in, 82, 89
  historic sites and houses in, 80–84
  hotels and motels in, 89–91
  map of, 83
  museums of, 88
  music, 89
  nightlife in, 92
  parks and gardens in, 87
  religious sites in, 82
  restaurants in, 91–92
  spectator sports in, 88
  tours in, 86–87
  transportation in, 85
  winter sports in, 37, 38, 81, 86–88
Spectator sports, 12, 60–61, 88
Speedboat regatta, 88
Stage. *See* Drama
Stationery, handcrafted, 137
Steak houses, 75
Summer sports, 11, 60, 102–103
Swimming, 60, 68, 69, 86, 126, 142, 144
Swiss restaurant, 133
Symphony orchestras, 32, 66, 129

Taxes, 3–4, 7
Taxis, 55–56, 120, 156
  tipping of, 15
Telephones, 17, 55, 85, 97, 119–120, 140, 156–157, 168, 182–183, 195, 201
Tennis, 11, 58, 60

Time zones, 16
Tipping, 15
Tobacco-growing, 166
Tobogganing, 59
Torngat Mountains, 201
Tourist information, 1–2, 54–55, 85, 97, 119, 138–140, 156, 168, 182, 187–188, 195, 200
Tours, 58–59, 86–87, 98–99, 122–123, 141–142, 158, 189, 201
  of power stations, 170, 196, 201
  of Sigma Mines, 183
  snowmobile, 37
Train travel, 54, 85, 96, 119, 156, 167–168, 182, 187, 200
Traveler's checks, 15
Trois-Rivières, 166, 169, 170, 172, 174, 176
Twain, Mark, 63

Université de Montreal, 49
Université Laval, 117

Vegetarian restaurant, 75–76
Viennese restaurant, 164
Visual arts, 33–34, 116
  ice sculpture, 121
  See also Art galleries; Museums—art

War of 1812, Quebec and, 46, 80, 112
Whale-watching, 141–142, 195–196
Wildlife reserves, 11, 99–102, 124, 136, 142, 170–171, 183, 189, 196
ZECS, 179
Windsurfing, 87, 103
Winter sports, 11, 36, 60, 88, 102
  See also Skiing
Wolfe, James, 23–24, 46, 112–116, 123, 128
Wood-carving, 84

Youth hostels, 14, 70, 108–109, 121, 131, 148, 176, 192, 199
YWCAs, 70, 121, 131

Zoos, 53, 59, 81, 87, 123, 189